W9-CSO-598

The Power of Critical Theory

Liberating Adult Learning and Teaching

Stephen D. Brookfield

JOSSEY-BASS
A Wiley Imprint
www.josseybass.com

Published by Jossey-Bass
A Wiley Imprint
989 Market Street, San Francisco, CA 94103-1741   www.josseybass.com

Published simultaneously in original paperback in the United Kingdom by The Open University Press
as *The Power of Critical Theory for Adult Learning and Teaching*.

Jossey-Bass books and products are available through most bookstores. To contact Jossey-Bass directly
call our Customer Care Department within the U.S. at 800-956-7739, outside the U.S. at 317-572-3986
or fax 317-572-4002.

Jossey-Bass also publishes its books in a variety of electronic formats. Some content that appears in
print may not be available in electronic books.

Library of Congress Cataloging-in-Publication Data

Brookfield, Stephen
    The power of critical theory : liberating adult learning and teaching / Stephen D. Brookfield.–
1st ed.
        p. cm.
    Includes bibliographical references and index.
    ISBN 0-7879-5601-5 (alk. paper)
    1. Adult learning.   2. Adult education.   3. Critical theory.   I. Title.
    LC5225.L42B77 2005
    374'.001–dc22   2004016014

Printed in the United States of America
FIRST EDITION
HB Printing   10 9 8 7 6 5 4 3 2 1

Contents

The Jossey-Bass Higher and
Adult Education Series

Preface

A couple of years ago, one of the most dispiriting things that can happen to a teacher happened to me. I had just finished teaching a semester-long course on the philosophy of adult education, a substantial portion of which had focused on critical theory. I had asked students to engage with key figures in critical theory such as Marx, Gramsci, Habermas, and Foucault, mostly by reading secondary texts that summarized these writers' ideas and placed them in an adult educational context. As part of the course, students wrote essays and gave presentations in which they considered how their experiences as adult learners or adult educators were illuminated by critical theory. As students were leaving the last class of the semester, I overheard one say to another, "I still don't see why we had to read all this critical theory. What's Gramsci got to do with adult education?"

Since I had just spent a good part of four months arguing for critical theory as a useful lens through which adult educators could view their practice, this comment took the wind right out of my sails. This student had written the required assignments, participated in the required team presentations, and successfully passed the course. Yet, clearly, all this had happened without any real connection being made between that student's practice and the critical tradition. This book is my attempt to deal with that student's complaint. Its overarching purpose is to try to convince adult educators that critical theory should be considered seriously as a perspective that can help them make some sense of the dilemmas, contradictions, and frustrations they experience in their work.

In a sense, this book is attempting to put the *critical* back into *critical thinking* by emphasizing how thinking critically is an inherently political process. Critical thinking is a dominant discourse in adult education, usually characterized by a particular understanding of what this intellectual process involves. To think critically is mostly defined as the process of unearthing, and then researching, the assumptions one is operating under, primarily by taking different perspectives on familiar, taken-for-granted beliefs and behaviors. As I argue in Chapter One, this notion of criticality draws on a number of intellectual traditions, including analytic philosophy, pragmatism, constructivism, psychoanalysis, and critical theory. The first of these traditions—analytic philosophy—is the one that most strongly frames how critical thinking is currently conceived and taught in contemporary higher and adult education. From this perspective, to be critical is to be skilled at argument analysis, to recognize false inferences and logical fallacies, to be able to distinguish bias from fact, opinion from evidence, and so on. These are valuable, even essential, intellectual functions, but they focus on cognitive processes to the neglect of social and political critique.

In this book I focus on a very different tradition informing critical thinking, the tradition of critical theory. Critical theory views thinking critically as being able to identify, and then to challenge and change, the process by which a grossly iniquitous society uses dominant ideology to convince people this is a normal state of affairs. As a body of work, critical theory is grounded in three core assumptions regarding the way the world is organized:

1. That apparently open, Western democracies are actually highly unequal societies in which economic inequity, racism, and class discrimination are empirical realities
2. That the way this state of affairs is reproduced and seems to be normal, natural, and inevitable (thereby heading off potential challenges to the system) is through the dissemination of dominant ideology
3. That critical theory attempts to understand this state of affairs as a necessary prelude to changing it

Dominant ideology comprises the set of broadly accepted beliefs and practices that frame how people make sense of their experiences and live their lives. When it works effectively, it ensures that an unequal, racist, and sexist society is able to reproduce itself with minimal opposition. Its chief function is to convince people that the world is organized the way it is for the best of all reasons and that society works in the best interests of all. Critical theory regards dominant ideology as inherently manipulative and duplicitous. From the perspective of critical theory, a critical adult is one who can discern how the ethic of capitalism, and the logic of bureaucratic rationality, push people into ways of living that perpetuate economic, racial, and gender oppression. Additionally, and crucially, critical theory views a critical adult as one who takes action to create more democratic, collectivist economic and social forms. Some in the tradition (for example, Cornel West) link social change to democratic socialism; others (for example, Erich Fromm), to socialist humanism. Clearly, then, the way critical theory defines being critical is far more politicized than the way humanistic psychology—until recently the dominant discourse in adult education—regards this idea.

My previous books have been concerned mostly with explaining general approaches toward the development of critical thinking and have given relatively little attention to exploring the theoretical traditions informing this practice. In developing my own understanding of practice, I have drawn on diverse intellectual traditions in the effort to get adult learners and adult educators to recognize, research, and challenge their assumptions. As someone who is very interested in practice, and who loves to try and untangle pedagogic problems and puzzles, I have usually written for educators who share this passion. My intuition is that people who buy my books are mostly looking for helpful suggestions on how to create and conduct adult and higher educational activities. Over the years I have received much confirmation of that intuition from people who liked the practicality of some of my earlier books.

But now I have the chance to talk some theory. In *The Power of Critical Theory* I take the opportunity to fill in some of the theoretical background to my earlier work by outlining one of the chief theoretical traditions informing the ideas of critical thinking and critical reflection. I am far from agreeing with everything that critical theory or every critical theorist says; indeed, critical theory's emphasis on critiquing its own presuppositions is one of its features that I find most appealing. To adapt the title of one of Cornel West's essays, "The Indispensability Yet Insufficiency of Marxist Theory," critical theory is indispensable though insufficient for a full understanding of the critical process. However, although critical theory has received considerable attention in some scholarly quarters of adult education, it is the discourses of liberal humanism and human capital theory that hold sway in the wider world of practice. Critical theory remains balkanized, regarded by most adult education practitioners as the province of a few, overly theoretical, leftist intellectuals. I suspect that many in the field think it has little to do with what they see as the "real" world of adult education as practiced in adult basic education, adult undergraduate degree completion programs, corporate training, and so on. One intent of this book is to help alter this perception by establishing critical theory as a dominant and legitimate interpretive perspective in the field, one that should be seen as relevant and helpful by adult educators who regard themselves as mainstream practitioners.

Any attempt to argue that critical theory can illuminate the everyday practices of adult educators faces formidable obstacles. Critical theory has as a priority the critique of capitalism, an ideology viewed by many as coterminous with the best that America stands for. Its intellectual genesis is in Marxism, a fact that is hardly likely to endear it to the vast majority who view Marx as fundamentally un-American. Critical theory views socialism not as repressive thought control or relentless subservience to totalitarian leaders but, in Fromm's terms, as "one of the most significant, idealistic and moral movements of our age" (Fromm, 1956a, p. 247). In fact Habermas at one point declares that "socialism and liberty are identical" (1992a, p. 75). To put it mildly, these are not sentiments that would receive broad support today, at least in the United States. Opponents of critical theory have effectively equated socialism with state totalitarianism, in which freedom of thought, individual creativity, and disagreement with one's leaders are all rigidly suppressed. Critical theory's repeated denunciations of the evils of totalitarian socialism go mostly unheard. Because the theory involves a dialogue with Marx and because it views democracy as intertwined with socialism, it is sometimes stigmatized as a kind of authoritarian, Stalinist creed. From this viewpoint a critical theorist is portrayed as someone interested only in muting the vibrant colors of individuality, liberty, and freedom that comprise the American dream until they form a grey anonymous smudge.

Hackles are raised even higher when people realize that critical theory even questions the idea of democratic majority rule and dares to suggest that the majority might not always be right.

Not only does critical theory have these ideological barriers to overcome before it can be taken seriously by skeptical practitioners, it also creates barriers by its mode of communication. Many people, myself included, find the texts of critical theory at best complex and challenging, at worst impenetrable. *The Power of Critical Theory* is my attempt to provide adult educators with an accessible overview of critical theory's central ideas without oversimplifying them. I have tried to create a point of entry into the critical tradition that does not distort its central themes and that uses the words of its proponents wherever possible. In trying to make my explanations of critical theory as comprehensible as possible, I was heartened by Angela Davis' and bell hooks' insistence that a theory can hardly inspire action if it is expressed in terms that only a few highly trained scholars can understand. However, I know that there are dangers in trying to write in accessible and comprehensible ways. One can sometimes be so concerned with making things accessible that the power and complexity of the original analysis is lost. It is also possible to end up speaking too much for people rather than letting them speak for themselves.

To try and avoid these dangers of neutering the powerful work of the theorists discussed and of diminishing their voices, I have used as many direct quotes as possible drawn from the theorists' works. Some readers will probably find this off-putting and wish that I'd just give my own summary of key concepts. But I believe that past a certain point it is intellectually dangerous to summarize another's ideas. So I have erred in favor of quoting too much from original texts rather than quoting too little. I do not want readers to leave any of the book's chapters without having read a large number of direct quotes from the works of the authors reviewed. In this endeavor I was encouraged by recent books interpreting the work of Marx, Gramsci, Freire, and Habermas for adult educators written by Allman (2000; 2001) and Morrow and Torres (2002). I agree with Morrow and Torres that critical theorists "have suffered from simplistic, selective interpretations—whether by critics or friends" (2002, p. 16) and that it is important "to rather meticulously reconstruct their positions in their own terminology with direct quotes, rather than relying primarily on our interpretation of what they mean" (2002, p. 16).

Organization of the Book

The book begins with a discussion in Chapter One of some of the central ideas of critical theory. It lays out why reading critical theory is important, examines different interpretations of criticality, and positions critical theory as a response to Marx. Drawing on Max Horkheimer's classic text "Critical Theory" (1995), Chapter One reviews five characteristics of critical theory then argues that a critical theory of adult learning must focus on exploring a number of learning tasks and on implementing a self-critical posture. An overview of these different learning tasks follows in Chapter Two. Here I argue that a critical theory of adult learning must focus on understanding how adults learn to challenge ideology, contest hegemony, unmask power, overcome alienation, learn liberation, reclaim reason, and practice democracy. Each of these tasks then becomes the focus of one of the succeeding chapters in the book.

The first of these tasks—challenging ideology—is the focus of Chapter Three. This chapter argues that ideology is the central concept in critical theory and establishes ideology critique as a major adult learning project. It reviews classic statements by Adorno, Horkheimer, and Althusser on how ideology functions but also examines ethnographic studies of how people resist ideological conditioning. Chapter Four looks at the idea of hegemony, a concept that emphasizes that adults are active learners of ideology and willing partners in their own oppression. It explores the work of Antonio Gramsci, in particular his analysis of how people learn critical consciousness and his concept of the organic intellectual. The chapter concludes with a brief review of some contemporary attempts by adult educators to work as directive persuaders and organizers, a formulation Gramsci used to describe the role of the organic intellectual.

The phenomenon of power is the focus of Chapter Five, and the work of Michel Foucault receives particular attention. Foucault argued that power is exercised in all social situations (including adult education) and that it is inextricably intertwined with the ability to define what counts as knowledge. His ideas on disciplinary power, mechanisms of surveillance, and the establishment of regimes of truth are applied in a number of adult education contexts. Chapter Six explores the notion of alienation, particularly through Erich Fromm's descriptions of twentieth-century life. Fromm broadened Marx's analysis to argue that alienation is a universal phenomenon that extends far beyond the industrial working class. Contemporary forms of alienation are evident in the ways adults develop a "marketing orientation" to life and see the development of identity as equivalent to assembling and marketing an attractive "personality package." Fromm also chronicles the decline of critical thinking as people succumb to "automaton conformity" and engage in pseudothinking, that is, thinking that uncritically espouses what people imagine the majority opinion to be. The chapter ends by reviewing Fromm's ideas on how adult educators can combat these tendencies by teaching a "structuralized worldview" and helping people learn habits of democratic process.

In Chapter Seven we encounter the idea of one-dimensional thought as articulated by Herbert Marcuse. Adults exhibit one-dimensional thought when their learning is focused on how to make current systems work more efficiently, rather than asking "big" questions such as How should we live? or What does it mean to act ethically? As a practicing educator, Marcuse suggests several specific ways adult educators can help people escape one-dimensional thought. One is through providing opportunities for people to have powerful and estranging aesthetic engagements. Marcuse believes in the transformative power of art and argues that it can temporarily take people out of everyday reality and then allow them to reenter it with a newly critical perspective. Another possibility is to teach abstract, conceptual thought, which Marcuse regards as a potentially revolutionary form of cognition. A third is to practice liberating tolerance, an approach that involves exposing learners only to alternative and dissenting perspectives. Marcuse contrasts liberating tolerance with repressive tolerance, which appears to open up curricula while actually closing them down. Applying his idea of "repressive tolerance" to contemporary diversity initiatives suggests that these only serve to underscore the dominance of the Eurocentric center.

Chapters Eight and Nine review the relevance of Jürgen Habermas for adult education practice. Habermas is probably the critical

theorist best known to adult educators, and his work has significantly influenced debates on transformative learning. I divide his
work into two different projects—reclaiming reason and practicing
democracy. Chapter Eight explores how reason can help us face the
three crises Habermas believes are undermining democracy:
the collapse of the public sphere, the decline of civil society, and the
invasion of the lifeworld. Habermas believes that true reason—
reason employed to build participatory democracy—can help us
learn our way out of these crises. In Chapter Nine I examine further his views on the similarities between democratic processes and
particular speech forms. It is Habermas' contention that adults are
constantly learning what he calls "communicative action," and that
this form of communication carries within it a democratic impulse.
The chapter also includes a summary of his ideas on the development of adult moral consciousness and his description of the role
of adult learning in social evolution.

Chapters Ten and Eleven turn a critical eye on the work summarized in Chapters One through Nine. These first nine chapters
undoubtedly reflect a Eurocentric perspective, and they emphasize class as a central construct. In Chapters Ten and Eleven I
review the central contentions of critical theory through the contemporary lenses of race and gender. Chapter Ten takes Lucius
Outlaw's idea that bodies of knowledge are always racialized and
explores how adult education literature is racialized in favor of
European White males such as myself. Two ways in which the field
could be racialized in favor of African Americans are then explored. The first option focuses on African American attempts to
take the critical theory tradition and rework some of its central
ideas so that they serve the interests of African Americans. Lucius
Outlaw and Cornel West are particularly prominent here. The second option is to develop an Africentric paradigm for adult education that conceptualizes its practice in terms of African cultural
values. Here the work of Scipio J. Colin III is at the forefront.

Chapter Eleven focuses on the masculinist emphasis in critical
theory and the lack of any sustained gender analysis. It begins with
the attempts of mostly White feminists to build on the work of
Marx, Foucault, and Habermas by broadening the analysis of ideology to include patriarchy and gender oppression. One educational implementation of critical theory—critical pedagogy—has
been critiqued as a strongly masculinist discourse, and that per-

spective is summarized here. The chapter concludes with a review of the work of two African American feminists, bell hooks and Angela Davis. These two writers share some similarities. Both critique the attempted domination of feminist discourse by White women, both draw explicitly on the critical theory tradition, both argue for multiracial and cross-gender alliances, and both argue that for theory to have any effect it must be written accessibly. Some of hooks' classroom practices are described, and it becomes clear that many of these challenge conventional adult educational wisdom. The chapter ends by summarizing Angela Davis' assertions that any analysis of women's issues must always be tied to a critique of capitalism and that truly transformative adult education can only happen through collective struggle and multiracial alliances.

Chapter Twelve changes the tone and focus of the book somewhat by reviewing adult educational practices rather than theoretical analyses. It begins with a brief statement of what it means to teach critically, then moves into a discussion of the different methodological approaches suggested by different critical theorists. The chapter ends with a personal reflection on my own attempts to teach critical theory and the resistance this often occasions.

Acknowledgments

Reading unpublished work for no reason other than a desire to help the author is an act of true colleagueship. I was lucky to find some true colleagues who spent considerable time reading draft chapters of this book and giving me their critiques. So, in alphabetical order, let me thank Gary Cale of Jackson Community College (Jackson, Michigan), Tom Heaney of National Louis University (Chicago), Jack Mezirow, professor emeritus of Teachers College (New York), Stephen Preskill of the University of New Mexico, and Michael Welton recently of Mount Saint Vincent University (Halifax, Nova Scotia). All these colleagues read a large part of the first draft of this book and their suggestions, critiques, and encouragement were essential to its completion. I can only hope that some time in the future I have the chance to repay my debt to them. Cornel West of Princeton University, Robert Kegan of Harvard University, and Mark Tennant of the University of Technology, Sydney (Australia), were all kind enough to read the completed manuscript and endorse its publication. I would also like to thank Nadira Charaniya of Springfield College (Massachusetts) and Elizabeth Hayes of the University of Wisconsin-Madison who reviewed the text for Jossey-Bass and made many useful suggestions.

In addition, four other colleagues helped me develop specific chapters in the text. Scipio J. Colin III of National Louis University (Chicago) provided a supportive critique of Chapter Ten, "Racializing Criticality." Gabriele Stroschen of De Paul University (Chicago) read and critiqued the Chapter Six, "Overcoming Alienation." John Holst of the University of St. Thomas gave me some good ideas regarding the flow of Chapter Four, "Contesting Hegemony." Elizabeth Tisdell of Pennsylvania State University helpfully reviewed the theoretical base for Chapter Eleven, "Gendering Criticality."

Two of the doctoral students in my course "Critical Theory and the Practice of Adult Education" at Harvard University Graduate School of Education kept telling me this would be a helpful and necessary book. Susan Klimczak and Chris Lanier read and commented on several early drafts of the books' chapters and reinforced my commitment to finishing it. So thanks to them for their encouragement. Conversations with Kevin Sealey of Teachers College, Columbia University, moved forward my engagement with Cornel West's work, contained mostly within Chapter Ten. Of course, all these colleagues should be excused any responsibility for the inaccuracies, inconsistencies, and omissions that are in here. I claim those for myself.

The writing of *The Power of Critical Theory* was helped considerably by the University of St. Thomas allowing me to split my sabbatical year over two consecutive spring semesters. This allowed me to write a first draft in spring 2003, field test it with various groups of students in fall 2003, and then completely revise and rewrite a second draft in spring 2004. Susan Anderson, Pam Nice, Rob Riley, and Miriam Williams were all supportive of this novel idea of a "split" sabbatical. I would also like to thank the following journals for allowing me to publish my thoughts in progress in the form of articles within their pages: *Adult Education Quarterly*, the *Canadian Journal for the Study of Adult Education*, the *Harvard Educational Review*, *Teachers College Record*, and the *Journal of Transformative Education*. David Brightman, my editor at Jossey-Bass was, as ever, an unfailing source of support and constructive critique.

Finally, thanks to Kim, Molly, and Colin (the 99ers) for everything.

The Author

Stephen D. Brookfield

The father of Molly and Colin, and the husband of Kim, Stephen D. Brookfield is currently Distinguished Professor at the University of St. Thomas in Minneapolis-St. Paul, Minnesota. He also serves as consultant to the adult education doctoral program at National Louis University in Chicago. Prior to moving to Minnesota, he spent ten years as professor in the Department of Higher and Adult Education at Teachers College, Columbia University, where he is still adjunct professor.

He received his B.A. degree (1970) from Coventry University in modern studies, his M.A. degree (1974) from the University of Reading in sociology, and his Ph.D. degree (1980) from the University of Leicester in adult education. He also holds a postgraduate diploma (1971) from the University of London, Chelsea College, in modern social and cultural studies and a postgraduate diploma (1977) from the University of Nottingham in adult education. In 1991 he was awarded an honorary doctor of letters degree from the University System of New Hampshire for his contributions to understanding adult learning. In 2003 he was awarded an honorary doctorate from Concordia University for his contributions to adult education practice.

Stephen began his teaching career in 1970 and has held appointments at colleges of further, technical, adult, and higher education in the United Kingdom and at universities in Canada (University of British Columbia) and the United States (Columbia University, Teachers College, and the University of St. Thomas). In 1989 he was visiting fellow at the Institute for Technical and Adult Teacher Education in what is now the University of Technology, Sydney, Australia. In 2001 he received the Leadership Award from the Association for Continuing Higher Education (ACHE) for "extraordinary contributions to the general field of continuing education on a national and international level." In 2002 he was visiting professor at Harvard University Graduate School of Education. In 2003–2004 he was the Helen Le Baron Hilton Chair at Iowa State University. He has run numerous workshops on teaching, adult learning, and critical thinking around the world and delivered many keynote addresses at regional, national, and international education conferences.

He is a three-time winner of the Cyril O. Houle World Award for Literature in Adult Education: in 1986 for his book *Understanding and Facilitating Adult Learning: A Comprehensive Analysis of Principles and Effective Practices* (1986), in 1989 for *Developing Critical Thinkers: Challenging Adults to Explore Alternative Ways of Thinking and Acting* (1987), and in 1996 for *Becoming a Critically Reflective Teacher* (1995). *Understanding and Facilitating Adult Learning* also won the 1986 Imogene E. Okes Award for Outstanding Research in Adult Education. These awards were all presented by the American Association for Adult and Continuing Education. His book (coauthored with Stephen Preskill) *Discussion as a Way of Teaching: Tools and Techniques for Democratic Classrooms* (1999) was an Educational Studies Association Critics' Choice for 1999. His other books are *Adult Learners, Adult Education and the Community* (1984), *Self-Directed Learning: From Theory to Practice* (1985), *Learning Democracy: Eduard Lindeman on Adult Education and Social Change* (1987), *Training Educators of Adults: The Theory and Practice of Graduate Adult Education* (1988), and *The Skillful Teacher: On Technique, Trust, and Responsiveness in the Classroom* (1990).

Chapter One

Exploring the Meaning of Critical Theory for Adult Learning

Theory is a dangerous word, one that should not be used lightly. Acting on what they believe are accurate theories of human nature or political development, people have started wars, committed murder, and sanctioned torture. As Zinn (1990) observes, "How we think is . . . a matter of life and death" (p. 2). Sometimes those who use the word *theory* give off a whiff of self-importance, as if telling the reader "look out, here comes something truly profound." Monty Python's Flying Circus hilariously parodied the theorist's tendency to portentousness in a skit involving John Cleese as Miss Anne Elk, the proud possessor of a new theory concerning the brontosaurus. After archly and repeatedly declaring to a TV interviewer that she has her very own theory, Miss Elk reveals (after considerable coaxing by Graham Chapman the interviewer) the substance of the theory: the brontosaurus was thin at one end, much, much thicker in the middle, and then thin at the other end. The sketch ends with Miss Elk trying in vain to disclose her second theory.

It is not only the Monty Python team that mocks the pretensions of theorists. Given what theorists see as the contextual, splintered nature of reality, postmodern analysis views large-scale theory generation as a naïve and self-deluding modernist project, as so much wasted effort. Postmodernism contends that the world is essentially fragmented and that what passes for theoretical generalizations are really only context-specific insights produced by particular discourse communities. Academics aware of this critique who are leery about appearing out of date are tempted to abandon any attempt even to speak or write the word *theory*. After all, if everything is local, par ticu-lar, idiosyncratic, then isn't trying to build generalizable theories a waste of time? That I wrote this book means, obviously, that I believe the answer to this question is "not really" and that any abandonment of theory is premature. But a book with a focus on theoretical expec-tation must begin by outlining how the author understands this activ-ity and by justifying why this is still a worthwhile effort rather than a comedic diversion. That is this chapter's intent.

What Is Theory?

If you have the temerity to title a book *The Power of Critical Theory: Liberating Adult Learning and Teaching,* you may create in some read-ers the expectation that a comprehensive explanatory framework accounting for all aspects of adult learning will spring forth. I want to counter this expectation at the outset. What I am trying to do is review one particular theoretical framework—critical theory—and explore the implications this work has for our understanding of adult learning and practice of adult education. Inevitably, in focus-ing on one tradition, others are discounted. The critical theory tra-dition draws on Marxist scholarship to illuminate the ways in which people accept as normal a world characterized by massive in-equities and the systemic exploitation of the many by the few. For adult educators the tradition helps us understand how people learn to perceive and challenge this situation. A critical approach to understanding adult learning sees it as comprising a number of crucial tasks such as learning how to perceive and challenge dom-inant ideology, unmask power, contest hegemony, overcome alien-ation, pursue liberation, reclaim reason, and practice democracy. A theoretical tradition concerned primarily with learning critical con-sciousness will obviously neglect some kinds of instrumental or technical learning. A critical theory of adult learning may strive to be as comprehensive as possible in describing and explaining the development of social and political awareness, but it should not be expected to account for the full range of learning activities evident in adults.

I also want to warn against the unjustified valorization or reifi-cation of theory, against the idea that theorizing is a high-status intellectual process restricted to a talented few. Theorizing should not be thought of as a process restricted to the academy and the preserve of the intelligentsia, but rather as an inevitability of sentient existence. A theory is nothing more (or less) than a set of explanatory understandings that help us make sense of some aspect of the world. To the extent that making sense of existence is a natural human activity, it is accurate to say that we are all theorists and that we all theorize; in Gramsci's (1971, p. 9) terms, "all men are intellectuals" (he would surely say "all people" were he writing today). Interpreting, predicting, explaining, and making meaning are acts we engage in whether or not we set out deliberately to do so, or whether or not we use these terms to describe what we're doing. So theory is not the preserve of university professors who disseminate it in refereed journals and scholarly monographs. It is produced and abandoned, refined and discarded, through everyday conversations, whether these are spoken or written, live or asynchronous. To quote Gramsci (1971) again, each person is a theorist because she or he "participates in a particular conception of the world, has a conscious line of moral conduct, and therefore contributes to sustain a conception of the world or to modify it, that is to bring into being new modes of thought" (p. 9). Thinking this way challenges the idea of theory as a restrictive professional discourse, the understanding of which requires specialist training in the philosophy and methodology of science. Although theorizing in the natural and social sciences can be richly elaborate and sophisticated requiring the development of specialized terminology, its difference from the quotidian theorizing of everyday action is one of degree, not of kind.

Theory can be more or less formal, wider or deeper in scope, and expressed in a range of ways, but its basic thrust—to make sense of the world, communicate that understanding to others, and thereby enable us to take informed action—stays constant. Theory is eminently practical. Our actions as people, and as educators, are often based on understandings we hold about how the world works. The more deliberate and intentional an action is, the more likely it is to be theoretical. To this extent theory is inherently teleological; that is, it imbues human actions with purpose. We act in certain ways because we believe this will lead to predictable consequences. Of course, our theory can be bad or wrong—inaccurate and assimilated uncritically from authority figures. We can act on understandings that consistently lead us into harmful situations yet remain committed to our theory because we are convinced we haven't understood it or its implications properly. But always in the midst of practice, of action, of judgment and decision, is theory.

The Utility of Theory

In an eloquent passage in *Teaching to Transgress* (1994), bell hooks testifies to the way theory saved her life. In describing her need to make sense of her own family's dynamics, she writes, "I came to theory because I was hurting—the pain within me was so intense that I could not go on living. I came to theory desperate, wanting to comprehend—to grasp what was happening around and within me. Most importantly, I wanted to make the hurt go away. I saw in theory then a location for healing" (p. 59). In his review of critical theory and poststructuralism, Poster (1989) too notes that "critical theory springs from an assumption that we live amidst a world of pain, that much can be done to alleviate that pain, and that theory has a crucial role to play in that process" (p. 3). Both hooks and Poster demonstrate the utilitarian base to much theorizing, in this case the alleviation of pain. Theorizing—generating provisional explanations that help us understand and act in the world—helps us breathe clearly when we feel stifled by the smog of confusion. We theorize so we can understand what's happening to us and so that we can take informed actions. Our hope is that we can justify the time spent theorizing by developing insights that will be useful to us. The everyday theories of action that frame our practice as adult educators are highly functional. They are not usually developed for their intellectual elegance or enduring conceptual beauty; indeed, they are brutally abandoned when they cease to be helpful to us. If they're useful we keep them, if they're not we dump them.

How exactly might we judge the utility of a critical theory of adult learning? In other words, what leads us to keep it or dump it? Three considerations suggest themselves. First, a theory is useful if it helps explain a piece of the world to us. This explanation will probably be provisional and replaced at a later date by one that seems even more accurate, that accounts for unresolved contradictions and complexities, and that covers a greater range of instances. From this point of view, theorizing is a form of meaning making, born of a desire to create explanations that impose conceptual order on reality, however artificial this order might later turn out to be. There is a direct connection here to Mezirow's (1991a) work on transformative learning which posits a developmental trajectory of adult meaning making as people develop meaning perspectives (broad frames of reference that shape how we see the world) that are increasingly comprehensive and discriminating. So a theory is useful to the extent that it provides us with understandings that illuminate what we observe and experience.

Clearly, just getting a better sense of why things are the way they are is often helpful. Even if we realize that our problems are reflections of structural contradictions that we can do little about individually, knowing that we are not their cause is crucial to our well-being. One of the earliest myths educators, including adult educators, learn is the myth that, in Britzman's (1991) words, "everything depends on the teacher." If we embrace this myth, then we are quick to believe that every time things go wrong (for example, students are hostile to, or apathetic about, curriculum and learning activities that we feel should animate their enthusiasm), it is because we are somehow at fault for not being sufficiently sensitive to students' experiences and learning styles or being less than fully charismatic. When a theoretical insight concerning hegemony (the process by which we embrace ideas and practices that keep us enslaved) helps us understand our practice in a new way, it often takes a great weight of potential guilt off our shoulders. There is no shame in admitting that we need theoretical insights to help us understand how the same destructive scenarios keep emerging in our lives, despite our best efforts to prevent these. Without theoretical help it is easy to fall prey to the danger of unjustified self-laceration as we fail to see how many of our private troubles are produced by systemic constraints and contradictions.

So reading theory helps us name or rename aspects of our experience that elude or puzzle us. When we read an explanation that interprets a paradoxical experience in a new or more revealing way, the experience often becomes more comprehensible. As a result we feel the world is more accessible, more open to our influence. When someone else's words illuminate or confirm a privately realized insight, we feel affirmed and recognized. Seeing a personal insight stated as a theoretical proposition makes us more likely to take seriously our own reasoning and judgments. Theory can also prevent us from falling victim to the traps of relativism and isolationism that bedevil adult educational practice. Through studying theory that has sprung from situations and concerns outside our circle of practice, we gain insight into those features of our work that are context-specific and those that are more generic. Embedded as we are in our cultures, histories, and contexts, it is easy for us to slip into the habit of generalizing from the particular. By offering unfamiliar interpretations of familiar events, theory can jar us in a productive way and suggest other ways of working.

Without attention to theory, we can easily remain fixated on the particular puzzles of our own practice. Critical theory helps us understand that these puzzles are not necessarily procedural kinks or pedagogic tangles of our own making that we need to take responsibility for unraveling. Instead they are sometimes politically sculpted situations illustrating the internal contradictions of the capitalist system in which we work. We come to see that these situations are the predictable consequence of trying to do something highly complex (help adults learn) within a system that is organized according to bureaucratic rationality and modes of factory production. Such a system ignores complexity and assumes, for example, that learning takes place at predictable times each week, in the same location, and follows the rationale of a curriculum divided into discrete and manageable units. We come to realize, too, how the inequities of race, class, and gender play themselves out in front of our eyes, reflecting dynamics that seem beyond our influence.

This first criterion of theoretical utility is basically representational. It springs from modernist epistemology that holds that our minds can construct increasingly accurate pictures of the world. As Bagnall (1999) puts it, modernist epistemology is "open to an infinite progression of ever more perfect representations of the material world, each one more general and more powerful than that or those it replaced, but always carrying with it the presupposition of further fallibility" (p. 23). This epistemology has come under increasing attack to the extent that postmodernism scorns any attempts to theorize beyond the individual case as hopeless acts of self-deception. Nonetheless, despite postmodernist skepticism adult educators display a remarkable tenacity in their desire to theorize and to use this theorizing to improve their practice. Indeed, one of the most frequently voiced complaints about critical deconstructions of adult educational practice is that these demonstrate practitioners' shortcomings, particularly their oppressive behaviors, without offering any suggestions as to how these failings might be addressed. Reading critiques that only leave us feeling foolish, misguided, or guilty, and that contain no hope for remaking our practice in more democratic ways, condemns us to nihilism or cynicism. In rejecting such demoralization throughout his life, it is no accident that Paulo Freire titled one of his last texts *Pedagogy of Hope* (1994).

A second way a theory can be judged as useful is the extent that it helps us understand not just how the world is but also how it might be changed for the better. (Of course, how one defines *better* is framed by one's class, culture, race, sexual preference, and ideology, among other things.) One of the strongest hopes of critical theory is that consideration of its understandings will prompt social and political change, often of a revolutionary nature. As Fay (1987) puts it, "A critical theory wants to explain a social order in such a way that it becomes itself the catalyst which leads to the transformation of this social order" (p. 27). So as well as providing different and helpful images of our practice that help us place what we do in wider social and political contexts, we can also ask of theory that it assist us in doing good work. Given that we all have only so much passion and commitment to draw on (we are not inexhaustible wells of energy), we need to be as sure as we can that such energy as we have is being deployed to greatest effect. This is what public intellectual and social critic Cornel West argues in his dialogue with bell hooks (hooks and West, 1991). For West, theory is "an indispensable weapon in struggle because it provides certain kinds of understanding, certain kinds of illumination, certain kinds of insights that are requisite if we are to act effectively" (hooks and West, 1991, p. 34). So it is reasonable to expect a critical theory of adult learning to suggest ways that adult education can contribute to building a society organized according to democratic values of fairness, justice, and compassion. In Horkheimer's (1995) terms, "the issue . . . is not just the theory of emancipation; it is the practice of it as well" (p. 233). In the critical tradition, theoretical utility is judged by criteria that are normatively based in a philosophical vision of the good, fully emancipated society. As we shall see in the next section, this emphasis on normative values is central to critical theory. Critical theory aims to help bring about a society of freedom and justice, a set of "beautiful consequences" as pragmatists might say. Consequently, we can assess critical theory's usefulness by judging how well it offers us guidance on the very practical matters of naming and fighting those enemies that are opposed to these consequences (Newman, 1994).

Third, a theory can offer us a form of radical hope that helps us stand against the danger of energy-sapping, radical pessimism. When we start to analyze the power and persistence of dominant ideologies, we can quickly reach the conclusion that there is little anyone can do to stand against the massive twin pillars of capitalism and bureaucratic rationality or against the monolith of the military-industrial complex. Knowing about the strength and persistence of the forces that use education to transmit dominant cultural values can leave us feeling puny and alone. Knowing that challenging dominant ideology risks bringing punishment down on our heads is depressing and frightening. It is easy to become demoralized when one realizes the strength of the opposition. As capitalism becomes truly global and exerts its influence through multinational corporations across state boundaries, it becomes harder and harder to envisage how citizens can stand against capitalism's encroachment into civil society.

This is where a critical theory of adult learning can help outline a pedagogy of hope, one where the possibility of democratic transformation of education and society is still alive. The fact that critical theory and the Frankfurt School's work exists at all, and that it has galvanized the energies of people across the world, is evidence that the dominant ideology of capitalism is not as pervasively stifling as we sometimes believe. If part of critical theory's purpose is to help adults realize the ways dominant ideology limits and circumscribes what people feel is possible in life, then raising awareness of how this happens provides "the necessary theoretical opening for understanding how an educative process might enable people to give up their illusions" (Welton, 1995, p. 13). Hence, critical theory can be deemed effective to the extent that it keeps alive the hope that the world can be changed to make it fairer and more compassionate.

I don't want to suggest, however, that for a theory to be useful it must generate neatly encapsulated formulations and implications for practice—standardized models, techniques, and approaches that can be easily applied across adult educational contexts. As Shalin (1992) wryly observes, "Things themselves do not suffer theory gladly and are sure to spoil our best faith efforts" (p. 268). Perhaps the most we can reasonably hope for is that those who understand their work through the lens of critical theory might document publicly the ways this understanding shapes, or at least influences, that work. An exemplar in this regard is Ira Shor, who has consistently outlined how his own practice of critical pedagogy is built upon the critical theory tradition in general and the thought of Paulo Freire in particular. In a series of finely written books (1987a, 1992, 1996), Shor offers compelling yet highly practical images of educational practice that have inspired many to experiment with different approaches in their own work (Shor, 1987b; Shor and Pari, 1999, 2000). His vignettes of apathetic students, rundown premises, learners' hostility to participatory approaches, and teachers' depression in the face of these factors are immediately recognizable to any educator who has tried to act on the insights of critical theory. In describing his responses to these vignettes, Shor provides numerous helpful suggestions that are rich in context-specific, illustrative detail, with no implication that these should be copied or reproduced. Yet the creativity he displays probably encourages many readers to break with their own tried and tested ways of doing things and serves as a point of departure for some useful experimentation. One concrete example of this in graduate adult education is the attempt by students and faculty at National Louis University in Chicago to create a democratic doctorate in adult education, drawing explicitly on some of Shor's suggestions (Avila and others, 2000).

In a review of several adult educational texts on teaching practices, Hayes (1993) opines that "it has always seemed to me somewhat unreasonable to expect teachers to tackle the formidable task of empowerment with few concrete tools" (p. 183). I agree with her sentiments. Whilst I support theorists' reluctance to prescribe standardized responses to complex, contradictory, and politically sculpted situations, I don't believe that those who write about theory can just throw up their hands and say, "Sorry, don't look to us for help in responding to these problems. Our job is done once we've analyzed them." To turn one's back on matters of practice and separate these from theoretical analysis is a denial of the idea of praxis—the constant intersection of opposites such as analysis and action—that is so central to the critical theory tradition. I have always felt it is a cop-out to refuse to discuss adult educational practice, particularly when one's analysis derives from an intellectual tradition that says the point of understanding the world is to be able to change it. After all, critical theory and its contemporary educational applications such as critical pedagogy are grounded in an activist desire to fight oppression, injustice, and bigotry and create a fairer, more compassionate world. Central to this tradition is a concern with highly practical projects—the practice of penetrating ideology, countering hegemony, and working democratically. Given that luminaries in the critical canon such as Gramsci were more than ready to describe in great detail the specifics of revolutionary strategy (for example, the creation and functioning of the factory council organization), it is surprising that such a deep suspicion of documenting practice (while not reifying it) has crept into adult educational interpretations of critical theory.

A refusal by theorists to dirty their hands with the specifics of practice is epistemologically untenable. Like it or not, we are all theorists and our formal and informal theories of practice inevitably frame how we approach helping adults learn. Conversely, our theoretical quests are usually initiated by our desires to explain and resolve the practical contradictions and tangles that consume our energies. The formal theory that appears in books and journals may be a more codified, regulated, and abstracted form of thinking about general problems, but it is not different in kind from the understandings embedded in our own local decisions and actions.

The Meaning of Criticality in Critical Theory

This is a book not just about theory but about a particular type of theory—critical theory. This takes us into deep waters indeed, since the term *critical* is deeply perverse in the plurality of connotations and interpretations (some of them contradictory) it provokes. Nonetheless, what this book is trying to do is explore a theory of adult learning that could be described as critical. Obviously, then, I need to explain exactly what this term means.

Criticality is a contested idea, one with a variety of meanings each claimed by different groups for very different purposes. How the term *critical* is used inevitably reflects the ideology and world-view of the user. As an example, consider the different ways people understand what it means to learn in a critical way at the workplace. Following the work of Argyris (1982), critical learning, thinking, and reflection are represented by executives' use of lateral, divergent thinking strategies and double loop learning methods. Here adult workers are deemed to learn critically when they examine the assumptions that govern business decisions by checking whether or not these decisions are grounded in an accurately assessed view of market realities. Inferential ladders are scrutinized for the false rungs that lead business teams into, for example, a disastrous choice regarding the way in which a brand image upsets a certain group of potential customers. The consequence of this exercise in critical thought is an increase in profits and productivity, and a decrease in industrial sabotage and worker absenteeism. Capitalism is left unchallenged as more creative or humanistic ways are found to organize production or sell services. The free market is infused with a social democratic warmth that curtails its worst excesses. The ideological and structural premises of the capitalist workplace remain intact.

For others, critical learning in a business setting cannot occur without an explicit critique of capitalism (Collins, 1991; Simon, Dippo, and Schenke, 1991; Mojab and Gorman, 2003). This kind of critical learning at the workplace involves workers fighting the immoral practice of relocating plants to countries where pollution controls are much looser, unions are banned, and labor is much cheaper. It challenges the demonizing of union members as corrupt Stalinist obstructionists engaged in a consistent misuse of power and explores the conditions under which successful organizing takes place. It investigates the ways in which profits are distributed and the conditions under which those profits are generated. It points out and queries the legitimation of capitalist ideology through changes in language; for example, the creeping and ever more widespread use of phrases such as "buying into" or "creating ownership" of an idea, the description of students as "customers," or the use of euphemisms such as "downsizing" or worse, "rightsizing" (with its implication that firing people restores some sort of natural ecological balance to the market) to soften and make palatable the reality of people losing their livelihoods, homes, marriages, selfrespect, and hope. In critical theory terms, the workplace is transformed when cooperative democracy and worker control replace the distribution of profits among shareholders and when workplace learning focuses on the worker's exercise of her creative capacities in terms she herself defines. In Horkheimer's (1995) words, "Critical thinking . . . is motivated today by the effort to abolish the opposition between the individual's purposefulness, spontaneity, and rationality, and those work-process relationships on which society is built" (p. 210). The factory councils in Turin, the Clydeside Shipbuilding (Scotland) sit-in, the 1968 occupation of the Renault factory outside Paris—these would be examples of workplace learning in this perspective.

How is it that the same term can be used to refer to such different activities? To understand the concept of criticality properly we need to disentangle the different, and often conflicting, intellectual traditions informing its use. Four predominant traditions inform criticality: ideology critique as seen in neo-Marxism and the work of the Frankfurt School of Critical Social Theory (the primary tradition examined in this book), psychoanalysis and psychotherapy, analytic philosophy and logic, and pragmatist constructivism.

Four Traditions of Criticality

In a provocative essay, "Making Critical Thinking Critical," Kincheloe (2000) argues that the political and ethical dimensions integral to criticality have been forgotten in contemporary programs of critical thinking. To him, criticality is grounded in the work of the Frankfurt School of Critical Social Theory and the ideas of Adorno (1973), Horkheimer (1974, 1995), and Marcuse (1964). Critical thinking is really "the ability of individuals to disengage themselves from the tacit assumptions of discursive practices and power relations in order to exert more conscious control over their everyday lives" (p. 24). This kind of critical distancing from, and then oppositional reengagement with, the dominant culture is the central learning task of adulthood, according to the Frankfurt School, who used the term *ideology critique* to describe this activity. When I talk of criticality and critical theory in this book, it is the ideology critique tradition I am chiefly invoking. As a learning process, ideology critique describes the ways in which people learn to recognize how uncritically accepted and unjust dominant ideologies are embedded in everyday situations and practices. As an educational activity, ideology critique focuses on helping people come to an awareness of how capitalism shapes social relations and imposes— often without our knowledge—belief systems and assumptions (that is, ideologies) that justify and maintain economic and political inequity.

An important element in the ideology critique tradition is the concept of hegemony which explains the way in which people are convinced to embrace dominant ideologies as always being in their own best interests. One of the theorists of hegemony, Antonio Gramsci, points out that because people learn hegemonic values, ideas, and practices, and because schools and other cultural institutions play a major role in presenting these ideas as the natural order of things, hegemony must always be understood as an educational phenomenon. For Jack Mezirow—probably the most influential contemporary theorist of adult learning—doing ideology critique is equivalent to what he calls "systemic" critical reflection that focuses on probing sociocultural distortions (Mezirow, 1991b). Mezirow argues that ideology critique is appropriate for critical reflection on external ideologies such as communism, capitalism, or fascism or for reflection on our own "economic, ecological, educational, linguistic, political, religious, bureaucratic, or other taken-for-granted cultural systems" (Mezirow, 1998, p. 193). Ideology critique contains within it the promise of social transformation and frames the work of influential activist adult educators such as Freire, Tawney, Williams, Horton, Coady, and Tomkins.

A second more psychoanalytically and psychotherapeutically inclined tradition emphasizes criticality in adulthood as the identification and reappraisal of inhibitions acquired in childhood as a result of various traumas. Mezirow (1981) writes of "the emancipatory process of becoming critically aware of how and why the structure of psycho-cultural assumptions has come to constrain the way we see ourselves and our relationships" (p. 6). Using the framework of transformative learning, theorists like Gould (1990) emphasize the process whereby adults come to realize how childhood inhibitions serve to frustrate them from realizing their full development as persons. This realization is the first step to slaying these inhibiting demons, laying them to rest, and living in a more integrated, authentic manner. Different theorists emphasize variously the extent to which the development of new social structures is a precondition of a newly constituted, integrated personality. Carl Rogers (1961), for example, sees significant personal learning and personal development as occurring through individual and group therapy and does not address wider political factors—an omission he regretted in his last book, *A Way of Being* (Rogers, 1980). Others, such as Erich Fromm (1941) and Ronald Laing (1960), argue that personality is socially and politically sculpted. These theorists view schizophrenia and mental illness as socially produced phenomena representing the internal contradictions of capitalism. To them the rise of totalitarian and fascist regimes is made possible by the way ideologies structure personality types that yearn for order, predictability, and externally imposed controls. This tradition is also clearly present in Mezirow's (1991a) groundbreaking theoretical work. To radical psychologists such as Laing and neo-Marxists like Fromm, individual and social transformation cannot be separated. For the personality to be reconstituted, insane and inhumane social forms need to be replaced by congenial social and economic structures, and the contradictions of capitalism need to be reconciled. In *Marx's Concept of Man* (1961), Fromm argues that the young Marx was convinced that the chief benefit of socialist revolution would be the transformation of the personality, the creation of a new kind of humanitarian citizen.

A third tradition shaping how criticality is thought and spoken about is that of analytic philosophy and logic. Here learning to be critical describes the process by which we become more skillful in argument analysis. In this tradition we act critically when we recognize logical fallacies, when we distinguish between bias and fact, opinion and evidence, uninformed judgment and valid inference, and when we become skilled at using different forms of reasoning (inductive, deductive, analogical, and so on). This tradition is often very much in evidence in texts on critical thinking (Stice, 1987; Norris and Ennis, 1989) the intent of which is to improve skills of analysis and argument disconnected from any particular ideological critique. In Wittgenstein's (1953) terms, social relations are understood as word games, and social understanding involves unpacking the multiple meanings and uses of language. Social action in this tradition is akin to participating in speech acts (Searle, 1969). Two British adult educators working in this tradition—Kenneth Lawson (1975) and Ralph Patterson (1979)—have produced provocative deconstructions of the concepts of adult learning, adulthood, and adult education. This tradition's concern for linguistic analysis as the defining characteristic of critical thinking seems, on the surface, far removed from Horkheimer's (1995) contention that "the critical attitude . . . is wholly distrustful of the rules of conduct with which society as presently constituted provides each of its members" (p. 207).

Finally, a fourth tradition that many invoke when defining criticality is that of pragmatist constructivism. This tradition emphasizes the way people learn how to construct and deconstruct their own experiences and meanings. Constructivism rejects universals and generalizable truths and focuses instead on the variability of how people make interpretations of their experience. This strand of thought maintains that events happen to us but that experiences are constructed by us. Pragmatism emphasizes the importance of continuous experimentation to bring about better (in pragmatist terms, more beautiful) social forms. It argues that in building a democratic society we experiment, change, and discover our own and others' fallibility. Democracy is the political form embraced by pragmatism since it fosters experimentation with diversity. Cherryholmes (1999) writes that "pragmatism requires democracy" since "social openness, inclusiveness, tolerance, and experimentation generate more outcomes than closed, exclusive, and intolerant deliberations" (p. 39). Elements of these two traditions are evident in parts of John Dewey's (1938) work and they have filtered, via the work of Eduard Lindeman ([1926] 1961), into adult education's concern with helping people understand their experience and with the field's preference for experiential methods. In Myles Horton's (1990) renowned work at Highlander Folk School, a largely constructivist approach was allied with a tradition of ideology critique to help activists realize that their own experience—properly analyzed in a collaborative but critical way—could be an invaluable resource in their fight for social justice.

My own understanding of criticality draws on all these traditions, but the first of these—ideology critique—is undoubtedly the most prominent. However, I also believe that it is possible to argue a concept of criticality that blends elements of pragmatism into the critical theory traditions. This stance, which might be called critical pragmatism, is one that accepts the essential accuracy and usefulness of the reading of society embedded within ideology critique. It also allies itself with the struggle to create a world in which one's race, class, and gender do not frame the limits within which one can experience life. However, it is also skeptical of any claims to foundationalism or essentialism, that is, to the belief that there is one, and only one, way to conceive of and create such a society. This fusion of critical theory and pragmatism is not to everyone's taste. Indeed, several of those associated with the critical tradition reject entirely the idea that pragmatism has any liberatory dimension. In his introduction to a reissued volume of Horkheimer's (1995) essays, Stanley Aronowitz condemns pragmatism as subversive of, and antithetical to, social and political critique, describing it as "the theory of nontheory" and claiming that "it leaves no room for critical theory" (pp. xv–xvi). In *Eclipse of Reason* ([1947] 1974), Horkheimer himself denounced pragmatism as a form of scientism that put all its faith in improvement through systematic experimentation and therefore represented the intellectual "counterpart of modern industrialism" (p. 50). The result of pragmatism's focus on the experimental improvement of contemporary conditions meant that "speculative thought is altogether liquidated" (p. 103). Gramsci (1971) too regarded pragmatism's focus on practice as undertheorized and inherently conservative, leading "to the justification of conservative and reactionary movements" (p. 373).

I believe, however, that the pragmatic tradition is not as destructive to criticality as Horkheimer, Aronowitz, and Gramsci argue. If we conceive of pragmatism as the flexible pursuit of beautiful consequences, it is reasonable to argue that the most beautiful social consequences of all are those of freedom and justice presupposed by Horkheimer himself as the defining necessities of critical theory

(1995, p. 230, 242). Taking a pragmatic slant on critical theory argues for a defensible flexibility regarding ways these values might be realized and encourages a self-critical, self-referential stance (claimed by some as integral to the critical tradition). It also reaffirms the creation of democratic forms of life as the central project of theory. The concern to democratize production to serve the whole community and the desire to reconfigure the workplace as a site for the exercise of human creativity are the meeting points for critical theory and pragmatism. The contemporary critical theorist Jürgen Habermas himself acknowledged this, arguing that his work could be interpreted as building on American pragmatism. In a 1985 interview he declared that "I have for a long time identified myself with that radical democratic mentality which is present in the best American traditions and articulated in American pragmatism" (p. 198). Shalin (1992) too argues that Habermas' theory of communicative action is "an attempt to invigorate critical theory by merging the Continental and Anglo-Saxon traditions and bringing the pragmatist perspective to bear on the project of emancipation through reason" (p. 244).

Perhaps the most sustained attempt to reinvent pragmatism as a critical philosophy is Cornel West's (1999a) passionate enunciation of prophetic pragmatism. The prophetic element in this philosophy "harks back to the Jewish and Christian traditions of prophets who brought urgent and compassionate critique to bear on the evils of their day" (p. 171). The pragmatic element "understands pragmatism as a political form of cultural criticism and locates politics in the everyday experience of ordinary people" (p. 151). West argues that "the emancipatory social experimentation that sits at the center of prophetic pragmatist politics closely resembles the radical democratic elements of Marxist theory, yet its flexibility shuns any dogmatic, a priori or monistic pronouncements" (pp. 151–152). For him, the twin pillars of prophetic pragmatism are "critical temper as a way of struggle and democratic faith as a way of life" (p. 186), with the pragmatist spirit ensuring that the certitudes of critical theory never become reified, never placed beyond healthy criticism. Despite Gramsci's rejection of pragmatism, West contends that "Gramsci exemplifies the critical spirit and oppositional sentiments of prophetic pragmatism" (p. 169), and he goes so far as to invoke Gramsci's concept of organic intellectuals in describing prophetic pragmatists as those who "relate ideas to action by means of creating, constituting or consolidating constituencies for moral aims and political purposes" (p. 146).

Marxism and Critical Theory

In this section I want to position critical theory as part of a wider intellectual debate concerning the correct response to and updating of Marxist analysis in the centuries following his death. Marx is the towering intellectual figure—simultaneously foundation and fulcrum—for the writers who fall into the category of what most people now call critical theory. In several ways his work shapes much of the work in this tradition. Many of its most important analytical categories—false consciousness, commodification, objectification, alienation—are derived from Marx's interpretations of Enlightenment thought and his dialogue with Hegel. Wiggerhaus' (1994) massive survey of the Frankfurt School makes clear that Horkheimer, Marcuse, and Fromm drew particularly on the "early" Marx's critique of the alienation and diminution of humanity produced by capitalism. In adult education, Habermas' work (which has been so influential on Mezirow's development of transformative learning theory) is in many ways a talking back to Marx. Yet, although Marx's ideas undergird one strand of transformative learning theory (that drawing on critical theory's concern with personal liberation), he is rarely mentioned in American adult education. Other than Holst's (2002) analysis, no major American text in the field takes Marxism as its conceptual center. Perhaps this is because American adult educators are fearful of being branded as subversive, communistic, overtly political, or concerned only with sectional class interests if they invoke his name. In other English-speaking countries, adult educators are more ready to engage with Marx as writers such as Law (1992), Mayo (1998), Welton (1995), Allman (2000, 2001), and Youngman (2000), amongst others, demonstrate. Welton (1995) argues that "the consequences of forgetting Marx for the construction of a critical theory of adult learning are enormous, inevitably binding us to an individualistic model of learning" (p. 19).

One of the difficulties with remembering Marx is the "knee-jerk 'marxophobia'" (McLaren, 1997, p. 172) faced by those who draw, however critically or circumspectly, on his work. Marxophobia holds that even to mention Marx is to engage in un-American behavior and by implication to support the genocide and repression exhibited by totalitarian communist regimes throughout history. Despite repeated attempts by all the Frankfurt School theorists to disassociate Marxist analysis from the rigidity of state totalitarianism, popular opinion equates Marx with repression, standardization, bureaucratization, and denial of creativity or liberty. One reason for this, as West (1982) points out, is the immediate association of Marxism with Stalinist centralization in particular and Soviet society in general. West remarks that "it is no accident that in American lingo Marxism is synonymous with Sovietism. It is as if the only Christianity that Americans were ever exposed to was that of Jerry Falwell's Moral Majority" (p. 139).

Yet, though critical theory can be conceived as a constant conversation with Marx, it is not a simple replication of Marxism. As McLaren points out, "Many if not most critical educators work outside the orthodox Marxian tradition and do not consider capitalism an irrevocable evil" (McLaren, 1997, p. 172). Erich Fromm, amongst other critical theorists, pointed out that it is also possible to find cracks and crevices in a capitalist system: "One must admit that 'capitalism' is in itself a complex and constantly changing structure which still permits of a good deal of non-conformity and of personal latitude" (1956b, p. 132). In the critical theory tradition, it is perfectly possible to find a Marxist analysis useful without by implication endorsing the Gulag or Chinese cultural revolution. Indeed, Marcuse, West, Davis, and others draw attention to the democratic impulse in Marx, while Fromm sees Marx as concerned chiefly with spiritual liberation.

If critical theory can be understood as a critical engagement with Marx, then a critical theory of adult learning must begin by acknowledging the centrality of Marxist concepts. This is not the stretch it might first appear to those nervously suffering Marxophobia. As an example, think of the criticisms made by many continuing educators in higher education to the effect that accelerated learning programs are used as cash cows to prop up colleges faced by sagging enrollments of traditional-aged students. By processing as many adult students as quickly as possible through the institution, such institutions are displaying a commodification of learning. Commodification—the process by which a human quality or relationship becomes regarded as a product, good, or commodity to be bought and sold on the open market—is a Marxist notion connected to his other ideas of objectification, fetishization, and exchange value. It is the key concept used by Shumar in his book *College for Sale* (1997), the subtitle of which is *A Critique of the Commodification of Higher Education.* So a criticism that many mainstream adult educators would feel very comfortable making can be traced back to Marxist analysis.

Youngman's (2000) analysis of adult education and development also illustrates the enduring relevance of Marxist modes of analysis for illuminating specific adult teaching and learning situations. Early in his book he argues that "Marxist social theory . . . provides a coherent foundation for comprehending adult education and development at both the micro and micro levels of analysis" (p. 9) and supports this by demonstrating how a computing class at a private commercial college in Harare can be analyzed using tools of class analysis, colonialism, and the development of capitalism in Africa. The class is organized to produce the skilled labor Zimbabwe needs to compete in the global economy. The location is partly a result of pressure from the World Bank and International Monetary Fund to create more private adult education organizations. The curricular materials are provided by an American transnational corporation, and participation in the class is determined by the economic situation of the learners. Relations between students in the class and between students and the teacher are structured by patterns of class, race, gender, and ethnicity, which themselves reflect Zimbabwe's colonial heritage. Hence, to Youngman "the everyday activity and experience of the adult educator and adult learners in this class are shaped by the wider economic and political realities of Zimbabwe and its place in world economy" (p. 10).

As well as providing critical theory with many of its central concepts, Marx also influences its forms of discourse. His alternation between polemic and scientism, between philosophizing about the need to create the conditions under which people can realize their creativity and humanity and demonstrating the immutable laws of history focused on the predictable crises of capitalism, has framed the style in which much subsequent critical theory is written. His grounding of social and political analysis in the realization of an explicit social ideal has also meant that critical theory after Marx springs explicitly from a normative vision of the good society. In his often quoted eleventh thesis on Feuerbach in which he argued that the point of philosophy was to change the world (not just interpret it), Marx underpins the intent of critical theory to act as a catalyst for revolutionary social change. Youngman (2000) argues that this activism is clearly evident in "the long-standing heritage within radical adult education in capitalist societies that has been based explicitly on Marxist theory" (p. 33) and further maintains that "since the early days of Marxism there has been a close connection between Marxist theory and the practice of adult education" (p. 32). As evidence of this, he cites Marx's involvement with the German Workers' Education Association, Gramsci's role in organizing workers' factory councils of Turin, and the creation by American Marxist socialists of the Working People's College in 1907.

With the fall of the Berlin Wall and the disintegration of the Union of Soviet Socialist Republics, many came to believe that Marxism had been intellectually discredited. Yet Marx's ideas refuse to disappear. In asking *Why Read Marx Today?* Wolff (2002) notes that the lectures his book is based on consistently attract standing-room-only audiences. Any time someone acknowledges that society is structured economically to favor a fortunate few, or any time someone observes that the rich get richer while the poor get poorer, they are probably drawing on a Marxist framework. When the debate about the North American Free Trade Agreement (NAFTA) rages, and critics point out how free trade across national boundaries chiefly allows corporations to get richer by exploiting new markets while reducing costs through the exploitation of cheap, non-unionized labor, Marx's influence is present. An interesting example of his enduring influence is seen in the fact that one of the most prominent contemporary African American thinkers, Cornel West, continues to engage with Marxist ideas (West, 1991). Certainly, Marx's influence hovers over the field of critical theory as elaborated by the Frankfurt School. Thinkers identified with this school (such as Adorno, Horkheimer, Marcuse, and Fromm) believed Marx's ideas could indeed breathe vigorously on the shores of the twentieth century, and they tried to restate and reinterpret the meaning of those ideas for a world Marx could not foresee. This reframing was done in a characteristically critical way. As Jay (1973) observes, "One of the essential characteristics of critical theory from its inception had been a refusal to consider Marxism a closed body of received truths" (p. 254).

This was just as well since the twentieth century was mounting many challenges to Marxism. The Bolshevik Revolution of 1917 had occurred in a predominantly rural (rather than urban) society and been a political coup d'état engineered by intellectual émigrés rather than a mass uprising springing from the urban proletariat as expected. Furthermore, the Russian Revolution had not led to a domino effect. Despite the working class being used as cannon fodder in World War I, there had been no revolutionary flame spontaneously combusting throughout the rest of Europe and beyond. Those societies that purported to operate according to Marxist principles were transmogrifying into ones characterized by totalitarian repression and the kind of worker alienation ascribed to capitalism. In the most advanced capitalist societies such as the United States, large sections of the working class seemed eager to enjoy the fruits of the capitalist system rather than destroy it. And on top of this there was the rise of fascism and Nazism. Faced with these and other realities, the Frankfurt School theorists took Marx's analytical categories and tried both to critique and use them as the departure point for the creation of entirely new categories. These categories would comprise a critical theory of social, political, and human development for the modern era.

The Frankfurt School is the shorthand descriptor for the Institute of Social Research established in 1923 in Frankfurt, Germany. It attracted and sponsored work done by, amongst others, Max Horkheimer (the Institute's director from 1930), Erich Fromm, Herbert Marcuse, and Theodor Adorno (who became codirector in 1955). As Nazism took over German life, the Institute moved to Geneva (in 1933) and then New York (in 1935). In 1953 it returned to Frankfurt, but after Adorno and Horkheimer's deaths (in 1969 and 1973, respectively) the Institute's distinctive intellectual project—to interpret, critique, and reframe the relevance of Marxist thought for contemporary industrial society—declined. Amongst contemporary thinkers Jürgen Habermas (who was once Adorno's assistant) is the most well known intellectual heir of the school's legacy. The Frankfurt School's work branched into two complementary lines of inquiry—ideology critique and psychoanalysis—both of which were identified in the previous section as important contributors to the critical tradition. The first of these—ideology critique—is the dominant tradition invoked in this book.

What Is So Critical About Critical Theory? Five Distinctive Characteristics

How does a critical theory differ from other kinds of theories? This is the key question addressed by Max Horkheimer in his classic 1937 essay, "Traditional and Critical Theory" (1995), and his analysis remains pertinent today. Although Horkheimer acknowledges that critical theory contains elements of what he calls traditional (that is, positivist) theory, there are important differences. The first of these is that critical theory is firmly grounded in a particular political analysis. Hence "critical theory does not have one doctrinal substance today, another tomorrow" (p. 234). This is because its primary unit of analysis—the conflicting relationship between social classes within an economy based on the exchange of commodities—remains stable, at least until society has been radically transformed. A "single existential judgment" (p. 227) is at the heart of critical theory. This is that the commodity exchange economy comprising capitalism will inevitably generate a series of tensions created by the desire of some of the people for emancipation and the wish of others to prevent this desire being realized. Horkheimer was pessimistic regarding the possibility for emancipation, believing that this would finally be suppressed and humanity driven into "a new barbarism" (p. 227). However, his pessimism did not mean that people should fall into quietism or conformism. Instead, he contended that the theory itself assumed that those who subscribed to it would fight against this creeping barbarism: "Every part of the theory presupposes the critique of the existing order and the struggle against it along the lines determined by the theory itself" (p. 229). So the starting point of Horkheimer's analysis is that the commodity exchange economy that dominates social relations must be reconfigured so that people can realize their humanity and freedom.

In the commodity exchange economy (an idea borrowed from Marx), the dynamic of exchange—I give you this, you give me that in return—determines all human relationships. The exchange value of a thing (what it's worth in monetary terms) overshadows its use value (its value assessed by how it helps satisfy a human need or desire). For example, the exchange value of gold (what people will pay to own a gold necklace) is a socially determined phenomenon that has little to do with its use value (which would be determined by the functions it could be used for, such as producing reliable teeth fillings). The exchange value of learning to read in adulthood (how such learning will help the adult become more successful in the job market) overshadows its use value (how it helps the adult develop self-confidence, draw new meanings from life, and be opened to new perspectives on the world). Although the use value of learning is important to adult learners and adult educators, it is primarily the exchange value that policy makers and purse holders consider when determining whether or not programs should be funded and how they should be evaluated.

In the exchange economy, goods and products are primarily produced for the profit their exchange value will bring their manufacturers. One important dimension of the exchange economy is the way that inanimate objects and goods become "fetishized," to use Marx's term. We start to think that these objects and goods contain some innate financial value or monetary worth that has been magically determined by forces beyond our recognition. Of course, this worth does not exist independently inside the product. In reality it is an expression of how much someone is willing to pay for it (in exchange economy terms, what goods or money we will exchange to own the product).

In the exchange economy it is not only products and goods that seem to acquire an apparently innate worth (which is really determined by market forces). Our labor—including our intellectual labor of learning and teaching—also becomes an object thought to have some intrinsic value. We exchange labor for money and money for goods, and in the process our labor becomes a thing, a commodity just like the goods we exchange money for. Hence we come to regard our labor power—our ability to work—as if it were a thing existing outside of us, no different in kind from other goods and products. When the objects or commodities we exchange become abstract entities or things to us, existing in an apparently separate universe in which their worth is determined by mysterious outside forces, this is called commodity fetishism. Because of commodity fetishism we sell our labor power—our learning—as if it were a commodity just like any other artifact. A transformative adult learning experience, such as going to college and finding one's worldview radically altered, becomes viewed by us as the pursuit of a qualification that can be exchanged for higher salary and status.

In this process a major source of our identity and sense of self-worth—our labor—is turned into an abstract object, commodified. Our relationships too become fetishized, assuming in our eyes "the phantastic form of a relationship between things" (Marx, 1973, p. 72). Hence in adult education we talk of the teaching-learning relationship and the development of adult educational procedures or curricula as if these existed as objects in a world located outside our emotions or being. The role of the adult educator engaged in good practices becomes detached from who we are as people, our histories and experiences. The exchange dynamic of capitalism even invades our emotional lives. We talk of making emotional investments, as if emotions were things we could float on the stock market of significant personal relationships. Attention and tenderness are exchanged for sex, affection for support. Parental concern toward children is exchanged for the promise of being looked after in old age. Habermas (1987a) describes this invasion of our personal lives by capitalist processes of exchange as the colonization of the lifeworld.

A second distinctive characteristic of critical theory is its concern to provide people with knowledge and understandings intended to free them from oppression. The point of theory is to generate knowledge that will change, not just interpret, the world. In this way, Horkheimer argues, critical theory truly qualifies for that most overused of adjectives, "transformative." There is no presupposition of theory being distanced from social intervention or political action. On the contrary, the converse is true. Critical theory *requires* such intervention. Its explicit intent is to galvanize people into replacing capitalism with truly democratic social arrangements. One important measure of the theory's validity, therefore, is its capacity to inspire action. In the evaluation literature, this is referred to as *consequential validity*, that is, validity that "asks for assessments of who benefits and who is harmed by an inquiry, measurement or method" (Patton, 2002, p. 548). The knowledge the theory produces can be considered useful to the extent that it helps change the behavior of its unit of analysis (people acting in society).

Geuss (1981) summarizes this view by describing critical theory as a "reflective theory which gives agents a kind of knowledge inherently productive of enlightenment and emancipation" (p. 2). To Horkheimer (1995) "its goal is man's emancipation from slavery" (p. 246) though he warned against a simplistic translation of the theory's tenets into schemes for emancipatory action. In his view, "philosophy must not be turned into propaganda, even for the best possible purposes . . . philosophy is not interested in issuing commands" ([1947] 1974, p. 184). In terms echoing Freire's later warnings regarding unreflective activism, Horkheimer declared that "action for action's sake is in no way superior to thought for thought's sake, and is perhaps even inferior to it" ([1947] 1974, p. vi). But the fact remains that critical theory is clearly transformative and exists to bring about social change. The research tradition most strongly identified with adult education— participatory research—is very much an exemplification of this idea. Participatory researchers make no pretense to detached observation. Their purpose is to help adults research their communities with a view to changing them in directions they (the adult citizens concerned) determine.

Horkheimer goes on to argue that a third crucial difference between critical theory and other kinds is that it breaks down the separation of subject and object, of researcher and focus of research, found in traditional theories. The validity of critical theory derives partly from the fact that its subjects—human beings, specifically those diminished by the workings of capitalism— support the philosophical vision of society inherent within the theory. The theory's utility depends partly on people recognizing that it expresses accurately the yearnings they have for a better more authentic way to live. As Geuss (1981) observes, this is clearly not the case with positivist approaches to studying the physical, chemical, and biological world. Traditional scientific theory has no requirement to secure the agreement of its objects of study. Asking atomic particles or types of flora whether or not they give free assent to the accuracy of the way they are described is nonsensical. An important indicator of the validity of a critical theory of adult learning, therefore, is the extent to which adults believe that the theory captures their hopes and dreams.

The fact that it is normatively grounded is critical theory's fourth defining feature. Not only does the theory criticize current society, it also envisages a fairer, less alienated, more democratic world. In Benhabib's (1986) terms, the project of critical theory is situated somewhere between social science and practical philosophy. Empirical investigation and utopian speculation are intimately connected. The critique undertaken of existing social, political, and economic conditions springs from and depends on the form of the alternative society envisioned. Unlike traditional theories that are empirically grounded in an attempt to generate increasingly accurate descriptions of the world as it exists, critical theory tries to generate a specific vision of the world as it might be. It springs from a distinct philosophical vision of what it means to live as a developed person, as a mature adult struggling to realize one's humanity through the creation of a society that is just, fair, and compassionate. This vision holds individual identity to be socially and culturally formed. Adult development is viewed as a collective process since one person's humanity cannot be realized at the expense of others' interests. Given critical theory's insistence that opportunities for development do not remain the preserve of the privileged few, the theory inevitably links adult development to the extension of economic democracy.

This grounding of critical theory in a preconfigured vision and set of values opens it to the criticism that it is not a genuine theory at all but a set of preferences, prescriptions, and platitudes— "Marxist flower power" as a onetime colleague of mine characterized it. Horkheimer (1995) himself acknowledges this criticism commenting that "although critical theory at no point proceeds arbitrarily and in chance fashion, it appears, to prevailing modes of thought, to be speculative, one-sided and useless . . . biased and unjust" (p. 218). He notes that this leads critics of the theory to portray it as "an aimless intellectual game, half conceptual poetry, half impotent expression of states of mind" (p. 209). After all, basing a theory on the "single existential judgment" of critiquing and transforming the commodity exchange economy does predetermine the focus of study. Yet it is not that simple.

In fact, trying to realize the philosophical and social vision of critical theory is enormously complicated. The industrial proletariat that figures so centrally in Marx's analysis has expanded into third-world peasantry (some of whom work in the first world) as capital has become increasingly mobile. As Collini (2000) notes in commenting on the internationalizing of class conflict, "The 'proletariat' of global capitalism mostly have different colored skins from those of the global bourgeoisie" (p. 12). The seductive promise of a life full of more and better consumer goods has managed to blunt revolutionary impulses among those working-class adults who might be regarded as the engine of social change. Indeed, in Western capitalist societies the last years of the twentieth century saw a decline in political institutions, such as trade and labor unions, organized to serve working-class interests. The analytical terrain on which critical theory is fought out has also grown more complicated. Race and gender have attained an equal prominence with social class as units of analysis. Poststructuralism has challenged our simple understanding of the exercise of sovereign or state power so that we are more aware of how we exercise censorship, surveillance, and discipline on ourselves. And postmodernism's emphasis on the idiosyncratic and uncontrollable nature of experience seems to undercut the possibility of critical awareness, freedom, and emancipation so central to critical theory's project. As society has fragmented by race, culture, and gender, so too the possible configurations of what freedom looks like have expanded. In and out of cyberspace, the ways human agency and social preferences are exercised are, at least potentially, infinitely diverse. This contemporary emphasis on difference and diversity is one reason to reexamine pragmatism as a tradition that embraces experimentation and emphasizes the different ways people think about realizing their humanity.

Of course, once we start using terms such as *realizing humanity* we have to acknowledge that these are culturally loaded, their meanings reflecting the class, gender, race, and ideology of those using them. The images generated by these terms vary greatly depending on the cultural milieu of the definer, with some images having much greater status than others. To some the classical concert hall has much more cache as an appropriate place to realize one's humanity through artistic creativity than, say, the mosh pit. To others, free market capitalism is seen as a more mature way to encourage freedom and creative energy than, say, state socialism. Additionally, postmodern analysis calls into question the idea that people contain a coherent identity waiting to be developed, arguing instead that this view represents a misplaced modernist confidence in the basic rationality and ultimate perfectibility of human beings. In postmodernism each of us is "fragmented among a plurality of partial identities, identity being only provisionally determined and underdetermined, and therefore open to the contingent addition of further partial identities" (Bagnall, 1999, p. 107). Faith in people's capacity to become more humane, and society's ability to organize itself along more compassionate lines, is shattered by the continuing existence of horrors such as genocide and ethnic cleansing. In Bagnall's words, postmodernism suggests that "morally, individuals appear to be capable of anything at all, so long as it is sanctioned by the frameworks of belief within which they are operating" (p. 108). To the extent that critical theory posits the creation of a more just and compassionate society as a pursuable ideal, it is unashamedly modernist.

This brings us to the fifth and final intriguing and distinctive element of critical theory, the fact that verification of the theory is impossible until the social vision it inspires is realized. In other words, we won't know whether critical theory is true or false until the world it envisages is created and we can judge its relative humanity and compassion. Horkheimer (1995) puts it this way: "In regard to the essential kind of change at which the critical theory aims, there can be no corresponding concrete perception of it until it actually comes about. If the proof of the pudding is in the eating, the eating here is still in the future" (p. 220). Traditional theories can usually be assessed by reference to the world as it is now or in the near future. Alternatively, the physical world can be manipulated where possible to create conditions under which the predictions of the theory can be tested for accuracy. By way of contrast, Horkheimer warns that the struggle to create the conditions under which the vision of critical theory can be tested is a long, sometimes violent, often revolutionary struggle.

Outlining Critical Theory's Relevance for Adult Learning

So how does all this connect to adult learning? And how, in particular, can adult learning theory be reframed in the light of critical theory? For me, two elements are central. First, and most importantly, we can focus on the dimensions of learning central to the chief concern of critical theory. This concern might be expressed as the desire to understand how the reproduction of blatantly unequal structures based on massive economic disparity is accepted as the natural order of things by adults within successive generations. What does critical theory tell us about how adults learn to accept and then challenge this state of affairs? Second, we can explore the way critical theory applies the critical reflection on assumptions—often claimed to be a distinctive characteristic both of adult learning and of adult education practice—on itself. Let me take each of these elements in turn.

The Centrality of Learning

Critical theory is usually not written in terms immediately recognizable to those of us primarily interested in adult learning. Yet, an analysis of adult learning is usually implicit in critical theory's propositions. Welton (1991, 1993, 1995) is perhaps the most forceful expositor of how critical theory, specifically that associated with Jürgen Habermas, threads a theory of adult learning through its analysis. Subsumed within the general desire of critical theory to understand and then challenge the continuous reproduction of social, political, and economic domination are a number of related concerns. One of these is to investigate how dominant ideologies educate people to believe certain ways of organizing society are in their own best interests when the opposite is true. Another is to illuminate how the spirit of capitalism, and of technical and bureaucratic rationality, enters into and distorts everyday relationships (what Habermas calls the colonization of the lifeworld by the system). A third (and this is particularly important to a theory of adult learning) is to understand how people learn to identify and then oppose the ideological forces and social processes that oppress them.

A theory of adult learning originating in these general concerns of critical theory would attempt to answer a series of more specific questions focused on the way people learn to awaken and then act on their human agency. These questions would ask how people learn to challenge beliefs and structures that serve the interests of the few against the well-being of the many. Some of these specific questions might be:

How do adults learn forms of reasoning that challenge dominant ideology and that question the social, cultural, and political forms that ideology justifies?

How do adults learn to interpret their experiences in ways that emphasize their connectedness to others and lead them to see the need for solidarity and collective organization?

How do adults learn to unmask the flow of power in their lives and communities?

How do adults learn of the existence of hegemony—the process whereby people learn to embrace ideas, practices, and institutions that actually work against their own best interests—and of their own complicity in its continued existence? And, once aware of it, how do they contest its all-pervasive effects?

How do adults learn to defend the lifeworld (the set of understandings and assumptions that frame how people live with each other) and civil society (the relationships, associations, and institutions not directly under state control within which people form relationships and develop identities) against the intrusion of capitalist ethics, market forces, and bureaucratic rationality?

How do adults learn to think critically by recognizing when an embrace of alternative views is actually supporting the status quo it appears to be challenging?

How do adults learn to recognize, accept, and exercise whatever freedom they have to change the world?

How do adults learn the practice of democracy with all its contradictions and disciplines?

As should be clear from these questions, a critical theory of adult learning is inevitably also a theory of social and political learning.

It studies the systems and forces that shape adults' lives and oppose adults' attempts to challenge ideology, recognize hegemony, unmask power, defend the lifeworld, and develop agency. Such a theory must recognize its explicitly political character. It must focus consistently on political matters such as the way formal learning is structured and limited by the unequal exercise of power. It must not shy away from connecting adult learning efforts to the creation of political forms, particularly the extension of economic democracy across barriers of race, class, and gender. It must understand adult education as a political process in which certain interests and agendas are always pursued at the expense of others, in which curriculum inevitably promotes some content as "better" than some other, and in which evaluation is an exercise of the power by some to judge the efforts of others. Critical theory springs from the desire to extend democratic socialist values and processes, to create a world in which a commitment to the common good is the foundation of individual well-being and development. A critical theory of adult learning will always come back to the ways in which adults learn to do this.

A Critical Posture Toward Critical Theory

The second element a critical theory of adult learning should display is a self-critical stance toward its own propositions. Just as critical theory illuminates the way that positivism and Enlightenment rationality are cultural artifacts rather than universal truths—forms of understanding created in a particular time and place—so we must understand critical theory itself as the product of a particular social, political, and intellectual milieu. For critical theory to be critical, it must be on guard against its own ossification and entombment as a "grand theory" meant to explain all social interaction, for all people and for all time. A critical stance toward critical theory entails a productive skepticism regarding its universality and accuracy. This means that those engaged in theory building must apply the same standards of critical analysis to their own theory as they do to theory developed by those energetically pursuing capitalism and subscribing to bureaucratic rationality. Predictably, those within critical theory who ask uncomfortable questions and point out the theory's negative consequences risk being ostracized as intellectually unsound pariahs. Critical theory has its share of Stalinists who will not tolerate deviation from the party line.

Howard Zinn, a prominent American historian, points out that those who challenge the social order are just as capable of creating their own orthodoxies as are dominant groups. He writes, "The experience of our century tells us that the old orthodoxies, the traditional ideologies, the neatly tied bundles of ideas—capitalism, socialism, democracy—need to be untied, so that we can play and experiment with all the ingredients, add others, and create new combinations in looser bundles" (1990, p. 8). Zinn urges us to make declarations of independence from rigid dogmas, and it is precisely this self-critical posture toward its own propositions that a critical theory of adult learning must display. This self-critical stance is not unfamiliar within critical theory; after all, the theory itself began as an attempt to reformulate Marxist thought in conditions Marx had not foreseen. As Bronner and Kellner (1989) observe, "Inspired by the dialectical tradition of Hegel and Marx, critical theory is intrinsically open to development and revision" (p. 2). Even as strong a Marxist as Antonio Gramsci observed that Marxism "tends to become an ideology in the worst sense of the word, that is to say a dogmatic system of eternal and absolute truths" (1971, p. 407). In a 1918 article in *Il Grido del Popolo* (The People's Cry), Gramsci warned that Marx "is not a Messiah who left a string of parables laden with categorical imperatives, with absolute unquestionable norms beyond the categories of time and space" (1988, p. 36). He believed that the value of Marxist ideas was always a provisional value. In Gramsci's stance toward Marx, we can see how critical theory stands consistently for a rejection of unchanging dogma and is watchful for its own deification.

It is easy to forget this and to allow critical theory to become subject to the very reification it condemns. For example, Oberg and Underwood (1992) noted that when they enthusiastically introduced critical theory to preservice teachers as a new way for them to understand their experiences, this perspective served to "function in the same debilitating way as the other frames already discarded, separating students from the daily events of their own practice and directing their attention to someone else's construction of their reality" (p. 166). Those of us convinced of the accuracy of critical theory's perspective can easily force this on learners and colleagues in a self-defeating way. Our insistence that we have found *the* one truly accurate way of understanding the world can smack of condescending triumphalism, particularly if we dismiss all criticism of our perspective as ideologically motivated propaganda. There should be no contradiction in critiquing critical theory. It is quite possible to accept, provisionally, the basic accuracy and utility of explanatory frameworks drawn from the critical theory tradition, while at the same time doing our best to challenge these. This is the purpose of books such as Mills' *The Marxists* (1962), Eagleton's *Ideology* (1991), Fay's *Critical Social Science* (1987), and Kellner's *Critical Theory, Marxism, and Modernity* (1989), all of which exemplify Marcuse's (1989) contention that "critical theory is, last but not least, critical of itself and of the social forces that make up its own basis" (p. 72).

The strenuous effort to disprove the validity of one's own ideas on the assumption that what's left after this effort is over must have intrinsic merit is essentially an application of Popper's (1959) principle of falsifiability, which to me is one of the elements of traditional theories that Horkheimer (1995, p. 242) acknowledges is part of a critical attitude. Theorizing critically requires that we be self-critical, that we turn a self-referential and skeptical eye on our own tentative conclusions. As Kellner (1989) declares, "If critical theory is going to remain on the cutting edge of social theory, then it must be subject to the sort of critique which it applies to traditional theories and must move beyond previous inadequate or obsolete positions" (p. 2). Hegemony, ideology, alienation, the lifeworld, commodification—these concepts may help us understand our experiences, but if something comes along that makes more sense and explains things more clearly, then we should be ready to seize it. This second element of critical theory draws partly from the tradition of analytic philosophy but particularly from the pragmatic tradition with its emphasis on contingency and fallibility. Pragmatism holds that all theory, indeed all practice, is provisional and open to reformulation. Its inclination is to experimentation, to undercutting its own foundations. Partly it anticipates postmodernism in encouraging an ironic skepticism regarding claims to universal explanations and in delighting in playing with unpredictable possibilities. But a pragmatic inclination can be deployed in the service of social justice in the manner articulated by Cornel West. For West, "One sign of commitment . . . is always the degree to which one is willing to be self-critical and self-questioning, because that's a sign that you're serious about generating the conditions for the possibility of overcoming the suffering that you're after" (West, 1999b, p. 295).

One of the temptations facing those who draw on critical theory is the development of an overconfidence regarding the accuracy of their analysis (of course, the same is true of proponents of traditional theory and positivism). A sense of triumphalism can creep into an analysis that purports to penetrate the ideological veil drawn over everyday life to reveal the hegemonic reality lurking beneath. This can then translate into an attitude of condescension toward those whose consciousness has yet to be raised and who have yet to see how they are colluding in their own oppression. There are also "no-go" areas that tend to be immune from critical scrutiny. For example, capitalism is often viewed as uncontestedly, irredeemably, and completely evil. A book such as James Loewen's *Lies My Teacher Told Me* (1995) that admits that capitalism, whilst creating and maintaining enormous social inequity and justifying genocide in the pursuit of expanded markets, might also have produced some benefits is the exception rather than the rule.

An interesting example of a sympathetically critical stance toward critical theory is Fay's *Critical Social Science* (1987). In his analysis Fay summarizes the criticisms most commonly made of critical theory: "That it is inherently unresponsive to empirical evidence; that it starts with the a priori assumption that it has 'the answer' to which it necessarily holds no matter what occurs; that it is inherently subjectivistic because it irreducibly contains a moral element; and that the goal of transforming society is incompatible with the objectivity required to study it with scientific rigor" (p. 5). His response to these criticisms is not to dismiss them as attacks made by politically compromised enemies seeking to defuse critical theory of its revolutionary power. Instead, after laying out his own arguments for the relevance and accuracy of critical theory, he attempts to critique the overly rationalistic and utopian dimensions to the ideas he has just espoused. In doing this, Fay models the kind of critical approach to criticality I am arguing should be integral to critical theorizing.

Put briefly, Fay argues that critical theory downplays the constraining influence of tradition, culture, and history, tending to view these as inherently conservative forces. Yet, as he points out, a tradition such as a populist skepticism of wealthy political leaders is inherently emancipatory. He also acknowledges that there is a great deal of critical theorizing that is not directly associated with the Frankfurt School, even if it is framed by similar concerns. For him it is important to broaden critical analysis beyond Germany. He quotes as examples of this contention figures as diverse as the psychoanalyst R. D. Laing and the ex-director of the Highlander Research Center (well known to adult educators) John Gaventa. In the book you are now reading, the insights of figures such as Foucault, Gramsci, Williams, West, hooks, and Althusser for adult learning are reviewed, yet none of these worked at the Frankfurt School, though to different degrees their work either responds to or builds upon Marx's ideas. Finally, Fay breaks with those who dismiss calls for empirical verification as a misplaced application of positivist technical-rationality to a critical epistemology. He aligns himself with Marcuse's (1964) view that where its judgments of the possibility of liberation are concerned, critical theory "has to demonstrate the objective validity of these judgments and the demonstration has to proceed on empirical grounds" (p. xi). Fay argues that predictive possibilities are inherent in critical theory's formulations and that the accuracy of these can be assessed by public reference to empirical evidence. In other words, we should not be afraid of studying how far social and educational experiments influenced by critical theory operate in the real world.

It is important to reemphasize that infusing critical theory with the spirit of self-critical inquiry was a hallmark of Frankfurt School writers. Jay (1973) makes the point that critical theory developed dialogically, through a critical engagement with other philosophical systems, and that this gave it "its essentially open-ended, probing, unfinished quality" (p. 41). In his survey of the Frankfurt School, Held (1980) writes regarding Horkheimer and Adorno that "it is ironic that they were attacked in the 1960s for their political pessimism and lack of practical involvement, but, after their deaths, for their supposed encouragement of 'terrorism' and 'political irresponsibility'" (p. 39). Indeed, to many sympathetic to the

Frankfurt School's line of analysis one of the most frustrating developments was Horkheimer's, Adorno's, and (to a lesser degree)
Marcuse's pessimism regarding the possibility of revolutionary
change and human liberation. These three thinkers refused to
hold out the promise of false emancipatory hope when everything
they observed empirically convinced them of the enduring imper-
meability of the forces of social control. The same independence
of thought, unwillingness to toe any predetermined ideological
line, and readiness to reverse previous positions in the face of new
evidence or theorizing are characteristic of many of the theorists
surveyed in this book such as Foucault, Habermas, and West.

Because of its exercise of internal criticism, critical theory has
undergone a number of important reformulations over the years.
First, class is no longer the only or sometimes even the primary
unit of analysis amongst those who identify themselves as critical
theorists. Though it remains crucial, it is usually linked with race
and gender in the holy trinity of contemporary ideology critique.
Second, Foucault's (1980) analysis of power has alerted us to the
way that sovereign power (power clearly exercised by some central authority such as the politburo, the military junta, the king,
the cabinet, the party's central committee, and so on) has been
partially displaced by the exercise of disciplinary power (self-
discipline exercised by subjects themselves who conduct their own
self-censorship and self-surveillance at their own sites of life and
practice). Third, postmodern critique has called into question the
modernist underpinnings of critical theory, particularly those
aspects that emphasize the unproblematic possibility of individual
and collective liberation, emancipation, and transformation.
Fourth, the legacy of critical pragmatism has encouraged a skepticism regarding any attempt to plunder methods and approaches
that are apparently successful in one political context (such as
Freire's approach to conscientization and problem-posing education developed in rural northeast Brazil) and then to parachute
them into quite different settings (such as American colleges and
universities).

In this chapter I have argued that the starting point for exploring critical theory's relevance for adult learning is to elaborate the
dimensions of learning embedded in the chief concerns of critical

theory. I have acknowledged that these concerns are normatively grounded in a social-philosophical vision of a democratic society that tries to realize values of freedom, fairness, justice, and compassion (the fact that these values may sometimes be in contradiction will be discussed later). The next stage in exploring this theory is to illuminate in more detail what the learning tasks of a critical theory might be and how they intersect.

Chapter Two

The Learning Tasks of Critical Theory

In this chapter I want to provide an overview of the adult learning tasks that are embedded in critical theory. I argued in Chapter One that critical theory is normatively grounded in a vision of a society in which people live collectively in ways that encourage the free exercise of their creativity without foreclosing that of others. In such a society people see their individual well-being as integrally bound up with that of the collective. They act toward each other with generosity and compassion and are ever alert to the presence of injustice, inequity, and oppression. Creating such a society can be understood as entailing a series of learning tasks: learning to recognize and challenge ideology that attempts to portray the exploitation of the many by the few as a natural state of affairs, learning to uncover and counter hegemony, learning to unmask power, learning to overcome alienation and thereby accept freedom, learning to pursue liberation, learning to reclaim reason, and learning to practice democracy. These learning tasks are, of course, interrelated and any separation of them is mostly for analytical purposes. After all, the categories we use to make sense of our experiences are shaped by dominant ideology. We cannot pursue liberation without uncovering and then challenging the hegemony of capitalist values and practices. And, of course, a central component of hegemony is the dissemination of an ideology that serves the interests of the few while purporting to represent the many. But separating these tasks and concepts in order that we may understand their interrelationships better is defensible.

Challenging Ideology

The first, and arguably the preeminent, learning task embedded in critical theory is that of challenging ideology. In his analysis of critical theory, Geuss (1981) writes that "the very heart of the critical theory of society is its criticism of ideology. Their ideology is what prevents the agents in the society from correctly perceiving their true situation and real interests; if they are to free themselves from social repression, the agents must rid themselves of ideological illusion" (pp. 2–3). Clearly, then, a critical theory approach to adult learning must begin by exploring how adults learn to resist ideological manipulation. Yet the concept of ideology is complex and contested, in McLellan's (1986) judgment "the most elusive concept in the whole of social science" (p. 1). However, though the term is used in multiple ways, it has a distinctive meaning within the critical tradition. This tradition builds on Marx's view that the relations of production and material conditions of society determine people's consciousness. As Eagleton writes, from a critical theory viewpoint, ideology "signifies ideas and beliefs which help to legitimate the interests of a ruling group or class specifically by distortion and dissimulation" (Eagleton, 1991, p. 30). Critical theory sees ideology as inherently duplicitous, as a system of false beliefs that justify practices and structures that keep people unknowingly in servitude. Eagleton takes issue with this view arguing that ideologies are not, by definition, false and that a condition of their gaining continued acceptance is that they contain elements that are broadly seen as true (a point also made by Gramsci). He also unmasks the condescension underlying the "ideology as false consciousness" position: "To believe that immense numbers of people would live and sometimes die in the name of ideas which were absolutely vacuous and absurd is to take up an unpleasantly demeaning attitude towards ordinary men and women" (p. 12).

Yet the fact remains that within the critical theory tradition the predominant understanding of ideology has very distinct connotations of oppression and domination, of its being used to subjugate and hoodwink people into accepting as normal and justifiable an artificially created and permanent state of inequity. To quote Eagleton (1991) again, "The study of ideology is among other things an inquiry into the ways in which people may come to invest in their own unhappiness" (p. xiii). Critical theory views ideology as the broadly accepted set of values, beliefs, myths, explanations, and justifications that appears self-evidently true, empirically accurate, personally relevant, and morally desirable to a majority of the populace. The function of this ideology is to maintain an unjust social and political order. Ideology does this by convincing people that existing social arrangements are naturally ordained and obviously work for the good of all. As Marx and Engels (1970) write, the ruling class aims "to represent its interest as the common interest of all the members of society . . . it has to give its ideas the form of universality and represent them as the only rational, universally valid ones" (p. 66).

Ideologies are hard to detect since they are embedded in language, social habits, and cultural forms that combine to shape the way we think about the world. They appear as common sense, as givens, rather than as beliefs that are deliberately skewed to support the interests of a powerful minority. On closer examination, however, we see that a degree of deliberation undergirds what appear as accidentally emergent belief systems. As Fromm (1968) puts it, "Ideologies are ready-made thought-commodities spread by the press, the orators, the ideologists in order to manipulate the mass of people for purposes which have nothing to do with the ideology, and are very often exactly the opposite" (p. 153). Understanding this process—how ideology works to support the power of a minority while appearing to advance the interests of all—is one of the central ideas in Marx and Engels' *The German Ideology* (1970). They write, "The ideas of the ruling class are in every epoch the ruling ideas: i.e. the class which is the ruling material force of society is at the same time its ruling intellectual force . . . the class which has the means of material production at its disposal, has control at the same time over the means of mental production" (p. 64). The individuals comprising this ruling class exercise dominion not just over the production and distribution of material goods. They "rule also as thinkers, as producers of ideas, and regulate the production and distribution of the ideas of their age" (p. 64). In recent years poststructuralists such as Foucault have clarified how knowledge and power entwine to create regimes of truth—dominant ideas, frameworks of analysis, and forms of discourse that shape how we think about the world.

In critical theory, understanding and challenging the workings of ideology has been a dominant concern, one often expressed as "ideology critique." Ideology critique is an activity springing from the Enlightenment conviction that living fully as an adult means acting on the basis of instincts, impulses, and desires that are truly our own, rather than implanted in us. Since capitalism will do its utmost to convince us that we should live in ways that support its workings, ideology critique holds that we cannot be fully adult unless we attempt to unearth and challenge the ideology that justifies this system. In doing this we come to see that the inclinations, biases, hunches, and apparently intuitive ways of experiencing reality that we regard as unique to us are actually socially learned. What we consider to be our idiosyncratic perspectives and dispositions are now realized to be, in Marcuse's (1964) terms, "ideologically sedimented." Ideology critique helps us understand how we learn political ideals, morality, and social philosophy within the institutions of civil society such as schools, associations, clubs, family, and friendship networks. It also shows us that the constructs and categories we use to understand our daily experiences are ideologically framed. What Williams (1977) calls our "structures of feeling" are seen in ideology critique as socially induced, learned from the cultural group and social class to which we belong. So doing ideology critique involves adults in becoming aware of how ideology lives within them as well as understanding how it buttresses the structures of the outside world that work against them. What strikes us as the normal order of things is suddenly revealed through ideology critique as a constructed reality that protects the interests of the powerful.

In the critical theory tradition, then, ideology critique is the basic tool for helping adults learn to penetrate the givens of everyday reality to reveal the inequity and oppression that lurk beneath. Given that ideology critique is the central project of the Frankfurt School, a critical theory approach to adult learning should have at its core an understanding of how adults learn to recognize the predominance of ideology in their everyday thoughts and actions and in the institutions of civil society. It should also illuminate how adults learn to challenge ideology that serves the interests of the few against the well-being of the many.

Contesting Hegemony

In a doctoral class titled Theoretical Foundations of Critical Pedagogy that I taught with my colleague Seehwa Cho at the University of St. Thomas, an intriguing question was posed to the students by Seehwa. "How many of you think that a working class revolution is possible in the USA?" she asked the group, all of whom were educational or community activists. Not a single person, myself included, raised a hand to answer in the affirmative. "Right there, that's hegemony," Seehwa declared, pointing out that when the possibility of large-scale social upheaval is foreclosed even by those with activist inclinations, there is little need for the state to make complicated arrangements to retain power and enforce control.

Hegemony is an idea that understands the maintenance of political control as involving adult education and learning. It describes the way that people learn to accept as natural and in their own best interest an unjust social order. As Antonio Gramsci (who is the thinker most associated with the idea) points out, "Every relationship of hegemony is necessarily an educational relationship" (1995, p. 157). People learn to embrace as commonsense wisdom certain beliefs and political conditions that work against their interests and serve those of the powerful. If hegemony works as it should, then there is no need for the state to employ coercive forms of control—heavy policing, curfews, torture, assassination squads—to maintain social order. Instead of people opposing and fighting unjust structures and dominant beliefs, they learn to regard them as preordained, part of the cultural air they breathe.

In a society in which people learn attitudes and values from entertainment media, and in which media outlets choose what counts as news and which social crises merit debate, the mass media are obviously central to the smooth functioning of hegemony. Herman and Chomsky (1988) describe the role the mass media play in this regard as being that of manufacturing consent. This phrase—manufacturing consent—could serve as a good shorthand descriptor of the concept of hegemony. By manufacturing consent Herman and Chomsky mean that media present as normal a version of reality in which large-scale structural inequities are never mentioned, let alone challenged, and which people largely accept as an empirically accurate, neutral reality. Political issues, questions, and debate are reduced to personal issues and conflicts (witness the amount of airtime devoted to the Clarence Thomas confirmation hearings, the Clinton-Lewinsky affair, or the personal demonizing of Saddam Hussein). They contend that five filters operate to ensure that the media never challenge the hegemony of capitalist ideas and practices: (1) the media are themselves huge capitalist corporations, (2) the media's survival depends on attracting advertising from other companies, (3) the media's reliance on government and business experts, (4) the media's awareness of the likelihood of complaints from powerful interests if these interests' activities are portrayed unfavorably, and (5) the propagation of anticommunism as a national ideology.

The subtle tenacity and adaptability of hegemony lies in the fact that it is very difficult to peel away layers of oppression to uncover a small cabal clearly conspiring to keep the majority silent and disenfranchised. If there is any conspiracy at work here, it is the conspiracy of the normal. The ideas and practices of hegemony—the stock opinions, conventional wisdoms, and common-sense ways of behaving in particular situations that we take for granted—are part and parcel of everyday life. It is not as if these are being forced on us against our will. The dark irony, the cruelty of hegemony, is that adults take pride in learning and acting on the beliefs and assumptions that work to enslave them. In learning diligently to live by these assumptions, people become their own jailers. By incorporating the concept of hegemony into the analysis of ideology, Gramsci widens our understanding of how ideology contributes to the maintenance of social control. The emphasis shifts from understanding how the state or sovereign imposes a view of the world on a neutral, skeptical, or resentful populace to understanding how people are willing partners with the ruling group by actively colluding in their own oppression. Indeed, helping adults learn to embrace oppression is the central educational task of hegemony.

The concept of hegemony becomes ever more relevant in the twenty-first century as multinational corporations take the place of governments as determinants of history and economics. Multinationals are cloaked in secrecy, accountable only to a closed community of stockholders, and operate with little public scrutiny. They are extremely malleable in their capacity to move across national boundaries in their search for new markets and cheaper labor and in their ability to respond to new social conditions, political shifts, technological developments, and demographic changes. Their survival rests on people learning to believe that the products and services multinationals offer fulfill genuine needs and are endemic to a happy, fully adult life. The parallels with hegemony's emphasis on people learning to embrace ideas that seem natural and desirable, but that actually serve the interests of others, are clear.

The concept of hegemony also extends our understanding of power, in some ways anticipating Foucault's (1980) much later work in this area. Foucault argued that in contemporary society power works in much more subtle ways than previously acknowledged, and that it should be understood as a circulation or flow around society rather than as something statically imposed from above. In his view we have moved from the exercise of sovereign power (power clearly exercised by a recognizable central controlling force) to the exercise of disciplinary power (power exercised on ourselves by ourselves). Because we learn self-discipline, undertake self-surveillance, and exercise self-censorship, there is little need for dominant groups to force ideas or behaviors on us. The parallel here is with hegemony's emphasis on getting people to learn and love their place. Gramsci and Foucault both see adults as colluding in their own servitude thereby removing the state's need to enforce this.

Gramsci's concept of hegemony is chilling stuff. Hegemony is powerful yet adaptable, able to reconfigure itself, skillfully incorporate resistance, and give just enough away to its opponents to keep them quiescent while remaining more or less intact. Yet Gramsci also opened up the possibility of opposition, of replacing a minority ruling-class hegemony with a majority proletarian hegemony. If hegemony is in constant flux and understood partly as a process of negotiation between oppressor and oppressed, then chinks and contradictions (some of which reflect the internal contradictions of capitalism) inevitably appear. Williams (1977) underscores this view arguing that hegemony "does not just passively exist as a form of dominance. It has continually to be renewed, defended and modified. It is also continually resisted, limited, altered, challenged by pressures not at all its own" (p. 112). This point also predates Foucault's emphasis on the possibility of adults learning to resist disciplinary power at the local site at which it is exercised. Foucault (1980) hypothesizes that "there are no relations of power without resistances; the latter are all the more real and effective because they are formed right at the point where relations of power are exercised" (p. 142). So although hegemony exists, it is never a total blanket smothering all opposition.

Where and how does opposition to hegemony arise? Popular culture was one site of oppositional practice for Gramsci, the workplace (particularly the factory councils) another. The labor movement, the environmental movement, alternative political parties such as the Green Party, antiracist initiatives, the feminist classroom, community action projects supported by adult and popular education centers (such as the Lindeman Center in Chicago, the Freire Center in Minneapolis, or the Highlander Center in Tennessee attempts to teach the deconstruction of media images in schools and colleges), all these are examples of educational counterhegemony, premised on the conviction that adults can learn to recognize when they are being manipulated. Even the World Wide Web can be used creatively as an adult educational tool to mobilize and coordinate global protests against imperialist invasions, capitalism, and transnational trade negotiations, rather than as the advertising tool of software giants who can control access to it.

Given the centrality of hegemony to ideological analysis, a critical theory approach to adult learning should help us understand how adults learn to recognize hegemony in the beliefs and assumptions they live by and the structures they live within. It should also examine how adults learn to contest hegemony individually and collectively by striving to replace it with a system of beliefs and practices that represents the interests of the majority.

Unmasking Power

Power is omnipresent in human existence, evident as much in the minutiae of interpersonal relationships as in large-scale political arrangements. One can deny its existence, but critical theory holds that its influence can never be erased. Typical of this is Foucault's (1980) insistence that "power is 'already there,' that one is never 'outside' it, that there are no 'margins' for those who break with the system to gambol in" (p. 141). Part of becoming adult is learning to recognize the play of power in our lives and the ways it is used and abused. It is a mistake to think of power in wholly negative terms, as only being exercised to keep people in line. A sense of possessing power—of having the energy, intelligence, resources, and opportunity to act on the world—is a precondition of intentional social change. When the power of the individual comes to be seen as inexorably embedded in the power of the collective (for example, in a social class, a culture, a gender, a race, a social movement), then the possibility of large-scale social change, even of revolution, comes dramatically alive. This is what Mary Parker Follett (1924a, 1924b) described as "power with" rather than "power over" and also what some refer to as empowerment. Interestingly, in an ironic demonstration of how hegemony incorporates and tames potentially disruptive ideas, empowerment has now been claimed by figures on the political right to justify their support of free market capitalism.

A critical theory understanding of adult learning should investigate how people learn to recognize the flow of power in their lives and communities, how they come to appreciate that power is inscribed (to use one of Foucault's favorite terms) in their everyday reasoning and actions, and how they try to redirect it to serve the interests of the many rather than the few. Unmasking power is particularly difficult given that its configuration and exercise is justified by and embedded in prevailing ways of thinking and speaking, what Foucault called "regimes of truth." For example, the widespread use of Darwinian metaphors (such as survival of the fittest) or mythic images of the self-made man (implying that any male can become president) creates a justification of existing power arrangements, whatever form these take. Furthermore, existing power imbalances are then seen as reflecting the natural order of things. After all, if the fittest really do survive then the ones who are in positions of power must be there by virtue of their innate strength or superior intelligence since this has obviously allowed them to rise to the top. Holding political power thus comes to contain its own justification. Those exercising it seem to do so by evolutionary right. They are the ones who appear to be left standing after the weeding out of those weaklings unfit to handle its stresses and requirements.

A concern to explore how adults learn to unmask power has an honorable tradition in adult education predating by many

decades the poststructuralist analyses of Foucault. Eduard Lindeman spent much of his life arguing for adult education as "the
operating alternative for dominance, dictatorship and violence"
([1937] 1987b, p. 6) believing that "adult education is the answer
to blind prejudice and demagoguery" ([1944] 1987c, p. 115). He
urged a network of neighborhood discussion groups as the most
effective hedge a society could evolve against the danger of creeping totalitarianism. A major tradition in North American and European adult education is to ally the field with social movements
concerned to empower working-class adults through organizations
such as trade unions, factory councils, worker cooperatives, and
other collectivist groupings. The thread that ties together such
lionized initiatives as the Highlander Folk School, the Antigonish
movement, Ruskin College, and Freireian culture circles is the concern to unmask and then confront power structures that stand
against working-class interests. This is partly achieved by helping
so-called "ordinary" people appreciate and act on the power they
already have. Adults learning the possibilities of their own power
through sharing knowledge, experiences, tactics, strategies, successes, and failures is one pole of radical and liberatory adult education. Learning to face down and subvert power structures, and
to experiment with forms of collective organization and democratic process, is the other. So a theme that runs through various
strands of adult educational literature is the importance of learning to develop agency—the capacity to exert influence on the
world through the exercise of individual and collective power.

One of the earliest attempts to theorize how people experience
being powerful and how this sense is differentially distributed was
McClusky's (1963, 1970) power/load/margin formula. McClusky
posited that at any time of life adults have a load that they carry
made up of social tasks they need to perform and internal aspirations and desires they want to realize. Power is defined as the resources, abilities, and allies adults can call upon to help them carry
this load. The greater the margin between the large amounts of
power adults possess and the smallness of the load they have to
carry, the more options for growth they have open to them. This
is a highly psychologized approach to understanding power, but it
does have the merit of conceptualizing power as access to resources. Thinking of power as bound up with the number and di-

versity of resources people can call on in the pursuit of their goals inevitably leads one to ask how it is that these resources are differentially distributed and tapped. This takes one straight into political and economic analysis.

Another area of adult learning that has the understanding of power at its center is self-directed learning. The massive amount of research conducted on self-directed learning in adults has at its core the study of how adults exercise power and control over their own educational activities. Although critics such as Collins (1991) argue forcefully that self-directed learning has degenerated into a reductionistic concern with the techniques of learning contracts and the technology of online instruction, others (Brookfield, 1993; Hammond and Collins, 1991) believe that a concern to unmask and confront power lies at the heart of this form of learning. Mezirow's (1991a, 1991b, 1998) theory of transformative learning and the many follow-up studies this has inspired (Taylor, 1997) also has as a central focus understanding how reframing a meaning scheme or meaning perspective brings with it an increased sense of power. Here power is regarded as the ability to understand and take action in the world in a way that feels authentically grounded in critical reflection.

In sum, then, one contribution of critical theory to understanding adult learning is to explore how adults learn to recognize and unmask power relations and inequities embedded in ideology and inscribed in their everyday lives. It investigates how adults learn to decide when power is being exercised responsibly and how they learn to defend themselves against its unjust and arbitrary use. It also studies how adults learn to develop the sense of powerful agency—of possessing the desire, resources, and capacity to come together with others in purposeful collective action. Finally, critical theory examines critically its own articulation of power, taking into account the poststructuralist contention that power is exercised in more diffuse and contradictory ways than critical theory has traditionally allowed for.

Overcoming Alienation

One of the most enduring concepts in Marxism is that of alienation. We are alienated, in Marx's view, when we work and live in ways that estrange us from who we really are. When we are unable to realize our innate creativity in the workplace, and when the work we do leaves us too tired to explore that creativity outside work, then we are in a state of alienation that stands against our freedom. Freedom is possible only in a nonalienated world, one in which we can choose how to act in ways that have not been foreclosed for us. Hence alienation is antithetical to freedom, and the abolition of the former is essential to the realization of the latter. The study of how this might happen was the life's work of Erich Fromm.

Unlike alienation, which is a word associated with a fairly rarified world of novelists, poets, philosophers, and theologians, freedom is a word that most people invoke fairly regularly as they lament its absence or celebrate its presence in their lives. Freedom is the flip side of alienation. By implication the removal of alienation allows for the possibility of freedom, for the unmanipulated exercise of one's creative powers. As such, claiming freedom and overcoming alienation are inextricably intertwined. Freedom is also a truly sacred word, one in the name of which countless people have lost their lives. For most of us in the Western first world, freedom is an uncontested good, something to go to war over and endure enormous pain and sacrifice to defend. Of all the ideas in the grand narrative of the Enlightenment, it is perhaps the most powerful and the most cherished. Governments invoke it to justify their policies, people see the search for it as the guiding principle of their lives, and its promise galvanizes social movements. Claiming freedom, then, could be said to be a central task of adulthood, something we spend a lifetime learning how to do as we try to escape our alienated lives. As such, it must occupy a prominent place in any critical theory of adult learning.

Of course from a postmodernist perspective freedom is a naïve and problematic notion, precisely because of its Enlightenment origins. From an Enlightenment perspective freedom is seen as exercised by independent selves able to make choices and take decisions that match their own personalities and preferences. McLaren (1995) regards this view of human conduct as "the magnificent enlightenment swindle of the autonomous, stable and self-contained ego that is supposed to be able to act independently of its own history" (p. 204). This Enlightenment ideal of freedom is grounded in the conception of the individual self as a person who acts as an integrated whole to realize her or his innermost desires in a unique and authentic way. Usher, Bryant, and Johnston (1997) describe this as "the classical scientific self—individualised, undifferentiated, an essentially abstract entity, the 'monological' self" (p. 94).

Postmodernism and critical theory both share a suspicion of this deracinated view of human conduct. Both question the idea that people act as autonomous entities in realizing core desires or discovering core identities. Postmodernism contends that because our lives are embedded in social and cultural contexts that constantly shift and fragment, freedom has no universal face. How freedom is conceived and lived varies enormously with time and location. Indeed, for freedom to be valued by a group, its members must share a set of cultural influences that can be traced back to the Enlightenment. Critical theory holds that individual conduct must always be understood as shaped by dominant ideology. From this perspective even when we think we are exercising our freedom as individuals, we are living out ideological battles and contradictions. This sets critical theory at odds with existentialism. To existentialists, freedom is something we are fated to claim through the exercise of choice. Life continually forces choices on us, and we have no option other than to act on these in ways that reveal our essential selves. To deny that we have this freedom is to live in bad faith, to pretend that our choices have nothing to do with who we are but are inevitably shaped by wider forces.

For the second half of the twentieth century, the creation and defense of freedom as central to a nonalienated life was the major concern of social critics as diverse as Hannah Arendt, George Orwell, and Erich Fromm, all of whom were united in their concern for the threat totalitarianism posed to the realization of humanity. Fromm's *Escape from Freedom* (1941), written at the height of fascism, explored how humans try to avoid the responsibility of freedom. Since freedom involves us making choices, taking actions, and living by commitments for which we take responsibility, and since doing these things is discomforting and difficult, Fromm argued that people avoid them by embracing totalitarian dictatorships or becoming willing automatons in the industrial machine. Ideologies such as fascism or totalitarian communism that allow people to identify with a larger identity and that purport to direct people's actions to some larger predefined purpose are, in Fromm's view, immensely appealing to those afraid to live with the burden of freedom. Fromm, Arendt, and Orwell were primarily concerned with political totalitarianism, the tendency of governments and state institutions to attempt to control all aspects of life and feeling. To political totalitarianism, critical theory added the threat of economic totalitarianism, the tendency of capitalism to dominate all aspects of people's existence by making the acquisition of goods and services the raison d'être of life. Economic totalitarianism is seen in the growth of multinational corporations and the globalization of desire. Through the skillful manipulation of images across national borders, multinationals work to create a globally shared consensus of what constitutes beauty and the good life and what it means to be fully human (drinking coca-cola and eating Big Macs while strolling the Great Wall of China or drifting down the Amazon). To the contemporary French thinker Baudrillard (1975, 1983), people's interaction with these images, symbols, and representations of desire (what he terms "simulacra") is the chief way they experience reality.

Fromm is one of the critical theorists most associated with analyzing freedom, largely through his classic work *Escape From Freedom* (1941), published outside the United States under the title *The Fear of Freedom*. He argued that a major cause of contemporary alienation was an unwillingness of people to take responsibility for their own actions. People are alienated because they fear their freedom and seek ways to escape the necessity to make choices that inevitably lead to certain consequences. In non-Fascist societies the attempt to escape freedom is seen most prominently in the flight into automaton conformity, a flight that people hope will help them feel unalienated. Automaton conformity is a particularly contemporary form of alienation that represents people's desire to think and act as part of an anonymous mass. Its logic is that the majority is always right, so to achieve happiness one must always discover what the majority thinks and then follow that. In a state of automaton conformity, people strive diligently to mimic what they believe to be commonsense views and to behave in ways that ensure they blend in with the majority. As with Foucault's notion of disciplinary power, people are exercising a perverted form of agency on themselves to ensure they stay in line. This kind of conformity signified the apotheosis of alienation for Fromm, and much of his energy was devoted to understanding how it might be overcome.

A critical theory of adult learning will explore several questions concerning how alienation might be overcome to allow the exercise of true freedom. How do people learn to develop a sense of free agency where they feel they possess the desire, capacity, and resources to shape the world according to their desires? How do adults learn to recognize the varying degrees of freedom that can be experienced in different contexts? How do they learn to detect when they're living a life that is supposedly free, but that is in reality shaped by their alienating attempt to satisfy needs manufactured by corporate advertising? How do adults learn to fight the alienating forces and obstacles that prevent them from claiming freedom? How do they live with the sense of failure and frustration this struggle sometimes induces? How do people learn to reconcile their desire to act freely with cultural constraints or collective disapproval? How do adults learn to live with the responsibility and fear of freedom Fromm explored? How do they learn to question socially constructed images and metaphors of freedom (such as the free press or the free market) that disguise the control exercised by powerful political economic and political forces? How do people learn to live with a perceived absence of freedom? And, finally, what kinds of adult educational approaches and conditions tend to foster a sense of freedom in participants?

These are modernist questions springing from the Enlightenment vision of people acting to realize their humanity in a society exhibiting the fewest possible inequities and injustices. In addressing them, however, I keep in mind postmodernism's skepticism regarding the concept of total freedom and its awareness of the oppression and atrocities committed in its name. Postmodernism reminds us that freedom is never absolute, always contextual, and that it should be the focus of continual critical analysis.

Learning Liberation

As Chapter One made clear, critical theory has as a central purpose the liberation of creativity from the demands of capitalism. For many the best chance for this liberation to occur is in mass social movements that will force large-scale social change. Individual liberation is seen as dependant on collective liberation. While agreeing with the importance of collective social movements, the critical theorist Herbert Marcuse also believed that attention should be paid to the possibility of individual liberation detached from the collectivity. He emphasized factors such as isolation, distance, separation, and privacy that other critical theorists are less drawn to. To him the inner revolution symbolized by the development of new sensibilities, aesthetic impulses, and imaginative powers is sometimes an important precursor to the outer revolution that calls for new forms of social, economic, and political organization.

How do adults learn to liberate themselves from dominant ideology? This is the question Marcuse addresses in books such as *One Dimensional Man* (1964), *An Essay on Liberation* (1969), and *The Aesthetic Dimension* (1978a). One-dimensional thought is a mental and social phenomenon very similar to the instrumentalization of reason described by Horkheimer in *The Eclipse of Reason* (1974). It is thought focused solely on making current systems work better, rather than thought that calls the legitimacy of these systems into question. Marcuse did not believe we could escape one-dimensional thought by relying on our own reasoning capacities. For him the creative force existed at a subliminal level, and its release could be triggered by aesthetic impulses. When adults experience deeply and powerfully a work of art such as a play, poem, picture, song, sculpture, or novel, they undergo a temporary estrangement from their everyday world. This estrangement is disturbing in a productive and revolutionary way. It opens adults to the realization that they could reorder their lives to live by a fundamentally different, more instinctual ethic. Marcuse called adults' development of a new sensibility "rebellious subjectivity."

What methods work best to develop rebellious subjectivity? One of its crucial dynamics, according to Marcuse, is the separation of adults from dominant values, commonsense opinions, and all the pressures that guide our thoughts and aesthetic responses into predetermined channels. This often requires adults to separate themselves temporarily from their peers. Isolation, detachment, and privacy are individual states that Marcuse stresses as potentially revolutionary. This is in stark contrast to much of critical theory which is suspicious of individual separation as an indulgence, a form of reflective luxury. In adult education circles, this suspicion of individualism often translates into an advocacy (sometimes uncritical) of collaborative, cohort-style learning formats.

The assumption of many involved in cohort learning programs is that a cohort represents an inherently supportive learning community that exhibits a concern for each member's welfare. But one of the dark sides of the cohort format is the often unacknowledged possibility of a form of groupthink developing. In cohort programs that involve a degree of participation, even of student-governance, there is a danger of a few strong voices defining the agenda early on in the cohort's history and of this agenda mimicking the dominant culture's ideology. Alternatively, when students meet as a group free from faculty interference to decide on which curricular or policy demands, requests or preferences they wish to present to faculty, there is the risk that dissenting, minority voices will be seen as obstructive, as getting in the way of a speedy resolution. Students' desire to come to consensus and thereby present a united front to faculty overrides the need to be alert to implicit pressures for ideological conformity.

Marcuse's position is that ideological domination permeates all interpersonal communications, including those of collaborative adult education groups. The logic of one-dimensional thought holds that cooperative team work and other forms of group activity often encouraged in cohort programs will automatically be directed toward making systems work better, rather than challenging the moral basis of those systems. Each person's belief in the basic efficacy regarding the way the adult education program and the larger society are organized is reinforced by contact with others in the program or society. So temporarily removing ourselves from the influence of others is a revolutionary act, a step into, rather than a retreat from, the real world. From this perspective accelerated learning programs that emphasize self-paced learning, individualized programs of study, or online instruction are raising the chances that learners might possibly experience the degree of separation from the mainstream body of learners necessary for the development of rebellious subjectivity.

Reclaiming Reason

To be able to reason—that is, to assess evidence, make predictions, judge arguments, recognize causality, and decide on actions where no clear choice is evident—is often presumed to be a mark of adulthood. A crucial element in reasoning within the critical tradition is the ability to do these things in ways that do not automatically support the logic of capitalism. But according to critical theorists such as Horkheimer, Adorno, and Marcuse, our capacity to reason has become what they describe as instrumentalized. In other words, we think reasoning is something we can legitimately only apply only to technical questions such as how to get to work on time, how to please our supervisor, how to get good grades in school, or how to access the best data source in a Web search. Reasoning about philosophical questions such as what constitutes living a moral life, what it means to organize society fairly, or what qualities should be prized above all others in personal relations becomes seen as inappropriate or off-limits. A major concern of critical theory is to reclaim reason as something to be applied in all spheres of life, particularly in deciding values by which we should live, not just in areas where technical decisions are called for.

One of the theorists most concerned with this reclamation of reason is Jürgen Habermas. Habermas believes that the instrumentalization of reason is linked to the disappearance of opportunities in our lives for us to meet with others to discuss small and large matters of mutual concern. He talks of the loss of the public sphere, the domain in which people used to come together and explore how to organize and conduct their communal affairs. Now that village gatherings and town meetings are rendered increasingly irrelevant by the advent of mass society and cyberspace, no contemporary equivalent of these places of association has emerged. In Habermas' view we are living increasingly privatized lives as civil society (the informal groupings we participate regularly in from car pools to parent organizations, churches to voluntary associations) declines. The overall result of these trends, according to Habermas, is the invasion of the lifeworld.

Lifeworld is a word that has begun to seep into the discourse of adult and higher education (Welton, 1995; Williamson, 1998; Sergiovanni, 1999) though it has yet to lodge itself in mainstream analysis. It is a term associated with the phenomenologist Alfred Schutz, who used it to describe the preconscious, taken-for-granted presuppositions, understandings, and perceptual filters that determine how we experience reality. As explained in Schutz's book with Luckmann (Schutz and Luckmann, 1973), the lifeworld is "the unquestioned ground of everything given in my experience, and the unquestionable frame in which all the problems I have to deal with are located" (p. 4). It is not something of which we are aware; rather, in the lifeworld "we designate everything which we experience as unquestionable; every state of affairs is for us unproblematic until further notice" (p. 4). A crucial aspect of the lifeworld is that it is intersubjective; in other words, it represents a set of shared meanings which make it possible for people to communicate with each other. The connections between lifeworld and ideology as a socially created structure of perception and feeling should be clear. The lifeworld is the unacknowledged frames of reference and sets of unquestioned assumptions that structure our actions and forms of reasoning.

Adult educators mostly know the term through various interpretations of the ideas of Habermas. Like Schutz, Habermas emphasizes the inaccessibility of the lifeworld, the way it forms a blurred and shadowy backdrop to all we think, speak, and do. For him "the lifeworld forms the indirect context of what is said, discussed, addressed in a situation . . . [it] is the intuitively present, in this sense familiar and transparent, and at the same time vast and incalculable web of presuppositions that have to be satisfied if an actual utterance is to be at all meaningful, that is valid, or invalid" (Habermas, 1987a, p. 131). However, Habermas argues that Schutz and Luckmann do not pay enough attention to the way in which the intersubjectivity of the lifeworld—our attempts at mutual comprehension and understanding—is determined by linguistic and communicative structures. To him the rules and patterns of speech we intuitively accept end up determining the lifeworld's shape. He proposes an everyday concept of the lifeworld that comprises the self-evident forms of reasoning and conversation that we use to come to common understandings. The unacknowledged rules and conventions that convince us that someone is saying something important comprise a symbolic structure. This structure frames how we form our identities, how we acquire cultural knowledge, and how we develop group solidarity.

What has most intrigued adult education theorists is the way Habermas argues that the lifeworld has become "uncoupled" from and then "colonized" by the system. The system comprises the social processes that regulate the exchange of power and money in society. These regulatory processes derive from capitalist ideology and from bureaucratic forms of administration. In contemporary society, system imperatives—rules and judgments that shape how we act—have invaded the lifeworld. These imperatives affect behavior, morality, and ethics and directly influence not only how we reason but how we live our lives as citizens, workers, and family members. An example of a capitalist system imperative might be correlating people's wisdom with their wealth (making the rich smarter than the rest of us). Or it might be equating success and happiness with the purchase of consumer goods. Examples of bureaucratic rationality system imperatives might be believing that a well-lived life should be ordered according to principles of time management (so that we program our days for thirty minutes of spiritual reflection here, forty minutes of deep, relationship-building conversation there), writing up family contracts as a way for parents to control the behavior of their children, or turning to professionally certified experts when we face difficulties in our relationships.

When these imperatives become reified, they are perceived as general beliefs and rules that have an existence independent of people's lives. In Habermas' terms they are uncoupled from our everyday experience and regarded as things apart. But being uncoupled does not mean they are without influence. Quite the contrary. Habermas proposes the thesis of internal colonization which states "that the subsystems of the economy and state become more and more complex as a consequence of capitalist growth, and penetrate ever deeper into the symbolic reproduction of the lifeworld" (1987, p. 367). Examples of this are the increased numbers of home offices for many middle-class workers made possible by the World Wide Web and the shift from a workforce composed chiefly of full-time employees to one with a large sector of part-time, self-employed (often of necessity) workers.

These changes have been accompanied by a reconfiguration of what constitutes a work site or work space. Is it the factory, the desk in the corner of the bedroom, the government office, the coffee shop, or the kitchen table? Once work is brought into the domestic setting, the lines between work and personal life become blurred. Forms of thinking and rules of social living derived from the capitalistic values and bureaucratic rationality evident in the domain of work come to invade our family lives, friendships, work relationships, and community involvements. These economic concerns become anchored in the lifeworld, shaping how people think about realizing their potential or taking control over their lives. Commenting on this thesis, Newman (1999) observes that "we find ourselves managing and judging everyday relationships, communications, actions and events, however inappropriate it may actually be, in terms of money and power. And we find more and more of our lives subject to control by the economy and the exercise of power through the political and legal structures" (p. 154).

How does Habermas' thought connect to a critical theory of adult learning? In an earlier and highly influential formulation of his theory of transformative learning, Mezirow (1981) developed the outlines of a critical theory of adult learning and education based on Habermas' theory of communicative action, especially his distinction between technical, communicative, and emancipatory domains of knowledge. Michael Welton (1995) and others built on, and sometimes disagreed with, Mezirow's engagement with Habermas in a volume titled *In Defense of the Lifeworld*. A critical theory of adult learning should begin by investigating how the lifeworld permeates and shapes our identities and how we learn to become aware of its presence in specific situations. Although Schutz and Habermas declare the logical impossibility of ever apprehending the lifeworld's exact presence, the very fact that they name the phenomenon undercuts somewhat the contention that it is, by definition, unknowable. To Welton and others (1995) a critical theory of adult learning would study how capitalism places system imperatives in the lifeworld and how adults learn to recognize that this is happening and thereby resist its momentum. Such a theory would seek to explore specific questions such as: How do adults learn to challenge consumer culture's definition of their needs and wants? How do they learn to recognize the cheapening of political discourse into sound bites and to contest the reality that those with the most funds have their voices heard the loudest? How do people learn to escape definitions of taste or beauty that tie these things to conspicuous consumption? How do we learn to reclaim domains of our lives that we have ceded to experts and to those who control and possess specialized knowledge? And, finally, how do we learn to sneak by the forces of segmentation and individuation that have cut us off from realizing our common interests and learn to rekindle the spirit and actuality of organizing collectively for the common good?

Practicing Democracy

Despite its origins in Marxism, contemporary critical theory (particularly that of Jürgen Habermas) is as interested in investigating the social ideal of democracy as that of socialism or communism. A theorist such as Marcuse, who was castigated during his life for being an antidemocrat and therefore anti-American, professed himself devoted to the project of realizing democracy despite the lack of any models of genuinely democratic societies. As Stalinism and totalitarian communism called the socialist dream into question, the Frankfurt School theorists stressed democracy's emphasis on the liberty humans need to enjoy if they are to take free actions that spring from their own desires and interests. Contemporary critical educators such as Greene (1988) argue that the political and economic conditions embedded in the democratic ideal mean that it can serve as an accessible and understandable springboard for radical practice in American education.

However, as with all grand narratives, the ideal of democracy can become reified and work to support capitalist hegemony. People can come to see the democratic process as existing independent of their daily lives and disconnected from their concerns. Yet they believe the democratic system is out there somewhere quietly working to ensure basic equity, defend free speech, and allow everyone an equal chance to participate in the political process. The fact that dissenting voices are sometimes heard reassures people that the system is working to give fair and equal representation to all points of view. This is the point of Marcuse's idea of repressive tolerance. By allowing a certain amount of social criticism in the name of free speech, the dominant group convinces the rest of the people that they live in a democracy. This reassuring conviction then blunts people's desire to pursue revolution and ensures that basic economic and political structures remain intact.

Adult education, particularly in the United States, has firmly embraced the democratic ideal. To describe an act of practice as democratic is to confer on it the adult educational "Good Housekeeping" seal of approval. Of all the ideas espoused as representing an authentic adult educational tradition, the idea that its practitioners should work to make their practice increasingly democratic is one of the most powerful. The words *democracy* or *democratic* are often used to justify and defend whatever practice adult educators subscribe to, serving as a kind of scriptural signaling. They are invoked to signify the progressive, leftist credentials of the speaker.

As with other grand narratives, the idea of democracy is malleable and slippery, with as many particular definitions and interpretations as it has utterers. It can be invoked so frequently and ritualistically that it becomes evacuated of any significant meaning. In this way *democracy* becomes a premature ultimate—a term that carries such reverence that, once invoked, any further serious discussion of its meaning is precluded. If we answer a question about our practice by replying that we did something because it was democratic, then the conversation often comes to a full stop. The word is so uncritically revered in adult education that it has become almost immune to critical scrutiny. Only by trying to live out the democratic process do the contradictions of this idea become manifest.

The American adult educator Eduard Lindeman was one of those who did try to take the understanding and analysis of democracy beyond ritualistic invocation. To Lindeman ([1935] 1987a) democracy was "one of the grandest words in the whole of human language" (p. 137) but also one of the least understood and most abused by hypocrites. He believed that most people "are democratically speaking, illiterate; they do not know how to operate in and through groups" (p. 150). This meant that they lacked the skill to deal respectfully with difference, live with unresolved conflict, and accept that proposed solutions to complex social problems should always be viewed as temporary, as contingent. Lindeman believed democracy is present when "ultimate power resides in the people, in the collectivity" (p. 147) so that a relationship of "power with" between people—"to be so related to you that our powers will be multiplied" (p. 144)—replaced that of "power over." He stressed, though, that democracy was not just a set of discourse patterns or decision-making protocols but that it also required an economic leveling. Political democracy required economic democracy, a point later emphasized repeatedly by Horton. For Lindeman "democracy will remain a grisly joke, but an ironic joke, unless we learn how to make it operate in an era of economics" (p. 144).

At its root, living democratically was seen by Lindeman as an adult learning process. It required its participants to study and become increasingly adept at practicing a number of democratic disciplines. These included learning to honor diversity, learning to live with the partial functioning of the democratic ideal, learning to avoid the trap of false antithesis (where we are forced to choose between either/or, mutually exclusive options), learning to accept the compatibility of ends and means (where we avoid the temptation to bypass the democratic process in the interests of reaching speedily a decision regarded as obviously right and necessary), learning to correlate the functioning of social institutions (health, education, and social services) with democratic purposes, learning collective forms of social and economic planning, learning to live with contrary decisions, and learning to appreciate the comedy inherent in democracy's contradictions. For Lindeman, then, learning democracy was a central task of adult life.

Lindeman's valorization of democracy has continued to exercise a strong influence, at least in American adult education. However, since his death the radical social critique embedded in parts of his work has largely been forgotten. These days he is usually placed in the mainstream of American pragmatism, well outside critical theory. Those parts of his writing containing an unequivocal condemnation of capitalism and individualism are rarely quoted. By way of contrast, his emphasis on group work as the crucible of democratic process and on the importance of experience to the adult education curriculum are well known. Yet to Lindeman adult education was first and foremost a social movement through which people learned collective forms of living and decision making. In his best known work, *The Meaning of Adult Education* ([1926] 1961), he wrote that "collectivism is the road to power, the predominant reality of adult life" and that an important purpose of adult education was "making the collective life an educational experience" (p. 43). This could not happen, however, as long as "warfare was the name of the game" in "the pervading economic structure of our civilization" (p. 26). This structure was based on "a doubtful competitive ethic . . . avowedly designed to benefit the crafty, the strong and the truculent" (p. 26). Effects of this structure of unbridled capitalism were nationalism and imperialism, both of which were "merely outward manifestations of this 'pseudo-power' which degrades us all" (p. 26).

I argue for Lindeman's inclusion in a critical theory of adult learning not because of his condemnation of capitalism. Lindeman was actually something of an economic centrist. In line with his desire to avoid binary reasoning, he rejected an absolutist commitment to socialism or capitalism, arguing that "when in any society all primary functions are performed by the government, and no room is left for private initiative and action, democracy will already have ceased to exist" (p. 166). However, as the most prominent American adult educator of his day and a continuing influence on contemporary thought, his location so clearly within the pragmatic tradition deserves our attention. As pointed out earlier, the connections explored by West and Habermas between some branches of critical theory and pragmatism's concern for democratic experimentation have been neglected. Yet, as Greene (1986, 1988) argues, pragmatists such as Dewey (and Lindeman) were well aware of "what would later be called 'hegemony,' or the ideological control, implicit in the dominant view of a given society" (1986, p. 434). As the chief adult educational interpreter of the pragmatic tradition, Lindeman's analysis of democratic processes and contradictions and his insistence that learning to deal with these were central tasks of adult life have important implications for a critical theory of adult learning.

Within the critical theory tradition, Jürgen Habermas is prominent in analyzing the processes and contradictions of democracy. A major concern of Habermas is to establish the conditions under which we can claim that decisions are arrived at in a truly democratic manner. As with Lindeman, Habermas is particularly interested in the way democratic process functions within small groups, and his thoughts on this have been described as a discourse theory of democracy. Habermas argues that we can establish an ideal speech situation—a set of conditions under which democratic discussion optimally takes place—that can guide the way we set up group conversations on important community issues and decisions. Although not a strict parallel with Lindeman's democratic disciplines, these ideal speech conditions contain the openness to new perspectives and the willingness temporarily to suspend one's own convictions that Lindeman also stresses. To Habermas it is important that we understand how decisions are arrived at democratically because only those decisions that are arrived at in this manner can hope to be perceived as legitimate by the populace. In his view we cannot be fully adult until we have learned these democratic forms of communication.

What tasks might a critical theory of adult education focus on where learning democracy is concerned? One might be to explore how adults become aware of and learn to live with the contradiction of subscribing both to freedom and democracy. As Baptiste (Baptiste and Brookfield, 1997) argues, democracy necessarily limits the exercise of freedom: "The freedom of interacting beings must be reciprocally regulated if their interactions are to be judged as being just. Ethical freedom is relative freedom" (p. 27). Living in association with others only works if we adjust our actions to take account of their presence. So in order to ensure equity, democrats must restrict the range of behaviors in which people can freely engage. This means adults must face the difficult task of learning to live with contrary decisions that Lindeman (Smith and Lindeman, 1951) identified as an important democratic discipline. They must also learn to be alert to the tyranny of the majority exposed by J. S. Mill (1961). In a famous passage from *On Liberty* (1859), Mill contended that when society mandates certain ways of thinking as democratically agreed or as desirable common sense, it "practices a social tyranny more formidable than many kinds of political oppression . . . it leaves fewer means of escape, penetrating much more deeply into the details of life, and enslaving the soul itself" (p. 191). This analysis of the oppressive control a majority can exercise in a democracy echoes Gramsci on the all-pervasive nature of hegemony and Foucault on power as inscribed in the choices and actions of everyday life.

A critical theory of adult learning might also investigate the general problem of how adults learn to live with the element of contingency inherent in the democratic process. Contingency—the acceptance of all understandings and solutions as partial, provisional, and continuously open to review and renegotiation—is often associated with postmodernism, as Bagnall's (1999) analysis of postmodern ideas, *Discovering Radical Contingency,* implies. Yet its roots are in pragmatism and that tradition's emphasis on continuous inquiry and experimentation as integral to democracy. Learning to live with this contingency is learning to accept that democracy is always a partially functioning ideal.

We can also study the disciplines and conditions identified by Lindeman and Habermas as necessary for participation in democratic discourse. How do adults learn to explore and respond to "otherness," to alterity, to the diversity of identities, values, desires, and expressive forms they encounter in democratic communication? How do they learn to avoid the premature closure of conversation occasioned by having to choose between mutually exclusive options? How do they learn to deal with decisions that run contrary to their desires until such time as these can be reexamined? More generally, how do adults in democratic process learn to deal with the distortions to that process that inevitably are produced by the differential power possessed by community members based on factors of race, class, and gender? How do they learn to break with cultural patterns of communication so they can slow down, remain silent, and listen carefully and attentively to what others are saying? Finally, how do democracy's participants learn to reflect critically on its practice?

This chapter has proposed that embedded in critical theory are seven adult learning tasks grounded in critical theory's central concerns—learning to challenge ideology, contest hegemony, unmask power, overcome alienation, pursue liberation, reclaim reason, and practice democracy. The rest of this volume explores these tasks in greater detail.

Chapter Three

Challenging Ideology

A while ago my wife and I were faced with choosing a junior high school for our daughter who was finishing sixth grade at her public elementary school (a Spanish immersion school in St. Paul). I didn't have to think twice about this decision. One particular public junior high leaped to mind with no conscious choice or weighing of alternatives on my part. Our friends spoke well of this school, and it had some of the best test scores in the area. Obviously, then, this was the school she should attend. This decision was ideological.

By ideological I mean that although the decision felt as if it had sprung fully formed out of my own instinctive sense of rightness, it was anything but spontaneous. In fact the decision was a manifestation of a set of largely unquestioned dominant beliefs and values that lived within me. These values and beliefs did not exist outside me as a sort of ideological smorgasbord from which I could choose a congenial blend. They *were* me. Obviously (whenever we catch ourselves saying "obviously" to ourselves we know ideology is lurking close by) our friends' judgment that this school was good could be trusted. After all, our friends are smart people (they must be or they wouldn't be our friends!) and whatever they agree on must be right.

It was only after my wife raised the possibility of our daughter attending other junior highs and started to challenge the sense of obviousness that attached itself to my school preference that I realized how two core ideological beliefs had framed what seemed like an unconscious, instinctive decision. These were that (1) the more a group of people agree about something (particularly if we see this group as our own peer or reference group), the more they are likely to be right, and (2) high test scores on the part of students are an accurate indicator of the intellectual productivity of a school, of the competence and dedication of its teachers, and of the relevance of its curriculum.

Of course, these beliefs might be right. After all, as Eagleton (1991) reminds us, ideology endures partly because it contains elements that people recognize as accurate in their experience. But just because large numbers of people believe something doesn't necessarily make it true. In this instance I never questioned the self-confirmatory dynamic of peer group communication ("You're my friend so what you say must be true otherwise the smartness of my choice of you as a friend is called into question") nor the fact that our friends came from a certain race and class. Neither was I bothered by the fact that I was commodifying learning by viewing it as a product, the value of which could be judged using an exchange economy indicator (the school's test scores). It didn't occur to me that the use value of learning (the meaning the learning had for students) was thereby being ignored.

The other thing that made these beliefs ideological was that their acceptance served to justify and reproduce an existing system, indeed a whole way of thinking about a sphere of human activity (education). In Chomsky's (1989) terms these were the "necessary illusions" that allowed the system to keep on running with the support of its members, even when massive disparities and inequities clearly existed. I accepted completely the assumption that the school district's much trumpeted indicator of a school's worth (its test scores) did indeed correlate with what happened inside that school. That a school's test scores might be more indicative of the economic character of the neighborhoods within which it was situated and of the desire of parents in this neighborhood to have their children score well and thereby retain the competitive advantage their class conferred on them did not really register. I knew this intellectually, but it didn't act as any kind of rational hedge or check against my instinctive sense of which school was right for my daughter.

When a belief seems natural and obvious and when it serves to reproduce existing systems, structures, and behaviors, it is ideological. Ideology is the system of ideas and values that reflects and supports the established order and that manifests itself in our everyday actions, decisions, and practices, usually without our being aware of its presence. When we are faced with choices in life and find ourselves turning without conscious deliberation to what seem like obvious, commonsense forms of reasoning, the chances are good that there is an ideological basis to these. The fact that these forms of reasoning seem almost effortless, suggesting a commonsense response in the same instant that we are confronted with a choice, is an important indication of their ideological nature.

These seemingly natural, obvious ideas have not just forced themselves onto our consciousness from some compartment in the brain labeled "decision-making center." Their immediacy springs from the fact that they represent the commonsense wisdom accepted by the majority in our class, race, and culture. In their apparent obviousness lie their subtle seductiveness and their hidden power. The truth is that these supposedly obvious ideas always serve some interests and oppose others. What seem like wise choices based on transparent truths often end up hurting us without our knowing quite how this has happened. Because ideology is so soaked into our existence, it seems objective and neutral, rather than partisan. This helps to explain how it manages to obscure the injuries it does us.

Ideology and Ideology Critique in Critical Theory

Ideology is the central concept in critical theory. It describes the system of beliefs, values, and practices that reflects and reproduces existing social structures, systems, and relations. Ideology maintains the power of a dominant group or class by portraying as universally true beliefs that serve the interests mainly of this dominant group. This is one of the most frequently quoted elements of Marx and Engel's analysis in *The German Ideology* (1970). The universalizing of sectional beliefs happens through acts of commission (as when schools and churches teach as the values of all society those that serve the interests of a privileged minority) and acts of omission (as when alternative beliefs are suppressed so people have no chance to consider them). As Eagleton (1991) writes, a critical theory perspective on ideology "draws attention to the ways in which specific ideas help to legitimize unjust and unnecessary forms of political domination" (p. 167).

Put colloquially, ideology is present when we shrug our shoulders in the face of misfortune and say "that's life." When I was growing up in England a popular phrase was "mustn't grumble." This was sometimes said in response to all manner of inconveniences, setbacks, and difficulties. "Mustn't grumble" was the universal salve to ease the pain of illness, unemployment, rising prices, falling wages, food shortages, power cuts, politically motivated bombings, unemployment, lack of access to decent health care, strikes, and the overall realization that life wasn't going to get any better. When people really believe that they "mustn't grumble," then the system is safe. Grumbling, on the other hand, challenges the system. If enough people grumble, they might start to hear each other making the low rumbling sound of protest and decide to seek each other out to do something about a situation. If "mustn't grumble" is ideology in action then "must grumble" is the start of ideology critique.

The Evil Twins of Ideology: Capitalism and Bureaucratic Rationality

To illustrate what might be called the "classic" tradition of ideology critique in critical theory, I want to examine the ideas of three thinkers—Max Horkheimer, Theodor Adorno, and Louis Althusser. Horkheimer and Adorno worked as researchers in the Frankfurt Institute for Social Research and are usually cited as key figures in histories of the Frankfurt School (Jay, 1973; Held 1980). Louis Althusser was a French Marxist who was influenced by Gramsci and who in turn influenced Foucault. In the following paragraphs I review the work of Horkheimer and Adorno, especially the two well-known books in which their ideas are most accessibly stated: *Dialectic of Enlightenment* (Horkheimer and Adorno, 1972) and *Eclipse of Reason* (Horkheimer, 1974). Both texts examine the ways in which thought and reasoning have become instrumentalized—disconnected from pondering universal questions such as how we should live and treat each other. When reason is instrumentalized, it is made subservient to practical utilitarian ends. Diverting reason from the study of universal questions, and attaching it only to the resolution of short term practical problems, serves to maintain capitalism and bolster bureaucratic rationality.

In the preface to *Dialectic of Enlightenment,* Horkheimer and Adorno write that we live in a world in which "thought becomes a commodity and language the means of promoting that commodity" (p. xii). Thought as a commodity concerns itself with solving problems defined as important by the ruling group, such as how to become more competitive and efficient in the global marketplace. The co-option of thought by the dominant order means that "there is no longer any available form of linguistic expression which has not tended toward accommodation to dominant currents of thought; and what a devalued language does not do automatically is proficiently executed by societal mechanisms" (p. xii). Thought is therefore viewed as being determined by the two central props of dominant ideology—capitalism and bureaucratic rationality.

The ideology of capitalism is analyzed extensively in *Dialectic of Enlightenment* (Horkheimer and Adorno, 1972). Following Marx, Horkheimer and Adorno argue that under capitalism the value of work has been commodified. In other words, labor is seen as being worth what people will pay for it so that well-remunerated labor is deemed inherently more valuable. In a commodified world people develop their identity and calculate their sense of self-worth in purely economic terms. They write (in masculinist terms common in the 1940s, itself an example of ideology!) that "the economic mask coincides completely with a man's inner character" so that people "judge themselves by their own market value and learn what they are from what happens to them in the capitalist economy" (p. 211). Moreover, people have become so seduced by the commodities produced by capitalism that their lives are geared to the pursuit of these. Commodities (or consumer goods) thus become "an ideological curtain behind which the real evil is concentrated" (p. xv) as people are enslaved by the myth of economic success. Consequently, "life in the late capitalist era is a constant initiation rite. Everyone must show that he wholly identifies himself with the power which is belaboring him . . . . Everyone can be happy if only he will capitulate fully and sacrifice his claim to happiness" (p. 153).

The ideology of bureaucratic rationality is explored in *Eclipse of Reason* (Horkheimer, [1947] 1974). This form of thought is seen in the belief that life can be ordered and organized into mutually exclusive, yet interlocking, categories. Horkheimer argues that adults' capacity to reason (surely a central concern of anyone interested in adult learning) has been dominated by the shift to what he calls formalized or subjective reason. This is an instrumental kind of reason, one "essentially concerned with means and ends, with the adequacy of procedures for purposes more or less taken for granted and supposedly self-explanatory" (p. 3). Formalized or subjective reasoning displays a dominance of means-end thinking. Reason is applied to solve problems of how to attain certain short-term social and economic objectives. In the scramble to achieve short-term ends, the application of reason to abstract universals such as justice, equality, and tolerance becomes increasingly impossible. When the habit of linking reason to the consideration of universal questions is lost, then reason "lends itself to ideological manipulation and to propagation of even the most blatant lies" (p. 23). When thinking becomes a tool to attain certain ends, it also becomes fetishized, that is, to have an existence and innate worth that exists separately of the thinker. Words become tools that are stripped of layers of meaning and dislocated from their history of social use. Witness the cases of *empowerment* or *transformative*. These two words describe the way oppressed people come together to take control of their lives and change prevailing power relations. Yet colloquial English has defused them of revolutionary or political connotations so that they are now applied to any situation in which people want to change things to their advantage. Horkheimer lamented that "as soon as a thought or word becomes a tool, one can dispense with actually 'thinking' it, that is, with going through the logical acts involved in verbal formulation of it" (p. 23).

This kind of short-term, instrumental reasoning is inherently conformist and clearly an ideological creation. Horkheimer writes that "to be reasonable means not to be obstinate, which in turn points to conformity with reality as it is" (Horkheimer, [1947] 1974, p. 10). Mustn't grumble, in other words. When thought has become instrumentalized, then being "reasonable," and by inference being thoughtful and wise, is the same as agreeing with the ideology of the dominant group. This predisposition for reason to be conformist means that thought is "compelled to justify itself by its usefulness to some established group rather than by its truth" (p. 86). Since the majority is the valorized established group in liberal democracies, people come to think that "the principle of the majority is often not only a substitute for but an improvement upon objective reason" (p. 26). So the majority principle (the assumption that if most people agree with an idea or course of action it is probably right—remember how my decision on school choice was right because all of my friends agreed with me?) becomes regarded as an inherently superior form of reasoning. The majority principle is based on the (to Horkheimer) patently false premise that "men are after all the best judge of their own interests" (p. 26). If people accept this premise, then it is but a short step to the majority principle becoming "a power of resistance to anything that does not conform" (p. 30).

It is easy to see the relevance of Horkheimer's analysis of reason for the kind of adult learning that occurs within formally organized adult and continuing education. The majority principle—the idea that people are the best judge of their own interests and therefore will probably request more of what they are already familiar with—plays itself out under the guise of a benevolent needs assessment by continuing education program developers. The mantra taught in graduate courses in adult education is that we plan adult and continuing education programs around learners' needs and that the first step of good program planning is therefore to do an assessment of what those needs are. Accepting adults' definition of their own needs (their "felt" needs as they are sometimes called) is clearly premised on the idea that people are always the best judge of their own interests. In practice, learners often express a desire for programs that are familiar and recognizable and decide what to learn by reviewing what others in their peer group are learning. Such an approach to program development certainly expresses "a power of resistance to anything that does not conform."

The problem for Horkheimer with the principle of a democratic majority representing people's interests is that these interests "are functions of blind or all too conscious economic forces" (Horkheimer, [1947] 1974, p. 28). Capitalism invades our psyche as "instinctual life in all its branches is increasingly adapted to the pursuit of commercial culture" (p. 112). This invasion extends even to those groups—labor unions—that might be expected to oppose it. Horkheimer viewed labor unions not as representatives of an anticapitalist movement that was trying to establish an alternative way of thinking about and doing work, but as ideological agents of capitalism. Labor leaders adopted a business ideology, worked to integrate workers into the social order, and commodified labor by viewing it as something to be managed, manipulated, advertised, and sold for the highest price. The union's job was to get the best possible deal for workers that the rules of the capitalist game allowed, rather than destroying the game and creating an entirely new kind of society. Without champions to challenge capitalism on their behalf, workers' minds were therefore "closed to dreams of a basically different world" (p. 150). The spread of instrumental, bureaucratic reason meant that workers "have learned to take social injustice—even inequity within their own group—as a powerful fact, and to take powerful facts as the only things to be respected" (p. 150).

Ideology and Ideological State Apparatuses

Building on *The German Ideology* (Marx and Engels, 1970) and echoing Gramsci's notion of hegemony, the French philosopher Louis Althusser deepened the understanding of ideology in his influential essay "Ideology and Ideological State Apparatuses" (1971). For Althusser ideology was a systematic form of thought control that ensured that people at all levels of the economic and social system accepted the system's basic reasonableness. Ideology intentionally obscured the fact that the system was based on certain values that furthered some interests over others. If ever the possibility of alternative values was seriously countenanced, then the system could be challenged. But if the system was accepted as a natural phenomenon needing no explanation or justification (because its essential rightness was so obvious), then the possibility of resistance evaporated.

Althusser believed that people lived naturally and spontaneously in ideology without realizing that fact. He wrote "those who are ideological believe themselves by definition outside ideology: one of the effects of ideology is the practical denigration of the ideological character of ideology by ideology: ideology never says, 'I am ideological'" (Althusser, 1971, p. 175). In Althusser's view we can claim in all sincerity to be neutral, objective, and free of ideological distortion when this is really an impossibility. This conviction of their own nonideological nature extends even to those who "manipulate the ruling ideology correctly for the agents of exploitation and repression, so that they, too, will provide for the domination of the ruling class 'in words' . . . all the agents of production, exploitation and repression, not to speak of the 'professionals of ideology' (Marx) must in one way or another be 'steeped' in this ideology in order to perform their tasks 'conscientiously'" (p. 133). To Althusser it was obvious that ideological managers would sincerely and strenuously deny the ideological character of their work.

How can people be so steeped in ideology without being aware of that fact? Althusser (1971) argued that this was made possible because "an ideology always exists in an apparatus, and its practice, or practices" (p. 166) and because "the 'ideas' of a human subject exist in his actions" (p. 168). These actions are then "inserted into practices governed by rituals of dominant ideology" (p. 182). In other words ideology lives and breathes in our daily decisions, routine behaviors, and small-scale interactions. This takes us into the world of Goffman and the framing of everyday rituals and also to Foucault's emphasis on the inscription of disciplinary power in the practices of daily life. Intimate gestures, routinzed professional conduct, conversational conventions, all reflect a wider ordering of power relations which is unconsciously confirmed in these practices. As Giddens (1991) argued twenty years after Althusser's essay, "the most subtle forms of ideology are buried in the modes in which concrete, day to day practices are organized" (p. 23). Ideology thus becomes less a clearly identifiable system of ideas and more a participation in actions, social games, and rituals which are themselves ideologically determined. People participate in these practices through what Althusser called ideological state apparatuses.

Althusser posited two types of socialization agencies that ensure the predominance of the ruling ideology: repressive state apparatuses (such as the legal system, police, and armed forces) and ideological state apparatuses (such as church, mass media, community associations) of which education is the most important. Ideological state apparatuses (his shorthand term for them was ISA's) exist mostly within civil society and ensure that the state reaches into and controls that part of life. His thesis was that "no class can hold state power over a long period without at the same time exercising its hegemony over and in the state ideological apparatuses" (1971,

p. 146). Education as an ideological state apparatus works to ensure the perpetuation of dominant ideology not so much by teaching values that support that ideology but more by immersing students in ideologically determined practices. These practices (such as chopping up the curriculum into discrete chunks to be absorbed, measuring students' learning and the quality of teaching by percentage improvement scores on standardized tests, and moving people in streams and age-based grades through a system at a pace and in a manner over which they have no control) are perceived as universal, rational, and obvious but actually support certain segmented ways of understanding and ordering the world.

By participating in the kinds of practices mentioned above, pupils learn "know how" "in forms which ensure subjection to the ruling ideology or the mastery of its 'practice'" (1971, p. 133). Educational institutions become analogs of capitalism in which "the relations of production in a capitalist social formation, i.e. the relations of exploited to exploiters and exploiters to exploited, are largely reproduced" (p. 156). The rules of good behavior, of morality, and of civic and professional conscience learned in school by students "actually mean rules of respect for the socio-technical division of labor and ultimately the rules of order established by class domination" (p. 132). Of course, ideology requires that this learning appear neutral so that education is falsely perceived as purged of or sidestepping ideology. Teachers believe that they are imparting values of self-determination to students who are making a free choice to accept or reject these. Neither group can see the ideological web in which it is caught.

Resisting Ideology

An initial reading of Horkheimer, Adorno, and Althusser can induce a pessimistic fit of the vapors. The situation they describe seems one of unrelieved hopelessness. If ideology is as powerful and seamless as it appears (to the extent that we can strenuously assert our freedom from it while being simultaneously deeply embedded in it), then what chance do we have of learning our way out? Yet, hope remains. Not all is doom and gloom from the tomb of ideological manipulation. After all, these three thinkers are all widely read and have been heavily influential. Can it be possible that millions of people have read them while all the time being unable to break free of an ideological stranglehold?

Despite their pessimism (understandable after being forced to flee Nazi Germany), Horkheimer and Adorno did admit of the possibility of resistance. Their reason for writing *Dialectic of Enlightenment* was "to prepare the way for a positive notion of enlightenment which will release it from entanglement in blind domination" (Horkheimer and Adorno, 1972, p. xvi), given that "social freedom is inseparable from enlightened thought" (p. xiii). In *Eclipse of Reason* Horkheimer saw a hope for people to reclaim reason as a force for democratic social change if they were able "to interpret accurately the profound changes now taking place in the public mind and in human nature" (Horkheimer, [1947] 1974, p. vi). He optimistically observed that "there is increasing awareness that the unbearable pressure upon the individual is not inevitable" (p. 160), citing in support of his contention the fact that "the intensification of repression in many parts of the world" (p. 160) testified to the fear those in power felt regarding the imminent possibility of change. Althusser, too, noted that ISA's never functioned completely smoothly as agencies of domination "because the resistance of the exploited classes is able to find means and occasions to express itself there" (1971, p. 147). As he succinctly put it, "Whoever says class struggle of the ruling class says resistance, revolt and class struggle of the ruled class" (p. 184). Even successfully communicated ideologies often contain contradictory elements—freedom, liberty, individuality—that challenge bureaucratic rationality.

So the tale of ideology is not just one of secret cabals of capitalist mind manipulators skillfully selling to gullible masses conspicuously false and distorted ideas which serve to secure the power elite's continuing supremacy. Instead ideology is a dynamic phenomenon. Writers such as Eagleton (1991), Williams (1977), and Zinn (1990) discuss ideology in terms of its being contested, fluctuating, negotiated, recreated, and continually redefined. Eagleton (1991) for instance, sees ideology as a "complex, conflictive field of meaning" containing themes that are "free floating, tugged now this way and now that in the struggle between contending powers" (p. 101). He views the Frankfurt School conception of ideology as too closed, arguing that Western capitalist societies mix and match pluralistic and sometimes contradictory ideological elements. For example liberal humanism's emphasis on freedom and autonomy makes room for "variousness, plurality, cultural relativity, concrete particularity" (p. 128). In everyday idioms such as "it takes all sorts," "take people as you find them," "we're all entitled to our point of view," he finds a celebration of difference and a rejection of monolithic orthodoxy that provides a fissure in the dyke of mainstream ideology. Also, as Willis (1999) points out, the meanings invested in cultural processes (such as advertising) and cultural commodities (such as TV programs) by their producers cannot be rigidly controlled or circumscribed. People create their own alternative readings that sometimes turn the intended meaning on its end.

It is surely also the case that institutions and groups deliberately and openly oppose dominant ideology in Western capitalism and live to tell the tale. Religious figures earn the opprobrium of political leaders for daring to find a social and political relevance in Christ's teachings. TV companies broadcast programs and publishers put out books that criticize the government or cast doubt on contemporary morality despite the efforts of lawyers and fundamentalist pressure groups to put them out of business. Subversion sometimes sells. And sometimes we gain a glimpse of alternative worlds in the most unlikely arenas. I well remember a *Donahue* show in which members of the American Communist party featured in the documentary *Seeing Red* were electronically parachuted into America's living rooms to talk in a direct and unedited way about the commitments and passions that had driven them to join the party in the 1930s and 1940s. Additionally, schools, colleges, and universities continue to develop programs and hire teachers who encourage students to propose alternative curricula, question prevailing values, puncture authority, organize social action, and think deeply about what the word *democracy* really means.

Ignoring the possibility that many teachers might *not* be ideological dupes working uncritically within the educational ideological state apparatus is one of the major shortcomings of Althusser's (1971) essay. Although he does acknowledge the likelihood of some "heroic" teachers working "against the ideology, the system and the practices in which they are trapped" (p. 157), he believes that such individuals are "rare" (his word). To him the majority of teachers are unaware of how their work could serve to nourish and maintain the ideological function of education. This seems heavily overstated and condescending, not to say empirically wrong. Thousands of committed teachers work within the education system trying to stretch things a little here, challenge conventional wisdom and practice a little there. The vast majority of teachers I know are certainly aware of the ideological dimensions of education, and of these a good many seek to skirt, question, or subvert this. At some adult educational conferences, one would be laughed out of court for trying to deny the ideological function of adult education.

In reading Althusser's essay, it is impossible to escape the seductively cozy sense of being offered the chance to become one of the elite few who can see through the ideological fog that has descended on the masses. It is as if critical theory is offered as a set of windshield wipers to sweep away the foggy condensation of false consciousness, myth, and distortion. There is sometimes a troubling touch of triumphalist arrogance about all this. It feels like critical theory is portrayed as an exclusive club comprising members who have penetrated an ideologically obscured reality inaccessible to ordinary people. Eagleton (1991) challenges this view of the masses as hoodwinked or duped into accepting patently false ideas. He repeatedly points out that for ideology to work successfully it must possess what its subjects recognize as a core of truth. In his view, "deeply persistent beliefs have to be supported to some extent, however meagerly, by the world our practical activity discloses to us" (p. 12). One thinks of Ronald Reagan's "morning in America" when reading Eagleton's observation that ruling ideologies "must engage significantly with the wants and desires that people already have, catching up genuine hopes and needs, reinflecting them in their own peculiar idiom and feeding them back to their subjects in ways which render these ideologies plausible and attractive" (p. 15). Successful ideologies "must communicate to their subjects a version of social reality which is real and recognizable enough not to be simply rejected out of hand" (p. 15).

So the jury is still out on the extent to which ideology operates as a seamless totalitarian pacifier. On the one hand stands Marcuse (1965a) arguing that repressive tolerance allows the expression of just enough dissent to give people the comfortable but misleading impression that they live in an open society. According to this argument, an expression of difference perversely ends up confirming the superiority of the norm. As an example of this, Horkheimer and Adorno (1972) point out in their essay on the culture industry that "whenever Orson Welles offends against the tricks of the trade he is forgiven because his departures from the norm are regarded as calculated mutations which serve all the more strongly to confirm the validity of the system" (p. 129). In the introduction to his analysis of American ideology, Zinn (1990) also presses the case for repressive tolerance in unequivocal terms. He argues that while the expression of some dissident ideas is allowed, this dissidence is "drowned in criticism and made disreputable . . . allowed to survive in the corners of the culture—emaciated but alive—and presented as evidence of our democracy, our tolerance, and our pluralism" (p. 4).

On the other hand, Zinn himself acknowledges that "we live in a country that, although controlled by wealth and power, has openings and possibilities missing in many other places," and he notes that "there is a long history in this country of rebellion against the establishment, of resistance to orthodoxy" (1990, p. 7). His enormously popular *A People's History of the United States* (1999), now in its twentieth anniversary edition and an historical best seller, chronicles this rebellion and resistance in convincing detail. Even as Barnes and Noble snuffs out the independently owned small bookstore, traditionally the crucible of alternative presses publishing dissident ideas, it contradictorily sells multiple copies of Zinn's works. In a Barnes and Noble store I recently visited, there were multiple works on the shelves by Marx, Engels, and Lenin (and not all in the "Used Books" section!). As I walked in another Barnes and Noble store, I was struck by a prominently displayed collection of copies of *The Cornel West Reader* (West, 1999a) containing his three essays on progressive Marxist theory. Subversion sometimes sells.

When we turn to the Internet, we undoubtedly find monopoly capitalism linking the use of this technology to its own ends. Irrespective of which search engine they choose, people are exposed to multiple corporate advertisements as soon as they log on. But we also find the Internet being used to coordinate mass protests such as the "Day Against Capitalism" demonstration in London and the disruption of the World Trade Organization talks in Seattle and Washington, D.C. If we take the case of critical theory as a counterhegemonic discourse, it is hard to deny the truth of Loewen's (1995) statement that "the upper class has hardly kept critical theory out of education. On the contrary, critical theorists dominate scholarship in the field. Their books get prominently published and well reviewed; education professors assign them to thousands of students every year" (p. 276). As he observes, if we accept the truth of the ideological domination thesis, then "the upper class seems to be falling down on the job" (p. 276).

So we are not faced with an unscaleable north face of the ideological Eiger. As Foley puts it, the tale of how ideology helps reproduce a social order is one "of gains and losses, of progress and retreat, and of a growing recognition of the *continually contested, complex, ambiguous and contradictory* nature of the struggle between domination and liberation" (1994, p. 129). A critical theory approach toward understanding adult learning is premised on the possibility of ideology critique and the existence of those contradictions, chinks, fissures, and crevices mentioned earlier. It is to the discovery and deepening of those chinks as a form of adult learning and educational practice that we now turn.

Adult Learning and Ideology Critique

Adult educators reading the previous few pages will probably have been struck by several things. First, they may be wondering how realistic it is to imagine that in adulthood we can start to stand outside ideology and critically examine the beliefs and values we learned in childhood. Second, they might be asking how the concept of ideology intersects with the idea of autonomous choice that lies at the heart of one of adult education's most revered concepts, that of adults as self-directed learners. And, third, they could well be concerned about the way their own practice might be a form of ideological manipulation. It is these three themes I now explore.

Adulthood as a Precondition for Ideology Critique

Drawing on various bodies of work on political learning, adult cognition, and intellectual development, a good case can be made that it is in adulthood that the incipient capacity for ideology critique stands the best chance of being realized. This is not to say that children don't notice contradictions. Children frequently say that adults in authority distort the truth to suit themselves, say one thing and do another, and send the message "do as I say not as I do." But developmentally, childhood and adolescence are usually presented as eras of dualistic thinking, of dividing the world into right and wrong, goodies and baddies. Not all subscribe to this view. A strong challenge is made by bell hooks (1994, p. 60) who tells of herself as a child "using theory as an intervention, as a way to challenge the status quo" in her own family. She cites Eagleton's contention that children make the best theorists since they have not yet been fully socialized into accepting as natural practices that clearly are unjust. This frees them to pose uncomfortable and embarrassing questions to adults about rituals and behaviors that they regard with a "wondering estrangement."

In adulthood, though, episodes during which adults challenge prevailing, supposedly obvious ideas and practices are rarely experienced as wondering estrangement. Ideology critique may be an estrangement, but it is a hurtful and painful one filled with cultural suicide, lost innocence, and social dislocation rather than wonder. If we study empirically based theoretical constructs such as dialectical thinking (Basseches, 1984), embedded logic, (Labouvie-Vief, 1980), practical intelligence (Sternberg and Wagner, 1986), and epistemic cognition (King and Kitchener, 1994), we see that it is in adulthood that the pile of empirical inconsistencies that call ideology into question mounts higher and higher until, like a tower of books that has one too many volumes placed on top of it, the whole stack of commonsense realities topples over.

Adulthood is a time when we are less and less able to hold the growing evidence of our discordant experiences at bay. The ideological beliefs we learned in childhood concerning the essential fairness of Western democracy, the importance of treating all members of society with equal respect, the assurance that if we work hard we will prosper, and that government always has the best interests of its people at heart are eroded for many of us by the experiences we keep having. The deep cynicism about politics and corporations that pollsters pessimistically report can, from the viewpoint of a critical theory of adult learning, be seen as a hopeful sign, as a giant teachable moment for ideology critique. Cynicism about leaders may indicate that the point of experiential overload has been reached for many adults who no longer believe that the world is organized to serve the interests of the many or that left to themselves things usually work out for the best.

That we should trust adults' knowledge and awareness of their condition was a familiar refrain of Myles Horton (1990), the activist and founder of the Highlander Folk School in Tennessee. Throughout his life Horton argued that adult educators and others in authority often underestimated the sophistication of so-called "ordinary" working people. Again and again he urged the importance of trusting people—particularly those that critical theory would have us believe are stupefied or ideologically hoodwinked—to know what was in their own best interests. He believed the oppressed saw their oppression clearly and that adult educators should help initiate a process whereby people could build on their common experiences of oppression to find ways to resist it. Adults were quite capable of detecting ideological manipulation. The adult educational task was to help them confront and challenge it.

In the contemporary era, the level of skepticism among the general populace regarding politicians' justifications for their actions during the Clinton administration (which was the administration in power when most of this book was written) was such that poll after poll supported Horton's view. Adults told pollsters that the strikes against foreign terrorism that were initiated at strategic moments during the Lewinski revelations and at particularly embarrassing times during the impeachment hearings were poorly orchestrated ideological dust storms designed to divert public attention from the president's problems. Popular skepticism was equally strong regarding the moralizing by Henry Hyde's impeachment committee to the effect that the impeachment hearings were a politically impartial event with no partisan desire by Republicans to humiliate a Democratic president. Neither did they swallow the Republican line that the hearings were initiated only to avert a constitutional crisis and preserve the dignity of the American political system. So, despite the power of the presidency and the prestige of the House of Representatives, very few people took the ideological meanings from these events that their framers intended. Reflective political skepticism and awareness of ideological manipulation far outweighed gullibility.

The Ideological Formation of Self-Directed Learning

A second theme in Horkheimer, Adorno, and Althusser's analyses that may strike many adult educators is the connection between the concept of ideology and the idea of self-direction, surely the jewel in the crown of contemporary adult learning theory. From Tough's (1971) hugely influential studies of adult learning projects through Knowles' (1984) placement of the tendency to self-directedness at the heart of andragogy to more recent critical evaluations of the idea (Candy 1991; Brockett, and Hiemstra, 1991; Hammond and Collins, 1991), self-direction has been argued as the distinguishing characteristic of adult learning and adult educational practice. The idea has inspired countless doctoral dissertations (mine included) and given rise to an annual conference devoted solely to its analysis. Part of its popularity is due to the promise it offers for discovering a distinctive form of adult cognition or identifying a distinctive methodological inclination exercised by adults toward their own learning. Partly its popularity is because the idea of rugged individuals making their own away across the frontier terrain of adult learning projects fits in so well with the notion of individualism (anyone can be president, we can all pull ourselves up by our own bootstraps) at the heart of American ideology.

Self-directed learning underscores the folklore of the self-made man or woman that elevates to near mythical status those who speak a narrative of succeeding against the odds through the sheer force of their individual efforts. This is the narrative often surrounding "adult learner of the year" awards bestowed on those who, purely by force of will and in the face of great hardship, claim their place at the table. This is the narrative that President Clinton's campaign team tapped expertly into in their video *The Man from Hope* shown at his nominating convention. That anyone can be president is celebrated as a prized tenet of American culture. That this takes enormous amounts of money and years of courting, and co-optation by, big business interests remains obscured.

Ideology critique calls into question the foundational belief that in self-directed learning adults make free, unfettered choices regarding their learning that reflect authentic desires felt deeply at the very core of their identity. Ideology critique also makes nonsense of self-directed learning's ideal of learners making autonomous choices among multiple possibilities. Instead it alerts us to the way that a concept like self-direction that is seemingly replete with ideals of liberty and freedom can end up serving repressive interests. For many learners and educators, the image of self-direction is of a self-contained, internally driven, capable adult learner working to achieve her or his goal in splendid isolation. The self is seen as a free-floating, autonomous, volitional agent able to make rational, authentic, and internally coherent choices about learning while remaining detached from social, cultural, and political formations. This idea of the self is what McLaren (1993) refers to as "the magnificent Enlightenment swindle of the autonomous, stable and self-contained ego that is supposed to be able to act independently of its own history, its own cultural and linguistic situatedness" (p. 121).

Ideology critique points out several problems with this notion of the self. First, it emphasizes that we cannot stand outside the social, cultural, and political streams within which we swim. In making what seem like purely personal, private choices about learning, we play out the sometimes contradictory ideological impulses within us. Second, ideology critique holds that conceiving self-direction as a form of learning emphasizing separateness leads us to equate it with selfishness, with the narcissistic pursuit of private ends regardless of the consequences of this pursuit for others. This is, of course, in perfect tune with capitalist ideology of the free market, which holds that those who deserve to survive and flourish naturally end up doing so.

A view of learning that regards people as self-contained, volitional beings scurrying around in individual projects is also one that works against collective and cooperative impulses. Citing an engagement in self-directed learning, people can deny the existence of common interests and human interdependence in favor of an obsessive focus on the self. Such a stance leaves unchallenged wider beliefs, norms, and structures and thereby reinforces the status quo. This concept of self-direction emphasizes a self that is sustained by its own internal momentum needing no external connections or supports. It erects as the ideal culmination of psychological development the independent, fully functioning person. Fortunately, this view of adults' developmental trajectories as leading inevitably toward the establishment of separate, autonomous selves has been challenged in recent years by work on gender (Belenky, Clinchy, Goldberger, and Tarule, 1986; Goldberger, Tarule, Clinchy, and Belenky, 1996) and critical psychology (Morss, 1996; Burman, 1994; Fox and Prilleltensky, 1997). This work questions the patriarchal notion that atomistc self-determination is both an educational ideal to be pursued as well as the natural end point of psychological development. In its place it advances a feminist valuing of interdependence and a socially constructed interpretation of identity.

So ideology critique questions the separatist emphasis of self-directed learning and demonstrates how this emphasis makes an engagement in common cause more difficult for people to contemplate. A separatist conception of self-direction severs the connection between private troubles and public issues (Mills, 1959) and obscures the fact that apparently private learning projects are ideologically framed. Policy makers can also use research into self-direction to justify cutting spending on adult education. After all, they can argue, if adult educators tell us that adult learners are naturally self-directed (unlike children who are dependent on teacher direction), then why bother making provision for their education? Won't they self-directedly take the initiative in planning and conducting their learning anyway? But atomistic, divisive interpretations of self-directed learning need not be the end of the story. As I have tried to argue elsewhere (Brookfield, 2000), if we can demonstrate convincingly the ideological dimensions of an idea that is routinely enshrined in programmatic mission statements and privileged in professional discourse, and if we can prevent interpretations of self-directed learning from sliding into an unproblematized focus on self-actualization, then we have a real chance to use this idea as a foundational element in building a critical practice of adult education.

Adult Education as an Ideological State Apparatus

A third point of connection between adult education and ideology critique is the analysis of adult education as an ideological state apparatus. Although Althusser's work on ideological state apparatuses (ISA's) was directed primarily at schools (as he pointed out, the power to compel attendance is a powerful weapon, not always present in adult education), it is possible to view adult educational programs and practices as ISA's and adult educators as professional ideologists. For example, while writing the first draft of this chapter, I was simultaneously teaching a graduate course on adult learning and adult educational theory. At least half of the course was devoted to an exploration of critical theory and radical adult education. The course was a pass/fail course and used discussion in large and small groups as the chief teaching method. Students were asked to spend approximately one-third of class time reading and critiquing each others' work in pairs or triads, and all written work was viewed as first-draft work constantly in process. On the surface, then, a dialogically taught course focusing in large part on ideology critique and hegemony, with Gramsci, Welton, Freire, and Horton on its reading list, seems an unlikely venue for the repressive functions of ISA's to play themselves out. Yet, one could argue that in important ways this is precisely what happened.

After all, the course commodified education in that the production of course "goods"—students' essays—was the focus of a great deal of effort. These goods were then subjected to the educational exchange economy. Students exchanged them with me for a grade I awarded, with their exchange value (the pass, fail, or incomplete grade they earned as course wages) arguably overshadowing their use value (the way these essays helped their authors understand their practice better, the theoretical illumination they provided for students, and so on). Students' learning was organized according to a top-down, input-output model of production. The top-down input was the reading for the course, my presentations in class, and my comments on students' papers. The output was whatever learning was judged by me to have occurred as recognized by the grade and evinced in students' essays and participant learning portfolios.

Learning was also organized according to a bureaucratic rationality with a clearly designated time (1:00 P.M. to 4:00 P.M. every fourth Saturday) and place (room 212). At times I myself functioned as a professional ideologist; after all, I chose the authors, concepts, theories, and readings that served as the official ideology of adult education. I also worked as an agent of domination, controlling the course of the classroom conversations and patterns of student participation through nods, smiles, frowns, and direct speech, as well as having the final say on when to switch activities, call a break, or call it quits for the day. Also, the course took place in a private college which worked to exclude interested parties on the basis of their inability to pay its high level of tuition or their inability to produce the correct cultural capital (master's degrees) with a certain predesignated exchange value (a GPA of at least 3.00). Clearly, then, subscribing to the surface forms of democratic adult education does not automatically stop particular practices functioning in the manner of ISA's.

Learning Ideology

Although Horkheimer, Adorno, and Althusser write about learning in the texts outlined above, they do so in very general terms. Their work is full of broad philosophical and sociological claims concerning the way capitalist and bureaucratic practices conspire to distort the process of learning. In their studies of anti-Semitism, authoritarianism, and the family, however, the Frankfurt School theorists do focus much more specifically on empirical studies, and it is to empirical work in learning ideology that I now wish to turn.

Viewed from one perspective, learning ideology is an oxymoron. If we accept the terms expressed earlier by Althusser and Giddens, one cannot learn ideology as one learns a new body of ideas, skills, or understandings, since ideology preexists in individuals' lives. According to this view, ideology is a sort of ancestral, preconscious memory that is embedded and replicated in everyday actions and inscribed in material practices. Perceived this way its acquisition is more a process of socialization into obviousness, rather than a deliberate act of learning. The intentional acquisition of skills, knowledge, and understanding implicit in most understandings of learning is absent from this notion of ideology. If ideology preexists, then the only learning involved is learning to perceive ideology's already existing presence. Of course, if we take a Gramscian turn, then the focus shifts to studying how people deliberately learn to embrace hegemonic ideas, thereby ensuring their own servitude.

However, my position is that it is possible to talk of learning ideology as an active and intentional process, even if those doing the learning are unable to foresee the consequences of their own actions. Some of the best support for this view comes from two classic ethnographies—one in middle England, one in south Texas—which document how adolescents simultaneously learn to challenge dominant ideology while being formed by it in ways they do not understand. Both these studies—Paul Willis' *Learning to Labor* (1981) and Douglas Foley's *Learning Capitalist Culture* (1990)—see learning ideology as a dialectical process concurrently involving reproduction and opposition. As Stanley Aronowitz comments in the Foreword to the American edition of *Learning to Labor,* "The kids become the genuine rebels from which political and social opportunists are made while at the same time, reproducing themselves as industrial workers. . . . People cannot be filled with ideology as a container is filled with water. They reproduce themselves in an antagonistic relation to the prevailing culture and ideological practices" (Willis, 1981, pp. xii–xiii).

The prevailing theme in *Learning to Labor* is ideological self-damnation. Willis studied male adolescents at secondary schools in Birmingham, England, as they negotiated the transition from school to the workplace and into their occupational role as manual laborers. In his focus on the "lads" in the school (who were distinguished by their disregard for authority and their contempt for academic study), Willis argues that working-class teenagers actively and enthusiastically embrace what they see as working-class oppositional ideas and practices, while being unaware that this same embrace ensures their subservience to the dominant order when they reach adulthood. Hence, "working class lads come to take a hand in their own damnation" (Willis, 1981, p. 3), yet "this damnation is experienced, paradoxically, as a form of true learning, appropriation and as a kind of resistance" (p. 113). In a poetic lament to the consequences of learning an apparent ideology of resistance, Willis asserts that "for a specific period in their lives the lads believe that they dwell in towers where grief can never come. That this period of impregnable confidence corresponds with the period when all the major decisions of their lives are settled to their disadvantage is one of the central contradictions of working class culture and social reproduction" (p. 107).

What are the components of the apparently oppositional ideology the lads learn? Four strong elements are learned freely within the lads peer group and reinforced by wider working-class culture. Self-direction—a theme familiar in adult education—is one that is particularly prized. The lads learn a self-directed disregard for orga-

nizational notions of time and space, constructing their own cal-
endar of the day and moving around the school at will. Another element is a learned skepticism concerning the value of mental work,
with mental labor equated with the kind of conformism and obe-
dience shown by the "earoles" (students willing to play by the rules
in the hopes of gaining semiskilled or skilled apprenticeships and
employment). Learning an instinctive disregard for mental effort
has implications for a critical theory of adult learning. Given that
any attempt to challenge ideology in adulthood requires a substantial intellectual effort, a learned resistance to critical analysis in
adolescence makes it much harder to do ideology critique later
in life. A third ideological element is a rejection of language as a
middle-class affectation, a bourgeois indulgence. As Gramsci, and
later Freire, point out, a precondition for working-class empowerment (short of violent revolution) is a critical appropriation of dominant language, so that one can use the master's tools to dismantle
the master's house (to use Audre Lorde's [1984] phrase). Learning
a contempt for language as an adolescent makes dismantling ideological obfuscation as an adult enormously difficult. A fourth ideological element—the acceptance of a patently unjust system as part
of the natural order of things—effectively nullifies potential resistance in adulthood. The lads recognize that they live in an unjust
world but see exploitation as "a random part of the human condition" (Willis, 1981, p. 165) as unpredictable as thunderstorms and
with no systemic common cause. This is clearly a contemporary
illustration in middle England of Horkheimer's ([1947] 1974) statement that workers "have learned to take social injustice—even
inequity within their own group—as a powerful fact, and to take
powerful facts as the only things to be respected" (p. 150).

Building on and sometimes critiquing Willis' work, Foley (1990)
spent over fourteen years studying ideological learning in a small
town in south Texas. He wanted to find out how young Mexicanos
"learn a materialistic culture that is intensely competitive, individualistic, and unegalitarian" (p. xv). The skepticism of intellectual
labor exhibited by Willis' lads was shared by the "vatos" (the lads'
Mexicano equivalent) who consequently moved into the world of
manual labor predisposed against the mental effort required to disentangle dominant ideology. Foley argued that this predisposition
was inculcated by school, which had convinced the vatos that "they

were dumb about books and learning standard English. Years of fail-ure had taught them to publicly reject, but privately internalize, the criticism of teachers" (p. 89). However, although Willis and Foley wished to illuminate processes of economic and cultural repro-duction, they avoid subscribing to a strict determinism. They believe that "there are many breaks, lags, antagonisms, deep struggles and real subversive logics within and behind cultural processes of repro-duction which fight for outcomes other than those which satisfy the system for the moment" (Willis, 1981, pp. 175–176).

As already indicated, Willis (1981) identified four distinct ide-ological elements the English lads learned—self-direction, resis-tance to mental work, a rejection of language, and the acceptance of injustice as part of the natural order of things. In a distinctively American context, a number of writers have explored the compo-nents—the curriculum if you like—of a specifically American ide-ology which the vatos and others across the United States learn. Gross (1980) proposes three simple ones: communism and social-ism are bad (a belief which leads people to equate the expansion of welfare, health, education, and housing with "creeping social-ism"), capitalism is good (seen most blatantly in the public rela-tions corporate commercials that suggest that the only reason businesses exist is to benefit humanity), and, contrarily, capitalism no longer exists (because it has been replaced by the mixed econ-omy which blends productive efficiency with a concern for social justice). West (1982) describes "the political unconscious of Amer-ican society" as "the sanctity of private property and the virtue of capital accumulation" (p. 132). In his view, "this ideology entailed an abiding distrust of institutional power, bureaucracy, and espe-cially the state; it also placed unprecedented emphasis on the wel-fare of people as isolated individuals" (p. 132).

The ideology of pluralism—the belief that we live in an open democracy characterized by freedom to choose among competing political allegiances and a free press—is proposed by Zinn (1990) as the dominant American ideology. He argues that people learn this ideology without learning the contrary position that our choices are actually very limited. We can choose between two cap-italist parties that differ only in the degree to which the extremes of capitalism should be moderated, and between newspapers, TV, and other media outlets controlled by a few billionaires (Rupert Murdoch, Ted Turner, and Bill Gates). Spring (1992) demonstrates how public education and mass media collude and sometimes collide in their attempts at ideological management (a term he learned from a Bulgarian political refugee who had been trained as an "ideological manager" under communism). Ideological management is defined as "the conscious exclusion or addition of information and ideas conveyed to the public by mass media . . . to shield the population from certain ideas and information or to teach particular moral, political, and social values" (1992, pp. 3–4).

Like Eagleton, these theorists stress that the ideology of liberal democracy contains elements that act as a hedge against the kind of unrestrained ideological management possible in a totalitarian state. Even ideological state apparatuses "maintain spaces and potential oppositions, keep alive issues, and prod nerves which capitalism would much rather were forgotten" (Willis, 1981, p. 176). Working within these agencies are employees who have a "commitment to professional goals which are finally and awkwardly independent from the functional needs of capitalism" (p. 176). To deny the opportunity for resistance and opposition, creativity and stubbornness, is in Willis' view "to condemn real people to the status of passive zombies, and actually cancel the future by default" (p. 186). In adulthood opportunities open up for people to challenge dominant ideology within the workplace, family, and community.

As Billig and others (1988) point out, ideology often contains internal contradictions or opposites: "It does not imprint single images but produces dilemmatic quandaries" (p. 146). Appreciating the essentially dilemmatic nature of ideology thereby becomes a major adult learning project, according to this view. The choices, decisions, interpretations, and judgments adults make on a daily basis reflect the way their consciousness fluctuates between opposing intellectual and social positions. We take actions that are framed by our understanding and attempts at partial reconciliation of contradictory concepts: free will versus determinism, the individual versus the collective, emotion versus rationality, creative artistry against technical necessity, and so on. Billig and others maintain this is particularly the case in societies where liberalism is a dominant ideology. Becoming aware of the dilemmatic nature of ideology can therefore be understood as a central task of adult learning in which people learn to think dialectically, a mode of cognition claimed by some to be distinctively adult.

Dialectical thinking is marked by the ability to move back and forth between contextually grounded, subjective modes of reasoning and universally objective rules and justifications. Schemas of research developed by researchers interested in dialectical thinking (Riegel, 1973; Basseches, 1984; Kramer, 1989) posit a developmentally predictable cognitive movement in adulthood toward being able to hold subjective and objective modes of reasoning in congenial tension. Adults accept that universal standards and rules are important guides for conduct and reasoning while acknowledging that context will inevitably distort these. One can believe that honesty is the best policy, that one should always tell the truth, and that full disclosure builds trust, while at the same time deciding that in certain situations it is best to tell white lies and hold back important information. Moreover, this holding of two contrary positions is not seen as schizophrenic, unethical, or contradictory but as appropriate to life in a complex, contrary, postmodern world. Researchers in dialectical thought argue that this ability is developmentally learned, a distinctive fact of adult cognition. Consequently, a tolerance for and appreciation of this local-universal tension is found chiefly in adults. If we give any credence to this considerable body of empirical work, then it becomes apparent that Horkheimer and Adorno's claims for the complete dominance of instrumental, subjective reasoning over its objective, universal counterpart are heavily overstated.

This chapter has examined critical theory's analysis of ideology, particularly the way ideology serves to justify and maintain inequity, but it has also argued that ideological control is never total, never successful in completely blanketing all opposition. The contradictory nature of ideological control—the way that dominance is exercised while at the same time containing contradictions that generate possibilities for resistance—is also at the center of Gramsci's concept of hegemony. Hegemony emphasizes the way people learn to embrace enthusiastically beliefs and practices that work against their own best interests, but it also allows for the possibility of opposing elements emerging, of counterhegemony. It is to this intriguing extension of the concept of ideological control that we now turn.

| Contesting Hegemony

Have you ever seen a friend or group of colleagues behave in a way which you knew was killing them slowly and decided in the interests of friendship to point this out to them? And have you ever found that your analysis of their behavior was met with scorn or disbelief and an increased desire by your friends to celebrate, and become even more committed to, these same behaviors? Then what you are witnessing may be something other than willfully irrational self-destruction. Instead, it could be hegemony in action. Hegemony is the process by which we learn to embrace enthusiastically a system of beliefs and practices that end up harming us and working to support the interests of others who have power over us. West (1982) describes a hegemonic culture as "a culture successful in persuading people to 'consent' to their oppression and exploitation" (p. 119). Hegemony describes the way we learn to love our servitude.

The theorist most associated with the term is Italian political economist Antonio Gramsci, described by Cornel West (1982) as "the most penetrating Marxist theorist of culture in this century" (p. 118). Gramsci was a founder member of the Italian Communist Party, a journalist for socialist newspapers, and a strategist for the factory council movement in 1920s Turin, which advocated direct worker control of industries such as the Fiat motor company. In 1926, while a Communist deputy in the Italian parliament, he was arrested by the fascist government (Mussolini had come to power in 1922) and placed under police supervision. In May 1928 he was tried as a political prisoner, with the prosecutor reportedly declaring that "for twenty years we must stop this brain from working." He spent the rest of his life in prison, interspersed with brief spells in hospital, until dying in 1937 in a sanitarium days after his full release finally became legal. There could hardly be a more dramatic illustration of Zinn's (1990) observation (quoted in Chapter One) that "how we think is . . . a matter of life and death" (p. 2).

Gramsci did not coin the term *hegemony*, indeed it is often associated chiefly with Lenin. Borg, Buttigieg, and Mayo (2002) observe that there is no "specific passage or section in Gramsci's massive opus wherein he succinctly and systematically expounds his concept of hegemony" (p. 1). This means that subsequent scholars such as Williams (1983) or Laclau and Mouffe (1985) have added their own shading to the concept. Generally speaking, discussions of hegemony locate the idea as a subtler, more encompassing, concept than ideology. As outlined by Marx and Engels in *The German Ideology* (1970), ideology explains how the ideas of the ruling class become universalized as the ideas of all. Hegemony widens this understanding of ideology so that instead of conceiving it as a system of dominant ideas deliberately designed to reinforce the power of the ruling class, it can be viewed as embedded in a system of practices— behaviors and actions that people learn to live out on a daily basis within personal relationships, institutions, work, and community. Ideology becomes hegemony when the dominant ideas are learned and lived in everyday decisions and judgments and when these ideas (reinforced by mass media images and messages) pervade the whole of existence. In many ways hegemony is the conceptual bridge between the Marxist notion of dominant ideology and Habermas' idea of the colonization of the lifeworld by capitalism and technical rationality. It emphasizes how the logic of capitalism, especially the logic of commodification discussed in Chapter One, seeps and soaks itself into all aspects of everyday life—culture, health care, recreation, even intimate relationships.

The important thing to remember about hegemony is that it works by consent. People are not forced against their will to assimilate dominant ideology. They learn do this, quite willingly, and in the process they believe that this ideology represents their best interests. Hegemony works when people actively welcome and support beliefs and practices that are actually hurting them. This means that the state or ruling class does not need to resort to force or coercion to keep order, which would be expensive and unpredictable. It is important to state, though, that Gramsci believed some form of hegemony was inevitable in every society. The crucial task was to make sure this hegemony was exercised on behalf of the many, rather than the few. His goal was to replace ruling-class hegemony with working-class, or proletarian, hegemony.

As we read Gramsci's elaboration of hegemony, there are several things we need to keep in mind. First, as with much critical theory appearing in English but written in other languages (Italian in this case), there is the problem of translation and the misunderstandings that can result from this. Second, most of his writing was done under harsh prison conditions, involving censorship by prison authorities, so it was necessary for him to use a kind of coded shorthand in his work (Marxism becoming "the philosophy of praxis" is the most quoted example). Third, as his letters (Gramsci, 1994) to his sister-in-law, wife, and friends indicate, Gramsci suffered constantly from increasingly serious illnesses, often untreated. Consequently, much of his work appeared only in note form, as outlines and sketches of future projects rather than as fully realized theoretical analyses. To this extent, the prosecutor quoted earlier could claim some success. Fourth, Gramsci was as much activist as theorist, concerned both before and after imprisonment to further the communist cause in Italy by offering strategic and tactical advice on specific initiatives. As well as the factory council movement, he was heavily engaged in the Institute of Proletarian Culture, magazines such as *The People's Cry* (*Il Grido del Popolo*) and *The New Order* (*L'Ordine Nuovo*), and the parliamentary work of the Italian Socialist and Communist Parties. As a result Gramsci's theoretical analysis is often embedded in the discussion of educational policies, theatrical events (he wrote a great deal of theatre criticism), and intellectual debates pertaining to Italian life in the 1920s and 1930s. The link between these local analyses and an analysis of generic tendencies in the twenty-first century is often hard to make. And, finally, as a Marxist activist writing for other Marxist activists, Gramsci's writing often assumes a level of knowledge of Marxist philosophy and of debates within Marxist scholarship denied to most general readers and most adult educators.

So why should those of us interested in adult learning read Gramsci? To me there seem to be three reasons. First, his understanding of hegemony as an educational relationship has justifiably captured the attention of adult educators. Hegemony—the process by which people learn to live and love the dominant system of beliefs and practices—is not imposed on them so much as it is learned by them. Hence, his most often quoted observation that "every relationship of hegemony is necessarily an educational relationship" (Gramsci, 1971, p. 350). For Gramsci a central feature of adulthood is learning hegemony. Second, in his writing on how to identify and oppose hegemony, he develops a theory of learning, particularly a theory of the formation and development of critical consciousness, that has relevance for contemporary work in transformative learning. Third, in sketching out the ways education can be used to contest ruling-class hegemony he develops the concept of the organic intellectual—an activist and persuader who emerges from an oppressed group to work with, and on behalf of, that group. This idea has been picked up by adult educators who see in it one way to think about their practice as catalysts of oppositional learning.

How Hegemony Works

In analyzing how the dominant class organizes, maintains, and defends its control, Gramsci emphasizes the all-pervasive nature of the process. Although he paid special attention to the influence of the mass media, he viewed the process of hegemony—of persuading people to accept they way things are—as infiltrating all aspects of life: "Everything which influences or is able to influence public opinion, directly or indirectly, belongs to it: libraries, schools, associations and clubs of various kinds, even architecture and the layout and names of streets" (Gramsci, 1985, p. 385). As Williams (1977) points out, "hegemony goes beyond ideology" by conceiving "the whole lived social process as practically organized by specific and dominant meanings and values" (p. 109). Hegemony is not just a system of ideas but "a saturation of the whole process of living . . . a whole body of practices and expectations, over the whole of living" (p. 111). It "constitutes a sense of reality for most people in the society . . . beyond which it is very difficult for most members of the society to move, in most areas of their lives" (p. 110). Knowing of hegemony makes it easier to understand how racism and sexism flourish unchallenged and unacknowledged. It is not so much that people go around loudly declaring bigotry, patriarchy, or homophobia, though this certainly happens. Rather, hegemony is lived out a thousand times a day in our intimate behaviors, glances, body postures, in the fleeting calculations we make on how to look at and speak to each other, and in the continuous micro-decisions that coalesce into a life.

In Gramsci's analysis, hegemony is evident in two domains. On a political level, the state exercises direct domination through "the apparatus of state coercive power which legally enforces discipline on those groups who do not consent either actively or passively" (Gramsci, 1971, p. 12). This is what Althusser (1971) subsequently referred to as the repressive state apparatus. State coercive power is a last resort, a fail-safe device in the event of hegemony failing to secure people's consent to their oppression. In civil society—"the ensemble of organisms commonly called private" (p. 12)—we see the workings of hegemony as ideological manipulation. Here hegemony is evident in the "spontaneous consent given by the great masses of the population to the general directions imposed on social life by the dominant fundamental group" (p. 12). If the workings of hegemony in civil society are successful, then the coercive apparatus of the state need never be called upon. The media, the schools, the churches, the networks of community associations through which we move, all serve to convince people that the way they live is a natural, preordained state that works in their best interests.

The idea that certain institutions in civil society convince the masses that the world is organized on their behalf (thereby concealing the gross inequity that really exists) finds expression much later in Althusser's concept of ideological state apparatuses. To re-emphasize the basic point—hegemony saturates all aspects of life and is constantly learned and relearned throughout life. If anything can be described as lifelong learning, it is this. The hegemonic relationship exists "throughout society as a whole and for every individual relative to other individuals. It exists between intellectual and non-intellectual sections of the population, between the rulers and ruled, elites and their followers, leaders and led, the vanguard and the body of the army" (Gramsci, 1971, p. 350).

As is probably evident by now, hegemony is a difficult concept to grasp. Of all the ideas I've discussed with groups of adult educators over the years, this is the one people have the hardest time understanding. Subtle and elusive, it seems to slide from our consciousness even as we think we have it. Think of trying to nail down Jell-O (in America) or blancmange (in England) and you have something of the struggle to get this concept clear. When the film *The Matrix* came out in 1999, Linda Kvamme, a participant in a graduate course I was teaching on adult learning theory, found the film helpful in illustrating how she understood the idea. This is entirely in keeping with the spirit of Gramsci's work, since he was fascinated with how narratives in popular culture both reinforced, and sometimes challenged, hegemony.

As we have seen, hegemony describes the process by which one group convinces another that being subordinate is a desirable state of affairs. The subordinate group enthusiastically embraces beliefs and practices that are slowly killing them. This is the premise of *The Matrix*. In the film, machines created from artificial intelligence maintain control of humans by saturating their consciousness with a manufactured reality, while keeping them imprisoned in pods. The humans live wholly in the realm of illusion which is experienced as convincingly real. The dominant group (the artificially intelligent machines) does not have to struggle to impose a way of life that the subordinated group (humans) would oppose if only they could understand their situation. Instead, the state of subordination is actively sought out and regarded as desirable.

For example, at one point in the film one of the few rebel humans (played by Joe Pantialano) who has become aware of the hegemonic Matrix decides to betray his small band of counter-hegemonic comrades (led by Lawrence Fishburne). As reward for his treachery, Pantialano asks the machines to return him to his previous state of blissful oppression where all aspects of his consciousness are controlled by the Matrix. Begging for our own oppression is what happens when hegemony works smoothly. Those who are exploited enter ideological prisons built by the exercise of their own free will. They choose their own cells, lock their cell doors behind them, and then throw the keys out of the cell window as far beyond retrieval as they can, all the while luxuriating in a gleeful sense of self-satisfaction at having completed a job well done. In a situation like this, there is no need for elites or state agencies to exercise coercive control. Not only will those being exploited work diligently to ensure their continued subservience, they will take great pride in so doing.

We can bring the concept of hegemony even closer to home by using as an example the metaphor of vocation. Think of how many of your colleagues, perhaps you yourself, speak of adult educational work in terms of fulfilling a vocation. The concept of adult education as vocation—of answering a calling and being in service to learners—appears irreproachable. Who could argue with the notion that good adult educators are selfless servants in the cause of adult learning? This seems praiseworthy indeed. It marks us out as special compared to those money-grubbers who serve corporate interests and global capitalism. I well remember leaving college in my early twenties and being told by a friend going into industry the riches he expected to earn by the time he was thirty and the kind of car he was going to buy as soon as he started work. My envious resentment of his good fortune was eased only by my self-congratulation concerning my choice of vocation. Unlike my mammon-worshipping friend, I would be helping students realize their full potential thereby increasing the amount of compassion and criticality in the world. "He may be saving money," I thought to myself, "but I'm saving imaginations, saving souls."

Viewed from another perspective, however, things are not quite so sunny. There is a dark side to this idea, notwithstanding its morally admirable aspects. Quite simply, this sense of vocation, of fulfilling a calling to the selfless service of others, opens educators to the possibility of exploitation and manipulation. Vocation becomes hegemonic when it is used to justify workers taking on responsibilities and duties that far exceed their energy or capacities and that destroy their health and personal relationships. In effect their self-destruction serves to keep a system going that is being increasingly starved of resources. If educators will kill themselves taking on more and more work in response to budgets being cut, and if they learn to take pride in this apparently selfless devotion to students, then the system is strengthened. Money can be channeled into corporate tax breaks and military expenditure as educators gladly give more and more for less and less.

Vocation becomes especially hegemonic when filtered through patriarchy, as is evident in predominantly female professions such as teaching. Again and again in my time as a university teacher, I have seen female faculty internalizing the ethic of vocation and being held to a higher standard regarding its realization than is the case with their male counterparts. Women professors in departments often become cast as the nurturers, known by students for their excellent teaching and advisement. Translated into academic reality, this means that women professors are willing to spend time working with students rather than locking themselves away in their offices writing articles and books in an effort to gain tenure. Since dominant ideology presumes men to be less relational, less prone to an ethic of care and compassion (in short, less moved by a sense of vocational calling), they receive less opprobrium for being unavailable to students.

Vocation becomes hegemonic when it is embedded in institutional culture and interpreted to mean that one should be willing to sacrifice one's mental and physical well-being to the cause of student learning (which translates into meaning "for the overall institutional good"). Imagine the scene: you're an overworked teacher who has too many students, too many administrative responsibilities, and too little time. A dean or department head comes to you and asks you to take on a section of students taught by a colleague going on sabbatical. Your supervisor explains it will only be for one semester until your colleague returns and that the students will really benefit from being able to work with you since you're such a good teacher. Then comes the kicker. Your supervisor informs you that the only other faculty member available to work with these students is Professor X. Now it just so happens that Professor X is a well-known idiot—a bigot with no sense of responsibility or compassion. You know you can't live with consigning these unfortunate students to the clutches of an incompetent. So you agree to take the students on but just for the one semester until your colleague returns from sabbatical. Then, at the end of the semester, you learn that your colleague has resigned the profession, or taken another position, and a budget freeze means that no new instructors will be hired. In the meantime you have formed relationships with the students temporarily assigned to you, and you just can't face abandoning them (which would be a betrayal of your sense of vocation). So now a temporary commitment has become permanent.

Cue the next semester. A representative of the faculty senate approaches you to chair a new college-wide committee on critical thinking across the curriculum. You have been chosen because of your knowledge of critical thinking, your ability to work with faculty from different disciplines, and the intellectual credibility you possess in the eyes of your colleagues. The argument is made that this new committee, properly chaired, could be of enormous benefit to the students. It would help generate a common understanding of and commitment to the practice of critical thinking across the university. Students would not be exposed to contradictory definitions of critical thinking, and critical abilities developed in earlier courses would be honed and refined, rather than just repeated, as students moved through the curriculum.

Now comes the killer argument. You are told that another person has lobbied vigorously for the chair—Professor Y. Professor Y is supported by a faction known to be hostile to critical thought and to regard its demonstration by students as an inappropriate challenge to teacher authority. This faction is hoping that by having Professor Y chair the committee the critical thinking across the curriculum initiative will effectively be killed. Professor Y is also known to be expert at divide-and-rule tactics and has a history of creating strife among previously harmonious committees. At this point (and very predictably), your sense of vocational calling kicks in and you find yourself agreeing. After all, the last thing you want to have happen is for the students to suffer because of the ill-thought-out and retrograde changes you know the committee will instigate. So now you have more students than you can possibly handle and more committee responsibilities than is reasonable, but you remind yourself that this is what fulfilling a vocation is all about. Astoundingly, you feel proud of this situation! After all, your acceptance of these additional responsibilities proves that you are dedicated to your students' well-being, truly worthy of the title "educator." You wear your enslavement with pride.

When vocation becomes hegemonic in this way it ensures that you start to think of any day on which you *don't* come home exhausted as a day when you have not been "all that you can be." If you have any energy left for your family, friends, or recreational pursuits, then you have failed to give your all to your students. If, however, all you can manage at the end of the day is to microwave a TV dinner and watch a rerun of "The Nanny," then you know you've done a good day's work. A state of burnout becomes a sign of your commitment to your vocation. Anything less than total exhaustion indicates a falling short of the mark of complete professionalism.

So what seems on the surface to be a politically neutral idea on which all reasonable persons could agree—that adult education is a vocation of service to learners calling for dedication and hard work—becomes manipulated to mean we should squeeze the work of two or three jobs into the space where one can fit comfortably. Lived out this way, adult education as vocation becomes a hegemonic concept, an idea that seems a morally desirable example of commonsense wisdom but that ends up working against educators' own best interests. The interests it serves within educational institutions are those of people who wish to run departments and divisions efficiently and profitably while spending the least amount of money and employing the smallest amount of staff they can get away with. On a broader scale, education as vocation becomes a metaphor that supports the commodification of learning, the turning of schools and colleges into centers of production concerned to minimize expenditure and maximize output. What is felt as a private moral commitment is actually a mechanism of control and a prop to the maintenance of the exchange economy. As long as teachers view taking on heavier and heavier workloads as examples of their vocational diligence, and as long as they take pride in the level of commitment this shows, then smaller and smaller resources can be devoted to education. These resources can then be diverted to fund tax breaks for the wealthy or to assist corporations who wish to skirt or reverse environmental controls.

The subtle power of hegemony, and the chief reason for its successful operation, is its all-pervasive, blanket nature. There seems no chance for opposition, no way to develop alternative possibilities. Defining the enemy, to use Newman's (1994) phrase, becomes impossible when the enemy is embedded in the thoughts one thinks, the actions one takes, and the relations one lives out on a daily basis. And even when hegemony is threatened, it is very adept at regrouping its forces to define and accommodate oppositional elements. Were it static and immovable, then the target would be clear. But hegemony is flexible, malleable, able to adjust and reconfigure its shape to try and block whatever revolutionary impulse emerges to challenge it. However, all is not doom and gloom from the tomb. The hegemonic blanket is never broad or deep enough to cover all parts of the body politic at all moments. Hegemony is always being contested, to a greater or lesser extent, by elements of those it seeks to dominate. So the hegemonic process is really a

constant process of realignment as challenges arise to the dominant group's control and as this group works to dampen these.

The contested nature of hegemony is emphasized by Williams
(1977) who writes that "it is never either total or exclusive. At any
time, forms of alternative or directly oppositional politics and culture exist as significant elements in the society" (p. 113). Of course,
hegemony is ever watchful for these elements, "especially alert and
responsive to the alternatives and opposition which question or
threaten its dominance" (p. 113). This means that "it has continually to be renewed, recreated, defended, and modified" at the same
time as "it is also continually resisted, limited, altered, challenged
by pressures not at all its own" (p. 112). Consequently, Williams
argues, "we have then to add to the concept of hegemony the concepts of counter-hegemony and alternative hegemony, which are
real and persistent elements of practice" (pp. 112–113). Adults
learn hegemony, to be sure, but they also have the capacity to
become critically aware of hegemony as they develop a revolutionary political consciousness.

Learning Critical Consciousness

Learning to think critically about power and control and learning
how to recognize one's class position and true political interests
are major adult learning projects for Gramsci. His discussion of
adult learning is placed firmly within his analysis of the development of working-class consciousness and the political impact of
coming to critical awareness. For him, the point is to understand
how workers learn an awareness of their oppression and how this
awareness helps them learn to organize for political transformation. The revolutionary party then becomes the adult educational
agency charged with fostering this learning. Such learning is not
easy since it involves adults deliberately distancing themselves from
their childhood experiences and coming to see these as culturally
constructed.

In his analysis of learning across the lifespan, Gramsci argues
that in childhood our consciousness is socially formed: "The child's
consciousness is not something individual (still less individuated),
it reflects the sector of civil society in which the child participates,

and the social relations which are formed within his family, his neighborhood, his village" (1971, p. 35). Thinking is always a social process and subject to the pressure to conform to the ideas prevailing in our class, racial, ethnic, and gender group. Gramsci writes that "in acquiring one's conception of the world one always belongs to a particular grouping which is that of all the social elements which share the same mode of thinking and acting. We are all conformists of some conformism or other, always man in the mass or collective man" (p. 324).

This emphasis on the socially constructed nature of learning is an outgrowth of Gramsci's Marxism. He argued that Marxism's "basic innovation [was] the demonstration that there is no abstract 'human nature,' fixed and immutable . . . . Human nature is the totality of all historically determined social relations" (1971, p. 133). He sounds a distinctly postmodern echo in his declaration that "all dogmatically unitary concepts are spurned and destroyed as expressions of the concept of 'man in general' or of 'human nature' immanent in every man" (p. 405). (Again, we must keep in mind the context in which Gramsci wrote when we read this sexist language.) Conceiving learning as always being embedded in society, and always reflective of particular group mores, means it is irrevocably contextual. One cannot speak of adult learning in a generic, abstract way or as a decontextualized model of stages or phases. Learning is relational, always framed by the interaction "of purely individual and subjective elements and of mass and objective or material elements with which the individual is in an active relationship" (p. 360). The focus and processes of learning spring from the social contexts of individuals' lives, and these change according to the political conditions under which they live.

Learning to recognize and challenge hegemony, for example, is linked to the development of political movements that fight class oppression, racism, sexism, and homophobia. This kind of learning is not individually decided and determined, nor is it a series of internal decisions or private mental acts made by individuals somehow abstracted out from the world in which they move. Instead, it is socially framed and, in Gramsci's view, linked to membership of a revolutionary party. The content of this learning (what people think is important to learn about contesting hegemony), the process of learning (the methods and approaches people use to learn how hegemony works and how it can be countered), and the cognition of learning (the concepts, categories, and interpretive forms that help people make sense of their learning about hegemony) all reflect the learner's situation—in contemporary terms, her location or positionality.

The major adult learning project that consumed Gramsci's attention was the way in which adult workers developed a revolutionary class consciousness and the way they then learned to act on this to change society and create a proletarian hegemony. This form of learning involved several activities recognizable to adult educators today: learning to think critically by challenging commonsense perceptions of the world (which were often organized to reflect the dominant group's ideas), learning to think independently as workers tried to distance themselves from prevailing habits of mind, and learning to blend revolutionary theory and practice. Gramsci studied these learning processes as they were lived out in the struggle for working-class revolution, and the adult learners he was most concerned with were political activists and organizers inside and outside the Italian Communist Party. But his analysis of adult learning has a contemporary resonance. Learning to think critically, for example, required the learner "to work out consciously and critically one's own conception of the world and thus, in connection with the labors of one's own brain, choose one's sphere of activity, take an active part in the creation of the history of the world, be one's own guide, refusing to accept passively and supinely from outside the moulding of one's personality" (1971, pp. 323–324).

How do adults learn to do this? To Gramsci the "elementary and primitive" phase of developing critical awareness "is to be found in the sense of being 'different' and 'apart,' in an instinctive feeling of independence [and] which progresses to the level of real possession of a single and coherent conception of the world" (1971, p. 333). Here we can see the lexicon of self-directedness so familiar within contemporary adult education, but of self-directedness as a deliberate break with, and a standing apart from, dominant ideology. In Gramsci's analysis the focus of self-directed learning is on adults learning a temporary critical detachment from the culture, rather than of their using the culture as a resource to support learning projects conceived within that culture. As we shall see in Chapter Seven,

Marcuse came to echo Gramsci's emphasis on the importance of a temporary detachment from commonsense, everyday experience, without building explicitly on Gramsci's analysis.

A precursor to any form of authentic self-directed adult learning, therefore, is the adult's perception of herself as an outsider. The exercise of independent thought has powerful political effects since "often an independent thinker has more influence than the whole of university institutions" (1971, p. 342). Gramsci is careful to point out, however, that independence of thought is not the same as the creation of original knowledge. Self-directedness in learning is evident in a powerful way, even if what is being learned is already known to others. Thus "to discover truth oneself, without external suggestions or assistance, is to create—even if the truth is an old one" (p. 33). This independent coming to truth represents "the phase of intellectual maturity in which one may discover new truth" (p. 33).

The "elementary and primitive" phase of learning a basic sense of independence and separateness is followed by a consciousness of one's own place in a hegemonic or counterhegemonic group. Gramsci wrote that working-class adults had two theoretical consciousnesses (or one contradictory consciousness). One of these was "superficially explicit or verbal . . . inherited from the past and uncritically absorbed" (1971, p. 333). This superficially explicit conception of the world comprised the dominant ideas of the time. It worked "powerfully enough to produce a situation in which the contradictory state of consciousness does not permit of any action, any decision or any choice, and produces a condition of moral and political passivity" (p. 333). This first superficial form of consciousness was hegemonic—a form of ideological control producing quietism and conformity. When circumstances conspired to have a group or class form itself into a movement to fight oppression, then the second consciousness—critical consciousness—began to emerge. Thus, for Gramsci, "critical understanding of self takes place therefore through a struggle of political 'hegemonies' and of opposing directions, first in the ethical field and then in that of politics proper, in order to arrive at the working out at a higher level of one's own conception of reality" (p. 333).

This is an unequivocal siting of adult critical reflection in political struggle. Gramsci is saying that criticality is learned in the context of working-class activism and that a truer conception of reality is realized as working-class adults understand their common situation and the need for collective action. It is a consciousness of solidarity on the part of the adult "which is implicit in his activity and which in reality unites him with all his fellow workers in the practical transformation of the world" (1971, p. 333). To understand Gramsci's analysis, in other words, requires us to acknowledge the adult educational power of the workers revolutionary party. It is the party that organizes the workers movement and, in so doing, triggers the development of critical consciousness. In this analysis adult educators are party members and activists, not classroom teachers who happen to have an interest in political change.

Adult Educators as Organic Intellectuals

As is clear from the above, Gramsci believed that the adult's progression from an "elementary and primitive" phase of realizing her potential independence to the awakening of critical consciousness depended on the person being involved in a political movement, more specifically, in the revolutionary party. The galvanizing of such a broad movement was partly the responsibility of party intellectuals. To Gramsci, one could not separate the learning of critical awareness by the working class from the catalytic activities of educators and intellectuals. Hence, "critical self-consciousness means, historically and politically, the creation of an elite of intellectuals" (1971, p. 335).

Before we look in detail at how Gramsci conceived of the adult educational work of these intellectuals, it is important to stress that he regarded intellectual processes—philosophizing, thinking, conceptualizing—as generic human activities. This idea is summarized in one of his most frequently quoted phrases: "All men are intellectuals . . . but not all men have in society the function of intellectuals" (p. 9). (As we read Gramsci we need to replace his use of "man" and "men" with the terms person and people.) Gramsci wanted to democratize how intellectual activity was regarded. He believed that "one cannot speak of non-intellectuals, because non-intellectuals do not exist" (1971, p. 9). All people are reasoning beings and therefore theorists. Each person carries on some form of intellectual activity because she or he "participates in a particular conception of the

world, has a conscious line of moral conduct, and therefore contributes to sustain a conception of the world or to modify it, that is
to bring into being new modes of thought" (p. 9).

Just as everyone is an intellectual in Gramsci's view, so everyone is a philosopher. Whenever people use language, whenever
they take action, whenever they develop guidelines of conduct,
"there is implicitly contained a conception of the world, a philosophy" (1971, p. 344). Speech acts and everyday behaviors are the
crucibles of philosophical thinking, not an acquaintance with
abstruse texts. Furthermore, Gramsci wanted to destroy the idea
that a cultured person is one acquainted with elite forms of aesthetic appreciation. To him "everybody is already cultured because
everybody thinks, everybody connects causes and effects" (1985,
p. 25) in ways framed by their culture. If this is true and everyone
is indeed a philosopher, then getting them to think critically does
not mean introducing them to some new form of higher order reasoning. It means, instead, adding a critical edge or dimension to
their already existing forms of conceptualizing. Hence, "it is not a
question of introducing from scratch a scientific form of thought
into everyone's individual life, but of renovating and making 'critical' an already existing activity" (1971, p. 331). Critical thinking
in this view is not an entirely new, higher-order cognitive activity
but a politicizing of what is already a naturally occurring process.

However, although everyone can be thought of as a philosopher engaging in intellectual activity, not everyone serves the social
function of being an intellectual. When Gramsci uses the word
"intellectual," he is not using it colloquially as many do to refer to
a group of sophisticated thinkers intimately familiar with multiple
literatures and supposedly operating at a higher theoretical level
than the rest of us. For him intellectual work was organizational
work on behalf of either the oppressor or the oppressed. Intellectuals were organizers, persuaders, and opinion leaders who worked
either to reproduce dominant ideology and secure the status quo
or to bring the masses to critical consciousness by organizing their
involvement in political struggle, primarily through the revolutionary party. The dominant group's intellectuals were deputies or
subalterns charged with maintaining that group's power by working in the institutions of civil society (schools, churches, community associations, and so on) to ensure that the dominant group's

conception of the world remained the accepted view of reality. Contrasted to these dominant intellectuals who were primarily concerned with ideological transmission and manipulation was a revolutionary group of intellectuals, organic intellectuals.

Organic intellectuals were "elites of a new type, which arise directly out of the masses, but remain in contact with them" (1971, p. 340). These intellectuals help the working class "to conquer ideologically the traditional intellectuals" by their "active participation in practical life as constructor, organizer, permanent persuader" (p. 10). These intellectuals distinguish themselves by having "worked out and made coherent the principles and the problems raised by the masses in their practical activity" (p. 330). They are able to formulate and communicate a strategy for political revolution in terms that the working class can understand, since they are themselves formed by working-class culture. The end result of this effort is the establishment of a new hegemony reflective of working-class interests.

The work of organic intellectuals results in "the theoretical aspect of the theory-practice nexus being distinguished concretely by the existence of a group of people 'specialized' in conceptual and philosophical elaboration of ideas" (1971, p. 334). In other words, a necessary trigger to workers coming to realize their true situation of oppression and deciding to change this through political action is a group of organic intellectuals. The existence of this group is crucial to the awakening of revolutionary fervor. Gramsci wrote that with regard to the dynamics of a large-scale political movement "innovation cannot come from the mass, or at least at the beginning, except through the mediation of an elite" (p. 335). Organic intellectuals have the responsibility to help people understand the existence of ruling-class hegemony and the importance of replacing this with proletarian hegemony. In order to do this, these intellectuals need a capacity for empathic identification with how it feels to be oppressed. They must inhabit the lifeworld of the masses "feeling the elementary passions of the people, understanding them and therefore explaining and justifying them" (p. 418).

This is why it is so difficult for well-meaning middle-class radicals to become organic intellectuals. Despite Freire's injunctions concerning the need for middle-class adult educators to commit class suicide so they can work in an authentic way with the peasantry and other oppressed groups (Freire, 1970), this transition is highly problematic. And what of attempts to commit racial, rather than class, suicide? How can White adult educators ever experience the systemic racism visited daily on non-Whites? As Holst (2002) points out, discussions of organic intellectuals that focus on Martin Luther King (the emblematic organic intellectual in Cornel West's view) tend to ignore the way the civil rights movement "produced organic intellectuals from the Black share-croppers and working class throughout the South" (p. 85). Also, from the Africentric adult education perspective outlined in Chapter Ten, it is clear that racial suicide by Whites is a meaningless idea. The central definitional component of Africentrism is that its proponents exhibit racial membership of the African Diaspora. Of course Whites can be supporters and allies of non-White struggles and may sometimes be invited to participate in them, but they cannot be movement organic intellectuals in Gramsci's terms. I read Gramsci as arguing that a condition of being an organic intellectual is the educator being a member of the racial or class group concerned and not a sympathetic fellow traveler, however well-intentioned. Myles Horton understood this when he insisted that the literacy teachers in the campaign to help St. John's islanders learn to read and write (so they could register to vote) should all be African American (Horton, 1990). No matter how sincere a White teacher might be, she lacked the racial membership to feel "the elementary passions of the people" which was a precondition of her being trusted by the people.

In his adumbration of the adult educator as organic intellectual, Gramsci is clearly operating from a very different conception than that of the adult educator as facilitator. To him the job of an organic intellectual is to "organize human masses and create the terrain on which men move, acquire consciousness of their position, struggle etc." (1971, p. 377). There is no pretence at neutrality or objectivity here, no compulsion to see the oppressor's point of view. The intellectual's task is to galvanize working-class opposition and translate this into an effective revolutionary party. In this analysis adult education is a site for political practice in which organic intellectuals can assist the working class in its revolutionary struggle. His idea of the adult educator as organic intellectual has been acknowledged by people as different as the Welsh cultural critic Raymond Williams (1977), the African-American philosopher Cornel West (1982)—who views Black pastors and preachers as organic intellectuals—and the aboriginal educator Rick Hesch (1995). To West (1982), adult educators who work as organic intellectuals "combine theory and action, and relate popular culture and religion to structural social change" (p. 121).

For Gramsci this organic intellectual work was part of a "war of position" to assist working-class adults in learning those elements of the dominant culture (at a very basic level, reading and writing) that would assist them in overthrowing that culture and establishing a new hegemony, a working-class proletarian hegemony. This kind of learning is very far removed from the learning as joyful self-actualization ethos that sometimes pervades adult and continuing education programs today. For Gramsci studying was a job, "and a very tiring one, with its own particular apprenticeship—involving muscles and nerves as well as intellect . . . a habit acquired with effort, tedium and even suffering" (1971, p. 42).

Contemporary Illuminations

Since Gramsci did not offer any detailed methodological template for adult educational practice (though he was highly detailed in his descriptions of the factory council's operations), there is no body of work applying his approaches to contemporary adult education comparable to the way in which, say, Paulo Freire's ideas have been interpreted for North American educators (Shor, 1987b; Shor and Pari, 1999; Shor and Pari, 2000). People don't claim to use a Gramscian protocol for adult education because one can't really be said to exist. This is probably a distinct advantage. As adult education commentators such as Mayo (1998) and Coben (1998) point out, the fragmentary, coded, and contradictory nature of Gramsci's writings, including his educational advice, make it possible for readers to draw multiple meanings from his words. In fact writers such as Entwistle (1979) have interpreted Gramsci as a highly conservative enthusiast of didactic teaching. This ambiguity is one plausible explanation for his influence. In the absence of specific and detailed methodological guidelines for adult education, one could say one was working in a Gramscian way, yet use a variety of approaches.

Where Gramsci is concerned, I believe it is more a case of working with a distinct purpose and spirit. The purpose is to develop critical consciousness among the people in order to combat ruling-class hegemony and replace this with proletarian hegemony. In this regard it is the revolutionary people's party—the "modern prince" (Gramsci, 1957)—that is the chief site for adult educational work. The spirit entails working out an uncompromising political agenda that informs one's adult educational practice. A Gramscian adult educator has a clear sense of who the enemy is and a sense of himself or herself as a directive persuader and organizer, rather than as a nondirective facilitator working to realize learners' agendas. A contemporary adult educator who seems to me to work in this spirit is the Australian Michael Newman. Newman positions adult educators as activists unable to avoid taking a stand and fated to declare allegiances. He does not place his discussion of adult learning in the context of a revolutionary workers party in the central way that Gramsci does, but he does declare very clearly his intent to work in a partisan fashion. Informed by a class analysis, he understands the adult educator's role to be that of a directive catalyst who chooses to take sides and works only to further the cause of certain groups. This unequivocal commitment to taking sides and to allying one's efforts to those who have the least power in an unequal struggle seems to me to embody Gramsci's notion of the adult educator as catalyst, persuader, and organizer.

Newman's elaboration of this position is best seen in two prize-winning books—*Defining the Enemy* (1994) and *Maeler's Regard* (1999). Both books are "driven by a touch of anger" (1999, p. 175) and strongly condemn what Newman calls the liberal-humanist hegemony in adult education. This hegemony, which focuses on helping people analyze their experiences to become aware of their assumptions, in his view leads inevitably to "the voluntary suppression of organized action" (1994, p. 108). To Newman a focus on self-understanding can lead to self-absorption. As a result, members of oppressed groups are encouraged to divert their attention away from the real problem of defining the enemy into a preoccupation with their experiences as victims. Newman clearly believes that it is crucial to replace the liberal-humanist hegemony with an activist hegemony aimed at creating genuine political and economic democracy. He states his case in the following terms:

"Rather than helping learners look at themselves, we should help them look at the thugs and the bigots, the people who do not care, the people who intrude, the people who misuse their authority . . . by doing this we can encourage people to be outward-looking, to be active and activist. We can help them focus their anger on the cause of their anger. And we can set up situations in which we and the people we are working with think, plan, learn and decide action" (1994, p. 144).

Newman grounds his conception of adult education in a familiar lexicon, that of helping adults think critically. However, his definition of critical thinking is distinctly unfamiliar to many adult educators. For him it is irrevocably linked to the exposure and overthrow of oppression, ruling-class hegemony, and capitalism. He wants to "restore to the word 'critical' the idea of laying blame; so that critical thinking should include identifying and exposing those who are duplicitous or dangerous or exploitative or monstrous or weak and who by being so cause harm to us and/or to others" (1994, pp. 53–54). Quoting the words of three South Africans—past political prisoner and then President Nelson Mandela, assassinated philosopher Rick Turner, and poet Alfred Temba Qabula—he argues that critical thought involves a clear-sighted and explicitly judgmental pointing of the finger of blame. Along with the act of laying blame comes the commitment to choose sides in a struggle and live with the implications of one's choice.

Not for Newman the concept of the adult educator as objectively detached, selfless servant of whatever learning needs adults define for themselves. Instead, "adult education for social justice will be oppositional, and the learning within that educational activity will be best constructed around an analysis of conflicts of interest and a definition of the oppositional forces in those conflicts. Learning for change is done by defining the enemy" (1999, p. 178). A major task of adult educators is to help learners identify the specific individuals, groups, and organizations that are the perpetrators of injustice and to find out their names, addresses, and bases of operation. Adult educators can help learners give substance to abstractions such as oppression and hegemony by researching whether the enemies identified are main or bit players, generals or foot soldiers. They can also study exactly how they wield power.

In the mode of organic intellectuals, Newman's adult educators will be directors, organizers, and permanent persuaders, working in solidarity with those who share a common oppression with a view to naming, confronting, and defeating the enemy perpetrating this situation.

Building on Newman's analysis, Grenadian born adult educator Ian Baptiste (2000) argues for an ethically grounded pedagogy of coercion in which adult educators help learners identify their "true enemies"—those who "intend, *on principle,* to frustrate the goals of their opponent because their opponent's goals stand in opposition to theirs" (p. 29). To Baptiste, adult educators often function as persuaders and organizers but choose not to acknowledge this. He argues that they already use forms of justifiable coercion but are queasy about admitting to that reality. In Baptiste's view it is naïve and empirically inaccurate for adult educators to insist that their job is not to take sides, not to force an agenda on learners. Like it or not (and Baptiste believes most of us do not like to acknowledge this), adult educators cannot help but be directive in their actions, despite avowals of neutrality or noninterference.

One of the most contentious aspects of Baptiste's writings is his insistence on the morality of coercion. Citing George S. Counts in his support, Baptiste believes that adult educators cannot avoid imposing their preferences and agendas on learners and that in certain instances it is important that they do this. Sometimes, in furtherance of legitimate agendas or to stop the perpetration of illegitimate ones, Baptiste argues that the adult educator must employ coercion. At other times, and for reasons that have to do with the adult educator's wish to stop any challenge to his authority, coercion is used but masked by a veneer of passive-aggressive, nondirective facilitation. We all know of situations in which we or our colleagues have said that "anything goes," while concurrently making it very clear (often through subtle, nonverbal cues) that the "anything" concerned needs to reflect our own preferences.

In Baptiste's view a pedagogy of measured coercion is justifiable if it uses "force sufficient to stop or curb the violence or injustice. The aim is not necessarily to annihilate the perpetrators but rather to render them incapable of continuing their pillage" (2000,

p. 43). To support his case, he describes a situation in which he worked with a number of community groups on the south side of Chicago to assist them in reviving an area ravaged by pollution and migration. As the neutral, independent facilitator, he was supposed to stay free of forming alliances with any of the groups involved. Citing his liberal humanist sensibilities, he describes how, in trying to stay neutral, "I succeeded only in playing into the hands of the government officials (and their lackeys in the community). They played me like a fiddle, pretending in public to be conciliatory, but wheeling and dealing in private" (p. 47).

In hindsight, Baptiste argues, the experience taught him that in situations where there is a clear imbalance of power, adult educators should take uncompromising stands on the side of those they see as oppressed. An inevitable consequence of doing this will be the necessity for them "to engage in some form of manipulation—some fencing, posturing, concealment, maneuvering, misinformation, and even all-out deception as the case demands" (2000, pp. 47–48). He points out that if adult educators do admit that manipulation is sometimes justified, then an important learning task becomes researching and practicing how to improve one's manipulative capacities. Through studying ethically justified manipulation, adult educators can "build a theory that can legitimize and guide our use of coercive restraint" (p. 49).

We can see in these accounts an illustration of how two contemporary adult educators work in the directive spirit of Gramsci's organic intellectuals. Although she does not use the lexicon of adult education to describe her organizing and activist work, I believe Angela Davis (whose ideas are considered in Chapter Eleven) is a third. In Newman and Baptiste's emphasis on the explicitly directive role of adult educators and the need for them to be clear and convincing about the political goals they work toward, we can discern Gramsci's idea of the adult educator as constructor, organizer, permanent persuader. Instead of starting with analyzing the learner's experience, "a kind of holy writ in adult education" (Newman, 1994, p. 94), adult education should start with analyzing the enemy. This is an analysis that springs from anger, from the adult educator's consciousness of people being violently mistreated and the need for them to organize politically to have any chance of stopping this. Adult educational work flowing from a Gramscian analysis will be infused with passion, and adult educators will have as part of their job to feel, understand, explain, and justify the elementary passions of adult learners. The overall task of adult education will be to fight a war of position in which adults are helped to acquire a consciousness of their oppression and to organize in solidarity to struggle against that situation.

| **Unmasking Power**

As a beginning adult educator, one of my earliest hopes was to organize classrooms that would be as open and democratic as possible. Adult education appealed to me as a field where the power of the teacher was emphasized far less than in the technical institutes where I had been working. With adults it seemed that classrooms could really be power-free zones, or at least ones in which power was shared equally by teachers and learners. In my first classes I set up discussion circles and was glad to find that I did not have to coerce people to speak. What a relief! Finally I had found a situation in which I could escape the responsibility of exercising power. Little did I know the extent of my naïveté.

The illusion that I had somehow escaped power stayed with me for many years. It was fortuitous that my instinctive preference for discussion circles fit so well with the ethos of the field. After all, democratically inclined discussion holds a central place in the pantheon of practices comprising the progressive-humanist approach beloved of so many in adult education. This approach is usually lauded for a mix of pedagogic and political reasons. Pedagogically, discussion is held to engage learners in participatory learning, which helps them come to a deeper understanding of the topics considered. Politically, discussion is supposed to provide an analog of democratic process, a space where all voices are heard and respected in equal measure. Mezirow (1991a) and Collins (1991), among others, invoke Habermas' ideal speech situation—which to many is exemplified in the rational discourse of respectful, democratic, open discussion—as the organizing concept for good adult educational practice.

My error was to confuse this ideal with reality. Just because my classrooms looked democratic did *not* mean learners felt themselves to be in a power-free zone. Had I reflected on my own autobiographical experiences of learning through discussion, I would perhaps have questioned my assumptions a little more. My own student memories of discussion groups are about as far removed from this tranquil, uncomplicated ideal as they could be. As a learner I rarely found participating in discussion to be a liberatory, democratizing experience; rather, I experienced discussion as a competitive ordeal, the occasion for a Darwinian-style survival of the loquaciously fittest. Much of my energy was consumed by performance anxiety. I knew I was supposed to perform brilliantly but was unsure what this brilliance was supposed to look like. Participating in discussion thus became translated into a form of competitive intellectual besting in which triumph was claimed by those who spoke most frequently or made the most brilliantly articulate and insightful comments. I knew I was engaged in the same kind of name-dropping that grips guests at an academic cocktail party as they struggle for recognition and status. My participation was framed by the need to speak as often and intelligently as I could, thereby impressing the teacher with how smart I was. The idea that I might be involved in a group creation of knowledge never occurred to me. I remember thinking that the conversation was in no sense open but that my tutor was using it as a means of checking the level of my understanding and familiarity with the course's content.

Had the work of Michel Foucault—the French social theorist—been available to me as an undergraduate, I would have understood better my feeling that in discussions I was under the surveillance of my peers and teachers and expected to perform according to some dimly sensed norm of what good participation looked like. I would also have realized that the discussion groups of which I was a member ran according to a regime of truth. Regimes of truth are "the types of discourse which it [society] accepts and makes function as true" (Foucault, 1980, p. 131), and they operate to support teachers in settings that appear to be power free. At the time I put my unhappy experience of discussion participation down to my own lack of intelligence and confidence, and dismissed any doubts I had that discussion might not be as democratically liberating as I'd supposed. When I subsequently began working as a teacher, my experiences as a participant in discussion meant nothing to me. I was going to teach through discussion because holding discussions was inherently democratic, a clear example of teacher power being used in an animating, liberating way to bring students into voice and provide them with a classroom analog of democracy.

In believing that power could be exercised unequivocally for either good or evil and that one could recognize emancipatory uses of power in practices such as discussion circles and learning journals in which adults' voices and experiences were affirmed, I was similar to many of my adult educational colleagues. Like them I viewed power as a Janus-like phenomenon, presenting two contradictory faces—repressive and liberatory. Repressive power is seen as constraining and coercing, bending its subjects to its will. Liberatory power animates and activates, helping people take control of their lives. Consequently, in adult education the release of liberatory power is prized as a core process. In the critical theory tradition, however, it is the repressive face of power that is most strikingly presented. Here the emphasis is on the ways state power is organized to lull people into submission to the dominant order, primarily through its organs of ideological manipulation (including adult education). This is the function of Althusser's ideological state apparatuses (ISA's). When ISA's fail to reproduce the dominant culture and secure consent to its continued hegemony, then repressive state apparatuses (the military, police, National Guard) are called into play to confront and quell revolution. Liberatory power is present in critical theory too, particularly in the analysis of workers' solidarity, revolutionary social movements, and the possibility of counterhegemony. But on the whole this face is less observable. Critical theory generates a Wagnerian wall of sound around the evils of repressive state power that sometimes drowns out the plaintive flute notes of power as a force for liberation.

In adult education, however, the converse is true. Here the liberatory face of power turns its gaze full force on the field. Adult educators talk emphatically of empowerment as a process through which adult learners find their voices and develop the self-confidence to take control of their lives. The possibility of converting "power over" learners into "power with" them (a formulation devised by Mary Parker Follett and popularized within adult educational circles by Lindeman) continues to this day to exercise a hold on educators' imaginations (Kreisberg, 1992). This determination to empower adults signifies to many adult educators what is distinctive and admirable about the field. Show up at a professional gathering of adult educators such as the American Association for Adult and Continuing Education, the National Institute for Adult Continuing Education (in the United Kingdom), or the Australian Association for Adult Education, and sooner or later conference participants will point with pride to the empowering aspects of their practice.

A critique of this bipolar approach to understanding power lies at the heart of the work of Michel Foucault, the French social theorist. Foucault is one of the most provocative voices of critique and dissonance internal to the critical tradition, and for progressively inclined adult educators his analysis of how apparently emancipatory adult educational practices often contain oppressive dimensions is particularly (but usefully) disturbing. In his view repression and liberation coexist to different degrees wherever power is present. Hence, "it would not be possible for power relations to exist without points of subordination which, by definition, are means of escape" (Foucault, 1982, p. 225). Furthermore, the simple classification of power as either good or evil is, for Foucault, hopelessly wrong. Power is far more complex, capable of being experienced as repressive and liberatory in the same situation. As we shall see in this chapter, Foucault shakes up the confident belief that power can be bent to our will so that it can be experienced by recipients the way we intend.

Foucault (who died in 1984) wrote historical analyses of madness, sexuality, punishment, and the way discourses emerge that construct dominant understandings of these. A unifying concern running through all his writings is the understanding of power. Foucault maintains that in modern society sovereign power (power exercised from above by a clearly discernible authority such as the monarch or the president) has been replaced by disciplinary power; that is, power that is exercised by people on themselves in the specific day-to-day practices of their lives. It is easy for adult educators to focus on sovereign power—the arrogant teacher, the unresponsive administrator, the co-opting of literacy training or workplace learning by the needs of capitalism voiced by corporations and governments, and so on. We often think of sovereign power as the enemy, and there is some comfort in feeling we have identified our enemy and can work to subvert or confront it. It is much harder for adult educators to focus on their collusion in and exercise of disciplinary power and surveillance. Reading Foucault should unnerve and unsettle any adult educator who feels she or he is clearly on the side of emancipatory goodness and truth. Foucault's work problematizes critical adult education in a productively disturbing way and in so doing helps adult educators guard against the arrogant certainty that they are free of any authoritarian or manipulative dimensions to their practice.

Let's return to the example of an adult education discussion group. Foucault can help us understand such a group as a complex mix of power-laden practices. His analysis prompts us to consider the way disciplinary power is exercised or the way participants feel subject to a certain form of surveillance while superficially inhabiting a liberatory space. In practices such as the raising of hands to signify one wants to speak, the way eye contact is made between students (or between students and teacher to confer the message that now a chosen participant can speak), the nods of participant and leader approval to register that a particularly insightful comment has been made, the preferred seating arrangement (usually a circle), and the form of speech and terminology that is approved, a norm is subtly, implicitly communicated regarding the "correct" or "appropriate" form of participation. The discussion group format has not removed teacher power, it has merely reconfigured it in a less overt manner and hidden it behind surface forms and processes that appear free. In fact, supposedly democratic, free discussion groups can function very effectively to bolster people's willingness to submit to authority. In Foucault's view this is only to be expected. He observes that modern society is so complex that a permanent army of police and informers would be necessary to make sure people accepted prevailing power relations. Since this is logistically impossible, he argues that overt surveillance has been replaced by self-surveillance—that we monitor and censor our own thoughts and behaviors in discussion groups and elsewhere.

Anyone who claims that adult education is about empowering adult learners (in my experience a majority of those who identify themselves as working within the field) must engage with Foucault's work. The fact that his writing is sometimes hard to follow means it is easy to give up on him. But the struggle to understand and apply him is worth it. Without an appreciation of Foucault's ideas, adult educators often end up with an incomplete and naïve understanding of how power manifests itself in adult educational processes. His work is crucial in helping us learn to recognize the presence of power in our daily practices, particularly the false face of apparently beneficent power exercised to help adult learners realize their full potential.

Foucault as a Critical Theorist?

The subheading above is posed as a question because Foucault is often placed outside critical theory and described as a poststructuralist or postmodernist. However, in a discussion of his intellectual formation, he recalls how "critical theory was hardly known in France and the Frankfurt School was practically unheard of" (Foucault, 1988a, p. 26) at the same time as it was producing some of its most important work. In that same interview, he shares how his line of analysis is very similar to that of critical theory and admits that "if I had been familiar with the Frankfurt School . . . I would not have said a number of stupid things that I did say and I would have avoided many of the detours which I made while trying to pursue my own humble path—when, meanwhile, avenues had been opened up by the Frankfurt School" (p. 26). In my view Foucault does meet the two conditions identified in Chapter One as integral to critical theory. First, he focuses on how existing power relations (such as dominant discourses and regimes of truth) reproduce themselves, and in doing so he draws on Marx. Although he does not consistently put Marx in the foreground, much of his work is in the form of a talking back to Marxist conceptions of sovereign power. Second, he adopts a self-critical attitude to his own theoretical formulations of power. Let me address each of these points in turn.

Given that citations of Marxist thought are rare in Foucault's work, it is easy to conclude that Foucault viewed Marx as an irrelevance. He certainly condemned those who uncritically viewed Marxist doctrine as representing a sort of Biblical, revealed truth of political economy that justified coercion and repression in the Soviet Union and elsewhere around the world. In an interview on intellectual history, he stated that he desired "the unburdening and liberation of Marx in relation to party dogma, which has constrained it, touted it, and brandished it for so long" (Foucault, 1988a, p. 45). Furthermore, precisely because the Left expected him to cite Marx in his footnotes, he gleefully declared that "I was careful to steer clear of that" (p. 46). In another interview in *Power/Knowledge* (1980), he admitted that he liked to play a game with his readers of using Marxist forms of analysis without revealing that this was his intent. In his own words, "I quote Marx without saying so" (p. 52). In this interview Foucault is quite explicit in acknowledging the ways in which Marx's work formed the background to his (Foucault's) own analysis of power. He declares, "It is impossible at the present time to write history without using a whole range of concepts directly or indirectly linked to Marx's thought and situating oneself within a horizon of thought which has been defined and described by Marx" (p. 53).

An example of Foucault's debt to Marx is his contention that the move from sovereign to disciplinary power is a function of the rise of capitalism. In his view, "the growth of a capitalist economy gave rise to the specific modality of disciplinary power" (1977a, p. 221) which "is exercised the way it is in order to maintain capitalist exploitation" (1977b, p. 216). To Foucault, "once capitalism had physically entrusted wealth, in the form of raw materials and means of production, to popular hands, it became absolutely essential to protect this wealth." This protective effort gave rise to a "formidable layer of moralization deposited on the nineteenth-century population" involving "immense campaigns to christianize the workers." In particular, it became "absolutely necessary to constitute the populace as a moral subject and to break its commerce with criminality." In other words, delinquency as a category describing antisocial, disruptive behavior was invented to keep behaviors such as stealing and malingering out of factories and thereby prevent production being threatened. This led to the segregation of delinquents—"vice-ridden instigators of grave social perils"—from the law-abiding majority of poor people (1980, p. 41).

Clearly, then, Foucault positions this part of his analysis in relation to Marx. However, he is critical of totalizing Marxist notions of economic determinism and of an oversimplistic reliance on the division between the material base of society and the ideological

superstructure. He questions the model of ideological manipulation and economic functionality in which "power is conceived
primarily in terms of the role it plays in the maintenance simultaneously of the relations of production and of a class domination"
(1980, p. 88) arguing that we need "a non-economic analysis of
power" (p. 89). To Foucault power is not always in a subordinate
position to the economy. Those with less income or consumer
goods are not always powerless. Neither is power a commodity to
be possessed. A starting point of his analysis is "that power is neither given, nor exchanged, nor recovered, but rather exercised,
and that it only exists in action" (p. 89). In Habermas' view·this
analysis "radicalizes Horkheimer and Adorno's critique of instrumental reason to make it a theory of the Eternal Return of power"
(Habermas, 1989a, p. 52). Cornel West too reminds us of Foucault's intellectual history: "Foucault cannot be understood without understanding his early years in the Communist Party, his
polemic against the French Left, the degree to which a Marxist culture was so deeply influential on the Left Bank, and Foucault's own
attempts to create new left space in relation to those various tendencies and elements" (West, 1993a, p. 95).

In this critical revisiting of Marx, Foucault displays the self-critical posture that I argued in Chapter One needs to be present if a
theory is to be called critical. He challenged any uncritical veneration of ideas arguing instead that "the only valid tribute to
thought . . . is precisely to use it, to deform it, to make it groan and
protest" (1980, p. 54). His own writings and interviews are pep-
pered with references to the hypothetical, tentative nature of his
work and to the way it is offered to the world to provoke responses,
initiate debate, and trigger refutation. Foucault believes that his
writing "does not have the function of a proof. It exists as a sort of
prelude, to explore the keyboard, sketch out the themes and see
how people react, what will be criticized, what will be misunder-
stood, and what will cause resentment" (1980, p. 193). He is also
quite ready to disavow his earlier work. At the end of an interview
with two geographers, he admits the merits of their criticism that
he has used spatial metaphors and geographical constructs without acknowledging their source, declaring that "I have enjoyed this
discussion with you because I've changed my mind since we started"
(1980, p. 77). Though Habermas (1987b) has criticized Foucault

for ignoring the normative basis of his own position and for making false generalities, he pays tribute to Foucault's relentless pursuit of contradictions within his own position, as well as in his analysis of how power invades the lifeworld. Referring to Foucault, Habermas writes that he appreciates "the earnestness with which he perseveres in productive contradictions" acknowledging that "only complex thought produces instructive contradictions" (1989a, p. 178).

The Centrality of Power to Human Relations

A central point in Foucault's analysis is that power is omnipresent, etched into the minutiae of our daily lives and exercised continually by those that critical theory usually describes as "the masses." This is in marked contrast to a view which sees power as possessed chiefly by a dominant elite, exercised from above and emanating from a central location that is clearly identifiable. To Foucault, "power reaches into the very grain of individuals, touches their bodies and inserts itself into their actions and attitudes, their discourses, learning processes and everyday lives" (1980, p. 39). Consequently, his study of power has concentrated on understanding its manifestation in everyday rituals and interactions. He studies power "at the extreme points of its exercise . . . where it installs itself and produces real effects" (p. 197). In adult education the extreme points of exercise are the configurations of specific practices—dialogic circles, learning journals, self-directed learning contracts, and so on—claimed to be distinctive to the field.

From a Foucaultian perspective, we learn far more about power in adult education by studying the microdynamics of particular learning groups in particular classrooms (the gestures, body postures, seating arrangements, facial tics, and phrases that learners and teachers commonly utter) than by investigating how adult education is funded. The growth of corporate training and human capital development may be important trends in the field, and the passing of adult educational legislation may seem an important political event, but Foucault maintains that this is not where power is primarily exercised. For him the only way to understand power is to investigate "how things work at the level of on-going subjugation, at the level of those continuous and uninterrupted processes which subject our bodies, govern our gestures, dictate our behaviors" (1980, p. 97).

So Foucault starts at the bottom, with the everyday thoughts and actions of "ordinary" people. He describes his method of focusing on everyday practices and behaviors as an ascending analysis of power. An ascending analysis begins by studying "infinitesimal mechanisms, which each have their own history, their own trajectory, their own techniques and tactics" and then describes how these are co-opted "by ever more general mechanisms and by forms of global domination" (Foucault, 1980, p. 99). This approach stands in marked contrast to a top-down analysis of power where a central supervisory agency is identified (for example one with responsibility for accrediting adult education programs), and the focus is on studying how this agency extends its control ever more widely by forcing people to behave in a certain way. Foucault believed that a top-down analysis was too deterministic and gave far too much weight to a dominant group's ability to make the world conform to its image.

In Foucault's view power relations are infinitely diverse and contextual. They originate in unpredictable ways at particular times and places. A dominant group does not set out to create a set of mechanisms of control designed to bolster its authority. What really happens is that members of this group begin to realize that specific practices have arisen that could "become economically advantageous and politically useful" (Foucault, 1980, p. 101) in maintaining the dominant group's position. Whenever a dominant group perceives that certain practices might prove useful to them then "as a natural consequence, all of a sudden, they came to be colonized and maintained by global mechanisms and the entire state system" (p. 101). So, in Foucault's view, the establishment of societal mechanisms of control is haphazard and accidental rather than deliberately organized. Those who desire to maintain the system as it is wait till a specific configuration of power relations and practices emerges that can be co-opted to support the functioning of that system. This serendipitous configuration is then seized upon and incorporated to serve ends that are often contradictory to the configuration's intent.

An adult educational example of this, discussed in Usher and Edwards' (1994) analysis of postmodern education, is the accreditation of adults' prior experiential learning. Acknowledging the validity of adults' prior learning experiences emerged originally as a countercultural, experimental practice. It was an innovative way of challenging the sterility and rigidity of formal conceptions of learning embedded in higher educational curricula. Proponents of recognizing prior learning for adults accused colleges and universities of denigrating and excluding the knowledge and experience adults brought to their studies. To them it was insulting to make adults take introductory courses in subjects where adult learners sometimes had more experience than the instructor. To challenge this position, some adult educators argued that people's everyday knowledge should be taken as seriously as the knowledge that was codified and transmitted within the academy. To this end they advocated the establishment of systems of portfolio assessment whereby adult learners could have their prior learning acknowledged and granted college credit.

Initially, the accreditation of adults' prior learning was regarded by many within academe as an irrelevant, soft option favored by a few wooly-minded liberals working in fringe institutions. To use a term of Foucault's, adults' experiential learning represented a subjugated knowledge, one of "a whole set of knowledges that have been disqualified as inadequate to their task or insufficiently elaborated: naïve knowledges, located low down on the hierarchy, beneath the required level of cognition or scientificity" (1980, p. 82). Over time, however, those in authority have realized that the practices associated with experiential learning present a happy set of circumstances ripe for co-opting in support of the dominant system.

In Foucault's analysis this is a predictable development. Subjugated knowledges "are no sooner accredited and put into circulation, than they run the risk of re-codification, recolonization" (1980, p. 86). This has arguably been the fate of some experiential learning initiatives placed within formal educational institutions. Initially, systems for accrediting prior learning flourish as oppositional practices. After a period of time, however, colleges start "to annex them, to take them back within the fold of their own discourse" (p. 86). Usher and Edwards (1994) suggest that "experiential learning is fast becoming a central object in a powerful and oppressive discourse" (p. 206) as governments bypass professional teachers to establish assessment and accreditation mechanisms that value certain forms of experience and learning (particularly those that are vocationally related to information technology) over others. In their view, "the turn to experience is a means of by-passing experienced practitioners and negating the power of their professional judgment . . . thereby transforming experience into a commodity to be exchanged for credit towards qualifications" (p. 204).

A Synaptic Economy of Power

Let us turn now to a fuller consideration of the way power is present in the smallest, apparently most inconsequential, human interaction. As we have seen, Foucault views power as something embedded in the everyday lives of citizens and in the everyday activities of adult learners and educators. He posits "a synaptic regime of power, a regime of its exercise *within* the social body, rather than *from above* it" (1980, p. 39). Power flows around the body politic and around the adult education classroom rather than being located at one clearly discernible point. Hence, "power must be analyzed as something which circulates, or rather as something which only functions in the form of a chain" (p. 98). It is continually in use, always being renewed, altered, and challenged by all those individuals who exercise it. Foucault writes that "power is employed and exercised through a net-like organization. And not only do individuals circulate between its threads; they are always in the position of simultaneously undergoing and exercising this power . . . individuals are the vehicles of power" (p. 98).

This view of power as all-pervasive and exercised by individuals at all levels challenges the discourse common in critical theory whereby power is used in a repressive way to enforce ideological manipulation. In the critical tradition view, those who possess power (the dominant group, power elite, or ruling class) use this possession to keep subjugated groups in place. But once we admit that "power is exercised rather than possessed" (Foucault, 1977a, p. 26), then the question of how one group maintains its hegemony over another becomes much harder to answer. Instead of identifying those social mechanisms that bend the masses to the will of an elite group, we have to shift our attention to studying how individuals' idiosyncratic and specific everyday actions keep a system going in the absence of force clearly exercised from above. Rejecting the notion that power is a commodity that is possessed only by those clearly identified as powerful also challenges the idea that social life, or adult educational practices, can be divided into opposing spheres of repression and freedom.

Foucault criticizes the belief that society at large, and adult educational practices in particular, contain zones of freedom uncontaminated by the presence of power. In his words, "It seems to me that power *is* already there, that one is never 'outside' it, that there are no 'margins' for those who break with the system to gambol in" (1980, p. 14). The omnipresence of power means we have to accept that all of us, at all times, are implicated in its workings. We must accept that "power is co-extensive with the social body; there are no spaces of primal liberty between the meshes of its network" (p. 142). The pride that I took in creating a power-free zone in my early days as an adult educator is, in Foucault's eyes, naïve and misplaced.

This is an analysis that many adult educators may reject entirely, arguing that in comparison with other fields of educational practice theirs is much freer. It is not uncommon to hear it argued that in adult educational settings learners have the chance to experience an open, democratic process liberated from the distortions and constraints imposed on them by the requirements of K–12 education. Those adult educators with humanistic, progressive, or radical sympathies take pride in their commitment to letting adult learners take control of their learning. They encourage adults to define their own curriculum, run their own classes, and evaluate their own progress. A belief in the possibility that adults can be responsible for their personal and political self-actualization seems inherently liberatory.

Foucault would have us think otherwise. To him power relations are manifest in all adult educational interactions, even those that seem the freest and most unconstrained. As an example, think of an adult educational practice that appears to equalize power relations, if not escape from them entirely—the circle. Some three decades ago a colleague of mine jokingly asked me the question "How do you recognize an adult educator at a party?" The response—"she's the one moving the chairs into a circle"—hit home, since almost my first action as an adult educator was to get to my first ever class early and move the chairs into a circle. In so doing I felt I had demonstrated admirably my commitment to honoring learners' voices and experiences and to removing my own coercive power from the educational setting.

The circle is so sacred and reified in adult education as to be an unchallengeable sign of practitioners' democratic purity and learner centeredness. However, following Foucault, it is quite possible to understand that the discussion circle may be experienced by participants as a situation in which the possibility of surveillance is dramatically heightened. Usher and Edwards (1994) write that while putting chairs in a circle "may create different discursive possibilities, it nonetheless simply reconfigures the regulation of students. They may not be so directly subject to the teacher/lecturer but they remain under the immediate scrutiny and surveillance of their peers . . . changing practices do not, then, do away with power but displace it and reconfigure it in different ways" (Usher and Edwards, 1994, p. 91). In a circle, students know that their lack of participation or their poorly articulated contribution will be all the more evident to their peers.

Gore (1993) builds on Foucault's work to argue that beneath the circle's democratic veneer there may exist a much more troubling and ambivalent reality. For learners who are confident, loquacious, and used to academic culture, the circle holds relatively few terrors. It is an experience that is congenial, authentic, and liberating. But for students who are shy, aware of their different skin color, physical appearance, or form of dress, unused to intellectual discourse, intimidated by disciplinary jargon and the culture of academe, or conscious of their accent or lack of vocabulary, the circle can be a painful and humiliating experience. These learners have been stripped of their right to privacy. They are denied the chance to check teachers out from a distance by watching them closely before deciding whether or not they can be trusted. This trust only develops over time as teachers are seen to act consistently, honestly, and fairly. Yet the circle, with its implicit pressure to participate and perform, may preclude the time and opportunity for this trust to develop. As such, it is a prime example of how apparently democratic practices can be experienced by their recipients as oppressive and dictatorial.

Disciplinary Power

Foucault subsumed many of his most important ideas within a single concept, that of disciplinary power. In seeking to illuminate the way power operates in complex, diverse, technologically advanced societies, he argued that the eighteenth and nineteenth centuries witnessed the rise of a new economy of power—disciplinary power. This new economy ensured "the circulation of effects of power through progressively finer channels, gaining access to individuals themselves, to their bodies, their gestures and all their daily actions" (1980, p. 152). Disciplinary power was in many ways more insidious, more sinister, than the workings of sovereign power, being based on "knowing the inside of people's minds" (1982, p. 214).

Although most people in the twenty-first century still think of power in sovereign terms (that is, as located in a clearly identifiable individual or political unit), Foucault believed that the economy of disciplinary power emerged two to three hundred years ago. This economy established "procedures which allowed the effects of power to circulate in a manner at once continuous, uninterrupted, adopted and 'individualized' throughout the entire social body" (1980, p. 119). Disciplinary power exhibits an "attentive malevolence" (1977a, p. 139) and is "a type of power which is constantly exercised by means of surveillance" (1980, p. 104). It is seen most explicitly in the functioning of prisons, but its mechanisms are also at play in schools, factories, social service agencies, and adult education. This form of power turns lifelong learning into a lifelong nightmare of "hierarchical surveillance, continuous registration, perpetual assessment and classification" (1977a, p. 220).

Consistent with his belief that power relations are not deliberately and skillfully engineered by a secretive, dominant elite, Foucault emphasized the element of arbitrary chance that lay behind the emergence of disciplinary power. As he sees it, "a multitude of often minor processes, of different origin and scattered location, [which] overlap, repeat, or imitate one another, support one another, distinguish themselves from one another according to their domain of application, converge and gradually produce the blueprint of a general method" (1977a, p. 138). The rationale informing the emergence of disciplinary power was the need to break up groups and collectivities into separate units that could be subjected to individual surveillance. These single units could then be inveigled into eventually surveying themselves. Surveillance would be more likely accepted if citizens could be persuaded that society itself was under constant internal threat and needed to be defended from all kinds of destabilizing forces (Foucault, 2003).

Disciplinary power exhibits spatial and temporal dimensions. It divides space "into as many sections as there are bodies or elements to be distributed . . . to be able at each moment to supervise the conduct of each individual, to assess it, to judge it, to calculate its qualities or merits" (2003, p. 143). Adult learners are separated into individual cubicles and study carrels, or behind individual computer terminals, working on individual projects. Examinations are taken, essays written, and graduate theses submitted as individual acts of intellectual labor. The collective learning represented by three or four adult graduate students collaboratively writing a dissertation or two or three adult education professors coauthoring scholarly articles is discouraged as a plagiaristic diversion of the intellectually weak. Disciplinary power also breaks down time "into separate and adjusted threads" (2003, p. 158) by arranging learning in a sequence of discrete stages. Training and practice are detached from each other, the curriculum is divided into elements for which predetermined amounts of time are allocated, and the timetable becomes the pivotal reference point for the organization of learners' and teachers' activities. Although he does not cite Foucault, Myles Horton sounds distinctly Foucaultian overtones in his critique of contemporary education: "You have things cut down to small units so you can analyze them, so you can control them, so you can have tests" (Horton, 2003, p. 225). To Horton, "the traditional way of dividing up classes—arithmetic, reading, grammar, language, geography, thirty minutes, thirty minutes, thirty minutes, etc.—that serves technological ends much better than it serves educational ends" (p. 225).

A central mechanism of disciplinary power is the examination. The examination has "the triple function of showing whether the subject has reached the level required, of guaranteeing that each subject undergoes the same apprenticeship and of differentiating the abilities of each individual" (Foucault, 1977a, p. 158). Those who go through a series of examinations have their lives fixed and recorded in documents that make up "a whole meticulous archive constituted in terms of bodies and days" (p. 189). People are sorted, classified, and differentiated by the examination, which functions as "a normalizing gaze, a surveillance that makes it possible to qualify, to classify and to punish" (p.184). When people's achievements and aptitudes are judged by the examination, then we enter "the age of examinatory justice" (p. 305) in which "the judges of normality are present everywhere" (p. 304). In other words, one's degree of normality depends on one's scores on a series of standardized tests.

Surveillance and the Panopticon

Why do drivers stay close to the speed limit when no highway patrol cars are to be seen? Perhaps because they assume that observing the limit ensures a safe trip. But probably the main concern is to avoid being caught speeding by unseen radar, hidden speed cameras, or unmarked police cars. We know these mechanisms of surveillance exist and that at any time they might be trained on us. As Foucault observes, "Surveillance is permanent in its effects, even if it is discontinuous in its action" (1977a, p. 201). We dare not risk accelerating beyond the prescribed speed because at the back of our minds there is always the risk that some hidden force will register our breach of the law. When we monitor our own conduct out of fear of being observed by an unseen, powerful gaze, then the perfect mechanism of control—self-surveillance—is operating.

Self-surveillance is the most important component of disciplinary power. In a society subject to disciplinary power, we discipline ourselves. There is no need for the coercive state apparatus to spend enormous amounts of time and money making sure we behave correctly since we are watching ourselves to make sure we don't step out of line. What makes us watch ourselves so assiduously is not an internal resolve to follow normal ways of thinking and acting, thereby avoiding a fall into disgrace. Instead, we watch ourselves because we sense that our attempt to stay close to the norm is itself being watched by another, all-seeing presence. We carry within us the sense that "out there," in some hidden, undiscoverable location, "they" are constantly observing us. It is hard to deviate from the norm if you feel your thoughts and actions are being recorded (figuratively and sometimes literally) by cameras hidden in every corner of your life.

For Foucault, "the perfect disciplinary apparatus would make it possible for a single gaze to see everything constantly" (Foucault, 1977a, p. 173) and for those being surveyed to be aware that at any time they may be subject to invisible scrutiny. Think of how when we ride alone in car park or hotel elevators we make sure we look "normal" and nonthreatening to the camera lens positioned in the top corner. This form of surveillance is based on the "principle of compulsory visibility" which "assures the hold of the power that is exercised over them" (p. 187). In Foucault's words, "It is the fact of constantly being seen, of being able always to be seen, that maintains the disciplined individual in all his subjection" (p. 187). As well as being very effective in keeping people in line, self-surveillance is also cheap. Foucault is almost rhapsodic in his appreciation of the utilitarian elegance of self-surveillance: "There is no need for arms, physical violence, material constraints. Just a gaze. An inspecting gaze, a gaze which each individual under its weight will end by interiorizing to the point that he is his own overseer, each individual thus exercising this surveillance over, and against, himself. A superb formula: power exercised continuously and for what turns out to be a minimal cost" (1980, p. 155).

The principle of compulsory visibility is most perfectly realized in the panopticon. Designed by Jeremy Bentham, the panopticon is a prison system in which hundreds of prison cells are organized in a circle around a single tower inhabited by two or three guards. Because the cells are backlit but the tower is not, the guards can see into all the cells but the prisoners cannot see into the tower. Consequently, any single prisoner can never be sure at any particular moment that he or she is not the object of surveillance. This is "an apparatus of total and circulating mistrust" (Foucault, 1980, p. 158) in which inmates themselves are the bearers of power. The system works on the facts of the visibility of the backlit inmate and the unverifiability of the disciplinary gaze from the darkened tower; "the inmate must never know whether he is being looked on at any moment; but he must be sure that he may always be so" (Foucault, 1977a, p. 201).

In Foucault's view, the panopticon is the organizing principle of disciplinary power in contemporary society, "a technological invention in the order of power comparable with the steam engine in the order of production" (1980, p. 151). Organizations and institutions throughout society induce in people "a state of conscious and permanent visibility that assures the automatic functioning of power" (1977a, p. 201). In car parks, high streets, workplaces, shops, hotels, airports, malls, banks, even schools and colleges, we can see cameras trained on us. We know that somewhere in a place we can't see a security guard has an image of us on one of a bank of screens. Of course, we can never be sure this guard has chosen to look at the particular screen containing our image or even that the guard has not temporarily gone to the bathroom. But we can never be absolutely sure he or she is not there. Better to be safe than sorry, then, and behave as if we were being watched.

Foucault is explicit in his belief that the panopticon pervades education just as much as any other human activity. In his words, "a relation of surveillance, defined and regulated, is inscribed at the heart of the practice of teaching, not as an additional or adjacent part, but as a mechanism that is inherent to it and which increases its efficiency" (1977a, p. 176). Examinations, timetables, student of the month awards, gold stars, end-of-term reports, student workbooks, and learning portfolios all combine to make learners aware that their presence within the system is being monitored constantly. An awareness of this fact by the "lads" featured in Willis' study (1981) of English secondary education (described in Chapter Three) was so strong that they spent a good part of their lives scheming to avoid it. By finding places where they were confident of being unobserved and by creating their own timetables of activity which had little to do with the school's functioning, they were able to reduce the effects of disciplinary time and space.

In a fascinating application of Foucault's ideas to the practice of adult education, Boshier and Wilson (1998) argue that Web-based courses (often thought to be learner centered, decentralized, and flexible) can function in a panoptic fashion. Participation in chat room discussion is mandated and observed by the webmaster who creates an archival paper trail documenting the learner's activities. Boshier and Wilson quote one site where irony is used to let students know they are being observed: "Our club-wielding Pinkerton agents, who keep us informed about the daily activities of suspicious History 102 students, inform us that quite a few rebels decided to postpone viewing Lecture 21 for a few days" (Boshier and Wilson, 1998, p. 46). Students know that a meticulous and comprehensive record of the

Web sites they access (including even e-mail messages they send then delete) can be recreated at any time in the future. So an educational process often touted as freeing adult learners from the need to attend courses at particular physical locations and pre-set times and praised as allowing them to set their own pace for learning can easily replicate some of the surveillance mechanisms of the panopticon.

Power, Knowledge, and Truth

One of the reasons Foucault's work is so interesting to educators is that it constantly illuminates the relationship between power and knowledge. Whoever is in a position of power is able to create knowledge supporting that power relationship. Whatever a society accepts as knowledge or truth inevitably ends up strengthening the power of some and limiting the power of others. Foucault repeatedly states that "the exercise of power perpetually creates knowledge and conversely knowledge constantly induces effects of power . . . it is not possible for power to be exercised without knowledge, it is impossible for knowledge not to engender power" (1980, p. 52). If this is so, then one of the social institutions identified as having the prime function of creating knowledge and truth—education (including adult education)—inevitably comes under scrutiny. After all, it is in educational institutions that people learn standards for determining truth and are taught whatever comprises the official knowledge (Apple, 2000) of that society.

According to Foucault knowledge is socially produced by a number of connected mechanisms. He writes that there is "an administration of knowledge, a politics of knowledge, relations of power which pass via knowledge" (1980, p. 69) all of which combine to label some knowledge as legitimate, some as unreliable. These mechanisms determine how knowledge is accumulated by prescribing correct procedures for observing, researching, and recording data and for disseminating the results of investigations. Such mechanisms of knowledge production are really control devices, and those with the greatest command of them are able to create dominant discourses and regimes of truth (two terms very much associated with Foucault).

A dominant discourse comprises a particular language and a distinctive worldview in which some things are regarded as inherently more important or true than others. A discourse is partly a set of concepts that are held in common by those participating in that discourse community. It includes rules for judging what are good or bad, acceptable or inappropriate contributions and procedures that are applied to determine who may be allowed to join the discourse community. Dominant discourses inevitably reflect and support existing power structures and are vital to them. According to Foucault, "Relations of power cannot themselves be established, consolidated nor implemented without the production, accumulation, circulation and functioning of a discourse. There can be no possible exercise of power without a certain economy of discourse" (1980, p. 93).

It is rare, however, for there to be only one all-powerful discourse in a community. Dominant and peripheral discourses are sometimes at odds with each other, and subjugated or minority discourses can occasionally hold sway in particular social enclaves. For example, in the field of contemporary adult education there are a number of dominant discourses. Those of human capital development, self-direction, experiential learning, and liberal humanism are perhaps the most prominent. Perusing the program brochure for the annual American Association of Adult and Continuing Education (AAACE) convention is instructive in the way the association gives prominence to these. However, attend the annual Adult Education Research Conference (AERC), and the dominant discourses are those of critical theory and postmodernism. In fact, those participating in the discourses honored at AAACE sometimes say they feel regarded as pariahs or unsophisticates when participating in AERC discourses.

When particular discourses coincide and overlap, they comprise what Foucault calls a regime of truth. In a frequently quoted passage, Foucault maintains that: "each society has its regime of truth, its 'general politics' of truth; that is, the types of discourse which it accepts and makes function as true; the mechanisms and instances which enable one to distinguish true and false statements, the means by which each is sanctioned; the techniques and procedures accorded value in the acquisition of truth; the status of those who are charged with saying what counts as true" (1980, p. 133)

Of course, when Foucault uses the term *truth* it is not to describe ideas or knowledge that exhibit some inherent universal accuracy or undeniable empirical correctness. Truth is a term that describes the system that decides that certain forms of discourse should be allowed. Hence, truth is "a system of ordered procedures for the production, regulation, distribution, circulation and operation of statements" (1980, p. 133).

Foucault's writings on the connections between truth, discourse, and power move us right away from thinking of knowledge as something that is pursued and produced for its own sake by energetic individuals enthusiastically dedicated to the wider edification of humankind. Instead, knowledge becomes seen as a social product. We start to wonder how it happens that particular writings, ideas, and people emerge as important in a particular field (such as adult education). Foucault prompts us to ask why certain adult educational books get published, why certain questions seem to come naturally to the forefront in professional conversations, how contributors to handbooks of adult education are chosen, why certain adult educational journals become more venerated than others, and how it is that certain concepts and theories come to frame the research activities of others in a field. He encourages us to link the emergence of new research agendas or theoretical frameworks in the field to the way these support, or at least do not challenge, the politics of truth that exist within the social or academic community of adult education.

Power, Resistance, and the Role of Adult Educators

Up to now the regulatory dimensions of power in Foucault's work have been stressed. One danger in doing this is to slip into thinking of power as wholly repressive or constraining. Foucault is constantly on the alert for this misconception since, in his view, power does not just prevent things happening, it also "produces effects at the level of desire" (1980, p. 59). He states his argument as follows: "If power were anything but repressive, if it never did anything but to say no, do you really think one would be brought to obey it? What makes power hold good, what makes it accepted, is simply the fact that . . . it traverses and produces things, it induces pleasure, forms knowledge, produces discourse" (p. 119). Power must therefore be considered "as a productive network which runs through the whole social body, much more than as a negative instance whose function is repression" (p. 119).

If exercising power is pleasurable, then this must apply to the exercise of disciplinary as well as sovereign power. When people take pleasure in disciplining themselves (for example when a learner completes a learning contract early and celebrates this speedy adherence to the specific requirements of the contract), we are very close to witnessing hegemony. Gramsci's idea of hegemony as the learner's willing embrace of ideas, values, and practices that actually work against her freedom is very close to Foucault's idea of the pleasurable exercise of disciplinary power. In both hegemony and disciplinary power, the consent of people to these processes is paramount. They take pride in the efficiency with which they learn appropriate boundaries, avoid "inappropriate" critique, and keep themselves in line. Both constructs emphasize learners' collusion in their own control and their feelings of satisfaction and pleasure at successfully ensuring their complete incarceration.

Another desire that power produces is a desire to resist manipulation and fight oppression. One of the most common reactions to reading Foucault on the way possibilities for surveillance are woven into all aspects of life is to feel defeated by the omnipresence of power. It is easy to despair of ever unraveling the interwoven and shifting configurations of power and knowledge. This unrelieved pessimism is unwarranted in the light of two aspects of Foucault's work. First, there are elements in his analysis that stress the empirical inevitability of resistance. Indeed, it is his position that resistance is a necessary correlate of power so that power can only exist if the possibility of resistance exists contemporaneously. He writes, "In the relations of power, there is of necessity the possibility of resistance, for if there were no possibility of resistance— of violent resistance, of escape, of ruse, of strategies that reverse the situation—there would be no relations of power" (Foucault, 1987, p. 12). Although dominant discourses and regimes of truth insert themselves into the most detailed elements of our daily thoughts and behaviors, he also believes these can be countered at these points of insertion. Second, Foucault's own life illustrated how citizens could intervene as activists to effect change with regard to specific causes. Let me examine these two aspects, dealing first with the possibility of resistance.

According to Foucault, resistance is so central to power relations that it constitutes a plausible starting point for the analysis of power: "In order to understand what power relations are about, perhaps we should investigate the forms of resistance and attempts made to disassociate these relations" (1982, p. 211). Power always implies the possibility of resistance. Hence, "at the heart of power relations and as a permanent condition of their existence there is an insubordination and a certain essential obstinacy on the part of the principles of freedom" (p. 225). Foucault argued it was mistaken to think that the omnipresence of power meant that people were pawns in some larger game of chess devised by the dominant group. In his view, "to say that one can never be 'outside' power does not mean that one is trapped and condemned to defeat no matter what" (1980, p. 142). Power and resistance are contemporaneous, one always exists as the flip side of the other: "There are no relations of power without resistances; the latter are all the more real and effective because they are formed right at the point where relations are exercised" (p. 142). In one of his interviews, he contends that "all my analyses . . . . Show the arbitrariness of institutions and show which space of freedom we can still enjoy and how many changes can still be made" (1988b, p. 11).

So even as he illustrates dramatically the all-pervasive nature of power and dominant discourses, Foucault holds out the promise of resistance. If power relations are ubiquitous, so is freedom: "If there are relations of power throughout every social field it is because there is freedom everywhere" (1987, p. 12). Clearly, then, in Foucault's view resistance to the exercise of power is a predictable certainty. In his words, "there is no relationship of power without the means of escape or possible flight [because] every power relationship implies . . . a strategy of struggle" (1982, p. 225). Moreover, the switch from monolithic sovereign power to splintered disciplinary power sometimes makes resistance seem more feasible to activists who can work at the local level on specific projects. Resistance "exists all the more by being in the same place as power; hence, like power, resistance is multiple and can be integrated in global strategies" (p. 225). The fact that overthrowing the state, reversing the history of patriarchy, or ending racism are not the only options for those resisting power opens up the possibility of smaller scale acts of opposition. A good example of this is Angela Davis' analysis, based mostly on her own experience of incarceration, of the ways in which prisons (set up as instruments of social control) produce their own points of resistance. Because many prison guards come from the same social group as prisoners, they assist in smuggling in messages and contraband articles from outside and allow prohibited conversation between prisoners. If convicts realize the arbitrary nature of their incarceration, they are sometimes transformed into militant adult educators engaged in "patient educational efforts in the realm of exposing the specific oppressive structures of the penal system in their relation to the larger oppression of the social system" (Davis, 1971a, p. 26).

It is also the case that the effects of power relations are often unpredictable and contradictory, unintentionally generating possibilities for resistance. Foucault maintained that wherever dominant discourses and regimes of truth exist "there are always also movements in the opposite direction, whereby strategies which coordinate relations of power produce new effects and advance into hitherto unaffected domains" (1980, p. 200). As an example of this consider how the World Wide Web has allowed oppositional groups to organize effectively or how hackers have been able to wreak havoc in the world of international business by their interventions.

So the advent of disciplinary power does not snuff out opposition or smooth over conflict. On the contrary, its workings allow for "innumerable points of confrontation, focuses of instability, each of which has its own risks of conflict, of struggles and of an at least temporary inversion of power relations" (Foucault, 1977a, p. 26). Just as disciplinary power exerts pressure on people, so "they themselves, in their struggle against it, resist the grip it has on them" (p. 26). This form of control does not produce a society hermetically sealed against incursions. There are always hairline cracks in the foundation stones of social order. It is to the widening of these cracks (particularly where penal reform was concerned) that Foucault devoted much of his energy.

As biographies such as Macey's (1993), Miller's (1993), and Eribon's (1991) demonstrate, Foucault was constantly involved in campaigns directed toward exposing the mechanisms of control that lay behind a range of human service operations, particularly those contained within the penal system. His life exemplified his belief that intellectuals are not passive, detached observers and recorders of culture and society. What observation they do conduct should be undertaken, in Foucault's view, to illuminate for others the specific mechanisms and strategies that those in power use to maintain existing systems. Specifically, intellectuals are to provide instruments of analysis that would help others locate lines of strength and weakness in power configurations. The role of theory is "to analyze the specificity of mechanisms of power, to locate the connections and extensions, to build little by little a strategic knowledge" (Foucault, 1980, p. 145). Building on his contention that politics is war conducted by other means (a deliberate inversion of Clauzewitz's dictum that war is politics conducted by other means), Foucault hoped that intellectuals would produce "a topographical and geographical survey of the battlefield" (p. 62) comprising power relations. In this way Foucault echoes Gramsci on the practical uses of theory in the struggle against power: "In this sense theory does not express, translate, or serve to apply practice: it is practice" (1996, p. 75).

In describing intellectual activity, Foucault comes close to invoking Gramsci's notion of organic intellectuals as educators, persuaders, and activists working within specific social movements of which they are members. Foucault declared that "a new mode of the 'connection between theory and practice' has been established. Intellectuals have got used to working . . . within specific sectors, at the precise points where their own conditions of life or work situate them" (1980, p. 126). He reconceptualizes theorizing as a local and regional "struggle against power, a struggle aimed at revealing and undermining power where it is invisible and insidious" (1977b, p. 208). Any analysis of power that theorists undertake should be understood as an act of solidarity with those who struggle against it, a contribution to some kind of specific social, cultural, or political intervention. Drawing a topographical map of power's operation is "an activity conducted alongside those who struggle for power, and not their illumination from a safe distance" (p. 208). The purpose of illuminating exactly how power works in obscure and hidden ways to uphold the status quo is "to sap power, to take power" (p. 208).

So, instead of working on behalf of massive constructs such as humanity, the working class, women, the oppressed, or a broad social movement, educators could fruitfully direct their energies toward specific projects. Educational reforms, teaching practices, housing policies, psychiatric protocols, prison organizations all offer opportunities for intellectuals to intervene in ways that contravene dominant power. In Foucault's case this involved him working for penal reform through the Prison Information Group, joining the Jaubert commission to investigate the arrest and beating of the science journalist, Alain Jaubert, and being arrested himself at many demonstrations supporting prison hunger strikers, North African immigrants, and Klaus Croissant (a German lawyer who defended the Baader-Meinhof terrorist gang). He helped establish the socialist newspaper *Liberation* and refused to meet then President of France Valéry Giscard d'Estaing if he (Foucault) was not allowed to raise the case of Christian Ranucci who had been guillotined for murder. He also worked on causes outside France by publicizing the struggles of Soviet dissidents, supporting the "Boat for Vietnam" committee to provide relief for Vietnamese boat people, and joining a convoy to take supplies to Warsaw during the struggle of the Solidarity movement to challenge the legitimacy of the Soviet-installed Polish regime. Foucault lived his belief that "theory does not express, translate, or serve to apply practice: it is practice" (1982, p. 208).

Foucault and Adult Learning Practices

What can we draw from Foucault's work in building a critical theory of adult learning? Perhaps the overriding insight is the need to study how adults learn to recognize that they are themselves agents of power, perpetually channeling disciplinary power, but also possessing the capacity to subvert dominant power relations. Many adults (including many adult educators) either maintain that they have no power over others or that they can choose when and when not to exercise it. Foucault views such confidence with amusement. He sketches out a theory of power as a circular flow that draws all into its currents. Choosing whether or not to exercise power is, in his eyes, an illusion. In reality we are fated to exercise power. If we accept the view that exercising power is unavoidable, then a critical theory of adult learning would study how it is that adults become aware of that fact and what happens to them when they do. More specifically, such a theory would have as a prime purpose the critical analysis of adult educational practices that purport either to be power-free or that attempt to democratize power.

Using Foucault's technique of ascending analysis, it is revealing to examine common adult educational practices that are celebrated for their intent to involve all participants equally. We do not
need Foucault to help us recognize the exercise of sovereign power
in adult education. This is seen in the lecturer who treats a group
of adults as if they were ten year olds, allowing few questions and
no unauthorized interruptions; the instructor who tells adults students they will drop a whole letter grade each time they are late for
class; the teacher who tells an adult student (herself a mother) that
because she missed a class she must bring a note from her aging
father excusing her absence. This kind of sovereign power is easily detected and usually discredited by those within the field who
see themselves as "true" adult educators dedicated to empowering
learners in a respectful way. What Foucault helps us recognize is
that another more subtle form of power—disciplinary power—is
often present in practices that are usually thought of as democratic
and participatory.

The circle and the accreditation of prior learning are two
examples of student-centered adult education that have already
been mentioned as sometimes embodying disciplinary power.
Other prime candidates for the label of power-free practices might
be the use of learning journals (introduced to honor adults' experiences and help them develop their own voices), the use of learning contracts (designed to cede to adults the power to choose,
design, and evaluate their learning), and teaching through discussion (intended to avoid the tendency of adult educators to
move to center stage as didactic transmitters of content in the classroom). Each of these practices appears to avoid the reproduction
of dominant power and to constitute the "temporary inversion of
power relations" (1977a, p. 26) Foucault predicts. Yet, even as these
practices are celebrated for their emancipatory intent and spirit of
self-actualization, we can apply Foucault's ideas to generate a very
different perspective on them.

Individualizing instruction via learning journals and learning
contracts can be interpreted as an instance of disciplinary power
that helps the system "be able at each moment to supervise the
conduct of each individual, to assess it, to judge it, to calculate its
qualities and merits" (Foucault, 1977a, p. 143). Through learning
contracts adult learners become their own overseers. They set cri-

teria for judging the worth of any work they produce, and they also set a timetable for the achievement of their contract's specified objectives. Good adult students devote themselves to producing proper examples of the specified work on time and hold themselves accountable to meet the conditions of the contract to the best of their abilities. To use a term introduced earlier in the book, the contract becomes reified and assumes an identity and presence separate from the intents that framed it. As a controlling influence hovering over learners, it directs many of their actions.

Learning journals also lend themselves to becoming instruments of surveillance. After all, they could arguably be said to be based on "knowing the inside of people's minds" (Foucault, 1982, p. 214) since their explicit intent is to externalize people's innermost reflections. A norm of "transformativity" often hovers in the background to direct the way such journals are written. Learners who sense that their teacher is a strong advocate of experiential methods may pick up the implicit message that good journals reveal dramatic, private episodes that lead to transformative insights. Adults who don't have anything painful, traumatic, or exciting to confess can easily feel that their journal is not quite what the teacher ordered, that it strays too far from this transformative norm. Not being able to produce revelations of sufficient intensity, they may decide to invent some. Or, they may start to paint a quite ordinary experience with a sheen of transformative significance. A lack of dramatic experiences or insights to relate may be perceived by students as a sign of failure— an indication that their lives are somehow incomplete and lived at a level that is insufficiently self-aware or exciting. The idea of transformativity thus constitutes a hidden but powerful norm for journal writing that is enforced by the "judges of normality" (Foucault, 1977a, p. 304), that is, by the teachers who read and grade these journals.

As mentioned at the beginning of the chapter, discussion as a way of learning is often experienced by learners as a sort of performance theater, a situation in which their acting is also watched by the judges of normality. These judges (the discussion leaders) monitor the extent to which adults are participating in the conversation in a suitable manner. Foucault argues that "the universal reign of the normative") means that each person "subjects to it his body, his gestures, his behavior, his aptitudes, his achievements"

(1977a, p. 304). Many adult discussion groups are certainly influenced by an unexpressed but influential norm of what constitutes good discussion. This norm holds that in the best discussions everyone speaks intelligently and articulately for roughly equal amounts of time, and all conversation is focused on the topic at hand. Silence is rare. Conversation focuses only on relevant issues with a suitably sophisticated level of discourse. Talk flows scintillatingly and seamlessly from topic to topic. Everyone listens attentively and respectfully to everyone else's contributions. People make their comments in a way that is informed, thoughtful, insightful, and unfailingly courteous. The Algonquin round table or a Bloomsbury dinner party are the exemplars the norm implies and the ones toward which learners and leaders direct their discussion performances.

Discussion leaders as judges of normality overtly reinforce the power of this norm by establishing criteria for participation that operationalize the norm's rules of conduct. Assigning part of a grade for "participation," without defining what participation means, activates the norm's influence over participants. Learners immediately interpret participation as doing their best to exemplify this norm. They carefully rehearse stunningly insightful contributions that will make them sound like Cornel West or Gertrude Stein. The norm is covertly reinforced by discussion teachers deploying a range of subtle, nonverbal behaviors that signify approval or disapproval of participants' efforts to exemplify the norm. Through nods, frowns, eye contact (or the lack of it), sighs of frustration or pity, grunts of agreement, disbelieving intakes of breath at the obvious stupidity or astounding profundity of a particular comment, and a wide range of other gestures, discussion leaders communicate to the group when they are close to or moving away from the norm. Unless discussion leaders redefine criteria for discussion participation to challenge this norm, adult learners will work assiduously to gear their behavior toward its realization.

This chapter has argued that Foucault's analysis of power is squarely in the critical tradition despite the belief of some that Foucault is really a postmodernist who challenges the Enlightenment foundations of criticality. Reading Foucault helps us understand how apparently liberatory practices can actually work subtly to perpetuate existing power relations. He cautions adult educators who pride themselves on their participatory approaches that they can inadvertently reinforce the discriminatory practices they seek to challenge. Foucault undermines adult educators' confidence that the world can be divided into good guys (democratic adult educators who subvert dominant power through experiential, dialogic practices) and bad guys (behaviorally inclined trainers who reproduce dominant ideology and practices by forcing corporate agendas on adult learners). If the Gramscian approach to adult education explored in the previous chapter helps us name the enemy, a Foucaultian approach makes us aware that the enemy is sometimes ourselves.

| **Overcoming Alienation**

Many people, quite understandably, approach critical theory with some trepidation. Part of this wariness is due to the content of the theory itself, part of it due to the manner of its expression. Work your way past the Marxophobia mentioned in Chapter One, and you still have to contend with a German philosophical tradition grounded in the complexities of Hegel. Accessible is about the last word that springs to mind when critical theory is mentioned. The seven habits of highly effective theorists it's not. But, as with most bodies of theory, an occasional writer stands out as an accessible public intellectual, one who can be read profitably (a term with capitalist overtones that Fromm would strongly object to) by a broader audience. In critical theory Erich Fromm is such a writer. His comment in the Foreword to *The Art of Loving* (1956b) that in order "to avoid unnecessary complications I have tried to deal with the problem in a language which is non technical as far as this is possible" (p. vii) could apply to most of his work. He strove constantly for an accessibility and consistency of tone, interpreting ideas drawn from the critical tradition in terms comprehensible to the average reader. As a consequence his work has been read by millions who would be very suspicious of opening works such as *Selections from the Prison Notebooks, The German Ideology,* or *Lenin and Philosophy.*

Perhaps as a consequence of his accessibility, Fromm has not enjoyed the same critical acclaim as his contemporaries, sometimes being regarded as "Frankfurt Lite." In view of postmodernism's deconstruction of the idea of the unitary, essential self, Fromm's belief in the possibility of each individual possessing a unique, core essence can appear comic. Fromm confidently proposed "the existence of a self, of a core in our personality which is unchangeable and which persists throughout life in spite of varying circumstances, and regardless of certain changes in opinions and feelings" (1956b, p. 123). This core was "the reality behind the word 'I'" and the reality "on which our conviction of our own identity is based" (p. 123). Such declarations are laughable to those of a postmodern bent given their notion of identity as socially labile. As Bagnall (1999) records, a tenet of postmodernism is that identity is so malleable it can be constituted and reconstituted at will. The same person can think and behave in entirely contradictory ways depending on the situation. Fromm's confidence concerning the stability of a core identity looks hopelessly naïve to contemporary postmodern sensibilities.

Fromm has probably also been neglected because of his dated sexist language. He talks constantly of the needs, desires, hopes, and potential of "man," refers to the individual person or worker as "he" and "his," and instead of people talks of "men." Even allowing for the literary conventions of the mid-twentieth century, the omission of any mention of women is striking. More than most in the tradition, Fromm uses "man" to refer to all humanity, arguing that such a convention "has a long tradition in humanist thinking" (1976, p. 10). In his defense, it is important to remember that he was not writing in his first language and that "in German one uses the word *Mensch* to refer to the non-sex differentiated being" (p. 10).

Fromm's view of gender and sexuality is also very much of his time and may go some way to explaining his relative absence from criticalist adult education texts. He sees the integrated, healthy personality as a fusion of masculine and feminine features. The masculine character exhibits "qualities of penetration, guidance, activity, discipline and adventurousness" while the feminine character has "qualities of productive receptiveness, protection, realism, endurance, motherliness" (1956b, p. 36). Even for his caveat that "in each individual both characteristics are blended" (p. 37), it is hard to imagine many contemporary critical theorists taking such an essentialist perspective on gender. Fromm did modify this stance somewhat toward the end of his life arguing in *To Have or To Be* (1976) that a healthy personality is "a synthesis in which both sides of the polarity lose their mutual antagonism and, instead, color each other" (p. 144). However, given the emergence in the last three decades of queer theory, gay, lesbian, bisexual and transgender studies, it is a shock to encounter the comment that in contrast to the ideal, androgynous union of feminine and masculine qualities "homosexual deviation is a failure to attain this polarized union, and thus the homosexual suffers from the pain of never resolved separateness" (p. 34).

Toward the end of his life, Fromm did have his consciousness raised regarding his sexist language. In the preface to *To Have or To Be* (1976), he thanks a female colleague "for convincing me that the use of language in this respect is far more important than I used to think" and states his belief that in that book "I have avoided all 'male-oriented' language" (p. 10). He also pays more explicit attention to patriarchy, declaring that "women must be liberated from patriarchal domination" (p. 186), though that phrasing itself could be taken as a subtle example of patriarchy with its implication that it is men's responsibility to bring about this liberation. The chief significance of the women's liberation movement, in his view, was its "threat to the principle of power on which contemporary society (capitalist and communist alike) lives" (p. 188).

If one can get past these drawbacks, Fromm's essential radicalism needs to be recognized. Make no bones about it, his analysis of contemporary society and his belief that adult education is crucial to a sane society are grounded explicitly in a Marxist analysis of capitalism, particularly the alienated nature of work and learning. In *Beyond the Chains of Illusion* (1962), Fromm is unequivocal in his admiring description of *The Communist Manifesto* as "a brilliant and lucid analysis of history" (p. 15), and throughout the rest of his work he frequently praises and calls attention to what he calls "the real Marx, the radical humanist" not "the vulgar forgery presented by Soviet communism" (1976, p. 25). Certainly his own summation of the central concerns of his life show their derivation from Marxist analysis. Hence, in the Preface to *The Revolution of Hope* (1968), he states "this book, like all my previous work, attempts to distinguish between individual and social reality and the ideologies that misuse and 'co-opt' valuable ideas for the purpose of supporting the *status quo*" (p. vii).

For Fromm, learning to penetrate ideological obfuscation, and thereby overcome the alienation this obfuscation induced, was *the* learning task of adulthood. Working firmly within the "ideology as false consciousness" perspective, Fromm observed that through "a complicated process of indoctrination, rewards, punishments, and fitting ideology . . . most people believe they are following their own will and are unaware that their will itself is conditioned and manipulated" (1976, p. 83). Adult education as a force for resistance can make people aware of ideological manipulation and educate them for participatory democracy. In such a democracy, people "regain control over the social and economic system" to make "optimal human development and not maximal production the criterion for all planning" (1968, p. 101). The point of democratic life in Fromm's view is to reorganize the workplace to make it a site for the exercise of human creativity.

Of all the theorists associated with the Frankfurt School, Fromm is probably the one who in his time was read by the largest number of readers, including many non-Marxists well outside the critical tradition. Why should this be the case? Perhaps one reason is that he draped his writing in the cloak of humanism as well as Marxism, frequently citing a commitment to radical humanism. To contemporary adult educators, humanism is a benign, friendly word associated with notions of self-actualization or the fully functioning adult and drawing on Rogers, Maslow, and Allport. A humanistic perspective on adult education is usually interpreted as one that emphasizes respect for each adult learner's individuality and that seeks to help her realize her potential to the fullest extent possible. There is less attention to the political underpinnings of adult education practice and to the way political economy makes self-actualization a luxury for a certain social class. In contrast to this, Fromm's normative humanism is a militant, Marxist humanism, one that contends that each human's realization of potential entails the abolition of capitalist alienation and the creation of democratic socialism. But because they are called humanist, Fromm's ideas beckon enticingly to adult educators who would not dream of touching anything remotely considered Marxist.

Fromm viewed himself as a social psychologist and his work emphasizes the psychology of the individual as much as social critique. But his analysis always insists that both psychological and sociological understandings need to coexist if contemporary life is to be fully understood. His writings on psychology, particularly in such books as *The Art of Loving* (1956b), exhibit a tone and terminology that make them congenial reading for those adult educators influenced by American, rather than European, intellectual traditions. Consider the Whitmanesque and Emersonian echoes of the following meditation on the aim of life which appeared in *The Sane Society:* "The aim of life is to live it intensely, to be fully born, to be fully awake. To emerge from the ideas of infantile grandiosity into the conviction of one's real though limited strength; to be able to accept the paradox that every one of us is the most important thing in the universe—and at the same time not more important than a fly or a blade of grass" (1956a, p. 204). Adult educators schooled in developmental and humanistic psychology and familiar with Perry, Kohlberg, Rogers, and Knowles will accept quite happily Fromm's contention that mentally healthy people are those who are able "to tolerate uncertainty about the most important questions with which life confronts us—and yet to have faith in our thought and feeling, in as much as they are truly ours" (p. 204).

In this chapter I want to argue that this congeniality of tone makes Fromm's work the statement of critical theory that is most accessible to a North American audience used to thinking in terms of the psychology of the individual adult learner. That Fromm can write in terms acceptable to a chiefly nonpolitical audience and that he can do this while unapologetically showing how this work is grounded in a Marxist influenced critique of capitalism makes him very important to the critical theory tradition in North American adult education. This is particularly so given that Fromm clearly saw a direct link between a healthy society free from capitalist alienation and a strong system of adult education. In his major book interpreting Marxism for a popular audience, *The Sane Society* (1956a), he wrote that "a sane society must provide possibilities for adult education, much as it provides today for the schooling of children" (p. 346) and optimistically recorded that "adult education is spreading" (p. 207). If adults were to understand and confront their alienation, they needed to understand how history and psychology intersected to construct a social character prone to follow fascist or totalitarian leaders or to be subject to the influence of automaton conformity. The difficulties entailed by such a learning project could not be overcome by children or adolescents. In Fromm's opinion, "to really understand the problems in these fields, a person must have had a great deal more experience in living than he has had at college age. For many people the age of 30 or 40 is much more appropriate for learning" (p. 346).

Fromm's Debt to Marx

The chief outlines of Fromm's critique of contemporary society, and, by implication, of adult education, are drawn directly from Marxist thought, particularly Marx's outline of the way in which work in capitalist society has become objectified, that is, experienced by workers as separated from their creativity and identity. In 1961 Fromm published *Marx's Concept of Man,* a translation of Marx's *Economic and Philosophic Manuscripts,* with an interpretive commentary added by Fromm himself. The first manuscript translated is "Alienated Labor," Marx's classic statement on the way in which capitalist economics means that "the individual worker sinks to the level of a commodity, and to a most miserable commodity" (Marx, 1961, p. 93). In this essay Marx describes the development of monopoly capitalism and the decline of the individual entrepreneur. In capitalist economies, "the necessary result of competition is the accumulation of capital in a few hands" (p. 93), a development Marx viewed as "a restoration of monopoly in a more terrible form" (p. 93).

The injuries of monopoly capitalism surface repeatedly in Fromm's work. Even in widely popular books written for a mass audience such as *The Art of Loving* (1956b), he writes that under modern capitalism "we witness an ever-increasing process of centralization and concentration of capital" in which "the ownership of capital invested in these enterprises is more and more separated from the function of managing them" (p. 84). When the owners of capital can command labor to produce goods that increase the return on the owner's investment, then a hierarchy emerges in which "amassed things, that which is dead, are of superior value to labor, to human powers, to that which is alive" (p. 84). Work under such a system is physically exhausting, mentally debasing, and creatively moribund. Most damningly, it is also spiritually demeaning. Since people work for someone else, their labor becomes converted into someone else's property. The artifacts produced by people's labor have nothing of their own creativity or identity contained within them. In Marx's words, "The object produced by labor, its product, now stands opposed to it as an *alien being,* as a *power independent of* the producer. The product of labor is labor which has been embodied in an object and turned into a physical thing; this product is an *objectification* of labor. The performance of work is at the same time its objectification" (Marx, 1961, p. 95).

Using Fromm's analysis as a starting point, it is quite possible to interpret adult learning processes through the lens of objectification. In mandatory continuing education, compulsory training, and the required participation of employees in human resource development programs, it is easy to see how learning undertaken to satisfy external authorities ceases to become the adult learner's intellectual project. Very frequently, the products and measures of learning—essays, test scores, papers, exams—take on physical forms and stand apart from the learner. The exam does not measure the adult's engagement in creative work as a means of broadening or confirming her identity. Instead, it exerts a coercive pressure requiring her to improve her performance according to criteria she had no hand in proposing and has little chance of affecting. Myles Horton, the renowned adult educational activist, expressed his disdain for the demeaning way in which contemporary education "has got to be something that can be tested or controlled" resulting in the learner "being handled like a machine with predictable results" (Horton, 2003, p. 225).

When labor is objectified, something peculiar happens to the worker's emotions. Workers feel more and more disconnected from their work which itself starts to be thought of as something separate from themselves, something outside their sphere of influence. In a famous quote from the "Alienated Labor" manuscript, Marx writes that "the more the worker expends himself in work, the more powerful becomes the world of objects which he creates in face of himself, the poorer he becomes in his inner life, and the less he belongs to himself" (Marx, 1961, p. 96). In devoting themselves to the production of objects, workers somehow find that their own identity has diminished as the power of the objects they produce has increased. Like the demented ventriloquist who sees his doll gain life and start to control him, so "the worker puts his life into the object, and his life then belongs no longer to himself but to the object [which] sets itself against him as an alien and hostile force" (p. 96). The tragedy of contemporary life is not just that workers are exploited and dominated by the owners of production but also that they are overwhelmed by the world of objects itself which now becomes experienced "as an alien and hostile world" (p. 99).

It is because of their suspicion of how learning can become objectified and experienced by adults as irrelevant to their real needs and inner yearnings that so many adult educators have stressed and continue to insist on the voluntary underpinnings of genuine adult education. From Lindeman ([1926] 1961) to Horton (1990), a school of adult education has contended that adult education only happens when adults opt voluntarily for a program of learning they have helped design. This tradition regards mandatory adult education as an oxymoron. It focuses instead on how adult education can help learners develop skills and knowledge that will help them understand and change the communities in which they live. This learning happens through a collaborative analysis of adults' experiences during which roles of teacher and learner interchange among participants. Adult educators who attempt to follow this tradition do their best to replicate the features of participatory democracy, with all participants actively involved in deciding aspects of what and how to learn.

The Marxist concepts of objectification, commodification, and alienation surface again and again in Fromm's work, constantly underpinning his own normative humanism. In commenting on Marx, Fromm argued that Marxism was less a political creed, more "a spiritual existentialism in secular language" (1961, p. 5). To Fromm, "Marx's aim was that of the spiritual emancipation of man, of his liberation from the chains of economic determinism, of restituting him in his human wholeness, of enabling him to find unity and harmony with his fellow man and with nature" (p. 3). Fromm believed that Marx was not concerned primarily with equalizing income. His main interest was in stopping work from being an alienating experience. He quotes Marx's comments in volume one of *Capital* that methods of production under capitalism "mutilate the laborer into a fragment of a man, degrade him to the level of an appendage of a machine, destroy every remnant of charm in his work and turn it into a hated toil" (p. 52). So for Fromm, "Marx's central criticism of capitalism is not the injustice in the distribution of wealth; it is the perversion of labor into forced, alienated, meaningless labor" (p. 42).

In fact Fromm's analysis of alienation deepened and broadened Marx's initial exposition of the idea. Fromm contended that Marx underestimated the intensity and pervasiveness of alienation which had become "the fate of the vast majority of people, especially of the ever increasing segment of the population which manipulate symbols and men, rather than machines" (Fromm, 1961, p. 56). In contemporary society, people "worship things, the machines which produce things—and in this alienated world they feel as strangers and quite alone" (p. 57). In such works as *Escape from Freedom* (1941), *Man for Himself* (1947), and *The Sane Society* (1956a), Fromm illustrates the power of the concept of alienation, extending it from the world of work into the domains of politics, recreation, and intimate relationships. Commodification has distorted even our language to the point that our "speech style indicates the prevailing high degree of alienation" (1976, p. 31) we feel. Fromm asks us to consider the colloquial phrase "I have a problem" and the commodification this signifies. He writes that "by saying '*I have*' a problem instead of '*I am troubled,*' subjective experience is eliminated; the *I* of experience is replaced by the *it* of possession . . . I have transformed *myself* into 'a problem' and am now owned by my creation" (p. 31). This commodification of language further ensures that in all aspects of modern life "one experiences oneself as a commodity or, rather, simultaneously as the seller *and* the commodity to be sold" (p. 146).

As a counter to alienation, Fromm (1965) proposed a version of socialism that he called humanistic or communitarian socialism. This kind of socialism did not stress the equalization of income or distribution of profits. Its emphasis was on the creation of a workplace in which workers controlled the pace and form of production. Instead of being separated from each other and denied the opportunity to exercise their own creative energies, workers in a truly socialist system experience work as an associative and creative activity. Fromm traces this version of socialism to what he claims are the humanistic underpinnings of Marx's version of socialism. He writes that "the principle goal of socialism for Marx is the recognition and realization of man's true needs, which will be possible only when production serves man and capital ceases to create and exploit the false needs of man" (1961, p. 59). To Fromm, socialism is more about human creativity then economic arrangements. It is "a form of production and an organization of society in which man can overcome alienation from his product, from his work, from his fellow man, from himself and from nature" (p. 59). A socialist society is one in which people feel connected to each other, able to discover and exercise their own creative impulses, and aware of their relationship to the natural environment. In such a society, a person will be able to "return to himself and grasp the world with his own powers thus becoming one with the world" (p. 59).

In many ways, Fromm anticipates Habermas' later articulation of socialism as a system enabling people to have the freest conversation possible about how they wish to live. In an interview Habermas declares that "socialism is only useful if it serves as the idea of the epitome of the necessary conditions for emancipated forms of life, about which the participants themselves would have to reach understanding" (Habermas, 1994, p. 113). Similarly, Fromm stresses the participatory and democratic aspects of socialism as a system in which people participate in a continuous conversation about their aspirations and how these might be realized given limited resources. It is not an enormous stretch to see in Fromm's vision of communitarian socialism a larger sketch of the processes that would be observable in adult education classrooms striving to realize some principles of participatory democracy. In such classrooms the object would be to make adult education serve the true needs of learners instead of satisfying their false needs. False needs will be those that uncritically mimic the aspirations of the dominant culture such as learning to compete more effectively against other learners, learning skills that allow people to acquire more and more possessions they do not really need, or learning how to adapt one's thinking and behavior to prevailing mores and cultural patterns. In seeking to overcome the individual adult's alienation from learning and from her fellow learners, an adult classroom would emphasize cooperative ways of working. It would regard the individual pursuit of truth, beauty, and knowledge as the exception to the collaborative rule. Adult education as communitarian socialism would be dialogic, an attempt to create a continuous conversation among learners about the direction of learning in which all voices would be heard equally.

Fromm was careful to distinguish communitarian socialism from state socialism which "leaves the worker in bondage" (1956a, p. 285). He was stinging in his criticism of rigidly totalitarian states that declared themselves to be socialist but that actually perverted ideals of socialism. Such perversions prevented those in the noncommunist world from giving any consideration to the links between democracy and socialism. To Fromm, "socialism is incompatible with a bureaucratic, thing-centered, consumption-oriented social system, that is incompatible with the materialism and cerebralization that characterize the Soviet, like the capitalist, system" (1976, p. 157). An important purpose of socialism was "the elimination of the secret rule of those who, though few in number, wield great economic power without any responsibility to those whose fate depends in their decisions" (1941, p. 299). Such an arbitrary and unjust exercise of power was as characteristic of totalitarian state socialism as it was of capitalism. What Fromm believed in was "a rational economic system serving the purposes of the people" (p. 299) which would "replace manipulation of men by active co-operation" (p. 300).

Some of his strongest statements concerning the need for socialism appeared in the post-McCarthy era at the height of the cold war. In a text published a year after the Cuban Missile Crisis, he refers to the socialist ideal as "the most important authentic spiritual movement in the Western world" (1962, p. 142). In *The Sane Society* (1956a), he calls socialism "one of the most significant, idealistic and moral movements of our age" (1956a, p. 247) arguing that where overcoming alienation is concerned "the only constructive solution is that of Socialism, which aims at a fundamental reorganization of our economic and social system . . . creating a social order in which human solidarity, reason and production are furthered rather than hobbled" (p. 277). A socialist workplace is one "in which every working person would be an active and responsible participant, where work would be attractive and meaningful, where capital would not employ labor, but labor would employ capital" (p. 283). In Fromm's analysis, learning at the workplace is clearly contiguous with learning to replace the production of goods that satisfy the false needs of people and create wealth for a small minority with a process whereby production enhances the person's sense that she is creating something both useful and beautiful.

The Social Character of Capitalism

Although Fromm clearly viewed Marx (along with Freud) as central to the critical tradition, he identified "important questions which were not dealt with adequately in Marxist theory" (1965, p. 233). One of the most important of these was "why is it that a society succeeds in gaining the allegiance of most of its members, even when they suffer under the system and even if their reason tells them that their allegiance is harmful to them?" (p. 233). Fromm's answer to this question lay in the concept of the social character, a central element of *The Sane Society*. Social character is "the nucleus of the character structure which is shared by most members of the same culture" (1956a, p. 78). Seen from the twenty-first century, with its emphasis on fragmented identities, virtual realities, and cultural diversity, social character is one of the weakest elements in Fromm's thought. Indeed, Fromm's whole emphasis on inherent human needs "like the striving for happiness, harmony love and freedom" (p. 81) appears faintly comic to contemporary sensibilities. Few adult educators today would state confidently, as Fromm did, that "there are certain factor's in man's nature which are fixed and unchangeable" (1941, p. 37) such as "the necessity to avoid isolation and moral aloneness" (p. 37), the need to cooperate with others (p. 35), and "the drive for freedom inherent in human nature" (p. xiv).

In stressing how human drives prompt people to resist ideological domination and take an active role in shaping their experiences and culture, however, Fromm does sound a more contemporary note. A human being "is not a blank sheet of paper on which culture writes its text" (1956a, p. 81) but someone with agency, who can stand against ideological manipulation. In fact, Fromm's ideas on the development of social character are perhaps best understood as describing a process of ideological formation through which people learn habits and dispositions that support the existing system. Fromm himself sometimes speaks of the concept this way. In a passage analyzing how social character ensures ideological domination, he writes that "it is the social character's function to mold and channel human energy within a given society for the purpose of the continued functioning of that society" (p. 79).

Under capitalism, social character takes on a particular formation. In his view, "modern capital needs men who cooperate smoothly and in large numbers; who want to consume more and more; and whose tastes are standardized and can be easily influenced and anticipated (1956b, p. 85). As capitalism developed, it required that each person "be molded into a person who was eager to spend most of his energy for the purpose of work, who acquired discipline, particularly orderliness and punctuality, to a degree unknown in most other cultures" (1956a, p. 80). This process of character formation had to be all enveloping so that people were not aware of any kind of manipulation. Hence, "the *necessity* for work, for punctuality and orderliness had to be transformed into an inner *drive* for these aims . . . society had to produce a social character in which these strivings were inherent" (p. 80). In this analysis Fromm sounds distinctly Foucaultian. In capitalism, workers discipline themselves to behave in ways that support the existing social and economic order. But this disposition is not something of which people are consciously aware. Foucault would say that the external gaze that ensures that people are punctual, driven, and assiduously following the rules has been successfully "interiorized"; that is, it is now experienced as a constituent element of the personality.

Contemporary capitalism has some important "characterological features," to use Fromm's phrase. First, the market requires people who are malleable in the extreme to serve as consumers of its products. The more malleable consumers are, the better they are suited to capitalism. Ideally, global capitalism is best served by large populations that equate living with consuming, that gain their identities from the purchase of certain branded products, and that shy away from buying anything too idiosyncratic. The greater the standardization of taste and consumption patterns across national boundaries, the more effectively production can be streamlined and commodities marketed. Thus, contemporary capitalism produces people "who want to consume more and more, and whose tastes are standardized and can be easily influenced and anticipated" (1956a, p. 110). Such people like nothing better than to buy the latest computer game and watch the latest Disney film while wearing similarly branded clothes and shoes, all the while knowing that across the world numerous others are simultaneously engaged in the same activity.

Ideological standardization is the second "characterological feature" of capitalism; "just as modern mass production methods require the standardization of commodities, so the social process requires standardization of man, and this standardization is called 'equality'" (Fromm, 1956b, p. 16). People's malleability as consumers is matched by their ideological malleability. The standardization of consumer taste extends into the social and political domain leading to a standardization of social behavior and political opinion. People are produced who are "willing to be commanded, to do what is expected, to fit into the social machine without friction" (p. 110). Such individuals crave conformity, to feel part of a mass that feels the same impulses and thinks the same thoughts in synchronization. They "are governed by the fear of the anonymous authority of conformity" (p. 102). This is the basic thesis of *Escape from Freedom* (1941), Fromm's attempt to explain the rise of fascist and totalitarian regimes.

Identifying and combating these two characterological features are important purposes for adult education. Fromm posed a clear choice for the future—"between robotism (of both the capitalist and communist variety) or Humanistic, Communitarian Socialism" (1956a, p. 363). Communitarian socialism would be based on sharing work, sharing experience, and sharing profits. Adult education could provide an opportunity for people to experience an analog of this system. If enough people participated in adult education that was a noncompetitive sharing of common experience, it could provide a template for creating wider social realignments that realized this cooperative impulse.

The Alienating Character of Capitalism

Fromm views the distinguishing character of capitalism as the elevation, to practically the exclusion of all else, of the economic domain of life. Its leitmotif is the use of people as if they were economic objects: "The owner of capital uses other men for the purpose of his own profit. . . a living human being, ceases to be an end in himself, and becomes the means for the economic interests of another man, or himself, or of an impersonal giant, the economic machine" (1956a, p. 93). A necessary corollary of assessing human worth in economic terms is the elevation of materialistic values over human values of compassion, skill, or creativity. Thus, "in the capitalistic hierarchy of values, capital stands higher than labor, amassed things higher than the manifestations of life. . . things are higher than man" (p. 95). Humanity is diminished as qualities such as a person's energy, skill, personality, and creativity become objectified—assets to be sold on the market of interpersonal relations. Under capitalism, "the market decides the value of these human qualities" with the result that "relations between human beings . . . assume the character of relations between things" (1941, p. 140). Each person "sells himself and feels himself to be a commodity" (p. 140).

In describing how the laws of the market corrupt personal relations, Fromm anticipates Habermas' ideas on the colonization of the lifeworld, a theme that has produced some provocative critiques of contemporary adult education (Welton, 1995; Newman, 1999). Fromm writes that in the United States today "our whole culture is based on the appetite for buying, on the idea of a mutually favorable exchange" (1956b, p. 3). Human communication and interpersonal feelings are distorted by the application of a cost-benefit analysis way of thinking to our relationships. The logic of the exchange economy pervades all aspects of life, and "in all social and personal relations the laws of the market are the rule" (1941, p. 139). This is because "in capitalistic society exchanging has become an end in itself" (1956a, p. 146), a metaphor for how we conceive the conduct of a well-conceived life. Thus, "the whole process of living is experienced analogously to the profitable investment of capital, my life and my person being the capital which is invested" (p. 148). Everyday life reflects this as people talk of how they have "invested" themselves in their marriages, children, and friendships.

Clearly, then, the most personal relationships are subject to this drive for exchange, and Fromm is pessimistic in his view of the possibility for love and friendship. A relationship between two people is typically "one between two machines, who use each other. . . everybody is to everybody else a commodity" (1956a, p. 139). Hence, "one speaks of human relations and one means the most in-human relations, those between alienated automatons" (p. 182). This is true even when talking of those who claim to be in love. In Fromm's view people "fall in love when they feel they have found the best object available on the market, considering the limitations of their own exchange value" (1956b, p. 3). When love is conceived as an exchange, then true intimacy—"union under the condition of preserving one's integrity" (p. 20)—is impossible. This is because "automatons cannot love" (p. 87). The best they can hope for is that "they can exchange their personality packages and hope for a fair bargain" (p. 87).

Another sign of an alienated life is an inability to engage wholly and authentically with a work of art. Fromm contends that when people in the contemporary era view a work of art or piece of entertainment their first response is to ask, "Is it worth the money we spent?" When people make major decisions in work, relationships, politics, and recreation they apply a cost-benefit analysis to "the concept of life as an enterprise which should show a profit" (1956a, p. 150). From this perspective a life well-lived is one showing a balance of happiness and fulfillment firmly in the black column. This turns the individual into a person concerned primarily with selling a personality, something Fromm viewed as the triumph of the marketing orientation in social life. To someone exhibiting a marketing orientation, "his body, his mind and his soul are his capital, and his task in life is to invest it favorably, to make a profit of himself. Human qualities like friendliness, courtesy, kindness, are transformed into commodities, into assets of the 'personality package' conducive to a higher price on the personality market" (1956a, p. 142). Certainly, in reviewing the prospectuses of some proprietary adult education centers, it is striking how many course titles invite adults to learn how to sell their personalities more effectively, whether that be through flirting, networking, or learning how to navigate organizational cultures.

As the metaphor of the market comes to pervade and dominate our worldview, Fromm believes that we feel that control of our lives has slipped out of our hands. After all, the market is a vast and inaccessible phenomenon, the intersection of millions of individual decisions made by strangers in places of which we know nothing. It is beset by seemingly unpredictable and uncontrollable crises that come out of nowhere—booms and busts, depressions, recessions and expansions. The indicator of the society's economic health—the stock market—becomes fetishized, viewed as a capricious being controlled by the whims of magical forces inaccessible to our influence. In this situation the individual becomes "an instrument in the hands of overwhelmingly strong forces outside of himself" (1941, p. 141), deeply affected by a sense of powerlessness.

When the market becomes the lens through which we view life, then the value of existence becomes determined by a series of calculations. Fromm believed that capitalism caused people to think of the world around them and each other as composed of standardized, abstract qualities. Under capitalism there is "an almost exclusive reference to the abstract qualities of things and people, and . . . a neglect of relating oneself to their concreteness and uniqueness" (1956a, p. 114). The individual is "experienced as the embodiment of a quantitative exchange value" (p. 116), something whose value can be assessed and tabulated. Not surprisingly, perhaps, bureaucrats in business, government, and labor unions feel free to "manipulate people as though they were figures, or things" (p. 126). In Fromm's view this cultural veneration of abstraction and quantification prepared the ground for moral outrages such as genocide. The Holocaust became viewed by its Nazi perpetrators as an abstract exercise in engineering in which the central logistical problem was how best to arrange the extermination of large numbers of objects that possessed no concrete, unique existence for them. This horror was made possible by the fact that "we live in figures and abstractions; since nothing is concrete, nothing is real. Everything is possible, factually and morally" (p. 120).

Dimensions of Alienation in Adult Life

Fromm relied heavily on Marx's idea of commodity fetishism to explain how alienation is experienced in contemporary society. Given McLaren and West's analysis of the Marxophobia rampant in American life, it is ironic that the Frankfurt School theorist whose work exhibits the widest popular appeal draws so consistently and explicitly on Marxist ideas and language. In terms drawn straight from Marx's manuscript on the subject, Fromm defines alienation as "a mode of experience in which the person experiences himself as an alien. . . estranged from himself. He does not experience himself as the center of his world, as the creator of his own acts" (1956a, p. 120). The roots of this sense of alienation lie in the nature of modern work, which requires that people pour their energy into making products which then assume an existence apart from them. In the contemporary workplace, the worker finds that "his life forces have flown into a thing" (p. 121) which becomes "something apart from himself, over and against him" (p. 122).

At the dawn of the twenty-first century, the concept of virtual reality is sometimes invoked to describe how many people experience the world. If this concept has any validity, then Fromm's analysis of alienation appears remarkably prescient. Alienation is a distancing of people from the world of feelings and sensuality so that they feel dominated by lifeless objects: "We are surrounded by things of whose nature and origin we know nothing. . . we live in a world of things, and our only connection with them is that we know how to manipulate or consume them" (1956a, p. 134). As an example, consider his description of travel as something experienced through the technological intermediary of the camera. The purpose of travel for many seems to be the production of photos or videotapes to view when they return home. The traveler "does not see anything at all, except through the intermediary of the camera" so that digitalized video records "are the substitute for the experience"(1956a, p. 136). Anyone who depends on computers to navigate through their work or life knows the miserable feeling of dependence on experts Fromm describes whenever the system shuts down: "The individual feels helplessly caught in a chaotic mass of data and with pathetic patience waits until the specialists have found out what to do and where to go" (1941, p. 276).

Fromm's extension of commodity fetishism into an analysis of rampant consumerism is still accurate half a century after it appeared. A major purpose of life under capitalism is to consume the commodities we produce, yet the experience of compulsive consumption is itself alienating. In the contemporary era, we experience "an ever increasing need for more things, for more consumption . . . but our craving for consumption has lost all connection with the real needs of man" (1956a, p. 134). We develop what Fromm calls the receptive orientation in which we desire "to have something new all the time, to live with a continuously open mouth as it were" (p. 136). Creativity, artistic expression, and personal fulfillment are equated with consuming more and more things. Fromm becomes positively lyrical in his description of how commodity fetishism becomes converted into the consumer ethic: "The world is one great object for our appetite, a big apple, a big bottle, a big breast; we are the suck-lers, the eternally expectant ones, the hopeful ones—and the eter-nally disappointed ones" (p. 166).

Education (including adult education) is, of course, no excep-tion to the process of commodification. The education system "generally tries to train people to *have* knowledge as a possession, by and large commensurate with the amount of property or social prestige they are likely to have in later life" (1976, p. 48). Educa-tional institutions "give each student a certain amount of cultural property" (p. 43) or a "luxury-knowledge package" (p. 49) with "the size of each package being in accord with the person's prob-able social prestige" (p. 49). Knowledge becomes equated with content, with "fixed clusters of thought, or whole theories" (p. 37) that students store. In this system teachers are reduced to "bureau-cratic dispensers of knowledge" (1968, p. 120). This commodified content, transmitted bureaucratically, is alienated from learners' lives and experiences: "The students and the content of the lec-tures remain strangers to each other, except that each student has become the owner of a collection of statements made by somebody else" (1976, p. 37).

Fromm also extended Marx's idea of commodity fetishism (the worship of things to the extent that they are imbued with magical qualities and powers) into the realm of political discourse, observ-ing that "the fetishism of words is as dangerous in the realm of po-litical ideology as it is in that of religious ideology" (1962, p. 159). Fromm feels that today words have become a substitute for concrete political action, so that making a speech is considered a significant act of social change. Yet language as a substitute for political inter-vention is illusory, allowing politicians to seem to be doing some-thing when actually doing nothing. Words don't change the world, deeds do; "the idea which remains a word only changes words" (1962, p. 177). A media and politically literate adult must be helped to see that "words have meaning only in the total context of deed and character; unless there is unity among these factors words serve to deceive—others and oneself; instead of revealing, they have the function of hiding" (1962, p. 159). In terms echoing Orwell's (1946) analysis of the perversions of political language, Fromm argues that a task of adult education must be to make adults aware of doublespeak, of when an utterance means exactly the opposite of what it purports to mean, as in "calling Franco and other dictators 'representatives of the free world'" (1962, p.160).

Fromm's analysis of political alienation looks back to J. S. Mill's ideas on the tyranny of the majority and forward to the contemporary perversion of political discourse by television advertising. Fromm argues that we are alienated politically when our political participation is reduced to being forced to choose between candidates we had no hand in selecting and who represent mammoth parties financed by giant, yet often invisible, corporate interests. Voters are blanketed by political commercials that dull the capacity for critical thought. Not surprisingly, "this situation gives the average citizen a deep sense of powerlessness in political matters" with the result that "political intelligence is reduced more and more" (1956a, p. 191). Given the current widespread cynicism regarding politics and the widespread dismissal of political commercials as propaganda, this may seem an overly pessimistic conclusion to draw. However, it is salutary to reflect on Fromm's warnings of the effects that the "increasing power of monopolistic capital" (1941, p. 141) have on the political process. Writing before the influence of corporate lobbyists and political action committees had become the accepted currency of politics, Fromm decried the fact that "an enormous though secret power over the whole society is exercised by a small group, on the decisions of which depends the fate of a large part of society" (p. 141).

In this part of his work, Fromm is outlining a political literacy project for adult education. Any socially responsible adult education program must include as part of its curriculum some offerings that show how those with the most capital attempt to purchase the greatest access to opinion-making organizations. Such a program would show that free speech is often bought speech, that getting one's ideas or opinions into the public sphere depends on having the capital to buy media outlets that can disseminate these ideas. Such a program would show how media must always be thought of as big businesses and how news divisions of major media outlets are heavily influenced by the interests of corporate sponsors. It would highlight the need networks feel to present news in an entertaining way so as to keep the maximum audience tuned in, thereby ensuring the charging of higher rates for commercials. In particular, Fromm's emphasis on how an unrepresentative minority

exerts disproportionate influence over political affairs clearly anticipates Newman's (1994) call to name the enemy. If, as Fromm says,
"an enormous though secret power over the whole society is exercised by a small group," and if this group can exert control over
political discourse out of all proportion to their size in the society,
then a crucial adult educational task becomes to conduct appropriate research and inquiry to name the members of this group.
In Newman's (1994) words, "We need to ask: who are the people,
what are the organizations promoting the reorganization of capitalism? Where do they operate? Can we name them and *do they
have an address?*" (p. 149).

Alienated politics is most tragically evident in the practice of
democracy, for many people the most hopeful grand narrative of the
twenty-first century. Fromm rejects the rhetoric of democracy as
liberation from tyranny, arguing instead that the democratic
process has transmogrified into the tyranny of the majority. In our
age of conformity, "the democratic method has more and more
assumed the meaning that a majority decision is necessarily right,
and morally superior to that of the minority, and hence has the
moral right to impose *its* will on the minority" (1956a, p. 340). He
cited with scorn the advertising slogan that "Ten Million Americans Can't Be Wrong" as evidence of how the epistemic distortion
of equating validity with majority opinion had spread through society. "Nothing is further from the truth" (1941, p. 14) he argued,
than to believe that agreement and consensus represent a higher
epistemological authority. To Fromm, "consensual validation as
such has no bearing whatsoever on reason or mental health"
(p. 15). In fact it often represents a deliberate suppression of critical thought through the exclusion of divergent opinions.

It is interesting to remember these words when we find ourselves practicing the difficult and contradictory process of trying
to democratize adult education classrooms. Adult educators committed to democratic process can easily find themselves turning
instinctively to the principle of majority vote when working with a
group of adults to decide collectively what and how to learn. Yet,
as Fromm points out, the majority opinion in an adult classroom
may stand firmly against anything that disturbs the familiarity of
teacher authority, didactic transmission of information, and curriculum being decided by omniscient strangers in far off places.

Shor's (1996) and Cale's (2001) studies illustrate how a majority of adults will usually choose not to rock the boat by challenging conventional thinking on race, class, or gender or by opting to explore political dynamics outside, and especially inside, the adult classroom. Cale's study of a writing class for adults shows how an apparent act of resistance—asking adults to take a measure of control in choosing what to learn—can end up reproducing dominant ideology. His students chose to avoid contentious racial issues and to stay close to home with familiar topics.

Here is one of the unresolvable tensions of critical practice: Can adult educators respect the agendas adults bring to a democratic negotiation of curriculum whilst contradictorily challenging these agendas by offering (and sometimes insisting on) radically different, politically contentious options for study? Fromm argues that adult educators must insist on paying attention to alternative, minority viewpoints. Otherwise the process of automaton conformity—of people choosing to think and do what they suppose everyone else thinks and does—runs rampant. Deliberately suppressing alternative perspectives because these have not been endorsed by majority opinion is one of the chief indicators that automaton conformity is in place and unchallenged.

Automaton Conformity

In Fromm's view alienation as a pervasive mode of existence is most evident in the phenomenon of automaton conformity. This idea is explained most fully in *Escape from Freedom* though its presence is felt in all Fromm's other writing. Automaton conformity describes the process of social manipulation that results in the adult striving to be exactly the same as he or she imagines the majority to be. When we succumb to such conformity, we become "cogs in the bureaucratic machine, with our thoughts, feelings, and tastes manipulated by the government industry and the mass communications that they control" (Fromm, 1976, p. 12). The flight into automaton conformity was one of the two possible responses Fromm identified to the fear of freedom (the other being to seek refuge in submission to fascist and totalitarian leaders).

In *Escape from Freedom* (titled *The Fear of Freedom* in England), Fromm argued that the decline of traditional mores and the growth of secularism had made people more and more aware of the fact that they were free to choose how to think and live. This recognition was a source of terror rather than pleasure to most people. The central thesis of *Escape from Freedom* is that "the process of growing human freedom . . . means growing isolation, insecurity, and thereby growing doubt concerning one's own role in the universe, the meaning of one's life, and with all that a growing feeling of one's own powerlessness and insignificance as an individual" (1941, p. 51). Faced with the void of freedom, people turn to two avenues of escape—"submission to a leader, as has happened in fascist countries, and the compulsive conforming as is prevalent in our own democracy" (p. 155).

Of these two avenues, it is automaton conformity that is the most subtle and intriguing, and ultimately the most alienating. The individual attempts to escape the burden of freedom "by transforming himself into a small cog in the machine, well fed, and well clothed . . . yet not a free man but an automaton" (1941, p. xii). By doing this people escape the anxiety produced by the awareness of their freedom; "if I am like everybody else, if I have no feelings or thoughts which make me different . . . I am saved; saved from the frightening experience of aloneness" (1956b, p. 13). The subtlety of automaton conformity is that the pressure to conform is applied internally, not externally, an example of disciplinary power in action; "people want to conform to a much higher degree than they are forced to conform, at least in the Western democracies" (p. 13). The authority one is submitting to by conforming is anonymous—the authority of imagined common sense, public opinion, conventional wisdom. Fromm sounds a distinctively Foucaultian note in his observation that "in anonymous authority both command and commander have become invisible" (1941, p. 190) with the power of public opinion obscured by social habit and political ideology. In this perspective information about the correct ways to think and act is inscribed in the cultural DNA.

Fromm's description of automaton conformity also echoes Gramsci's writing on hegemony. The power of anonymous authority comes from its all pervasive, yet invisible, nature. Like fish unaware of the water in which they live, citizens swim unsuspectingly in the ocean of anonymous authority. We are surrounded by an "atmosphere of subtle suggestion which actually pervades our whole social life . . . one never suspects that there is any order which one is expected to follow" (1941, p. 190). Under the enveloping influence of anonymous authority, "the individual ceases to be himself; he adopts entirely the kind of personality offered to him by cultural patterns and he . . . becomes exactly as all others are and as they expect him to be" (p. 208–209). Any anxiety people might feel about this kind of existence concerns whether or not they are sufficiently assiduous in pursuing and realizing the pattern of conformity. The automaton conformist's credo can be summarized thus: "I must conform, not be different, not 'stick out'; I must be ready and willing to change according to the changes in the pattern; I must not ask whether I am right or wrong, but whether I am adjusted, whether I am not 'peculiar,' not different" (1956a, p. 153).

Automaton conformity has crucial consequences, according to Fromm. One is the spread of pseudophenomena. Anticipating Baudrillard's (1983) concept of hyperreality and his contention that viewing representations of experience has replaced the direct experience of the sensuous world, Fromm argued that when people's opinions and reasons mimic dominant ideology we have pseudothinking (1941, p. 217), pseudoreasoning (p. 215), and the evolution of a pseudoself (p. 290). Connected to the emergence of pseudothought is the stamping out of original ideas and self-directed learning. Although freedom of thought, speech, and action are cornerstones of American ideology, Fromm believed that automaton conformity had worked to erase these elements from the culture. In his view, "original decision is a comparatively rare phenomenon in a society which supposedly makes individual decision the cornerstone of its existence" (1941, p. 225). We venerate the ideal of a society full of staunchly rugged individuals defending the right to think, say, and do whatever they wish, but the reality is that "we have become automatons who live under the illusion of being self-willing individuals . . . everybody and everything has become instrumentalised" (p. 279).

This decline in originality of thought and decision inevitably works to kill individual conscience and with it the possibility of morally inspired revolution. In *The Sane Society* (1956a), Fromm posed the rhetorical question "How can conscience develop when the principle of life is conformity?" (p. 173). To him, "conscience by its very nature is non-conforming" because its distinctive feature is that it allows a person "to say no, when everybody else says yes" (p. 173). When people are consumed by the need to conform, they cannot hear the voice of conscience, much less act on it. The pressure to conform is raised to almost irresistible levels in times of war when the expression of opposition to military action (as, for example, in the unilateral invasions of Vietnam or Iraq) can be stigmatized in the early stages of war as unpatriotic. In this atmosphere advocates of war strive to define dissent as either irrational or evil. This kind of unthinking agreement with calls to patriotism is much easier to ensure when we think of ourselves as things or commodities. After all, conscience has no place in the life of inert objects. Through automaton conformity we cede the responsibility for developing conscience and for conscientious objection to the judges of normality (echoes of Foucault again) that are everywhere. When the power of individual conscience is neutralized, then what is considered "normal" thought becomes the responsibility of specialists in psychoanalysis, psychiatry, and psychology who "tell you what the 'normal' person is, and, correspondingly, what is wrong with you; they devise the methods to help you adjust, be happy, be normal" (p. 168).

Automaton conformity inevitably results in a suppression of critical thinking. As we strive to conform to anonymous authority and as we feel increasingly powerless in the face of the massive structures (corporations, political parties, labor unions) and forces (advertising, political propaganda) confronting us, we lose the capacity to think critically. In Fromm's view, "these methods of dulling the capacity for critical thinking are more dangerous to our democracy than many of the open attacks against it" (1941, p. 150). We are unable to see the big picture, to realize that we are part of a system that operates deliberately to diminish our agency and suppress our ability to ask critical questions. It was clear to Fromm that a most effective "way of paralyzing the ability to think critically is the destruction of any kind of structuralized picture of the world" (p. 276). Life becomes seen as "composed of many little pieces, each separate from the other and lacking any sense as a whole" (p. 277).

In this analysis a crucial role is suggested for adult education, that of teaching a structuralized worldview. Fromm is here offering us a clear purpose for adult education, one that fits firmly within the tradition of adult education as a field of practice focused on helping adults learn democracy. A structuralized view of the world is one that emphasizes how individual decisions are framed by much broader social structures and economic forces. It requires a familiarity with history, political economy, and sociology. Fromm argued that the development of such a structuralized view was really only possible with adult learners. In his way of thinking, adults not only had a greater interest in developing such a perspective, but they also possessed the intellectual capability to do this in a way that was not possible for them in adolescence. An interpretation of Fromm's call to develop a structuralized picture of the world is something that Fromm's contemporary C. W. Mills attempted to provide. Like Fromm, Mills had written a popular text on Marxism (Mills, 1962), and like him he had thought deeply about the social purpose of adult education. In a slim pamphlet published by the Center for the Study of Liberal Education for Adults (Mills, 1954), Mills anticipates his own argument in *The Sociological Imagination* (1959)—that a structuralized view of the world emerges when adults learn "to turn personal troubles and concerns into social issues and rationally open problems" (1954, p. 12). If adults start to see situations in their private lives as concrete manifestations of broader social and political contradictions, they will see that changing their individual lives is impossible without political action. Hence, "to the extent that the adult college is effective, it is going to be political; its students are going to try to influence decisions of power" (p. 16).

Fromm and Mills both emphasized the necessity of adults understanding how the particular circumstances of their lives were produced by the intersection of political decisions, social and economic trends, and the workings of capital. Divorce, unemployment, unhappiness, and isolation must be interpreted not as the capricious workings of a cruel fate but as the result of decisions made by the (often secret) few in positions of enormous power. Factories close and jobs are lost not because the economy somehow catches a cold. These things happen because companies relocate to other states or countries where nonunionized labor is cheap and plentiful, or because governing boards decide to merge with other boards, or because by "downsizing" or "rightsizing" its operations a company's stockholder dividends are likely to be higher. Even the most private and traumatic tearings in the fabric of personal relationships, such as divorce, should be understood as social and political phenomena. The restlessness and unfulfilled desires that lie behind a divorce are manifestations of the receptive orientation that predispose people to want more and more with no prospect of achieving anything more than temporary satisfaction—the eternally expectant ones forever doomed to be the eternally disappointed ones, as Fromm put it. Alternatively, divorce, unhappiness, and isolation are the result of people needing to leave their home communities in search of work that will provide them with the financial means to satisfy their appetite for the commodities they feel are necessary to create the good life.

Teaching a structuralized view of the world moves adults away from magical consciousness (in Freire's terms) to an awareness of how ideology, culture, and economics intersect to shape individual lives. In Fromm's opinion possessing such an awareness is the necessary precursor to people deciding that alienating social arrangements could be reshaped by individual and collective will. So helping people develop a structuralized view of the world is one way Fromm believes adult education can lay the foundations for social action. Without learning this view, there is little chance that people can recognize, let alone oppose, "the consensus of stupidity" (1962, p. 182) that will most likely ensure environmental self-destruction. The task of adult education is to break the chains of illusion that bind people to an individualized view of life and to develop in them the capacity for reason—"the capacity to recognize the unreality of most of the ideas that man holds, and to penetrate to the reality veiled by the layers and layers of deception and ideologies" (1962, p. 179).

Adult Learning as Democratic Participation

Earlier I argued that Fromm's vision of a humanistic, communitarian socialism could serve as an analog for the conduct of the adult education classroom. If "human activity is paralyzed in the capitalist system," then the goal of socialism must be "to restore full humanity by restoring activity in all spheres of life" (1976, p. 99).

Politically, this meant the creation of a participatory democracy that would liberate people from the commodified, "having" mode of existence. Fromm proposed a network of face-to-face groups that would coalesce into town-meeting sized assemblies of not more than five hundred people. This network of assemblies would constitute a lower house to monitor and advise the elected legislature on a day-to-day basis.

Within these small face-to-face groups, adults would be enjoined to behave in ways appropriate to participatory democracy. In his outline for these processes, Fromm focuses quite concretely on the conditions and dispositions for dialogic learning. In participatory adult learning groups, members exhibit a disposition to help others learn because they regard their peers' learning as crucial to their own individual development. They strive to understand what others are saying and to "help the other to clarify his thought rather than to force him to defend formulations about which he may have his own doubts" (1968, p. 115). Adults in these groups are in a "being" mode of learning and strive for a loss of ego: "They respond spontaneously and productively; they forget about themselves, about the knowledge, the positions they have. Their egos do not stand in their own way . . . they carefully respond to the other person and that person's ideas. They give birth to new ideas because they are not holding on to anything" (1976, p. 42).

Although he does not reference Lindeman, Fromm is here reprising some of Lindeman's sentiments regarding the nature and function of adult discussion groups in a democratic society (Lindeman, [1935] 1987a; Smith and Lindeman, 1951) and then adding a more psychological sheen by focusing on the loss of ego. To a social psychologist like Fromm, slaying the individual ego and opposing capitalist commodification are two sides of the same coin. When adult learners in discussion groups are disposed to help others learn, they also help the other "to transcend his or her egocentricity" (1976, p. 42). In furthering the loss of ego, "the conversation ceases to be an exchange of commodities (information, knowledge, status) and becomes a dialogue in which it does not matter any more who is right" (p. 42). As the model of conversation as a combative posturing recedes, so "the duelists begin to dance together . . . with joy" (p. 42).

But Fromm argues that adult learning groups as analogs of participatory democracy are not just talking shops. They also impose two responsibilities on their participants. First, members of such groups must strive to ensure that they have access to all pertinent information. If organizational procedures or political constraints block this access, then adults need to become activists who seek out the relevant information they need to make good decisions and insist on its dissemination. Second, participants must all play an active role in decision making. Participatory democracy is hard work. It does not allow you to sit back and let others do your thinking, talking, and deciding for you. What is most likely to galvanize people into active involvement in decision making is a conviction that what they decide actually matters.

Fromm believed that "the knowledge that one's decision has an effect" (1976, p. 179) is crucial to the functioning of participatory democracy and the missing element in many superficially democratic formats. What is true for democratic experiments in the wider society is just as true for the adult classroom. A basic indication that a degree of democracy is in place is that the opinions adults express have some impact on the situation in which they find themselves. This does not mean that the will of the majority must, by definition, prevail. Indeed, the minority's perspective may be the more valid one (as would be the case in an insistence that dominant ideology obfuscates the extent of repressive power). But where hard-fought decisions emerge from true dialogue, the originators of those decisions need to know that they will have some effect. Otherwise, why bother?

At National Louis University in Chicago, where participants in the doctoral program in adult education constitute themselves as a governance assembly to discuss and generate curricular, evaluative, and programmatic options, knowing that one's words count is indeed significant. As described in Avila and others (2000) and Baptiste and Brookfield (1998), no matter what format the students' deliberations take, participants expend a great deal of energy on talking over their concerns and take the trouble to propose different protocols to guide their conversation, only because they believe that whatever they decide will be considered seriously by the power holders (the faculty) and stands a good chance of being implemented.

Radical Love and Adult Pedagogy

Although Fromm mentions adult education only occasionally in his work, we can interpret many of his ideas as offering some guidelines for its practice. When it comes to the work of teaching, Fromm has much to say in his small but immensely popular book, *The Art of Loving* (1956b). In this disquisition on the practice of love, Fromm explains the difficulties of creating loving relationships in terms of the constraining and contradictory social arrangements flowing from capitalism. In commenting on how the struggle for intimacy is made harder by capitalism's influence, he writes that "to analyze the nature of love is to discover its general absence today and to criticize the social conditions which are responsible for this absence" (p. 133).

One important component in the struggle for loving relationships under capitalism is the work of teachers. The best teachers of adults exhibit "being authority" and are "highly developed individuals who demonstrate by what they are . . . what human beings can be" (1976, p. 45). Fromm contends that teachers in the being mode are "bearers of significant spiritual qualities" (1956b, p. 117) but laments the fact that "we are losing that teaching which is the most important one for human development: the teaching which can only be given by the simple presence of a mature, loving person" (p. 117). A teaching based on presence, in other words a loving pedagogy, is relational. For an adult educator, such a pedagogy calls for overcoming a narcissistic preoccupation with one's own judgments and interpretations. Doing this ensures that one can give full attention to the learner's individual characteristics and experience. This giving of attention precipitates a giving of many other things—joy, understanding, interest, knowledge, humor, and sadness (p. 24)—that are returned with interest to the teacher. In the act of giving, teachers experience "the highest expression of potency" (p. 23) and the benefits of mutuality whereby "the teacher is taught by his students" (p. 25).

A loving pedagogy is a social rather than an individual process, but the social arrangements that make love possible are hard to find under capitalism. To Fromm, "the principle underlying capitalistic society and the principle of love are incompatible" (1956b, p. 131). This is because the exchange economy dynamic stands in straight opposition to the overcoming of narcissism and self-absorption. Under the exchange economy, we view a loving relationship as "a mutually favorable exchange" (p. 3), with love as something existing outside our core, a commodity we trade with others for a fair return. Love under capitalism is governed by the ethic of fairness, "the particular ethical contribution of capitalist society" (p. 129). Where love is concerned "'I give you as much as you give me' . . . is the prevalent ethical norm in capitalist society" (p. 129). A loving adult educator constrained by this ethic doles out parcels of love to those who offer love to the teacher, with the size of each parcel being determined by the amount of love directed by the learner toward the teacher. A loving society, and by implication a loving practice of adult education, is premised on an opposition to this tit-for-tat approach and attempts to escape the constraints imposed on teaching-learning relationships by the capitalist dynamic of exchange. Truly loving adult education is "the practice of a human power, which can be practiced only in freedom" (p. 22).

In Fromm's view learning to teach adults in a loving way is something that requires discipline, concentration, and, above all else, practice. Underlying the practice of any art—including adult education—is an unequivocal belief in its importance. To the practitioner, the practice of a loving adult pedagogy should be one of the most important learning projects in life. Fromm wrote that "a condition of learning something is a supreme concern with the mastery of the art" (1956b, p. 110). The neophyte practitioner should feel that "there must be nothing else in the world more important than the art" (p. 5). Adult educators who teach in this loving way begin by making a vocational commitment to a calling, in the manner described by Collins (1991) and Palmer (2000), and then apply objectivity and faith to all they do.

Objectivity is a concept much derided by contemporary critical theorists who claim that no adult educational practice can escape its situatedness or avoid political implications. In fact, when Fromm talks about objectivity, he is really talking about a mix of intersubjectivity (the empathic ability to see a situation from the viewpoint of the learner at its center) and bracketing (the attempt, never completely successful, to recognize and hold at bay one's own preconceptions, prejudices, and projections where certain adult learners are concerned). Objectivity entails "the overcoming of one's narcissism" (Fromm, 1956b, p. 118) and grants the adult educator the faculty "to see people and things as they are, objectively, and to be able to separate this objective picture from a picture which is formed by one's desires and fears" (p. 118). Striving to be objective inevitably leads to humility in adult educators regarding both their own capacities and the potential of their learners. Thus, in teaching adults "humility and objectivity are indivisible" (p. 120).

From humility springs faith, in particular a faith in the potential of people to build "a social order governed by the principles of equality, justice and love" (1956b, p. 125). The more experience adult educators have of their learners, and the longer they practice their craft, the greater the faith they develop in the importance of their work. Faith can also be thought of as a kind of critically informed insight regarding the complex dynamics of adult education practice. The more we struggle to overcome our narcissism and see our learners the way they really are, the more we are able to recognize which of our many impulses, instincts, and institutions are well grounded and should be taken seriously. This is faith produced by an intentional engagement in critical reflection. To Fromm such reflection leads to "a conviction rooted in one's own experience of thought or feeling" (p. 121) and "confidence in one's power of thought, observation and judgment" (p. 123).

Developing faith in the validity of our convictions and practices as adult educators is not, however, only a matter of critical analysis. It also calls forth courage. Faith "requires courage, the ability to take a risk, the readiness even to accept pain and disappointment" (1956b, p. 126). Risk, pain, and disappointment are endemic to critical practice. Partly this is because pursuing the tasks of critical practice—getting people to challenge ideology, contest hegemony, unmask power, and so on—represent adult education at its most unpredictable. Critical adult educators need great creativity and experimental flexibility as they seek to circumvent dominant practices and expectations. It takes a degree of nerve for an adult teacher to depart from tried and trusted pedagogic formats when adult learners bristle at being asked to take responsibility for their learning and regard deviation from a didactic norm as irresponsible, unprofessional conduct. Adult teachers have to call on their courage in the face of learners' conservatism and in the face of skepticism or hostility to critical practice voiced by colleagues, supervisors, and the wider society.

In a commodified society and similarly commodified adult education system, any new or troubling ideas and practices will necessarily produce resistance. In Fromm's view this is because the majority of adult learners are "having" type individuals who settle comfortably into commodified patterns of learning and education. Predictably, these adults "feel rather disturbed by new thoughts or ideas about a subject, because the new puts into question the fixed sum of information they have" (1976, p. 38). After all, to adults used to possessing "luxury-knowledge packages" any "ideas that cannot easily be pinned down (or penned down) are frightening" (p. 38). In response to such resistance, a critical adult educator must have the courage "to stick to one's convictions even though they are unpopular" (1956a, p. 127). To do what is right, to follow one's vocation (Collins, 1991) requires "the courage to judge certain values as of ultimate concern—and to take the jump and stake everything on these values" (Fromm, 1956b, p. 126). In staking everything on helping adults overcome the alienation inherent in capitalist society, and in urging the practice of radical love as an organizing principle for adult pedagogy, Fromm's work reaches out to us from across the millennial divide.

Chapter Seven

Learning Liberation

In the late 1960s and early 1970s—the era of the Hippies and Black Panthers, the French May 1968 revolution, Students for a Democratic Society, race riots in Watts, protests against the war in Vietnam, beatings of demonstrators at the Chicago Democratic Convention, and shootings at Kent State University—there was arguably no more famous public intellectual than Herbert Marcuse. This was particularly the case in education. Though he criticized aspects of the student movement's actions as "pubertarian revolt against the wrong target" (1972, p. 51) and was disturbed by the slogan of "do your own thing" (which he felt ignored the fact that some things contributed more to liberation than others), his effect on educational and social activists was massive. In a text published at the time, Marks (1970) noted that despite death threats from the Ku Klux Klan, contempt from *Pravda* (the Soviet state-sponsored newspaper), and attempts by the San Diego post of the American Legion to deprive him of his academic post, "he has nevertheless more general popularity than any other living philosopher" (p. 8). Like Fromm, Marcuse was read by millions, but unlike Fromm he was regarded as an instigator of and catalyst for oppositional social movements across the Western world. His emphasis on combating libidinal oppression, emancipating the senses, and striving for new aesthetic, sensuous, and moral sensibilities also fit perfectly the zeitgeist of the time that encouraged liberation through pharmaceutical and sexual experimentation. As Habermas (1983) acknowledged, Marcuse developed "striking arguments for a new political praxis that integrates sensuality, fantasy and desire" (p. 170).

Marcuse's power as a critical theorist was brought home to me a few years ago during a class I was teaching. I was talking about his idea of repressive tolerance and about how the contemporary emphasis on diversity could be interpreted as an example of the dominant culture's ability to seem to be opening itself up to dissenting views and different perspectives, when in fact it was subtly reasserting its control over public discourse. When we took a break an African American woman, a veteran of the civil rights movement still actively engaged in antiracist education, came up to me. "Marcuse was a beautiful man," she said, "as soon as you mentioned his name I knew I could trust you." What was it about the mention of Marcuse that engendered such goodwill? Perhaps it was his association with the Black Panther and communist activist Angela Davis. Davis, a student of Marcuse's at Brandeis and then at the University of California-San Diego, tells of her asking Marcuse to be the first to enter the registrar's office at UC-San Diego when the students wished to mount an occupation. This was an act that meant they could well be arrested and charged with breaking, entering, and trespassing. As she recalls, "Without a moment's hesitation, Herbert Marcuse agreed: 'Of course I'll do it.' There was no question in his mind. At that time he was about seventy-five years old. He was the first person to walk into the registrar's office" (Davis, 1998a, p. 317).

Perhaps, too, there was goodwill resulting from his placing hope in extraparliamentary direct action by the most disenfranchised members of society. He supported the Black Power movement as a "far more subversive universe of discourse" (Marcuse, 1969, p. 35) than the Hippie movement. In the language of Black militants, particularly their claiming of soul—"in its essence lily-white ever since Plato" (p. 36)—and their declaration that "Black is beautiful," Marcuse detected "the ingression of the aesthetic into the political" (p. 36). Black Power represented "a systematic linguistic rebellion, which smashes the ideological context in which the words are employed and defined, and places them in the opposite context—negation of the established one. Thus, the blacks 'take over' some of the most sublime and sublimated concepts of Western civilization, desublimate them and redefine them" (p. 35). To emerging African American scholars of the time such as Lucius T. Outlaw, Jr. (1996, p. xxvii), Marcuse's work was an entry point into critical theory that connected it to Black Nationalist critiques of White supremacy.

In the years since his death in 1979, however, Marcuse's influence has waned. From being viewed as a prophet of a qualitatively different society struggling to be born, he is now a historical figure, sidelined by the postmodern furor. Part of this may be due to the fact that there have been few new publications of material from the Marcuse archive in Frankfurt, though Kellner (1994) suggests a wealth of translatable material pertaining to issues of globalization and postmodernism exists there and has begun to issue some of this in a six-volume series (Marcuse, 2002). Whatever the reason, Marcuse has had little impact on adult learning theory. Compared to Habermas, Marcuse (like Fromm) is a nonfigure in adult education discourse. This is a shame, for several reasons. First, Marcuse has much to say on concepts that dominate contemporary adult education, such as self-directed learning and critical thinking. Second, his analysis of the way in which a tolerant embrace of a diversity of perspectives works to legitimize domination and repression challenges in fundamental ways practices that many progressive adult educators would heartily endorse. Third, he stresses aspects of adult learning such as inwardness, privacy, memory, and distance that receive little attention from others in the field. Fourth, he forces critical adult educators to take seriously the aesthetic dimension of life, not something that always springs to mind when one thinks of critical adult education.

Marcuse's insistence on the importance of individual isolation in learning to think critically and his belief that revolutionary struggle requires us to look inward to our deepest instinctual impulses add a very different tone to contemporary discussions of critical theory. Tied to his insistence on the importance of individual isolation and the need for people to create some distance from the dominant culture is his theory of aesthetics. Marcuse believed that individual artistic experiences could trigger a revolutionary estrangement from everyday life, thus nurturing the tendency to political critique. For Marcuse artistic experience threatened the political order, particularly where the work of art concerned was highly stylized, perhaps even a part of "highbrow" culture. In acknowledging the liberatory possibilities of art and in stressing the importance of "rebellious subjectivity" (Marcuse, 1978a, p. 7), Marcuse opposes critical theorists' instinctive dismissal of individual isolation as an apolitical and anti-revolutionary turn away from social commitment.

Marcuse's Critique of Marx

Like all the thinkers reviewed at any length in this book, Marcuse drew heavily on Marxist analysis and that of Marx's precursor Hegel (Marcuse, 1941). But his was a truly critical reappraisal of Marx, whom he regarded as overly optimistic and idealistic. In Marcuse's view, "Marx underrated the extent of the conquest of nature and of man, of the technological management of freedom and self-realization" (1965b, p. 112). In addition, Marxism had been co-opted and distorted by the Soviet Union to justify repression. In communist societies, "the theory that destroyed all ideology is used for the establishment of a new ideology" entailing "planning for the retention of government above and against the individuals" (1958, p. xiv). Marxism had become one more tool in the total administration of thought that characterized the technologically advanced societies in East and West alike. Finally, in Marcuse's view, "Marx was still too tied to the notion of a continuum of progress" (1970, p. 62) and did not appreciate enough the need for a complete qualitative change in the structure of human needs. For Marcuse such needs as "the need for calm, the need to be alone, with oneself or with others whom one has chosen oneself, the need for the beautiful, the need for 'undeserved' happiness" (p. 67) were potentially revolutionary, not individual indulgences.

One element of Marcuse's critique of how Marx's ideas were being distorted—the use of overly specialist leftist jargon—is particularly relevant for adult educators. Marcuse was frustrated by the slavish, repetitive, and ultimately uncritical invocation of Marxist concepts and slogans that he saw leftist activists and educators slipping into. He railed against "the distortion and falsification of Marxian theory through its *ritualization*" (1972, p. 33). By mechanically repeating a basic vocabulary—proletariat, exploitation, impoverishment were examples he gave—critically inclined activists only ensured "a petrification of Marxian theory into a rhetoric with hardly any relation to reality" (p. 34). Not only did this jargon petrify Marxism, it also ensured that educators and activists actually undercut the possibility of their reaching those they were trying to teach, whether in the adult classroom or social movements.

Among contemporary adult educators, the issue of whether or not a critical practice of adult education requires a separate language, untainted by the distortions of the dominant, capitalist culture, generates vigorous disagreement. Can we have a language of empowering practice, for example, when the very word *empowerment* has lost its radical democratic meaning? How can we galvanize transformative forces and movements when the word *transformative* is now used by some to describe the slightest changes in personal outlook or behavior? Although he acknowledged that specialized radical language was sometimes necessary for communication amongst a small cadre of activists, he was unequivocal in his criticism of those using a specialized "unrealistic language" of leftism to communicate with the masses (Marcuse, 1978b). While terms such as *counterhegemony, emancipatory praxis,* or *transformative agency* might be permissible shorthand for activists to use with each other, they were disastrous for wider education. Like it or not, he argued, "The 'people' speak a language which is all but closed to the concepts and propositions of Marxian theory" (Marcuse, 1972, p. 37).

Although he acknowledged that an aversion to "foreign words, 'big words,' etcetera" (Marcuse, 1972, p. 37) served to bind people to the language of the establishment, and consequently to the establishment itself, Marcuse saw little point in forcing the language of critical theory on them. Indeed, such an imposition was likely to turn people against radical ideas and kill the oppositional spirit embedded in radical language. In his words, "bombarding the people with these terms without translating them into the actual situation does not communicate Marxian theory . . . these words become identification labels for in-groups . . . they function as mere clichés—that is, they don't function at all. Their use as instant stimuli in a canned vocabulary kills their truth" (p. 39).

Marcuse's words have resonance for the literature of critical adult education. In our field as in most other areas of academic writing, a specialized form of discourse often develops. Sometimes this has reflected the field's desire to distance itself from other areas of educational practice and to carve out a piece of the world that is distinctively its own. Such was partly the case with the term *andragogy.* Sometimes rarefied language is necessary to capture the complexity and distinctiveness of processes that cannot easily be described in colloquial terms. *Hegemony* would be a good example of this. At other times, however, writers throw around terms that are understood only by an "in" group of ideologically sympathetic theorists, as a kind of coded, scriptural signaling.

Perhaps the most significant contribution Marcuse made to critical debate on Marxism was his questioning of the predominant orthodoxy of Marxist aesthetics. This orthodoxy, drawing on the idea that the material base of society determined the ideological, cultural, and artistic superstructure, held that "art represents the interests and world outlook of particular social classes" (1978a, p. ix). Marcuse rejected such a deterministic equation, arguing that "in contrast to orthodox Marxist aesthetics I see the political potential of art itself, in the aesthetic form as such . . . by virtue of its aesthetic form, art is largely autonomous vis-à-vis the given social relations. In its autonomy art both protests these relations, and at the same time transcends them" (p. ix). As we shall see later in this chapter, Marcuse believed that the stylized, formal aspects of "high" art could produce an estrangement with reality and that in this estrangement lay the truly revolutionary potential of art.

In defending individual creativity that produced art containing no explicit political message or intent, Marcuse broke with those who believe that the content of art should always serve a predetermined revolutionary purpose. He criticized the way that "Marxist aesthetics has shared in the devaluation of subjectivity, the denigration of romanticism as simply reactionary; the denunciation of 'decadent' art" (1978a, p. 6). For him overtly political art explicitly dedicated to raising people's consciousness of oppression and igniting the fires of change—agitprop theater, socialist realism, even the theater of the oppressed (Boal, 1985)—was actually less revolutionary than some forms of introspective poetry. This was because "the more immediately political the work of art, the more it reduces the power of estrangement and the radical, transcendent goals of change" (Marcuse, 1978a, p. xii). The films of Ken Loach or plays of Dario Fo would not be strongly revolutionary art, according to Marcuse, since their direct critique of current social conditions do not produce the experience of estrangement, of an altered sense of reality. As Marcuse acknowledged, the logic of his critique meant that "there may be more subversive potential in the poetry of Baudelaire and Rimbaud than in the didactic plays of Brecht" (p. xiii).

On a broader scale, Marcuse's critique of Marx reflects his contention that critical theory has lost its way in the world of cyberspace and technological domination. Originally developed as a guide to activating forces, such as the proletariat, that could overthrow the social order, Marxism was rendered less potent when no such forces clearly existed. To Marcuse, "the categories of critical social theory were developed during the period in which the need for refusal and subversion was embodied in the action of effective social forces" (1964, p. xiv). It contained an immanent critique; that is, the pathways to liberation could be detected within the contradictions of the existing society. Potentially revolutionary social forces immanent within society could be guided to create "more rational and freer institutions by abolishing the existing ones which had become obstacles to progress" (1964, p. 254). The transformative potential of working-class and other oppositional social movements "were the empirical grounds on which the theory was erected, and from these empirical grounds derived the idea of the liberation of *inherent* possibilities—the development, otherwise blocked and distorted, of material and intellectual productivity, faculties, and needs" (p. 254).

In the contemporary world, however, Marcuse believed that technological and administrative advances have combined "to institute new, more effective, and more pleasant forms of social control and social cohesion" (1964, p. xv). People live in "comfortable, smooth, reasonable, democratic unfreedom" (p. 1), the experience of which "makes servitude palatable and perhaps even unnoticeable" (p. 24). The weakness of critical theory in this situation is "its inability to demonstrate the liberating tendencies *within* the established society" (p. 254). The working class, the proletariat, are no longer active forces for revolutionary social change; indeed, they are often the most enthusiastic upholders of the status quo. Given that critical theory "analyzes society in the light of its used and unused or abused capabilities for improving the human condition" (p. x), Marcuse felt that a whole new analysis of liberatory forces and strategies was called for. In these strategies and forces was a distinctive role for adult education.

One-Dimensional Thought

At the core of Marcuse's work is his belief that we learn our own servitude and that we have learned to love our condition of oppression. In advanced industrial society, the most pernicious oppression of all is that of affluence. Lulled into stupefaction by the possession of consumer goods, we believe ourselves to be living in democratic freedom, when our needs have actually been manipulated to convince us we are happy. In reality, a condition of disaffection lurks beneath the carapace of everyday life. If we could just see our alienated state clearly, we would want to liberate ourselves from it. But we have learned to regard half-buried feelings of dissatisfaction as basically irrational symptoms of neurosis.

This vision of a society controlled by technological advances, consumer luxury, and smoothly functioning administration is most fully laid out in *One Dimensional Man* (1964), Marcuse's most celebrated book. Before examining this vision, it is important to state that Marcuse was no Luddite. He believed strongly in the power of technology to liberate people from the burdens of unnecessary toil and physical drudgery. In his opinion, "all the material and intellectual forces which could be put to work for the realization of a free society are at hand" (Marcuse, 1970, p. 64). That these resources are not used for this purpose "is to be attributed to the total mobilization of existing society against its own potential for liberation" (p. 64).

At the core of his critique is his contention that in the modern world technology has been used to create false needs—the need for stupefying work, for the consumption of consumer goods, and for the maintenance of a social order that is inherently repressive. Hence, "the liberating force of technology—the instrumentalization of things—turns into a fetter of liberation, the instrumentalization of man" (1964, p. 159). We live in a society characterized by "a non-terroristic economic-technical coordination which operates through the manipulation of needs by vested interests" (p. 3). These needs (particularly the need for consumer goods) are created by the dominant capitalist order and then internalized by us until they are indistinguishable from our most basic desires, so that we define ourselves, and the attainment of a fulfilled life, in terms of these needs. To Marcuse, "existing society is reproduced not only in the mind, the consciousness of men, but also in their senses; and no persuasion, no theory, no reasoning can break this prison . . . until the oppressive familiarity with the given object world is broken" (1972, p. 72). An intense encounter with a work of art is one way a sense of estrangement from oppressive familiarity can be instigated, thus laying the groundwork for the development of political awareness.

In the contemporary world, domination is so total and insidious that it has seeped into our synapses, into our most basic ways of apprehending reality: "The so-called consumer economy and the politics of corporate capitalism have created a second nature of man which ties him libidinally and aggressively to the commodity form" (1969, p. 11). The needs the system creates in people are "eminently stabilizing, conservative needs" (p. 11) that ensure we have a "deep rooted, 'organic' adaptation of the people to a terrible but profitably functioning society" (p. 17). In this society, it is hard to identify revolutionary forces, since to be dissatisfied is taken as a sign of inadequacy or psychological disturbance. When "the administered life becomes the good life of the whole" (1964, p. 255), then "the intellectual and emotional refusal 'to go along' appears neurotic and impotent" (p. 9). In times of war, for example, the refusal to "go along" with invasions of countries that pose no imminent threat is often portrayed as irrational and confused as well as unpatriotic.

What is the administered life? It is a life in which the urgent need to reproduce the existing order is felt at the deepest, most visceral, instinctual level. Keeping things as they are becomes a vital personal imperative. In the administered society, "the coordination of the individual with his society reaches into the very layers of the mind where the very concepts are elaborated which are designed to comprehend the established reality" (1964, p. 104). Marcuse contended that "administered human beings today reproduce their own repression and eschew a rupture with the given reality" (1978a, p. 71). Everything—needs, sensual experience, identity, emotions, all the subterranean dimensions of our being—serves the role of capital. The administered society turns "the entire human being—intelligence and senses—into an object of administration, geared to produce and reproduce not only the goals but also the values and the promises of the system" (1972, p. 14). How is such deep rooted psychic and sensual control established?

One-dimensional thought is the most pervasive mechanism of control. One-dimensional thought is instrumental thought focused on how to make the current system work better and perform more effectively. When people think this way, they start to conceive of the range of possibilities open to them in life within a framework predefined by the existing order. People assume that all is for the best in society, that things are arranged the way they are for a good reason, and that the current system works for the benefit of all. In this system, philosophical thought, even of an apparently critical kind, serves only to keep the system going. Hence, "the philosophic critique criticizes *within* the societal framework and stigmatizes non-positive actions as mere speculation, dreams or fantasies" (1964, p. 172). Problems of meaning and morality, such as how we should treat other people, what it means to act ethically, or how we can make sense of death, are defused of metaphysical dimensions and turned into operational difficulties to be addressed by techniques and programs. Thus, "the operational and behavioral point of view, practiced as a 'habit of thought' at large, becomes the view of the established universe of discourse and action, needs and aspirations" (p. 15).

When adults learn to keep their thought fixed within familiar boundaries, the status quo is easily maintained. A universe of discourse is created that is "populated by self-validating hypotheses which, incessantly and monopolistically repeated, become hypnotic definitions or dictations" (1964, p. 14). One-dimensional thought is circular even when it appears divergent. Any questions we ask always bring us back to the same point where we affirm the validity of the current system. This kind of thought is endlessly repetitive, so that "self-validating, analytical propositions appear which function like magic-ritual formulas" (p. 88). Its internal organization is so tight that "transgression of the discourse beyond the closed analytical structure is incorrect or propaganda" (p. 88). Thought that protests the given order of things is effectively anaesthetized by rejecting it as irrational or simply redefining it to fit the prevailing worldview.

Crucial to the successful maintenance of one-dimensional thought is the creation of false needs. These are needs "which are superimposed upon the individual by particular social interests in his repression: the needs which perpetuate evil, aggressiveness, misery and injustice. Their satisfaction . . . serves to arrest the development of his ability . . . to recognize the disease of the whole and grasp the chance of curing the disease. The result is euphoria in unhappiness" (1964, p. 5). Examples of such needs are the need "to behave and consume in accordance with the advertisements, to love and hate what others love and hate" (p. 5), the need "for stupefying work" (p. 7), and "for modes of relaxation which soothe and prolong this stupefaction" (p. 7). As long as adults are "kept incapable of being autonomous, indoctrinated and manipulated down to their very instincts" (p. 6), they are unable to recognize their own real needs in any meaningful sense. Any freedom of choice they experience is illusory, the deceptive liberty of "free competition at administered prices, a free press which censors itself, free choice between brands and gadgets" (p. 7).

One-dimensional thought ensures its own continuance when it trains people to feel a deep need to stay within their existing frameworks of analysis. Although avoiding divergent thinking seems like an individual decision, it is in reality a massive indoctrination effort intended to stop people questioning what they see around them. The purpose of this system-preserving effort is to ensure that "the needs and the satisfactions that serve the preservation of the Establishment are shared by the underlying population" (p. 8). The apogee of the administered society is reached when everyone shares the same deep-seated need to preserve the existing social order, but each believes this to be an idiosyncratic feature of their own personality. Social control is assured if "the transplantation of social into individual needs is so effective that the difference between them seems to be purely theoretical" (p. 8).

Language has an important place in one-dimensional thought. In fact, it is in language that the presence of such thought is most recognizable. In the administered society, "the determining function of the social system of meaning asserts itself . . . in a much more covert, unconscious, emotional manner, in the ordinary universe of discourse" (1964, p. 197). By the language we speak and the patterns of thought we employ, we commit ourselves to maintaining the current system. Marcuse's eloquence on this point is worth quoting at length:

> The established universe of discourse bears throughout the
> marks of the specific modes of domination, organization and

manipulation to which the members of a society are subjected. People depend for their living on bosses and politicians and jobs and neighbors who make them speak and mean as they do. . . . Under these circumstances, the spoken phrase is an expression of the individual who speaks it, *and* of those who make him speak as he does, *and* of whatever tension or contradiction may interrelate them. In speaking their own language, people also speak the language of their masters, benefactors, advertisers. Thus they do not only express themselves, their own knowledge, feelings, aspirations, but also something other than themselves" [1964, p. 193].

In Marcuse's analysis there is little that is private or personal about language. Language—the prime tool we use in the most private spheres of our lives to mediate and communicate reality—has been ravaged by the consumer society. Thus, when "describing to each other our loves and hatreds, sentiments and resentments, we must use the terms of our advertisements, movies, politicians and best sellers" (1964, p. 194). If this language is comprised of terms, metaphors, phrases, and sayings that confirm that all is for the best, then we are robbed of an important tool with which we can record our indignation and inspire others to change the world. When they are enclosed in language that focuses on tinkering with the system to make it work more smoothly, "the people, previously the ferment of social change, have 'moved up' to become the ferment of social cohesion" (1964, p. 256).

How does language function to cement one-dimensional thought? First, the system establishes certain habits of communication, patterns of talk, that close down the possibility of divergent thinking. This is the "authoritarian ritualization of discourse" (1964, p. 101) that trains people to mistake making pronouncements or sticking to the facts with the conduct of probing critical analysis. Language is imbued with a tone of certainty, and statements are uttered with a self-evident correctness that allows "no time and no space for a discussion which would project disruptive alternatives" (p. 101). This kind of language is antithetical to dialog and discussion since "it pronounces and, by virtue of the power of the apparatus, establishes facts—it is self-validating enunciation . . . it communicates decision, dictum, command" (p. 101). Can a more accurate description be imagined of the claim of the Fox News Network to provide "fair and unbiased" coverage of the invasion of Iraq?

More specifically, contemporary language kills abstract, conceptual thought by encouraging people to equate thinking with a focus only on specific, concrete, empirical concerns. To Marcuse, "the language which the man on the street actually speaks" offers "the token of a false concreteness" (1964, p. 174). It is a "purged language, purged . . . of the means for expressing any other contents than those furnished to the individuals by their society" (p. 174). These falsely concrete contents are an almost exclusive concern with making things work better, with perfecting and improving whatever is already in place. In adult education, for example, it is the language of quality, of improved service, of ensuring that the programs we create meet as fully as possible the wants and needs (to Marcuse, false needs) that adult learners express.

An important component of false concreteness is the removal of the universal elements in conceptual thought. Concepts are, by definition, universal ideas referring to abstractions under which various particulars are subsumed. Justice, love, fairness, compassion—all these concepts have meaning above and beyond their individual contexts and referents. When the abstract dimensions of these ideas are ignored, it becomes very difficult to judge how we should act by reference to some broader ideal. Whether a person or institution is behaving justly becomes something we decide in a purely situational way, possibly by comparing the behavior we're examining to other examples within our personal horizons. The last thing we think of doing is invoking a broad, abstract notion of justice and applying it to our little local difficulties. This is how "the methodological translation of the universal into the operational then becomes repressive reduction of thought" (1964, p. 108). For example, the public discussion of the morality of invading a country can quickly become obscured by a focus on situational imperatives such as the number of troops deployed from week to week, the exact civilian and military body count, and the amount of money spent supporting the war effort.

When abstract conceptual thought is purged from everyday language, two consequences ensue. First, it becomes increasingly difficult for people to conceive of radical alternatives. A narrow focus on false concreteness inhibits the breadth of imaginative thought necessary to create alternative possibilities. Second, without abstract concepts it becomes very difficult to generate radical, external criteria that can be applied to judge the conduct of everyday affairs.

In the absence of abstract concepts, "the criteria for judging a given state of affairs are those offered by . . . imposed by, the given state of affairs. The analysis is 'locked,' the range of judgment is confirmed within a context . . . in which their meaning, function, and development are determined" (1964, p. 115). So the prevention of abstract, conceptual thought and the promotion of false concreteness are important ways that education, including adult education, contributes to keeping things as they are. In Marcuse's terms, "language controls by reducing the linguistic forms and symbols of reflection, abstraction, development, contradiction; by substituting images for concepts" (1964, p. 103).

The picture Marcuse paints in *One Dimensional Man* of the administered society dominated by technology, consumerism, restricted language, and falsely concrete thought processes that only confirm the correctness of the existing order seems dismal indeed. In his view scientific management and rational production methods might have improved people's standards of living, but they have done so at a price—the destruction of nature and diminution of the soul—that people are not so much willing to pay as completely oblivious to. The adult educator Myles Horton echoed Marcuse in his belief that the all-encompassing nature of technology meant "man is grown into this all-encompassing machine and made a mechanistic device" (Horton, 2003, p. 222). Like Horton, Marcuse's analysis stresses the costs of technological envelopment. The administered society has extended its tentacles into the deepest recesses of the psyche to produce "the thorough assimilation of mind with facts, of thought with required behavior, of aspirations with reality" (Marcuse, 1964, p. 252). But documenting the ways in which the logic of domination infused language, thought, and sensibility was only one part of Marcuse's work. We need now to turn to another element of particular concern to adult educators: the possibility of people learning how to liberate themselves from the discourse, logic, and practice of domination.

Pathways to Liberation

One reason why Marcuse had such an influence in his time was because he offered a way out of the prospect of a society lulled into repressive consumerism by the delights of affluence. Even those such as Habermas (1983) who viewed his theoretical work as "somewhat meager" acknowledged that "as always, the discourse is affirmative" (p. 171) . Marcuse was a philosopher of hope as well as a chronicler of domination. He believed that "today there are tendencies in society—anarchically unorganized, spontaneous tendencies—that herald a total break with the dominant needs of repressive society" (Marcuse, 1970, p. 69). So while he documented oppression, he also explored social, educational, and cultural pathways to liberation. Even in a one-dimensional society he acknowledged that "there are still gaps and interstices in which heretical methods can be practiced without meaningless sacrifice, and still help the cause" (p. 76).

Some of the gaps, interstices, and pathways he explores contribute a new dimension to a critical theory of adult learning, emphasizing as they do aspects of learning—inwardness, isolation, memory, distance, and subjectivity—that usually receive little attention. For Marcuse social living in an administered society is dominated living. In the pressure to conform to common expectations, the chance for individual thought is lost. The only way people can come to a truly critical perspective is by distancing themselves in some manner from the stupefying influence of commonsense ways of thinking, feeling, and speaking. Isolation and separation—the conditions of true autonomy—are potentially revolutionary, the precursors to a commitment to social change.

The Revolutionary Significance of Distance and Privacy

The themes of autonomous learning and thinking are familiar within adult education, particularly in the discourse surrounding self-directed learning. The explosion of self-paced, online learning is often linked to the idea of the adult learner's autonomous exercise of control over how and when she learns. But the political dimensions to self-direction, and by implication to autonomy, have, with a couple of exceptions (Hammond and Collins, 1991; Brookfield, 2000), been ignored. To Marcuse, however, autonomous thought is a necessary condition for the development of any kind of social movement intended to resist domination. But because of technological domination and the consumerist manipulation of needs, "independence of thought, autonomy and the right to political opposition are being deprived of their basic critical function"

(1964, p. 1). The growth in automaton conformity (to use Fromm's term from the previous chapter) can only be reversed or challenged by the development of independent thought; "intellectual freedom would mean the restoration of individual thought now absorbed by mass communication and indoctrination" (p. 4).

In an era of total domination, how can true autonomy be realized? Here Marcuse turns to the liberating power of art, an avenue for social change well known to cultural workers in popular education through the theater of the oppressed, street art, community murals and video, independent film, rock and roll, punk, folk, hip-hop, and rap music. But it is not this kind of overtly political "people's" art that interests Marcuse. To him true autonomy—separation from the contaminating influences of conformity and consumerism—arises out of the individual's opportunity to abstract herself from the day-to-day reality of the surrounding culture. For an altered consciousness to develop, it is necessary for the adult to experience a fundamental estrangement from commonly accepted ways of thinking and feeling. Immersion in artistic experience is one way to induce this estrangement. Contact with certain artistic forms offers a pathway of separation, a way of breaking with the rhythms of normal life. This focus on inwardness, on subjectivity, as liberating is very much at odds with how contemporary activists think of the political function of art. Privacy, isolation, and inwardness have become suspicious ideas, indicating an irresponsible withdrawal from political commitment. How, then, can Marcuse regard them as liberating?

The answer lies in Marcuse's belief that domination is so total in this society that group creativity, collaborative artistic work, team productions, and other forms of collective activity have all been suffused with the dominant culture's belief that such activity should be directed toward making the system work better. When people get together, they do so to support, rather than challenge, the system. Each person's belief in the basic efficacy of the way society is organized is reinforced by contact with others in the society. So removing ourselves from the influence of others is a revolutionary act, a step into, rather than a retreat from, the real world.

In his analysis of liberating subjectivity, Marcuse stresses three things—memory, distance, and privacy. Memory is subversive because it signifies a temporary break with the current reality; "remembrance is a mode of dissociation from the given facts, a mode of 'mediation' which breaks, for short moments, the omnipresent power of the given facts. Memory recalls the terror and the hope that passed" (1964, p. 98). When we remember days of childhood bliss when the world seemed benign and beautiful, or when we re-member our first cruel realization that life is unfair, we reencounter a source of primal energy. Instead of being pleasant reverie, mem-ory is here seen as a route out of the usual way of experiencing everyday life and hence a source of the estrangement Marcuse feels is crucial to developing revolutionary consciousness. In his view the distance from daily existence that memory sometimes provides is key to the development of all forms independent, critical thought. The further we get from the quotidian, the better chance we have of breaking out of domination. As a general rule, "it is the sphere farthest removed from the concreteness of society which may show most clearly the extent of the conquest of thought by society" (1964, p. 104).

When we live our lives in association with others, it becomes dif-ficult to establish the necessary distance for autonomous thought. In all areas of our lives we are subject to "aggressive and exploitative socialization" (1978a, p. 5) that forces us into constant association with those who believe things are working just fine. For example, the contemporary emphasis on collaboration and teamwork, on being one of the team, on a successful marriage as comprising two people who make a good team (a bête noire of Fromm's) has "invaded the inner space of privacy and practically eliminated the possibility of that isolation in which the individual, thrown back on himself alone, can think and question and find" (1964, p. 244). To him, privacy is "the sole condition that, on the basis of satisfied vital needs, can give meaning to freedom and independence of thought" (p. 244). It is no accident, therefore, that for most people privacy "has long since become the most expensive commodity, available only to the very rich" (p. 244).

Marcuse's lamentation of the passing of privacy, and his stress on the revolutionary power of detachment and isolation, sits uneasily alongside the belief held by many adult educators that learning (par-ticularly critical learning) is inherently social. I have argued (Brook-field, 1995) that introspective analysis of a private and isolated sort leads us into perceptual dead ends. To me critical reflection is a social learning process in which we depend on others to be critical mirrors reflecting back to us aspects of our assumptive clusters we are unable to see. I have also (like many others) urged that true adult education is collaborative and collective, the building of a learning community in which the roles of teachers and learners are blurred. In my own practice, the three doctoral programs in which I have been involved as worker or cocreator (at Teachers College, National Louis University, and the University of St. Thomas) have all insisted on collaborative work as the norm, even to the extent of encouraging collaboratively written doctoral dissertations. I have felt that this cocreation of knowledge mirrored best practices in the field as seen in Freireian culture circles, the Highlander Folk School, social movements, and participatory research. For me isolation is usually a step backward, a retreat into the divisive, competitive, privatized creation of knowledge characteristic of capitalism. How on earth can privacy and isolation challenge the social order?

To Marcuse, my question is asinine. I should be asking instead, "How can we possibly challenge the social order *without* experiencing first the separation that isolation provides?" For example, experiencing art communally at a gallery, theater, poetry reading, or concert is, he argues, inherently conservative. Our responses to the art concerned are preconditioned by our awareness of the presence of others. But when a person experiences a deeply personal, completely private reaction to a work of art, she "steps out of the network of exchange relationships and exchange values, withdraws from the reality of bourgeois society, and enters another dimension of existence" (1978a, p. 4). This is the dimension of inwardness, of liberating subjectivity. Such subjectivity is liberating because we are moved by primal aesthetic and creative impulses, not the dictates of majority opinion or commonsense criteria of beauty. Privacy, inwardness, and isolation are all revolutionary because they play the role of "shifting the locus of the individual's realization from the domain of the performance principle and the profit motive to that of the inner resources of the human being: passion, imagination, conscience" (1978a, p. 5).

According to this logic, a truly critical practice of adult education would be concerned not just with locating itself within existing social movements. It would also be seeking to create opportunities for people to experience the privacy and isolation they need for memory, introspection, and meditation to trigger a rupture with present day experience. This rupture is not just a sort of spiritual awakening but an experiential dissonance that will jerk people into an awareness of how life could be different. Only with distance and privacy can a new sensibility develop that "would repel the instrumentalist rationality of capitalism" (1972, p. 64).

Marcuse believed that at the root of all striving for freedom is the need to emancipate the senses. Feeling, touch, sight, smell, and sound all contain sensuously uncontrollable qualities that stand against bureaucratic rationality. If adults are to be truly liberated, they need to be free at "the roots of social relationships . . . where individuals most directly and profoundly experience their world and themselves: in their *sensibility,* in their instinctual needs" (1972, p. 62). Marcuse grounds his emphasis on liberating sensibility in Marx's call in the *Education and Philosophic Manuscripts* (1961) for the complete emancipation of all human senses and qualities. In contrast to contemporary critical theorists who are skeptical of a focus on personal change, Marcuse is quite willing to stress that social change must be located in the individual's altered sensibility; "it is this primary experience itself which must change radically if social change is to be radical, qualitative change" (1972, p. 62). A new sensibility is "the vehicle for radical construction, for new ways of life. It has become a force in the *political* struggle for liberation" (p. 72).

Of course, altered individual sensibilities acting alone will not activate change; they need to be united in building a new society. There is "no individual liberation without the liberation of society" (p. 48), and individual acts of transgression "must incorporate the universal in the particular protest" (p. 49). Hence, nurturing the new sensibility is only the beginning of transformation; "the individual emancipation of the senses is supposed to be the beginning, even the foundation, of *universal* liberation, the free society is to take root in instinctual needs" (p. 72). But, equally, skipping individual consciousness and concerning oneself solely with the mechanics of collective action, is to leave out one half of the transformative equation. Altered social and economic arrangements will not free people unless there are corresponding alterations at the level of instinctual sensibilities. For Marcuse, "the individuals themselves must change in their very instincts and sensibilities if they are to build, in association, a *qualitatively* different society" (p. 74). This contention has important implications for formal programs of adult education, particularly those that emphasize changing the individual's sensibility through aesthetic immersion.

The Revolutionary Potential of Art

If there is any truth to Marcuse's argument regarding the power of aesthetic immersion to trigger a revolutionary estrangement from everyday experience, then adult education that concerns itself with liberating the senses through creative, artistic expression is potentially revolutionary. This is a switch for many critical adult educators who may be tempted to dismiss this kind of practice as elitist dilettantism. Recreational art or music appreciation is about as far as you can get from critical theory for many on the left who find it hard to think of these classes as potential crucibles for the development of revolutionary consciousness. But Marcuse's analysis challenges us to reverse our dismissal of aesthetic education as an irrelevant indulgence of middle-class, leisured learners. The key point, though, is that for liberal adult education to instigate a rupture with everyday experience, its programs would have to focus on fostering the isolation necessary for an immersion in aesthetics. Music or art appreciation would not be taught collectively as a group process in which people were introduced to the canon over a period of several weeks. Instead, the adult learner would receive minimal initiation into the criteria for judging artistic power and maximal immersion in an extended private engagement with art.

This still seems like a politically correct rationalization for the elitist enjoyment of an elitist individualized program of artistic study, and commentators such as Reitz (2000) have criticized Marcuse for what they see as the "ironically conservative political overtones" (p. 43) present in his work. To understand its political import, we need to examine Marcuse's contention that individual artistic experience represents rebellious, liberating subjectivity. Again and again he asserts that "the flight into 'inwardness' and the insistence on a private sphere may well serve as bulwarks against a society which administers all dimensions of human existence" (1978a, p. 38). Because they instigate a separation from the routinized, unthinking life, "inwardness and subjectivity may well become the inner and outer space for the subversion of experience, for the emergence of another universe" (p. 38). It is the tasting of a new form of experience that is inherently revolutionary, and the power to initiate this is "the critical, negating function of art" (1978a, p. 7). Art can induce "the transcendence of immediate reality" which "shatters the reified objectivity of established social relations and opens a new dimension of experience: rebirth of the rebellious subjectivity" (p. 7).

Marcuse is careful to recognize that "art cannot change the world" (1978a, p. 32) though he does believe that "it can contribute to changing the consciousness and drives of the men and women who could change the world" (p. 32). Art represents only "the promise of liberation" (1978a, p. 46) not its actuality, and "clearly, the fulfillment of this promise is not within the domain of art" (p. 46). What art does offer us, however, is a chance of breaking with the familiar, of inducing in us an awareness of other ways of being in the world. Art "opens the established reality to another dimension; that of possible liberation" (1972, p. 87). If radical political practice is focused on creating "a world different from and contrary to the established universe of discourse and behavior" (1969, p. 73), then art is one important prompt to this state of difference. What exists now for most people is a condition of voluntary servitude. Working to create a free society therefore "involves a break with the familiar, the routine ways of seeing, hearing, feeling, understanding things so that the organism may become receptive to the potential forms of a non aggressive, non exploitative world" (1969, p. 6). The political significance of art is that it helps us make this break with the ordinary. It helps us "find forms of communication that may break the aggressive rule of the established language and images over the mind and body of man—language and images which have long since become a means of domination, indoctrination, and deception" (1972, p. 79).

Art, then, gives us new forms of visual and spoken language and opens us to new ways of sensing and feeling. Learning these different forms of communication and perception is, for Marcuse, the inevitable precursor to social action. Adult education that focuses on developing artistic sensibility is regarded as full of revolutionary potential as Freireian culture circles, theater of the oppressed, participatory research, or education for party activism. This is why Marcuse felt that the development of the aesthetic dimension of life was as much part of political struggle as the democratizing of decision making, rejection of consumer culture, or the abolition of the exchange economy. A liberated society "presupposes a type of man with a different sensitivity" (1969, p. 21) possessing different language, gestures, and impulses and "guided by the imagination, mediating between the rational faculties and the sensuous needs" (p. 30).

For Marcuse, then, aesthetics is politics and adults who learn a new aesthetic sensibility are learning a new form of political consciousness. Indeed, learning a new sensibility is so crucial to liberating humanity that we can gauge the progress we are making in a revolution by reference to aesthetic as much as political or economic criteria. Hence, "the aesthetic dimension can serve as a sort of gauge for a free society" (1969, p. 27) with the demand for quiet and beauty "cleaning the earth from [sic] the very material garbage produced by the spirit of capitalism" (p. 28). Again, Marcuse is careful to specify that this sensibility must be thought of as a deeply personal phenomenon. He is not afraid to focus on the individual and does not regard this focus as apolitical or ignoring wider social and economic forces. Developing a new sensibility can only happen when the individual has privacy and distance from quotidian reality. People "require a degree of emancipation from immediate experience, of 'privacy'" (1972, p. 102) if they are to comprehend "the extreme aesthetic qualities of art" (p. 102).

As discussed earlier, the political power of art is not to be found in directly political images of revolution, struggle, and socialist victory. Marcuse declares that "art cannot represent the revolution" (1972, p. 103) since it "obeys a necessity, and has a freedom which is its own—not those of the revolution" (p.105). It is the rigidly stylized aspects of art, the way it adheres to a set of strict constraints that are wholly aesthetic, that is truly emancipatory. If art is "to pierce and comprehend the everyday reality, it must be subjugated to aesthetic stylization" (1978a, p. 122), to the tyranny of form. This sounds contradictory, for how can adhering to stylized artistic conventions liberate us? But Marcuse is very insistent on this point. Repeatedly he stresses how "the political potential of art lies only in its own aesthetic dimension" (1978a, p. xi) and how "the critical function of art, its contribution to the struggle for liberation, resides in the aesthetic form" (1978a, p. 8). The aesthetic form in painting, sculpture, music, drama, and poetry "reveals tabooed and repressed dimensions of reality" (p. 9) by conjuring up different "modes of perception, imagination, gestures—a feast of sensuousness which shatters everyday experience and anticipates a different reality principle" (1978a, p. 19).

When we submit to the aesthetic power of a work of art, we immerse ourselves in an experience in which different rules are present. There is a tyranny of form and structure present, "a necessity which demands that no line, no sound could be replaced" (1978a, p. 42). Because the rules of creative and artistic necessity are radically different from those governing social and economic necessity, works of art that adhere to aesthetic rules induce an estrangement from contemporary life. In this way "art breaks open a dimension inaccessible to other experiences, a dimension in which human beings, nature, and things no longer stand under the law of the established reality principle" (1978a, p. 72). The rules that make for effective art (effectiveness being defined as the capacity to induce an altered consciousness) are quite separate from the rules that make for effective adult education practice, to take one example. Art "has its own language and illuminates reality only through this other language" (p. 22).

Although he does not draw explicitly on Marcuse, Newman's (1999) provocative meditation on images of adult learning contains several examples of how immersion in the different language of artistic experience is inherently emancipatory. Describing the activities of Australian surfers, he notices how the different grammar of surfing—"sensing the currents, noting their distance from the rocks, maintaining their balance on a narrow piece of fibreglass, watching the water for unwelcome shadows" (p. 92)—induces an altered sense of reality. Referring to the intense concentration surfing induces, Newman declares that "this form of focused reverie can result in profound personal and political change" (p. 92). Later in his book he describes attending a production of Shakespeare's *The Tempest*, with Patrick Stewart (better known as Captain Jean Luc Picard in TV's *Star Trek: The Next Generation*) as Prospero. Newman writes that "Prospero uses conflict openly to generate learning and promote change" (p. 175) and sees him as "an eccentric and passionate learner and educator, driven by anger at injustice, a belief that the world could be a better place, and a readiness, given the opportunity, to intervene in order to shift people towards his view of the world" (p. 175). In Marcuse's terms, Prospero, like other dramatic protagonists, restructures our view of life "through concentration, exaggeration, emphasis on the essential, reordering of facts" (Marcuse, 1978a, p. 45) and other dramatic devices. In the hands of Shakespeare, Prospero, and Patrick Stewart, "the aesthetic transformation turns into an indictment— but also into a celebration of that which resists injustice and terror, and of that which can still be saved" (p. 45).

In contemplating artistic forms, Marcuse believes we catch glimpses of other realities, of what our world could be like if technological, social, and economic domination were removed. But these glimpses can only be apprehended through deliberately unreal artistic depictions. In a world in which the injunction to "get real" means to adapt yourself to the brutal reality of everyday life, the unreal expresses people's yearnings for a different world. To Marcuse, "the world of a work of art is 'unreal' in the ordinary sense of this word; it is a fictitious reality" (1978a, p. 54). However, in its fictitious or illusory form, art "contains more truth than does everyday reality . . . only in the illusory world do things appear as what they are and what they can be" (p. 54).

This is because what we name as reality is actually a state of servitude, a way of living in which the needs we feel, and the satisfactions we enjoy, are essentially false. If, on the one hand, capitalism produces deception, illusion, and mystification, then "art, on the other hand, does not conceal that which is—it reveals" (1978a, p. 56). When artistic immersion induces an intense engagement with the stylized representation of a painting, play, or poem, we are nudged toward a perception of life as "more as well as qualitatively 'other' than the established reality" (ibid.). From this perspective it is art that now holds empirical truth and "it is the given reality, the ordinary world which now appears as untrue, as false, as deceptive reality" (p. 56). When a play, song, or film draws us into a stylized "other" universe, we experience an estranged state of being in which we are liberated from the so-called reality of daily life; "the intensification of perception can go as far as to distort things so that the unspeakable is spoken, the otherwise invisible becomes visible, and the unbearable explodes" (1978a, p. 45).

Who produces art of such stylized intensity? Is it those who dedicate their life to socialist transformation? Not according to Marcuse. Those with no political consciousness can create just as powerful images of revolutionary other-worldness as lifelong revolutionaries. We cannot assume that working-class or minority artists produce art of greater revolutionary power than do the White bourgeoisie. In Marcuse's view, "the progressive character of art, its contribution to the struggle for liberation, cannot be measured by the artists' origins nor by the ideological horizon of their class" (1978a, p. 19). Whether or not art is progressive is determined by criteria intrinsic to the work itself, not by the artist's birthplace. Famously, Marcuse declared that "Marxist theory is not family research" (p. 19). The revolutionary significance of art lies solely in its transcendent power; "the radical qualities of art . . . are grounded precisely in the dimensions where art *transcends* its social determination and emancipates itself from the given universe of discourse and behavior while observing its overwhelming presence" (1978a, p. 6).

When Negativity Becomes Positive: Adult Education for Critical Thinking

If we live in a society in which thought is circumscribed within certain limits that justify the correctness of the existing order, then critical thought must by definition exist outside of and in opposition to these limits. This is Marcuse's position on what it means to be a critical thinker, and it is very far from the kind of positive cheerleading for critical thinking as a productive activity that I, amongst others, have written about (Brookfield, 1987a). Just as rebellious subjectivity can only develop at a distance from everyday experience, so critical thinking is distanced from the false concreteness of everyday reasoning. In his view, "an irreducible difference exists between the universe of everyday thinking and language on the one side, and that of philosophic thinking and language on the other" (1964, p. 178). The latter is conceptual in nature and deals with universals. Thus, "critical philosophic thought is necessarily transcendent and abstract" based on a "dissociation from the material practice" (p. 134) of everyday life. Critical thinking in this view, therefore, is inherently philosophical and conceptual.

In stressing the universal, conceptual elements of critical thinking, Marcuse is at odds with those adult educators like myself who have emphasized that the road to criticality begins with examining the specific experiences of adult learners. He challenges us to rethink our dismissal of conceptual analysis as an irrelevant game played only by ivory tower academics distanced from revolutionary struggle. In his view the anti-intellectual mistrust of theorizing "serves well the interests of the powers that be" (Marcuse, 1978b, p. 63). Marcuse views it as a tactical mistake for adult educators to focus only on communicating with learners through colloquial, street language in an effort to create a personal connection. In a dominated, administered society, street language—the metaphors, slang, and expressions of everyday life—is by definition falsely concrete. Daily language is imbued with the belief that we must always apply thought to making the existing system work more smoothly. It diverts people from considering the possibility of radically different ways of thinking and living. By this logic, abstract conceptual thought is inherently critical and critical thought is inherently abstract.

Not only does critical thinking operate at a necessary level of abstractness, it is also negative. As articulated by three of Marcuse's students, "negative thinking is first and foremost critical thinking" (Leiss, Ober, and Sherover, 1967, p. 424) because it "opposes the self-contentment of common sense which is so ready to embrace the given and to accept the established fact" (p. 424). Critical thinking focuses on what's wrong with what currently exists, on illuminating omissions, distortions, and falsities in current thinking. In Newman's (1994) terms, critical thinking is about laying blame. A negative appraisal of "commonsense" reasoning (such as the reasoning informing justifications for invading other countries) is the first step in developing a framework for the kind of thought that could replace what now exists. So what in the short term seems negative is in the long term positive. Marcuse argues that before we have the great liberation and the creation of what could be, we need the great refusal, the rejection of what is. Those participating in the great refusal "reject the rules of the game that is rigged against them, the ancient strategy of patience and persuasion, the reliance on the Good Will in the Establishment, its false and immoral comforts, its cruel affluence" (1969, p. 6). Saying "no" to a culture of domination is a positive act.

What kind of adult education can prepare adults to think crit-ically in this necessarily negative manner? First and foremost it will be a conceptually based adult education. Marcuse is certainly very ready to give all kinds of strategic advice on direct political action, but he never left behind his fundamental conviction that learning to think conceptually was as much part of the revolution as creating new political and economic structures. In the administered society of dominated thought, any kind of conceptual abstract reasoning is by definition critical. Hence, a fundamental task of adult education is to "provide the student with the conceptual instruments for a solid and thorough critique of the material and intellectual culture" (1969, p. 61).

As with his emphasis on the importance of isolation and privacy in the development of rebellious subjectivity, Marcuse's insistence on adults learning to think conceptually challenges practices lionized in adult education. In particular, his position seems to stand against the celebratory aspects of experiential learning. But if we accept the contention that most people's experiences are falsely concrete, then celebrating and dignifying them—even integrating them directly into the curriculum—only serves to legitimize the existing society. Experiential learning would have meaning for Marcuse only if it focused on deconstructing experiences and showing their one-dimensional nature and if it avoided the uncritical celebration of people's stories. From his perspective experiential learning would be learning to recognize how the ways we perceive and construct experience have been colonized by the dominant language of consumerism. Marcuse also seems to question the wisdom of "starting where the students are," long a prized tenet of the progressive canon. If where the students are is living a falsely concrete existence, then we need to get as far away from where they are as is possible, chiefly by insisting on conceptual analysis. The struggle to think conceptually is always a political struggle to Marcuse, not just a matter of intellectual development. Politics and cognitive movement are partners here in the development of revolutionary consciousness.

An important part of conceptual learning for Marcuse is the development of a new language. Although he rejects the ritualized invocation of Marxist jargon, he still feels that an important educational task is "the effort to free words (and thereby concepts) from the all but total distortion of their meanings by the Establishment"

(1969, p. 8). Developing new language is crucial if people are to learn to recognize their servitude and expose the comfortable consumerism to which they are enslaved. Language operates at the deepest levels of thought to frame the concepts adults use to name and interpret their experiences, and its control by the managers of the administered society effectively prevents any revolutionary awareness from emerging. Oppositional movements need "a language that reaches a population which has introjected the needs and values of their masters and managers and made them their own, thus reproducing the established system in their minds, their consciousness, their senses and instincts" (1972, p. 80). Consequently, the study of linguistics, as well as an immersion in the stylizations of art, could be understood as an important part of political adult education. When adults start to realize how language is socially formed and learned, they take a big step toward becoming politically literate (a theme Paulo Freire explored in his life and work). The creation of a new language is also an important moment of transition in a political movement; "if the radical opposition develops its own language, it protests spontaneously, subconsciously, against one of the most effective 'secret weapons' of domination and defamation" (1969, p. 74).

What does Marcuse think would be the features of an adult educational practice that developed the capacity for negative critical thinking and that encouraged rebuilding a language of liberation? For one thing there would be a clear distinction between adult educators and adult learners. Marcuse departs somewhat from the andragogical and collaborative traditions in the field to emphasize that adult educators cannot be as one with adult learners and that adults cannot liberate themselves without participating in formally planned programs of adult education. For him, "self-liberation is self-education but as such it presupposes education by others" (1972, p. 47). This is because society is organized to keep people away from disturbing ideas and to promote a state of happy stupefaction. Those lucky enough to have access to revolutionary knowledge and information "have a commitment to use their knowledge to help men and women realize and enjoy their truly human capabilities" (p. 47).

A program of adult education designed to reverse years of induced stupefaction would need to be highly organized and staffed by well-trained activists. Those who reach adulthood with little capacity for conceptual thought, and without access to a language untainted by metaphors and connotations of domination, will not have their sensibilities changed or imaginations awakened by a few workshops or courses. One class cannot undo a lifetime's ideological acculturation. Instead "the intensive indoctrination and management of the people call for an intensive counter-education and organization" (1972, p. 47). Those in charge of programs of counterindoctrination will be exercising leadership that is "educated and tested in the theory and practice of radical opposition" (p. 47). This kind of leadership will not be exercised in formal classrooms but within existing and nascent social movements. Here we see Marcuse at one with adult education activists and theorists such as Horton and Freire (1990) who see adult educators working within communities and social movements to help those adults involved learn skills of organization, advocacy, and tactical planning. To Marcuse, "the function of this leadership is to 'translate' spontaneous protest into organized action" (1972, p. 47).

There is also a role for adult educators to work as developers of consciousness. Marcuse does not believe that intellectuals who are not drawn from the working class are necessarily compromised. He acknowledges that leftist, middle-class intellectuals can form "catalyst groups" who "because of the privilege of their education and training—develop their intelligence, their theory, largely remote from the material process of production" (Marcuse, 1978b, p. 72). Once again isolation, separation, and distance are seen as constituting a form of revolutionary privacy. Although not a substitute for working-class activism, leftist middle-class intellectuals have as their main task "the development of consciousness—trying to counteract the management and control of consciousness by the established power structure" (p. 72).

Education as the Practice of Liberating Tolerance

As a practicing educator, Marcuse often returns to the dynamics of teaching and learning, particularly the tendency to embrace diverse curricular perspectives in the name of democracy. In one of the essays that is most unsettling to adult education, he argues that an all-embracing tolerance of diverse views always ends up legitimizing an unfair status quo. Marcuse's students observe that in their observation of him it became clear that "the essential element of Marcuse's teaching is that knowledge is partisan" (Leiss, Ober, and Sherover, 1967, p. 425). In their judgment he repeatedly emphasized "the role of the philosopher in challenging the beliefs and assumptions of ordinary life and indeed in abolishing the entire structure of established existence" (p. 425). This was done in a serious but not solemn way; "in informal lectures and informal discussions his teaching is generally spiced with irony and humor directed at the sacred cows of the Establishment . . . a characteristic of those who are truly serious" (p. 425). Marcuse's explicit partisanship is at odds with contemporary humanistic adult education sensibilities which emphasize the facilitator presenting students with an array of viewpoints and letting them make up their own minds. Marcuse's charismatic presence was also at odds with adult education's dislike of the cult of the personality. Angela Davis describes how "when Marcuse walked onto the platform, situated at the lowest level of the hall, his presence dominated everything. There was something imposing about him which evoked total silence and attention when he appeared, without his having to pronounce a single word. The students had a rare respect for him" (Davis, 1974, p. 134). The seriousness, even solemnity of his presence, seems light years away from the kind of dialogic interplay urged on adult educators by luminaries such as Lindeman, Freire, and Horton.

Marcuse certainly thought of education as a serious activity. To him "the struggle for a free and critical education becomes a vital part in the larger struggle for change" (1969, p. 61). He quotes the German activist Rudi Dutschke's idea of a long march through institutions, of activists "working against the established institutions while working in them" (1972, p. 55). Learning is central to this march as change agents learn how to program computers, to develop socially critical instructional materials that connect with learners of different levels, and to use the mass media as educational tools. Sometimes these agents are able to establish alternative educational systems—open schools, free universities, and so on. At other times they work within existing schools and colleges to help students recognize technological domination and its reproduction.

One of the chief inhibitors to developing this recognition in learners is teachers' willingness to run discussions and develop curricula in which a variety of perspectives are present. On the face of it, this hardly seems like a problem. Indeed, a broadening of curriculum to include radical ideas seems an important and obvious part of building a critical practice of adult education. In one of his most famous essays, however, Marcuse (1965a) argues that such tolerance is often repressive, not liberating. The central thesis of his essay—that "what is proclaimed and practiced as tolerance today, is in many of its most effective manifestations serving the cause of oppression" (p. 81)—extends the concept of hegemony and has important implications for the practice of adult education. When they experience repressive tolerance, adults mistakenly believe they live in an open society characterized by freedom of speech and expression. In such a society, adult learners assume they can freely choose to plan and conduct learning projects that spring from their innermost desires.

Repressive tolerance is the tolerance, in the name of impartiality, fairness, or even-handedness, of intolerable ideologies and practices, and the consequent marginalization of efforts for democratic social change. It is also a tolerance for just enough challenge to the system to convince people that they live in a truly open society, while still maintaining structural inequity. This tolerance of challenge and diversity functions as a kind of pressure cooker letting off enough steam to prevent the whole pot from boiling over. When repressive tolerance is in place, the apparent acceptance of all viewpoints only serves to reinforce an unfair status quo. This is because "tolerance is extended to policies, conditions and modes of behavior which should not be tolerated because they are impeding, if not destroying, the chances of creating an existence without fear and misery" (p. 82). In a society in which a small number of people hold a disproportionate amount of wealth and power, and in which ideological obfuscation ensures the reproduction of the system, tolerance only serves to reinforce the status quo. In Marcuse's words, "The conditions of tolerance are 'loaded' . . . determined and defined by the institutionalized inequality . . . i.e. by the class structure of society" (p. 85). When "false consciousness has become the general consciousness" (p. 110), tolerance ensures that alternative, oppositional perspectives are rendered ineffectual. When we have a "passive toleration of entrenched and established attitudes and ideas even if their damaging effect on man and nature

is evident" (p. 85), then the apparently benign "ideology of tolerance . . . in reality, favors and fortifies the conservation of the status quo of inequality and discrimination" (p. 123).

How does repressive tolerance work? Essentially, repressive tolerance is hegemonic, a taken for granted notion embedded in the
ideology of democracy. Corporations and media perpetuate the
idea of tolerance as democratic fairness, thereby creating a social
mentality which accepts that things are organized for the good of
all. But what counts as truth is predefined by these institutions so
that avenues of opposition are subtly closed off. Marcuse argues that
"under the rule of monopolistic media—themselves mere instruments of economic and political power—a mentality is created for
which right and wrong, true and false are predefined wherever they
affect the vital interests of the society" (p. 95). Language—in contemporary terms, discursive practices and relations—is controlled
to maintain oppression; "the meaning of words is rigidly stabilized
. . . the avenues of entrance are closed to the meaning of words and
ideas other than the established one" (p. 96).

Repressive tolerance masks its repression behind the façade of
open even-handedness. Alternative ideas are not banned. Critical
texts are published and critical messages circulated. The defenders
of the status quo can point to the existence of dissenting voices
(such as Marcuse's) as evidence of the open society we inhabit and
the active tolerance of a wide spectrum of ideologies. But the framing of meaning accomplished by hegemony is all. Sometimes the
meaning of radical texts is diluted by the fact the texts themselves
are hard to get or incredibly expensive. More likely the radical
meanings are neutered because they are framed as the expressions
of an obviously weird minority opinion. As Marcuse writes, "Other
words can be spoken and heard, other ideas can be expressed, but,
at the massive scale of the conservative majority . . . they are immediately 'evaluated' (i.e. automatically understood) in terms of the
public language—a language which determined 'a priori' the direction in which the thought process moves. Thus the process of reflection ends where it started: in the given conditions and relations" (p.
96). Like Fromm, Marcuse cites Orwell's analysis of language in
illustrating how words are used to mean their opposite. For example, the meaning of peace is redefined so that "preparing for war *is*

working for peace" (p. 96). Supporters of the 2003 unilateral American invasion of Iraq frequently used this formulation.

A crucial component of repressive tolerance is the metanarrative of democratic tolerance. This narrative is ideologically embedded in the way adult educators sometimes think of democratic discussion, where the intent is to honor and respect each learner's voice. But the implicit assumption that all contributions to a discussion carry equal weight can easily lead to a flattening of conversation. A discussion leader's concern to dignify each adult's personhood can result in a refusal to point out the ideologically skewed nature of particular contributions, let alone saying someone is wrong. In Marcuse's view, the ideology of democratic tolerance in adult discussion groups means that "the stupid opinion is treated with the same respect as the intelligent one, the misinformed may talk as long as the informed, and propaganda rides along with falsehood. This pure tolerance of sense and nonsense is justified by the democratic argument that nobody, neither group nor individual, is in possession of the truth and capable of defining what is right and wrong, good and bad" (p. 94). As we saw earlier, Marcuse's explanation for this is people's unfamiliarity with abstract, conceptual thought. False concreteness means that discussion participants are unable to think in terms of universal moral imperatives, reverting instead to a position in which any idea or practice is right or wrong depending on the circumstance.

Under repressive tolerance the airing of a radical perspective as one among many possible viewpoints on a situation always works to the detriment of that perspective. This is because participants are disposed to skepticism or hostility regarding new ideas due to their formative ideological conditioning. Thus "persuasion through discussion and the equal presentation of opposites (even where it is really equal) easily lose their liberating force as factors of understanding and learning; they are far more likely to strengthen the established thesis and to repel the alternatives" (p. 97). In a contemporary analysis of the discourse of multicultural inclusion, San Juan (2002) adopts a Marcusean posture by arguing that such discourse (and its related practices of celebrating diversity) only serve to affirm the legitimacy of the capitalist status quo. Heretically (at least to many adult educators) Marcuse even suggests that with some people discussion is a waste of time. In his view "there are in fact large groups in the population with whom discussion is hopeless" (1970, p. 102) owing to the rigidity of their opinions. So the best thing to do, in Marcuse's opinion, is avoid talking to them.

The only way to make democracy a reality, in Marcuse's view, is to have its participants in full possession of all relevant information. He argues that "the democratic argument implies a necessary condition, namely that the people must be capable of deliberating and choosing on the basis of knowledge, that they must have access to authentic information, and that, on this basis, their evaluation must be the result of autonomous thought" (p. 95). In stressing the necessity of adult autonomous thought, Marcuse takes us right to the idea of self-direction but a politicized interpretation of that idea that avoids collapsing into the self-indulgent reiteration of familiar ideas. For him self-direction exists when individuals are "freed from the repressive requirements of a struggle for existence in the interest of domination" (p. 105) and able to choose where best to exercise their creativity. In exhibiting the capacity to think autonomously, people are thus demonstrating their maturity. Marcuse quotes J. S. Mill's argument that democracy only works if those involved are "human beings in the maturity of their faculty . . . capable of being improved by free and equal discussion" (p. 86).

A crucial step toward autonomous thinking is to smash the myths of objectivity and impartiality that allow false consciousness to become mainstream consciousness. Marcuse believes that we must "break the established universe of meaning (and the practice enclosed within this universe)" (p. 98) so that people are "freed from the prevailing indoctrination (which is no longer recognized as indoctrination)" (p. 99). In a society living under false consciousness, people "are indoctrinated by the conditions under which they live and think and which they do not transcend" (p. 98). To help them emerge from this, they need to realize that truth is manipulated, that the "facts" "are established, mediated, by those who made them" (p. 99). They need to shed the tolerance for multiple truths, each of which is presumed to have its own integrity and internal validity, and realize instead that "there *is* an objective truth which can be discovered, ascertained only in learning and comprehending that which is and that which can be and ought to be done for the sake of improving the lot of mankind" (p. 88). This objective truth is a liberatory truth concerning the need to abolish the one-dimensional society, and it must always take precedence over a supposedly respectful, but ultimately repressive, tolerance of all viewpoints. To Marcuse "tolerance cannot be indiscriminate and equal . . . it cannot protect false words and wrong deeds which demonstrate that they contradict and counteract the possibilities of liberation" (p. 88).

The key point for Marcuse is that learning to break free of one-dimensional thought requires a necessary rupture with the appearance of facts and truth. This rupture "cannot be accomplished within the established framework of abstract tolerance and spurious objectivity because these are precisely the factors which precondition the mind *against* the rupture" (p. 99). Providing a smorgasbord of alternative views, traditions, and perspectives in the name of a pluralist tolerance of diversity only ensures that the radical ones are marginalized by the dominant consciousness. The only way to break with the face of spurious impartiality is to immerse adults fully and exclusively in a radically different perspective that challenges mainstream ideology and confronts the learner with "information slanted in the opposite direction" (p. 99). After all, "unless the student learns to think in the opposite direction, he will be inclined to place the facts into the predominant framework of values" (p. 113).

This forced rupture with mainstream reality will inevitably be castigated as undemocratic censorship, a criticism Marcuse expects as the predictable response of organized repression and indoctrination. But he is firm that "the ways should not be blocked on which a subversive majority could develop, and if they are blocked by organized repression and indoctrination, their reopening may require apparently undemocratic means" (p. 100). An intolerance of certain teaching practices (Marcuse does not specify which) may also be called for if students are to develop autonomous thought. He writes that "the restoration of freedom of thought may necessitate new and rigid restrictions on teachings and practices in the educational institutions which, by their very methods and concepts, serve to enclose the mind within the established universe of discourse and behavior—thereby precluding a priori a rational evaluation of the alternatives" (pp. 100–101).

In a society characterized by repressive tolerance, the dominant minority—particular corporations and the media—claim that an open marketplace for the dissemination of ideas by all exists, when in reality they exercise an ideological monopoly. To Marcuse, the free exchange of ideas is a myth since it is the White Right that has the purchasing power to buy control of the media. In such a situation the truly fair thing is to discriminate in favor of the Left, or racially grounded perspectives, and to give a preponderance of space to subtly discredited discourses such as Africentrism, feminism, queer theory, and postcolonialism. Because the roar of the corporate mainstream media drowns out dissenting voices, we need positive discrimination in favor of "the small and powerless minorities which struggle against the false consciousness and its beneficiaries" (Marcuse, 1965a, p. 110). These should be helped because "their continued existence is more important than the preservation of abused rights and liberties which grant constitutional powers to those who oppress these minorities" (p. 110). Hence, "the exercise of civil rights by those who don't have them presupposes the withdrawal of civil rights from those who prevent their exercise" (p. 110). This is a kind of community-sponsored intellectual affirmative action in favor of leftist perspectives; "withdrawal of tolerance from regressive movements, and discriminating tolerance in favor of progressive tendencies would be tantamount to the 'official' promotion of subversion" (p. 107).

So, for Marcuse, the end of a democratic access to objective truth justifies the means of censoring dominant, mainstream ideas and discriminating in favor of outlawed knowledges. Realizing the objective of tolerance calls "for intolerance toward prevailing policies, attitudes, opinions, and the extension of tolerance to policies, attitudes, and opinions which are outlawed or suppressed" (p. 81). Although early in the essay he states that "censorship of art and literature is regressive under all circumstances" (p. 89), twenty-one pages later, in outlining the necessary steps to stop the development of false consciousness, he argues that such efforts "must begin with stopping the words and images which feed this consciousness. To be sure this is censorship, even precensorship, but openly directed against the more or less hidden censorship that permeates the free media" (p. 111). Not only should words and images (literature and art) be censored, we also need to censor the right of speech and assembly. In an argument preceding contemporary "hate speech" policies, Marcuse stated that it was important to stop privileged groups preaching hateful intolerance but using the umbrella of tolerance of diversity as cover. A full and proper consideration of disallowed ideas can only happen by "the withdrawal of toleration of speech and assembly from groups and movements which promote aggressive policies, armament, chauvinism, discrimination on the grounds of race and religion, or which oppose the extension of public services, social security, medical care" (p. 100).

As can be imagined, Marcuse's vigorous assertion of the need to censor conservative viewpoints proved highly contentious and was responsible for much of the notoriety mentioned at the beginning of the chapter. But he points out that his own life has suffered the consequences of repressive tolerance. He writes that "if the Nazi movement had not been tolerated once it revealed its character, which was quite early, if it had not enjoyed the benefits of that democracy, then we probably would not have experienced the horrors of the Second World War and some other horrors as well" (Marcuse, 1970, p. 99). For him the example of Nazi Germany provides a powerful illustration of "an unequivocal position according to which we can say: here are moments that should not be tolerated if an improvement and pacification of human life is to be attained" (p. 99).

As a proponent of the view that critical theory is always critical of its own assumptions, it is not surprising that Marcuse's work challenges familiar practices suggested by a critical theory of adult learning. Adult educators in the critical tradition envisage teachers and learners engaged in a collaborative cocreation of knowledge as they embrace a diversity of perspectives and experiences. Marcuse adds some useful dissonance and counterpoint to this progressive symphony of tolerance, diversity, and collaboration. He reestablishes a justifiable difference between educators and learners. He forces us to pay attention to elements of subjectivity—isolation, distance, privacy, memory—that are too easily dismissed as examples of privatized ways of being and learning. He reestablishes the importance of aesthetics as a spur to adults' disengagement from the dominant culture, and as offering criteria we can use to build a liberated society. He challenges the self-evident truth

218 THE POWER OF CRITICAL THEORY

that a tolerant embrace of diverse views is inherently humanistic and democratic and confronts us with the uncomfortable proposition that there should be an intolerance of diversity, if diversity is set up to ensure that antidemocratic forces prevail. If diverse perspectives are reviewed against a backdrop in which one perspective is thrown into sharp relief, this does not equalize diversity. What is needed for true diversity is a total immersion in a completely different set of perspectives not widely accessible, as would happen, say, if an adult education doctoral program deliberately immersed its students only in an Africentric perspective.

Finally, Marcuse builds a bridge between critical theory and cultural studies with its focus on the dominating influence of popular culture. To Marcuse it is as important to study popular aesthetic forms—architecture, songs, commercials, films, magazines—as it is to study the distribution of wealth. In an era when adult educational practices are all too easily labeled as transformative or liberatory, we need to read Marcuse to see that liberation is not just a matter of opening ourselves to new perspectives or even of altering economic and political structures. Learning liberation in adulthood requires a deep-seated change in the ways we experience the world that takes place at an instinctual, sensual level.

Chapter Eight

Reclaiming Reason

In this and the following chapter, I review the work of Jürgen Habermas, the contemporary critical theorist who is most prominent in the consciousness of adult education. Over the course of his career, Habermas has been ready to connect critical theory to a wide range of contemporary concerns and events, most recently the September 11, 2001 attacks on the World Trade Center in New York (Borradori, Habermas, and Derrida, 2003). In the field of adult education, his ideas have been highly influential to the development of transformative learning theory (Mezirow, 1991a, 2000) and to other attempts to develop a critical theory of adult learning (Welton 1991, 1993, 1995, 2000, 2001, 2003; Collins 1991, 1998; Hart, 1990). One reason for his influence is that he connects directly to the Lindemanian strain of adult education that emphasizes discussion and dialog as quintessential practices in the field. A recent comparative analysis of Freire and Habermas points out that both these thinkers share a commitment to dialogical, communicative learning as a fundamentally democratic process (Morrow and Torres, 2002). In Morrow and Torres' view, Habermas, like Freire, articulates a "critical theory of society that seeks to bridge between revolutionary Marxism and reformist liberalism" (p. 3).

In this chapter I sketch out Habermas' place in the broader critical theory tradition and review his attempt to reclaim reason from the instrumentalized void it was exiled to in Horkheimer and Adorno's *Dialectic of Enlightenment* (1972). The bulk of the chapter examines the three crises Habermas believes Western societies are facing—the decline of the public sphere (the informal arenas in which citizens meet to talk through societal crises and issues), the threat to civil society (the organizations and associations, not directly controlled by the state or corporations, in which we live our lives), and the invasion of the lifeworld (the clusters of preconscious understandings that structure how we see the world and communicate our understandings to others). These crises all signify a loss in people's ability to apply reason to the discussion and resolution of common social problems. His analysis of how we can learn our way out of these crises through communicative action and deliberative democracy follow in Chapter Nine.

Habermas and Adult Education

It all started with Jack Mezirow. In 1981, in an article that filled in the theoretical background to his earlier work on perspective transformation, Mezirow published "A Critical Theory of Adult Learning and Education" (Mezirow, 1981). As an English adult educator, at that time working in London and Leicester as a researcher for the ill-fated national Advisory Council for Adult and Continuing Education (ACACE) of England and Wales, I read Mezirow's article with a sense of surprise. In my ethnocentric arrogance, I had assumed that things theoretical were the exclusive concern of European adult education and that American adult education was hopelessly fixated on empirical matters of practice. Little did I guess that in the following year I would be working as Mezirow's colleague at Teachers Colleague in New York and that he would become both a close personal friend (I was married in his apartment) and an important model for me of a scholar who conducted a continuous critical inquiry into his own theoretical positions.

That 1981 article had far-reaching consequences for adult education scholarship. For a significant number of adult educators, it offered a very different theoretical slant to the then almost exclusive focus on andragogy and self-directed learning. Subsequently, it ushered in a host of confirmatory studies (Taylor, 1997, 2000a, 2000b) designed to extend and refine Mezirow's theoretical insights. It also prompted a vigorous debate between Mezirow and his interpreters and critics (see for example, Collard and Law, 1989; Clark and Wilson, 1991; Tennant, 1993; Mezirow, 1989, 1991b, 1992, 1994b, 1997). Mezirow subsequently broadened his ideas into a full-blown theory of adult transformative learning (1990, 1991a, 2000) that has been enormously influential. Because of Jack Mezirow, scholarship in the field has become much more self-consciously theoretical.

What was surprising to many about Mezirow's 1981 article was the fact that his theory of adult learning explicated the ideas of a German intellectual—Jürgen Habermas—whose work had only recently appeared in English. In a series of books published in the 1970s (Habermas, 1970, 1971, 1973, 1975, 1979), Habermas developed a concept of democracy grounded in a theory of communication. He accepted critical theory's articulation of the extension of technocratic consciousness into everyday life but argued that a theory concerned with human liberation should replace the Marxist emphasis on how people organize and conduct their patterns of production with a focus on how they organize and conduct their patterns of communication. If we could understand the conditions necessary for people to participate in full, free, and equal discourse, Habermas argued, then we would have a theory—the theory of communicative action—that would guide the operation of democracy.

Mezirow's 1981 article took Habermas' concern with the emancipatory dimensions of communicative action, reinterpreted emancipatory action as adult perspective transformation, and linked this to contemporary adult educational ideas of self-directed learning and andragogy. In viewing these concepts through a Habermasian lens, Mezirow introduced adult educators who had been comfortable with the tradition of humanistic psychology to the realization that a more conflictual, Marxist-inclined approach to interpreting adult learning processes was possible. Since 1981 Mezirow has moved beyond Habermas' work and, in a manner echoing Habermas' own intellectual eclecticism, has crossed theoretical traditions as diverse as linguistics, information processing, artificial intelligence, and cognitive development. As Mezirow develops his ever-expanding theory of transformative learning, it has fallen to others to interpret the relevance of Habermas' constantly evolving body of work for adult education. Of these interpreters, Michael Welton is undoubtedly the most prominent.

In a series of articles and chapters, Welton (1991, 1993, 1995, 2000, 2001, 2003) has parlayed Habermas' own convoluted, dense, endlessly hyphenated prose into a passionate and lucid justification of adult educators' need to move beyond simplistic declarations of the importance of social transformation to "speak in a more self-limiting and precise way about the asymmetrical relationship between the system (state and work) and the lifeworld (civil society)" (Welton, 2001, p. 32). Giving up "the old Marxian dream of total change" (p. 32) is necessary in Habermas' (and Welton's) view if we are to work to achieve realistic and specific social changes in particular contexts. They argue that because the industrial working class is no longer the chief engine of revolutionary change our efforts at resistance must be located in social movements and grassroots activism across a wide range of issues. Habermas and Welton both believe this is the only realistic chance we have of preserving, let alone extending, the democratic process within civil society. They argue that learning how to defend the lifeworld against the system and how to restrict the increasing influence of steering mechanisms within the public sphere (ideas to be considered later in this chapter) are adult learning projects at the heart of twenty-first century democracy.

Locating Habermas in the Critical Theory Tradition

Habermas is the contemporary figure who most probably comes quickest to adult educators' minds when the term *critical theory* is mentioned, and there is no doubt that his ideas have been strongly influenced by that tradition. However, Habermas himself mentions many times that he was not formally schooled in the tradition (indeed, he belonged to the Hitler Youth in his early adolescence) and that knowledge of it came through his own self-education. In Habermas' view, the Frankfurt School never really existed as a cohesive group of scholars pursuing a distinctive intellectual project when it was located in Frankfurt. It was only during the 1930s exile of the school's members in New York that it really came to life (Habermas, 1985b, p. 68). Undeniably, though, Habermas' own intellectual journey and his autobiography are inextricably intertwined with critical theory. He was hired as Adorno's research assistant, came to occupy the Max Horkheimer Chair in Philosophy and Sociology at the Frankfurt Institute, and could speak about his personal conversations with Marcuse just before Marcuse's death (Habermas, 1992a).

Habermas' own positioning within critical theory is a complex matter. At times he refers to himself as a Marxist, declaring in one breath that "today I value being considered a Marxist" while in the next breath cautioning that "I'm not a Marxist in the sense of believing in Marxism as a sure-fire explanation" (1992a, p. 82). For him Marxism is a useful heuristic tool to understand the logic of capitalism's development, providing "the impetus and the analytical means to investigate the development of the relationship between democracy and capitalism" (p. 82). In Habermas' view, "the fundamental question posed by Marx" is "how capitalist expansion . . . affects the structure of the life-world" (1992a, p. 91). This question, as we shall see later in this chapter, is also fundamentally important to Habermas himself.

In line with Marx, Habermas sees theorizing as having an explicitly emancipatory intent. The purpose of theorizing about society is to understand the mechanisms and relations at play so that these can be altered to give greater opportunity for people to realize their creative potential. Historical materialism—Marx's theoretical understanding of how the organization of productive forces up to capitalism has shaped social evolution—is one such theory that helps us understand these mechanisms and relations. In Habermas' view the theory of historical materialism is bound up with humans' attempts to become more self-aware and "specifies the conditions under which reflection on the history of our species by members of this species has become objectively possible" (Habermas, 1973, p. 1). The theory's purpose is to galvanize the proletariat, and those bourgeois individuals who wish to aid the revolution, by providing insight into the process of revolutionary change. It "names those to whom this theory is addressed, who then with its aid can gain enlightenment about their emancipatory role in the process of history" (p. 2). In *Communication and the Evolution of Society* (1979), Habermas refers approvingly to historical materialism as "a theory that needs revision in many respects but whose potential for stimulation has still not been exhausted" (p. 94). He describes himself as engaged in a project to help it "attain more fully the goal it has set for itself" (p. 94), of providing guidelines for the creation of democratic socialism.

How does Habermas set about reconstructing Marxism for the twentieth and twenty-first centuries? Here the centrality of learning—particularly adult learning—clearly emerges. If a distinguishing characteristic of humans is their capacity to learn, then social science and educational theoreticians need to focus much more centrally on how adults learn to create a more moral, just democracy. Marx's mistake (to Habermas) was that he "localized the learning process impor- tant for evolution in the dimension of objectivating thought—of technical and organizational knowledge, of instrumental and strate- gic action, in short, of productive forces" (1979, p. 98). Concen- trating on how people learn to organize production efficiently and exploitatively is too restrictive a focus for adult learning theorists, given that the capacity for learning permeates all facets of adult life. In Habermas' view, "there are good reasons meanwhile for assum- ing that learning processes also take place in the dimension of moral insight, practical knowledge, communicative action, and the consensual regulation of action conflicts" (p. 98). If we are to pre- serve and extend the democratic process, we need to help adults learn how to anticipate and resolve the inevitable contradictions and tensions of democracy. So historical materialism should be broadened, in Habermas' view, to explore the "learning processes that are deposited in more mature forms of social integration, in new *productive relations,* that in turn first make possible the intro- duction of new productive forms" (p. 98).

For Habermas, then, "a critical theory of society can no longer be constructed in the exclusive form of a critique of political econ- omy" (1970, p. 120). It must broaden its concern to investigate mat- ters of morality and communication and how a democratic society might organize itself to promote the fullest and freest communica- tion possible amongst its members. Habermas has commented that "it was always my feeling that there was no adequate theory of democracy in Marxism" (1992a, p. 188) and that "the old Frankfurt school never took bourgeois democracy very seriously" (p. 99). So one thrust of his Marxist reconstruction is to reestablish the cre- ation of genuine democracy as the purpose of revolutionary change. This has led him to engage with American pragmatism, especially the work of Charles Pierce and his "radical-democratic humanism" or "logical socialism" (p. 189). Habermas acknowledges, "I have relied on this American version of the philosophy of praxis when the problem arises of compensating for the weaknesses of Marxism with respect to democratic theory" (p. 149). His debt to Pierce, Dewey, and other American pragmatists is evident in those times when he prefaces his observations with remarks like "as a good pragmatist" (Habermas 1985a, p. 198).

Habermas has also incorporated aspects of liberalism into his work, thus committing the ultimate betrayal of Marxism to many on the left. Acknowledging that "my Marxist friends are not entirely unjustified in accusing me of being a radical liberal" (1992a, p. 171), Habermas views the liberal ideal of personal freedom as an important criterion to employ when judging whether or not democracy exists. To him freedom is indivisible and universal and cannot be said to exist if any in a society are unfree. In his words, "the individual cannot be free unless all are free, and all cannot be free unless all are free in community" (p. 146). He is careful to distinguish freedom from anarchic selfishness, as in "do your own thing without regard to others." Freedom is a social relationship in which the rights one person takes to herself are extended to all others. Hence "freedom of choice in the last instance can only be thought in internal connection with a network of inter-personal relationships" (p. 146). It is present only "in the context of the communicative structures of a community, which ensures that the freedom of some is not achieved at the cost of the freedom of others" (p. 146).

The imperative of freedom applies equally to liberalism and socialism. For him "socialism and liberty are identical" (1992a, p. 75), and socialist theory is "an attempt . . . to indicate the necessary conditions which would have to be in place for emancipated life-forms to emerge" (p. 145). Socialism is a useful organizing idea that offers criteria we should consider when trying to organize society fairly. As such "it serves as the idea of the epitome of the necessary conditions for emancipated forms of life, about which the participants themselves would have to reach understanding" (Habermas, 1994, p. 113). This interpretation of socialism stresses its democratic imperatives, in the manner of Marcuse and Fromm, rather than the principle of collective ownership and control of the means of production. Socialism, for Habermas, is as much about establishing inclusive conversational forms as it is about nationalizing private industries.

In Habermas' view, critical theory not only overemphasizes the means of production but also stresses too much the way reason has become distorted under capitalism. To him, books such as *Eclipse of Reason* (Horkheimer, [1947] 1974) and *Dialectic of Enlightenment*

(Horkheimer and Adorno, 1972) "took refuge in an abstract critique of instrumental reason and made only a limited contribution to the empirical analysis of the over-complex reality of our society" (Habermas, 1992a, p. 56). Habermas does not agree with Horkheimer and Adorno that reason has been so totally instrumentalized that it has been denuded of all moral force. He is alarmed that *Dialectic of Enlightenment* (discussed in detail in Chapter Three) is forced "to oversimplify its image of modernity so astoundingly" (Habermas, 1987b, p. 112) in its effort to prove that "in cultural modernity, reason gets definitively stripped of its validity claim and assimilated to sheer power" (p. 112). He also makes the point that Horkheimer and Adorno use critical reason to prove the impossibility of using critical reason! In *Dialectic of Enlightenment,* the "description of the self-destruction of the critical capacity is paradoxical, because in the moment of description it still has to make use of the critique that has been declared dead" (Habermas, 1987b, p. 119).

Habermas places his own understanding of reason "much closer to the practical attitudes of Marcuse . . . to the idea that the life of theory is a project of practical reason, or conducted in its name" (Habermas, 1992a, p. 190). He declares his "special affinity with the existentialist, i.e. the Marcusean, variant of critical theory" (p. 150) that he believes affirms the possibility of reestablishing reason to serve the creation of a humane democracy. Marcuse beckons to Habermas because Marcuse "made appeals to future alternatives" (Habermas, 1985b, p. 67), "spoke a straight, affirmative language, easy to understand" (p. 69), and constantly displayed "one of his most admirable features—not to give into defeatism" (p. 76).

Leaving aside the reference to Marcuse's easy-to-understand language, Habermas' comments on Marcuse could apply equally to Habermas himself. If *Dialectic of Enlightenment* "holds out scarcely any prospect for an escape from the myth of purposive rationality that has turned into negative violence" (Habermas, 1987b, p. 114), then Habermas' own books set out to reclaim reason and place it at the center of his attempt to ground democracy in a theory of communication. In *Postmetaphysical Thinking* (Habermas, 1992b), he states as his aim "to defend and make fruitful for social theory a concept of reason that attends to the phenomenon of the lifeworld and permits the 'consciousness of society as a whole' . . . to be re-formulated on the basis of a theory of intersubjectivity" (p. 141). He disapproves of the radical critique "which equates reason as a whole with repression—and then fatalistically and ecstatically seeks refuge in something wholly Other" (p. 8). For him, dismissing reason as hopelessly compromised and the willing, uncritical servant of capitalism or technocracy is too simplistic. It throws the baby of critical reason applied in the cause of democracy out with the bath-water of compromised reason serving the cause of exploitation. Habermas' view of critical theory "retains a concept of reason which asserts itself simultaneously against both scientific mutilation and existentialist downgrading, and which is furthermore also critically applied to itself" (1992a, p. 55).

So the reclamation of reason as the heart of critical theory is a central theme in Habermas' work. Reason underscores his theory of communicative action, which focuses on the assessment of those validity claims (is what we say understandable, true, and sincere?) that Habermas believes are implicit in every speech act or utterance. His concept of the ideal speech situation—"a description of the conditions under which claims to truth and rightness can be discursively redeemed" (Habermas, 1992a, p. 171)—is, as we shall see in Chapter Nine, pivotal to his understanding of the place of reason in human communication. The ideal speech situation establishes an ideal of full, free, and equal discourse in which understandings and agreements are reached through the giving of reasons for action. He quite deliberately uses the ideal speech situation "to reconstruct the concept of reason, that is, a concept of communicative reason, which I would like to utilize against Adorno and Horkheimer's *Dialectic of Enlightenment*" (Habermas, 1992a, p. 93). The ideal of reason also lies at the heart of his discourse theory of deliberative democracy, which explores the reaching of decisions through rationally driven efforts to come to consensus. In fact reason, in Habermas' view, underlies the very survival of the species: "A species that depends for its survival on the structures of linguistic communication and co-operative, purposive-rational action must of necessity rely on reason. In the validity claims, however implicit, by means of which we are obliged to orientate ourselves in our communicative actions, a persistent, albeit repeatedly suppressed, claim of reason lies concealed" (p. 58).

Reason serves human emancipation, and critical theory's concern with emancipation is reaffirmed in Habermas' own work. He says he "cannot imagine any seriously critical social theory without an internal link to something like an emancipatory interest" (1992a, p. 193). Just as reason is a species-survival need, so is the desire for emancipation expressed as "the calling into question, and deepseated wish to throw off, relations which repress without necessity" (p. 194). The emancipatory drive for freedom is so "profoundly ingrained in the structure of human species . . . intimately built into the reproduction of human life" that it must be considered "part of the basic structure of the theory of cognitive interests" (p. 194). A critical theory of adult learning in a Habermasian key studies how people learn to realize this desire for freedom in their personal relationships and in the creation of genuinely democratic political forms. It also studies the forces and structures that attempt to prevent this freedom being realized.

Habermas connects the human striving for freedom with a version of ideology critique that is focused specifically on patterns and structures of communication. Ideology critique unmasks how ideas and theories that we accept as true, and definitions of what we consider reasonable conduct and aspirations, in reality serve to support the interests of the powerful. To Habermas, "ideology critique wants to show how . . . validity claims are determined by relationships of power" (1987b, p. 116). In a critical theory of communicative action, ideology critique reveals "the relations of power surreptitiously incorporated in the symbolic structures of speech and action" (Habermas, 1973, p. 12). Realizing how power relations are embedded in linguistic conventions is the necessary precursor to learning how to alter these same relations. In Habermas' view, "the relations of power embodied in systematically distorted communication can be attacked directly by the process of critique" with the resulting insights leading to "emancipation from unrecognized dependencies" (p. 9). Reason is claimed as crucial to freedom.

One of the central projects of critical theory is claiming freedom. Fromm, Marcuse, and Habermas are all concerned to release people from falsely created needs and help them make their own free choices regarding how they wish to think and live. Critics of critical theory, however, have often been very successful in framing it as a wholly materialistic discourse concerned only with economic arrangements. While it is true that critical theory springs from the desire to abolish the exchange economy of capitalism, the roots of that desire have less to do with creating worker cooperatives and redistributing wealth and more to do with allowing people to realize their creativity through the free choice of how they might use their labor. For Habermas, the whole point of people using reason to help rebuild civil society and the public sphere is so that they can then make free choices about the nature of that society and the issues they think are truly important. Given the valorization of freedom in American culture, a Habermasian emphasis on critical theory as the engine of freedom is a useful entry point into the critical tradition for many students.

Before leaving this discussion of Habermas' relationship to the critical theory tradition, it is important to note that Habermas stresses the self-critical nature of critical theory claimed in Chapter One as integral to criticality. In his estimation critical theory applies critical reason to its own propositions, which must always be considered provisional. He believes that critical theory "can only make pronouncements with a claim to propositional truth" (Habermas, 1992a, p. 101) and that we should conduct "the attempt to continue critical social theory in an unreservedly self-correcting and self-critical mode" (p. 212). Critical theory's lack of attention to empirical proof is a serious flaw in Habermas' opinion, and his own writing displays an astonishing grasp of empirical work in linguistics, anthropology, sociology, cognitive and developmental psychology, and economics. For him critical theory moves forward by engaging its critics on the one hand (something Habermas does constantly) and seeking empirical confirmation or refutation of its propositions on the other.

Problems Addressed by Critical Theory 1: The Decline of the Public Sphere

I read Habermas as a theorist of democracy who believes that a society is more or less democratic according to the processes its members use to come to decisions about matters that affect their lives. The more democratic the society, the fuller the information its citizens have access to and the fewer the distortions that constrain their communication. For Habermas democracy is all about communication—the freest, least-restricted communication possible. In his view the greater the freedom of conversation that people enjoy, the higher the chance that true critical reason—reason employed to create a just, humane democracy—will emerge.

Under contemporary industrial capitalism, however, certain social developments have inhibited the democratic way of life. Society has become too vast and complicated for everyone to sit round a table and talk about how they wish to arrange things. To use the terms that Habermas employs across his work, the public sphere has collapsed and both civil society and the lifeworld have become dominated by— steered by—mechanisms of money and power. Terms such as the *public sphere, lifeworld,* and so on are unfamiliar to many American adult educators and have prevented them from fully engaging with Habermas' work. But these concepts are so integral to his attempts to outline how democracy can be established that they cannot be avoided. I hope readers already familiar with these ideas will forgive my explication of their meaning in the rest of this chapter.

At the core of Habermas' concern about the loss of reason in modern life is the collapse of the public sphere. The public sphere is the civic space or "commons" in which adults come together to debate and decide their response to shared issues and problems. In simple terms it is like an enormous outdoor café full of people talking about concerns they share in common or a chat room in which people log on to register and exchange their views about something. Habermas sees the public sphere as "a network for communicating information and points of view; i.e. opinions expressing affirmative or negative attitudes" (Habermas, 1996, p. 360). The "streams of communication" that flow through this network "are, in the process, filtered and synthesized in such a way that they coalesce into bundles of topically specified *public* opinions" (p. 360). As people talk with varying degrees of informality about issues that affect them, viewpoints emerge that represent the chief clusters of their opinions and that are noticed by politicians, government officials, pollsters, media workers, and so on. As a result the opinions developed informally in the public sphere come to affect how more formal political and legislative deliberations are conducted. In this way the public sphere is "an intermediary between the political system, on the one hand, and the private sectors of the lifeworld and functional systems, on the other" (p. 373). This intermediary mech-

anism never coalesces into a formal system or structure. By definition the public sphere is fluid and resists calcification. Habermas
writes that "publics cannot harden into organizations or systems"
because their boundaries "remain permeable in principle" (p. 374).

Sometimes the public sphere is the site of brief conversations
among a few people, sometimes a more sustained discussion in a
larger group takes place. People talk episodically at subway stops,
in pubs, or on the street, but they also talk in the interstices of
larger public events—waiting in line for the cinema, at half-time
at football matches, in the corridors between sessions at academic
conferences, over coffee at a political congress. There is also a
more abstract form of talk that happens when readers, viewers, lis-
teners, and Internet users around the world connect with each
other through media and technology. These different levels of the
public sphere are interconnected and flow in and out of each
other so that "all the partial publics constituted by ordinary language remain porous to one another" (1996, p 374). Sometimes,
as Newman (1999) illustrates, adult educators can initiate an informal conversation (an episodic public sphere) that results in a coa-
lescence of opinion and a desire to do something about a situation
(what Habermas calls political will-formation).

In *The Structural Transformation of the Public Sphere* ([1962]
1989b), Habermas painstakingly traces how, as society becomes
ever larger and more differentiated into complex subsystems, "the
communicative network of a public made up of rationally debating private citizens has collapsed" (p. 247). The town meeting, village green gathering, or tribal circle cannot provide effective
forums for the kind of public discussion of community concerns
that lies at the heart of democracy. Yet democracy cannot exist
without a public sphere that allows people to talk out their feelings
and opinions and gather their political energies behind a particular movement for change. For Habermas "democratically constituted opinion and will-formation depends on the supply of
informal public opinions that, ideally, develop in structures of an
unsubverted political public sphere" (Habermas, 1996, p. 308).

In the absence of any arena in which adults can come together
to debate and engage in political will-formation (the development
of strands of opinion and the decision to act on these that sometimes
comes after prolonged discussion), we cannot accurately talk about

public opinion. This lack of a public sphere is a boon to governments that seek to steamroller a vision of the world they wish people to accept as self-evident. Conversely, a public sphere that debates long and hard about the morality of invading another country in the absence of any visible threat, or that keeps focusing on the legitimacy of policies enacted by a president who received votes from fewer citizens than his or her rival, is extremely inconvenient for a regime determined to damp down public criticism of its actions.

Habermas defines public opinion as an informed viewpoint on a particular issue that is offered by a group of people involved in that issue after they have engaged in a full consideration of all the relevant facts. In his view, however, true public opinion rarely develops. Instead of a full conversation and the emergence of political will-formation that real public opinion represents, we have a limited political discourse controlled by media institutions. In his words public opinion "has partly decomposed into the informal opinions of private citizens without a public and partly become concentrated into formal opinions of publistically effective institutions" ([1962] 1989b, p. 247). We have our personal longings and frustrations that we voice to family, friends, and colleagues or through occasional letters to editors, elected representatives, or public officials. Or, we have organizations, pressure groups, and institutions (corporations, government agencies, labor unions, professional associations, and so on) that disseminate the views of those who occupy the top positions in these groups, whether or not these views actually reflect the opinions of members. The mass media then either serve as the mouthpiece for these organizations or reframe their opinions to support the existing system. In line with earlier Frankfurt School critiques of media and popular culture, Habermas believes that "the electronic mass media of today is organized in such a way that it controls the loyalty of a depoliticised population" (Habermas, 1973, p. 4). In this way the public sphere is severely diminished. Lacking the communicative vehicles through which they can meet, discuss, and decide their responses to the ways economic and social forces are shaping their lives, adults are left privately vociferous but publicly voiceless.

The diminution of the public sphere is a theme threading throughout Habermas' work. It features as prominently in later books such as *Between Facts and Norms* (1996), *On the Pragmatics of Communica-*

tion (1998), and *The Postnational Constellation* (2001a) as it does in his earliest work (*The Structural Transformation of the Public Sphere* was originally published in Germany in 1962). With the growth of capitalism and the move from the industrial to the information society, the education system and class structure combine to force people into more and more specialized roles and functions leaving them less and less prepared for participation in public discourse. The logic of capitalistic economic development is that "the unavoidable division of labor results in an unequal distribution of information and expertise" (Habermas, 1996, p. 325). Some members of society, because of their class position, racial identity, and education, know more and have greater life chances than others. Inequities resulting from class and racial factors are further compounded by the way "the communications media intervene with a selectivity of their own in this social distribution of knowledge" (p. 325). For example, access to and technical knowledge of the workings of cyberspace are determined partly by people's education, income, occupation, and status. These determining factors reflect the wider organization of society for the benefit of certain groups. Without access to or knowledge of communication technology, large parts of the population are locked out of the public flow of communication. Without membership in an influential organization or pressure group, people have no channel through which to voice an opinion. In this situation "the structures of the public sphere reflect unavoidable asymmetries in the availability of information, that is, unequal chances to have access to the generation, validation, shaping, and presentation of messages" (Habermas, 1996, p. 225).

What are some of the consequences of the decline of the public sphere? One is the growth of a destructive privatism, a focus on the self. When people have no way to influence discussion and decisions in the wider society, they may as well pursue private goals without regard to the effects this pursuit has on others. In *Legitimation Crisis* (1975) Habermas describes the condition of a "structurally depoliticized public realm" (p. 37) in which administrative decisions are made independent of people's interests. We have the "application of institutions and procedures that are democratic in form, while the citizenry, in the midst of an objectively political society, enjoy the status of passive citizens with only the right to withhold acclamation" (p. 37). In such a situation civic privatism—"political abstinence combined with an orientation to career, leisure and consumption" (p. 37)—is bound to flourish. Habermas notes how a "familial-vocational privatism complements civic privatism" (Habermas, 1975, p. 75) by establishing "a family orientation with developed interests in consumption and leisure on the one hand, and (in) a career orientation suitable to status competition on the other" (p. 75). These forms of privatism are underscored by popular theories extolling the virtues of meritocracy, the rise of democratic elites, and the efficient workings of technocratic systems.

As well as encouraging the growth of a privatized attitude to life, the diminution of the public sphere neutralizes intellectual challenges to the dominant order. When intellectuals act as social critics to reveal and uncover the existence of social inequities, they need a public to receive, consider, and then sometimes act on such critiques. With no public to debate the arguments and evidence they offer, no commons in which their analyses can be heard, intellectuals are impotent, offering only the sorts of notes to a dying civilization or messages in bottles mentioned at the end of *Dialectic of Enlightenment, Eclipse of Reason,* or *One Dimensional Man.* By definition, intellectual work (particularly critical theory) is premised on the existence of a public sphere to receive it. Habermas writes that "when intellectuals, using arguments sharpened by rhetoric, intervene on behalf of rights that have been violated and truths that have been suppressed, reforms that are overdue and progress that has been delayed, they address themselves to a public sphere that is capable of response, alert and informed" (Habermas, 1989a, p. 73). This sphere can only exist when supported by constitutional safeguards that ensure and encourage the free expression of critical opinion. In order to perform their proper critical function, intellectuals "rely on a half way constitutional state" and on "a democracy that for its part survives only by virtue of the involvement of citizens who are as suspicious as they are combative" (p. 73).

Problems Addressed by Critical Theory 2: The Threat to Civil Society

In Habermas' analysis the decline of the public sphere is a function of a concurrent social development, the increasing precariousness of civil society. Civil society essentially comprises all those forms of collective human association not directly controlled by the state or corporations. Everything from car pools to professional organizations to alternative political movements is potentially part of civil society. Unlike the more amorphous and porous public sphere, civil society frequently organizes itself into groups with clearly designated hierarchies of communication and conditions for membership. The Adult Education Research Conference (AERC) and the Commission of Professors of Adult Education (CPAE) in their different ways show some of the variety of civil society. The AERC, with its nomadic annual wanderings across the North American continent, its lack of a formal membership, and its reliance on word of mouth to publicize its activities, is a loosely organized part of civil society. By way of contrast, the CPAE is more closely structured. To be part of the CPAE, one must satisfy certain conditions. For example, one needs to hold a job with the title "professor" and to teach university graduate courses in adult education. One also needs to be part of a larger, dues paying, professional organization (the American Association for Adult and Continuing Education) with its attendant qualifications for membership.

Habermas defines civil society as "composed of those more or less spontaneously emergent associations, organizations, and movements that, attuned to how societal problems resonate in the private life spheres, distill and transmit such reactions in amplified form to the public sphere" (Habermas, 1996, p. 367). In other words, the discussions people have within the organizations of civil society about particular problems that affect them help crystallize the topics and issues that are then considered in the wider public sphere. In the field of adult education, for example, some practitioners lament the infiltration of human capital perspectives into the ways programs are created and evaluated. Others are worried about the way adult literacy sometimes becomes a palliative to preserve an unequal system, rather than a force for social change, or the way literacy practitioners are treated as slave labor. The decline of voluntarism, the replacement of face-to-face learning by online instruction, the ascendance of efforts to certify, license, and professionalize the field, the denial of funding to more radical, alternative adult educational initiatives, and the general marginalization of provision for adult education (the last to be funded, the first to be cut)—all these are concerns that arise in that part of civil society we call adult education and that some within that sector try to "distill and transmit" to the larger public sphere as items for discussion.

Marginalized groupings within civil society are not, by the way, entirely powerless or without influence. Sometimes those organizations and movements that find themselves exiled to the periphery of civil society have "the advantage of greater sensitivity in detecting and identifying new problem situations" (Habermas, 1996, p. 381). Habermas cites as examples the way that certain issues (ecological threats, third world crises, feminism, multiculturalism) "were broached by intellectuals, concerned citizens, radical professionals, self-proclaimed 'advocates,' and the like" (p. 381) long before occupying space in an admittedly diminished public sphere. Also, as nongovernmental organizations (NGO's), environmental agencies, and activist groups across the world begin to coordinate their activities in opposition to global capitalism, there is increasing talk of the idea of international civil society. As with domestic civil society, the international counterpart also forces issues into the realm of the international public sphere ensuring that the agendas of formal institutional groupings such as the World Trade Organization (WTO) have to take account of international civil society's concerns. Given that the organizations of domestic and international civic society frequently generate issues that claim attention in the public sphere, Habermas argues that "the communicative structures of the public sphere must [rather] be kept intact by an energetic civil society" (1996, p. 369).

Unfortunately civil society is diminished as the political system of state power, and the economic system of the capitalistic pursuit of profit, become ever more dominant. In Newman's (1999) words, "Civil society may become what is left over in our lives after the parts that really matter have been taken out" (p. 150). When political and economic systems operate completely independently of civil society, then major decisions affecting our lives are taken by these systems with no chance for their merits to be questioned or for alternatives to be proposed or discussed. There is little point in joining a tenants' group or showing up at neighborhood meetings if all we are able to do is choose between options shaped and presented to us by political or business interests. Civic democracy is hardly alive when all we can decide on are matters that are relatively trivial. Spending inordinate amounts of time debating the shape of a new bus shelter while a local industrial plant pollutes the neighborhood's air, for example, is a pale version of the robust civil dialogue a democratic society requires.

When civil society is on the defensive, then the forces that determine how the political and economic systems run—what Habermas calls "steering mechanisms"—operate more or less unchallenged. The steering mechanisms of money (the pursuit of profit through the exchange economy) and power (the maintenance by dominant groups of a system of ideological and technocratic domination) start to encroach on civil society. For example, the market—the web of economic exchanges, price control mechanisms, cartel agreements, and patterns of consumption—impinges on our lives in ways that seem uncontrollable, beyond our influence. Boom and bust, recession and growth, help wanted signs, or long dole queues—all these seem random happenings. In Habermas' words economic crises "lose the character of a fate accessible to self-reflection and acquire the objectivity of inexplicable, contingent, natural events" (1975, p. 30). We also use market analogies—the "free market of ideas" is a good one—to structure the conversations we have in civil society and in the public sphere. The fallacy of this particular analogy is that market operations are not free at all. Those who exercise the greatest influence in the "free" market are often those who already have the greatest power. The same is true of conversation circles. Those used to speaking because they have the right accent, a facility in the dominant language, or because their education, money, skin color, gender, or social position ensure their opinions will be listened to, exercise a disproportionate influence.

Problems Addressed by Critical Theory 3: The Invasion of the Lifeworld

As well as encroaching on civil society, the steering mechanisms of money and power also invade the lifeworld. This is dangerous since "communication in a public sphere that recruits private persons from civil society depends on the spontaneous inputs from a lifeworld whose core private domains are intact" (Habermas, 1996, p. 417). If the lifeworld is controlled by money and power, then all the discussions we have in the public sphere and all the topics we

raise for discussion in the organizations of civil society are profoundly tainted and compromised without our ever being aware of
that fact.

Unlike the public sphere or civil society, which can at least be
seen physically (albeit sometimes fleetingly) in the form of conversations, gatherings, associations, and organizational activities,
the lifeworld is chiefly a mental, even a psychic, phenomenon. It
exists prereflectively, inside consciousness. Segments of the lifeworld can be glimpsed when they are thrown into sharp relief as
elements of situations we have to respond to, and this is where we
often see most clearly the encroachment of steering mechanisms.
But as the shadowy "horizon of shared, unproblematic beliefs"
(Habermas, 1996, p. 22), the lifeworld cannot be penetrated. In
Habermas' view it is by definition unknowable. The lifeworld is so
ingrained in our structures of perception and communication that
we cannot stand outside it and reflect back on it. It is "always
already there" to use a common Habermas phrase, "a context that
cannot be gotten behind and cannot in principle be exhausted"
(1987a, p. 133).

What exactly is the lifeworld? In one of the most quoted sentences from the second volume of *The Theory of Communicative
Action* (1987a), Habermas describes it as "the intuitively present,
in this sense familiar and transparent, and at the same time vast
and incalculable web of presuppositions that have to be satisfied if
an actual utterance is to be at all meaningful, that is, valid or invalid" (p. 131). As one graduate student dryly remarked to me
when I presented this definition, "That's not exactly helpful is it?"
A simpler definition on the same page is perhaps clearer: "The lifeworld forms the indirect context of what is said, discussed,
addressed in a situation" (p. 131). It is all those assumptions that
frame how we understand our experience of life and how we try to
convey that experience to others. Thus, "the lifeworld forms a horizon and at the same time offers a store of things taken for granted
in the given culture from which communicative participants draw
consensual interpretative patterns in their efforts at interpretation"
(Habermas, 1987b, p. 298). I think of the lifeworld as the background rules, assumptions, and commonsense understandings that
structure how we perceive the world and how we communicate that
perception to those around us. This kind of primordial, prereflec-

tive knowledge hovers on the periphery of consciousness, a shadowy frame to all we think and do.

The lifeworld is all-pervasive, the perceptual oxygen we breathe without ever really being aware of our rhythmic inhalations or the way they keep us alive. Because it "only exists in the distinctive, pre-reflexive form of background assumptions, background receptivities or background relations [it] dissolves and disappears before our eyes as soon as we try to take it up piece by piece" (Habermas, 1992a, p. 109). It saturates our conversations, forming "the horizon in which communicative actions are 'always already' moving" (Habermas 1987a, p. 119). The cultural knowledge embedded in the lifeworld is "always already familiar" (p. 132), representing "a storehouse of unquestioned cultural givens from which those participating in communication draw agreed-upon patterns of interpretation for use in their interpretive efforts" (Habermas, 1990, p. 135). So every time we communicate with another person, as I am trying to do with you by putting these marks on a page, we do so within a cluster, a web, of unwittingly shared understandings and unacknowledged ways of perceiving. Hence "as we engage in communicative action, the lifeworld embraces us as an unmediated certainty, out of whose immediate proximity we live and speak" (Habermas, 1996, p. 22).

A key element in Habermas' treatment of this idea is that "the lifeworld always remains in the background" (Habermas, 1987a, p. 131), impenetrable and unknowable. No matter how hard we try to uncover and examine it, we are doomed to perpetual frustration. This is because "the life-world is so unproblematic that we are simply incapable of making ourselves conscious of this or that part of it at will" (Habermas, 1992a, p. 110). If we try to identify and examine the cultural knowledge it contains, we see it vaporize just as it starts to assume shape: "No sooner has it been thematized, and thereby cast into the whirlpool of possible questions, than it decomposes" (Habermas, 1996, p. 23). To study the lifeworld's contours would be as impossible as a bigmouthed bass levitating out of a Minnesota lake and making a leisurely survey of the water's surface in mid-air to discern where the juiciest minnows are swimming or where the most predatory anglers are moored.

Again and again, across all his writing, Habermas emphasizes the enclosing totality that is the lifeworld. In *The Theory of Communicative*

Action (1987a), it is "a horizon behind which we cannot go . . . a totality with no reverse side" (p. 149); in *The New Conservatism* (1989a), "a background totality" and "a totalizing vortex" (p. 120); in *Postmetaphysical Thinking* (1992b), "a porous whole of familiarities that are prereflexively present" (p. 16); in *The Philosophical Discourse of Modernity* (1987b), "an intuitively known, unproblematic and unanalyzable, holistic background" (p. 298); and in *Between Facts and Norms* (1996), "a penetrating, yet latent and unnoticed presence . . . a sprawling, deeply set, and unshakable rock of background assumptions, loyalties, and skills" (p. 22). Although the lifeworld represents total enclosure, there are times we can breach its fences or stumble across gaps in its walls. Habermas allows the possibility of our becoming aware of the false knowledge, distorted assumptions, and self-destructive presuppositions the lifeworld contains when we are confronted with a particular situation that demands action.

In action situations—times when events impel us to respond—the lifeworld's horizon becomes a little less hazy and a segment of it "comes into view" (Habermas, 1987a, p. 132). Since adulthood entails "the constant upset of disappointment and contradiction, contingency and critique in everyday life" (1996, p. 22), there are plenty of opportunities for us to confront these different lifeworld segments. Situations constantly arise—jobs disappear, relationships fall apart, neighborhoods change, friends betray us (or we betray friends), those close to us fall seriously ill or die—that demand responses. As we work through these situations, we realize that lifeworld knowledge and assumptions are perhaps not the accurate, dependable realities we had imagined them to be. Even though the total lifeworld is preflectively known and "given to the experiencing subject as unquestionable" (1987a, p. 130), we can examine that segment of it thrown into sharp relief by the need to set goals and take action. Habermas writes that "in the light of an actual situation . . . the relevant segment of the lifeworld acquires the status of a contingent reality that could also be interpreted another way" (p. 131).

When adults deal with situations that demand actions from them, glimpses of the lifeworld become possible. Pieces of it also come into view in the process of what Habermas calls symbolic reproduction. The lifeworld is always being renewed and recreated as we involve ourselves in communicative action. On the one hand, "in fallibly interpreting a given situation" (Habermas 1996, p. 324), communicative actors (that is, adults trying to understand what's happening to them and hoping to reach agreements with others in the situation) "must draw from resources supplied by their lifeworld and not under their control" (p. 324). On the other hand, "actors are not simply at the mercy of their lifeworld. For the lifeworld can in turn reproduce itself only through communicative action" (p. 324). Its assumptions are strengthened and confirmed when we invoke them to explain our decisions and actions.

In communicative action our assumptions and intuitive preunderstandings are all the time being put to the test as we are asked tacitly to accept suggestions, justifications, and social arrangements that are presented to us as obvious fact. Habermas believes that "in communicative action, which requires taking yes/no positions on claims of rightfulness and truthfulness, no less than reactions to claims of truth and efficiency, the background knowledge of the lifeworld is submitted to ongoing tests across its entire breadth" (Habermas, 1987b, p. 321). Every time we are asked to nod our heads—literally or figuratively—to something that someone else says, or to the way a situation is framed for us, the lifeworld is put to a brief examination.

As any totalitarian leader sooner or later realizes, reproducing a closed system of ideas is a slippery business. Inevitably, unforeseen events eventually intervene to take the reproductive process out of the leadership's control. This is even more the case where what is being reproduced—understandings, assumptions, intuitions—is symbolic rather than material. It is much easier to reproduce material phenomena such as organizational rituals, institutional behaviors, or economic and community conventions than it is to control and reproduce shared meanings. Of course, "the symbolic reproduction of the lifeworld and its material reproduction are internally interdependent" (Habermas, 1987b, p. 322). After all, the smooth functioning of social institutions depends on people sharing an unspoken agreement to their legitimacy. Overall, then, the lifeworld strives to ensure continued social solidarity through the transmission of "culturally ingrained background assumptions" (1987b, p. 298).

The symbolic reproduction of the lifeworld fulfills three important functions—"the propagation of cultural traditions, the integration of groups by norms and values, and the socialization of succeeding generations" (Habermas, 1987b, p. 299). As a result of this reproduction, people draw from the lifeworld "consensual patterns of interpretation," "normatively reliable patterns of social relations," and "the competencies acquired in socialization processes" (p. 314). The first function of cultural reproduction "secures the continuity of tradition and a coherency of knowledge sufficient for the consensus needs of everyday practice" (p. 343). Thus the cultural frame in which we operate structures the way that "newly arising situations can be connected up with existing conditions in the world" (p. 343) and helps us decide what is the most appropriate response to a situation. The second function of social integration "takes care of the coordination of action by means of legitimately regulated interpersonal relationships and lends constancy to the identity of groups" (p. 344). This function ensures that we learn the habitual ways our group solves problems, sets goals, resolves disputes, and so on. The third function of socialization "secures the acquisition of generalized capacities for action for future generations and takes care of harmonizing individual life histories and collective life forms" (p. 344). Through socialization our individual identity becomes bound up with allegiances to groups, communities, and nation states.

Cultural reproduction, social integration, and socialization only happen as we communicate with each other. In this way the lifeworld "reproduces itself only through ongoing communicative actions" (Habermas, 1996, p. 32). All the speech acts and linguistic utterances we produce as we strive to understand each other's behaviors and try to come to communicative agreements serve to reproduce the lifeworld. So communicative action and lifeworld reproduction are contemporaneous: "The network of communicative action is nourished by resources of the lifeworld and is at the same time the medium by which concrete forms of life are reproduced" (Habermas, 1987b, p. 316).

As we have seen, points of entry into examining the lifeworld do exist. Adults can analyze situations demanding action, and they can also study the numerous everyday agreements they implicitly make as part of lifeworld reproduction. Habermas believes that philosophy can help examine these points of entry to discern when the lifeworld is being invaded by the steering mechanisms of money and power. Hence, one important task of philosophy is to "contribute to making us conscious of the deformations of the life-world" (Habermas, 1992b, p. 50). An example of this would be challenging the unspoken assumption that competition is a nat-ural survival mechanism. Habermas quotes as an example of ideo-logical domination "the idea that the capacity to compete on an international scale—whether in markets or in outer space—is indis-pensable for our very survival" (Habermas, 1987b, p. 367). Such a belief is "one of those everyday certitudes in which systemic con-straints are condensed" (p. 367). Philosophy might also alert us to the infiltration of the concept of retooling into the lexicon of adult education. Retooling the workforce through adult education turns adult education into something that always serves the system since workers are trained to perform the job functions the economy needs to work more efficiently. Retooling also dehumanizes people by viewing them as machines since retooling, like recalibration, is something one does to nonhuman objects.

The invasion of the lifeworld by administrative and economic systems is a matter of extreme concern to Habermas. He refers to an "arising awareness of the infiltration of capital into areas of life which until now were shielded from it by tradition, and within which the values of capitalist society (competition for status, pur-suit of gain, instrumentalization of existence) were not hitherto dominant" (Habermas, 1992a, p. 66). When we study situations of crisis in our lives, we can sometimes see just how much our instinc-tive ways of understanding have become shaped by capitalistic or bureaucratic ways of thinking. An intimate relationship falls apart and the partners lament their wasted emotional investment. Par-ents having trouble with their children are told to establish a series of contracts specifying duties, obligations, and expectations. We divide our days into work time, relaxation time, quality time, or family time, or we regard our marriages as work teams geared to the achievement of particular goals such as raising children or buy-ing a house. All these examples show how "the foundations of a lifeworld that is already rationalized are under assault" and alert us to the fact that "what is at stake is the symbolic reproduction of the life-world itself" (p. 117).

Habermas' analysis of the crises facing contemporary society is somber reading. The decline of the public sphere, the threat to civil society, and the invasion of the lifeworld are manifestations of a broader loss of social solidarity—in his view the truly endangered resource on the planet (Habermas, 1996, p. xlii). In *Theory and Practice* (1973), a collection of essays mostly published in the 1960s, he sounds a distinctively Marcusean note in his warning of how false needs and false freedom separate people from each other: "Scurvy and rickets are preserved today in the form of psychosomatic disturbances, hunger and drudgery in the wasteland of externally manipulated motivation in the satisfaction of needs which no longer 'are one's own'" (p. 196). In contemporary society the "anonymous compulsion of indirect manipulation" extends further and further to invade "ever more extensive domains of social life" (p. 196). Today social compulsions are felt as inner needs: "Directives lose their form of commands and are translated by means of sociotechnical manipulation in such a manner that those forced to obey, now well integrated, are allowed to do, in the consciousness of their freedom, what do they must" (p. 196).

The loss of solidarity and co-option of our inner needs by commerce and administration are compounded by the collapse of our belief that reason can be used to create a better world. In *Between Facts and Norms* (1996) Habermas declares that the twentieth century "has taught us the horror of existing unreason" and that, as a result, "the last remains of an essentialist trust in reason have been destroyed" (p. xli). With the rejection of reason, "politics has lost its orientation and self-confidence before a terrifying background" (p. xli). Ecological crises, north/south disparities, ethnic strife, and the collapse of socialism have all cast doubt on people's capacity to use reason to build a humane world. But this is just the surface of the problem. In Habermas' view, "the unrest has a still deeper source, namely, the sense that in the age of a completely secularized politics, the rule of law cannot be had or maintained without a radical democracy" (p. xlii). The prospects of such a democracy emerging are dim indeed as long as the tendencies outlined in this chapter remain unchallenged.

However, all is not lost in Habermas' view. In particular it is a disastrous mistake to replace a loss of trust in reason with a hurtling into unreason. If reason can be rescued from its co-option by money and power, then it can be used to build a more participatory democracy. Democracy is Habermas' response to domination and, as we shall see in the next chapter, he ties his interest in adult learning and his theory of communicative action to the idea of a truly deliberative democracy. Such a democracy would help counter "the depoliticization of the mass of the population" and go some way to reviving a public realm currently "confined to spectacles and acclamation" (Habermas, 1970, p. 75). Like Marcuse, Habermas sees the uncritical acceptance of the technocracy thesis—"a perspective in which the development of the social system seems to be determined by the logic of the scientific-technical progress" (p. 105)—as lying at the core of domination.

Technocracy acts as a force for domination by promoting the belief that life is principally a matter of technical adjustment. All problems—emotional, spiritual, and social—are fixable by the application of technology. This "dominant, rather glassy background ideology, which makes a fetish of science, is more irresistible and farther-reaching than ideologies of the old type" (1970, p. 111) because it secures "the repression of 'ethics' as such as a category of life" (p. 112). Hence, technocratic consciousness turns all questions concerning how to live into instrumental, rather than ethical or moral, questions. People set goals and make decisions as purely technical matters. As a result, "the reified models of the sciences migrate into the sociocultural lifeworld and gain objective power over the latter's self-understanding" (p. 113). Anticipating current controversies over genetic engineering by three decades or more, Habermas sketches out a frightening extension of technocratic domination in which "behavioral control could be instituted at an ever deeper level tomorrow through biotechnic intervention in the endocrine regulating system, not to mention the even greater consequences of intervening in the genetic transmission of inherited information" (p. 118).

As he sees societies growing larger and increasingly differentiated, Habermas offers the hypothesis that "the more complex the systems requiring steering become, the greater the probability of dysfunctional effects" (Habermas, 1989a, p. 51). For example, productive forces become devoted to destructive ends, invasions aimed at establishing peace produce terroristic backlashes, and attempts to plan society (transportation, health, education, welfare) backfire disastrously inducing more disruption than existed before. The increasing commercialization and bureaucratization of life generates "disturbances, pathological side-effects" (Habermas, 1992a, p. 112) in the lifeworld "and interferes with its symbolic reproduction" (p. 246). Although superficially reassured by technocratic logic, people are subject to a deeper unease. Habermas writes of the ways that "social conflicts . . . have been shifted over into the psychological and physical domains and internalized" (1989a, p. 59). People are plagued by the unspoken sense that economic, ethnic, or ecological disasters are likely to explode at any moment.

The preconscious awareness that pathological disturbances lie just under the surface of existence induce a feeling of hopelessness, what Habermas characterizes as "a certain *fin-de-siecle* mood, a sense that time is running out" (Habermas, 1989a, p. 189). In his view the dread that lurks, dimly sensed, in the periphery of life is reflected in the popularity of postmodern analysis. To him it is no accident that the theories gaining in influence today are those that illustrate how the forces from which modernity draws its utopian self-confidence "are in actuality turning autonomy into dependence, emancipation into oppression, and reason into rationality" (p. 51). In a theoretical alternative to the nihilism these theories can induce, Habermas draws on the affirmative strain of critical theory he admires Marcuse for preserving to propose a new model of democracy based on the innate need of humans to communicate. It is to his belief in the power of adult learning, his theory of communicative action, and his reaffirmation of the democratic dream that we now turn.

| **Learning Democracy**

In the previous chapter, you, the reader, may have been wondering exactly what happened to adult learning and education. In that chapter's detailing of the crisis tendencies Habermas sees in Western societies, the roles of adult learning and education in countering these received only passing attention. But now their place in the sun has arrived. In this chapter I want to outline the centrality of adult learning to Habermas' view of social evolution, to examine how his ideas of human discourse and communicative action entail a theory of adult learning, and to explore how for him the most important adult learning project of all—learning democracy—works to limit the destructive effects of the attacks on the public sphere, civil society, and the lifeworld.

The Centrality of Adult Learning

In the preceding chapter, I acknowledged Habermas' liking for the affirmative strain of critical theory represented by Marcuse who at one point declared "no one could be more of a democrat than I am," while also recognizing that "the true conditions of democracy still have to be created" (Marcuse, 1970, p. 80). Like Marcuse, Habermas has as one of his central projects the understanding and creation of the conditions for democracy. Central to this effort is adult learning. Habermas' hope for regenerating democracy resides in adults' capacity to learn, in particular, to learn how to recognize and expand the democratic processes inherent in human communication. Adult learning, for Habermas, is integral to communication and, therefore, contemporaneous with existence. Since

we all communicate, learning is a naturally occurring phenomenon that can only be prevented by some act of suppression initiated by an external force. In a world in which adults regularly
communicate, the most intriguing question for Habermas is not
how adult learning happens but how it doesn't happen! If learning is such an omnipresent part of adulthood, then the problem
that needs explaining is why it isn't everywhere. To quote a typically Habermasian turn of phrase, "not *learning,* but *not-learning* is
the phenomenon that calls for explanation" (Habermas, 1975,
p. 15).

The explanation Habermas proposes as to why adults are not
continually and conspicuously learning is that contemporary political and economic systems, and their various steering media,
attempt to foreclose the possibility of any learning that challenges
systemic imperatives. Since learning involves asking "why?" it is
potentially very threatening to the system and must be controlled.
If learning to ask why cannot be stopped at the outset, then the system tries to divert the energy generated by learning into channels
that confirm the legitimacy of the existing order. But make no mistake about it, in Habermas' view learning is what adults do all the
time, unless something actively prevents this from happening.
Adults have "an automatic inability not to learn" (1975, p. 15) that
is a defining feature of adult existence. Although he works within
a different intellectual tradition than many of those adult educators who research self-directed learning, Habermas agrees with
their contention that adults learn continuously and in a variety of
settings. This continuous learning happens whether or not these
adults are participating in formally sponsored and arranged programs of education.

Reflexive Adult Learning and Social Evolution

In *Legitimation Crisis* (1975), Habermas sketches out two broad
forms of learning—nonreflexive and reflexive—a distinction taken
up by Mezirow in his influential 1981 article. Nonreflexive learning is learning without a critical element. It is learning to submit
without resistance to rules of debate, argument assessment, and
decision-making processes that the dominant culture favors
because they cut off any prospect of challenge to that culture by

severing the connection between decision making and any deeper moral inquiry. Hence "non-reflexive learning takes place in action contexts in which implicitly raised theoretical and practical validity claims are naïvely taken for granted and accepted or rejected without discursive consideration" (Habermas, 1975, p. 15).

Reflexive learning, on the other hand, is learning tinged with criticality. In this kind of learning, we learn to question and challenge everyday practices or social arrangements by discussing with others the extent to which these can be justified. Reflexive learning is, therefore, inherently communicative. It involves comparing our experiences and opinions with those of other adults, and considering with them the merits of the evidence proposed to justify different beliefs or courses of action. Habermas expresses this idea rather convolutedly: "Reflexive learning takes place through discourses in which we thematize practical validity claims that have become problematic or have been rendered problematic through institutionalized doubt, and redeem or dismiss them on the basis of arguments" (1975, p. 15). Put more simply, reflexive learning involves us talking over with others the conflicting evidence available to us regarding whether or not things have been ordered the best way they could be in society, and whether or not corporations, bureaucracies, and governments act with the best interests of the people at heart.

The extent to which adults engage in reflexive learning is not a matter of chance but rather one of social determination. It depends on "whether the organizational principle of the society permits (a) differentiation between theoretical and practical questions and (b) transition from non-reflexive (pre-scientific) to reflexive learning" (1975, p. 15). For example, learning to question the distribution of resources or the right of certain groups to rule can be blocked or prevented outright if the lifeworld holds such learning to be deviant, immoral, or unpatriotic. In this way what look like self-directed learning projects are not individually determined at all but socially framed. Indeed, as a general rule, the development of an individual's reflective capacities is always culturally bounded; "since the cognitive development of the individual takes place under social boundary conditions, there is a circular process between societal and individual learning" (Habermas, 1979, p. 121).

One dimension of reflexive learning that does not appear much in the adult learning literature, but that is important to Habermas, is evolutionary learning. Habermas sees such learning as the overall lever for societal development, "the fundamental mechanism for social evolution in general" (Habermas, 1975, p. 15). Without a socially sanctioned engagement in learning, society remains in stasis. In reviewing historical and anthropological evidence, Habermas observes that "the initial state of archaic societies . . . could itself be changed only by constructive learning on the part of socialized individuals" (Habermas, 1979, p. 121). Consequently, it is in a society's best interests (assuming, of course, that evolution is a good thing) to organize evolutionary learning processes as well as relying on their natural emergence.

Two conditions need to be in place for evolutionary learning to occur: "On the one hand, unresolved system problems that represent challenges; on the other, new levels of learning that have already been achieved in world views and are latently available but not yet incorporated into action systems and thus remain institutionally inoperative" (Habermas, 1975, p. 122). The case of global warming represents one contemporary opportunity for evolutionary learning to occur, racial tension another, the African continent's AIDS epidemic a third. In each situation an unresolved system problem has emerged that clearly represents an enormous challenge to humankind. These are all system problems because they are either caused by the actions of people in a system run for economic profit or are naturally occurring but exacerbated to crisis levels by the desire of some for profit or the refusal of others in power to admit a problem exists. Some adults in civil society—activists, concerned professionals, intellectuals, and so on—have forced awareness of the need to learn new ways of responding to these crises into the public sphere. President Bush's refusal to sign the Kyoto Accord, race riots in downtown Cincinnati or Oldham, England, and the prevarications of pharmaceutical companies over whether or not to abandon their exorbitantly profitable pricing policy regarding the sale of AIDS-treatment drugs in poor third-world economies were all granted media space in the weeks and months surrounding my writing this paragraph.

At the same time that these "unresolved system problems" have emerged, activists have offered a variety of responses to them. To take the example of global warming, in the United States there have been proposals for alternative energy policies, for a move to smaller hybrid cars, for a massive increase in investment for public transportation, for more stringent requirements for fuel additives, for punitive taxation on those who buy gas guzzlers, and for an acceptance that air conditioning is a costly luxury—not a necessity—in the desert climate of California and Arizona. All these proposals have been successfully sidelined by the oil, gas, nuclear, and auto industries, and by an administration that includes prominent former figures in these industries amongst its senior public officials. However, Habermas is obstinate in his belief in the hopeful possibilities of learning and looks to history, particularly the move of archaic, preindustrial societies to organize productive systems, to provide evidence of a general theory of evolutionary learning.

To him it is clear that social progress depends on the organization and institutionalization of learning processes. As a society coheres into a unit with a shared sociocultural identity, it ensures that "learning processes are socially organized from the start, so that the results of learning can be handed down" (Habermas, 1979, p. 171). This explains the establishment of the education system, models of apprenticeship, and the transfer of knowledge in churches, families, and friendship networks. Such learning processes "are from the outset linguistically organized, so that the objectivity of the individual's experience is structurally entwined with the intersubjectivity of understanding among individuals" (p. 173). We learn in communities as social beings, and our development of knowledge depends on our ability to understand what others are telling and showing us. The ways I interpret my own experiences as an adult educator are not, therefore, idiosyncratic but rather draw on concepts and frameworks learned through conversation with other adult educators in person and through their writings.

Learning systems can also be created that institutionalize norms of critical skepticism as does, for example, the concept of critically reflective education for professional practice. Habermas' definition of this kind of practice involves the mix of credible practical experience and sociopolitical awareness that seems to me to characterize much writing on critically reflective adult education. Hence, adult education for critical professional practice is "the combination of competence and learning ability to permit the scrupulous handling of tentative technical knowledge and the context-sensitive, well-informed willingness to resist politically the dubious functional application or control of knowledge that one practices" (Habermas, 1970, p. 47). One is skilled in one's area of practice, in other words, but also skilled in recognizing when one's practice is being put at the service of the system and against the interests of its less powerful members.

Adult Learning as Communicative Action

Habermas' theory of communicative action is probably his most famous idea and, along with the invasion of the lifeworld, the part of his work best known in adult education. What is forgotten sometimes is just how central adult learning is to this theory. Habermas' ideas on communicative action "start from the trivial assumption that subjects capable of speech and action cannot help but learn" (Habermas, 1992a, p. 165). He moves, sometimes confusingly, between a normative view of communicative action as a chosen way of reaching agreement with the fewest possible distortions and manipulations, and communicative action as an unavoidable empirical reality existing almost irrespective of adults' intentions. He summarizes this latter view by declaring that "in everyday communicative practice, sociated individuals cannot avoid *also* employing everyday speech in a way that is oriented toward reaching understanding" (Habermas, 1994, p. 101). Hence, "whenever we mean what we say, we raise the claim that what is said is true, or right, or truthful" (p. 102). It is not that "people *want* to act communicatively but that they *have* to" (p. 111). Childrearing, education, friendships, work relationships, community action—"these are elementary social functions that can only be satisfied by means of communicative action" (p. 111).

Once again, the interesting question is less the conditions under which adults learn and more the conditions that prevent this wholly natural and predictable process from happening. If adults are not learning as they communicate, then something is getting in the way. Given that learning is, as we have seen, a social process dependent on our membership of speech communities in which we pursue intersubjective understanding, it is the lack of such communities that is often the problem. In Habermas' view, "reaching mutual understanding . . . depends on contexts characterized by a capacity for learning, both at the cultural and personal level" (Habermas, 1996, p. 324). These contexts exist in societies that exhibit "a discursive mode of sociation" but are prevented from emerging in societies that encourage "dogmatic worldviews and rigid patterns of socialization" (p. 324). In contexts that allow communicative action, the possibility of who will actually do the most learning is always open; "within a process of reaching mutual understanding, actual or potential, it is impossible to decide a priori who is to learn from whom" (Habermas, 1990, p. 26). This is a common idea in adult education, usually expressed in the hope that the roles of teachers and learners will move around in an adult learning group.

What exactly is communicative action? In Volume One of his massive *The Theory of Communicative Action* (1984), Habermas says such action happens when attempts by people to communicate "are coordinated not through egocentric calculations of success but through acts of reaching understanding" (p. 286). When we act communicatively, we try to step out of our normal frames of reference to see the world as someone else sees it. We make this effort because we live in a world full of different cultures, agendas, and ideologies. In a sense, living with others continually forces perspective-taking upon us. Life keeps presenting situations to us in which we need to reach common agreement with other people. The communicative action such agreements call for is premised on the disposition to try and understand another's point of view. Habermas writes that "in communicative action participants are not primarily oriented to their own individual successes; they pursue their individual goals under the condition that they can harmonize their plans of action on the basis of common situation definitions" (1984, p. 286). The ability to put aside egocentric calculations of success in a society run by money and power is a learned ability. Indeed, in Habermas' view, learning to do this is *the* adult learning task, made doubly difficult by the existence of schooling systems run according to the competitive ethic and by the spread of civic or familial privatism documented in the last chapter.

In Habermas' writings on the dialogic conditions necessary for communicative action to occur, there is a direct connection to adult education's traditional concern with discussion as the uniquely adult teaching and learning method. In communicative interactions "the participants coordinate their plans of action consensually, with the agreements reached at any point being evaluated in terms of the intersubjective recognition of validity claims (Habermas, 1990, p. 58). What we agree to or decide on in a conversation is based on our acknowledging that what others are saying has merit. Habermas writes that when people talk through an issue and come to shared understanding or decision, they "make three different claims to validity in their speech acts . . . claims to truth, claims to rightness, and claims to truthfulness" (1990, p. 58). In fact, "every speech act involves the raising of criticizable validity claims aimed at intersubjective recognition" (1996, p. 18).

Habermas' writings on communicative action have a functionalist, even a legalistic tone that can be off-putting to adult educators. Communicative action, validity claims, intersubjective recognition, and understanding—these are hardly terms we use to describe our daily practices to each other. When opening a conversation about how much milk we need to get today, or what is the best way for the United States to beat Portugal in a World Cup soccer match, or who is going to meet the school bus this afternoon, I would never think I was invoking something called validity claims. I might, after a moment or two of thinking about it, acknowledge that my partners in conversation are trying to communicate, so we could legitimately call ourselves communicative actors. And I might also grant the possibility that we're trying to understand each other's positions and come to common agreement. But raising validity claims? What's that got to do with getting milk?

Yet Habermas contends that raising validity claims is intrinsic to every human conversation. In his view, "anyone acting communicatively must, in performing any speech action, raise universal validity claims and suppose that they can be vindicated" (Habermas, 1979, p. 2). Validity claims are the basic conditions of speech that people strive to meet when they attempt to communicate in good faith with each other. If I struggle to understand what you're saying and try to make my comments to you as comprehensible as possible in return, then I am communicating in good faith. If I then try to connect to, build on, and take account of what you have said as I respond to you, I am likewise sincerely trying to develop some shared understandings. What Habermas calls communicative action—two or more people trying to come to an understanding or agreement—is premised on the good faith effort of those involved to speak in the most truthful, best informed way they can. Hence, "whenever we mean what we say, we raise the claim that what is said is true, or right, or truthful" (Habermas, 1994, p. 102). In communicative action then, "speaker and hearer know implicitly that each of them has to raise the aforementioned validity claims if there is to be communication at all (in the sense of action oriented to reaching understanding)" (Habermas, 1979, p. 4).

Two things are striking about this idea. First, not all conversational interactions are examples of communicative action. Indeed, in a society dominated by money and power, a great deal of communication will be the exact opposite of this kind of talk. People will speak to exploit or dominate others or to justify and support a system that legitimizes this domination. True communicative action is a rarity in life, something that deliberately needs to be fostered. This is where the role of adult education and the actions of adult educators become relevant. Within the dialogic tradition of adult education, there is a belief that speaking in the way that Habermas describes as communicative is something that adults can learn. There are, furthermore, the assumptions that adult educators can teach these orientations to speech, that they can create learning opportunities in which these ways of speaking are honored and practiced, and that they can do their best to model their commitment to these dialogic forms in their own educational actions. A book I wrote with Stephen Preskill, *Discussion as a Way of Teaching* (Brookfield and Preskill, 1999), is premised on the idea that dispositions of democratic discussion—the sorts of reciprocity and mutuality endemic to Habermas' notion of validity claims—can be taught and learned.

The second thing that is striking about communicative action is how its unabashed hope in the possibility of two or more people coming to understand each other's views and then agreeing on a common course of action stands firmly against postmodernism. From a postmodern perspective, Habermas is engaged on something of a fool's errand. If postmodernism teaches us anything (and teaching us something is too directive an activity for many in this orientation), it is that language can never be trusted. Logocentrism—the assumption that a central, unequivocal, discoverable meaning exists at the core of speech and writing—is completely rejected. Words are viewed instead as slippery, opaque, and contextual. From a postmodern perspective, the thoughts I have can never be expressed in words in exactly the way I think them. Furthermore, despite my best intentions to craft words that convey my meanings as transparently and accurately as possible, the meanings that you take from them will never be exactly what I intend. Your experiences and history will always skew how you understand the words I use and ensure that you invest them with connotations and meanings I never intended.

Despite the postmodern critique of his theory of communicative action, Habermas steadfastly refuses to ditch modernity's dream of using human reason to create a more humane world. Part of that dream is clearly bound up with the possibility of adults learning to speak to each other in honest and informed ways so that they can hold democratic conversations about important issues in a revived public sphere. Since, to Habermas, learning to talk in this way is the most important hope we have for creating a just society, there could hardly be anything more important in social life than adult education. Adult educators who possess the ability and inclination to create conversational settings in which people learn to base their communication on validity claims are precious resources indeed from Habermas' point of view. Before getting carried away regarding the planet-saving role of adult education, and particularly before getting any deeper into the nature of validity claims, I want to leave the theory of communicative action for a moment (but only for a moment) to return to the centrality of adult learning in Habermas' work, in particular to the way he interprets ego development as an adult learning process.

Adult Learning and the Development of Moral Consciousness

As well as viewing reflexive adult learning as the lever of social evolution, and arguing that adults learning to act communicatively is crucial to reviving the public sphere (and thereby expanding democracy), Habermas also sees the development of moral consciousness as a learning process that occurs primarily in adult life. This conviction is rooted in Habermas' early formulations of the interests people have in developing different kinds of knowledge. In *Knowledge and Human Interests* (1971), he presents his influential categorization of technical, communicative, and emancipatory knowledge, arguing that emancipatory knowledge—"analyses that free consciousness from its dependence on hypostatized powers" (1971, p. 313)—is a function of people's capacity to become reflective. To Habermas, "the emancipatory cognitive interest aims at the pursuit of reflection" (p. 314).

Without a capacity for critical reflection, we are unable to separate our identity from the steering mechanisms of money and power that have invaded the lifeworld. Our sense of who we are then becomes constructed in terms of how successfully our actions exemplify systemic imperatives. For example, we treat relationships as profit-making activities to which we can apply a cost-benefit analysis of the emotional dividends that accrue to us. In this way of thinking, a relationship is successful if its participants enjoy a good rate of return on their emotional investment in the form of ego aggrandizement, sexual favors, or receipt of unconditional positive regard. Becoming reflective is a necessary hedge against this tendency.

If ego development is a learning process that crosses the lifespan, then it is in its adult stages that the evolution of full moral consciousness potentially occurs. In *Moral Consciousness and Communicative Action* (1990), Habermas cites Kohlberg's work on adult moral development to support his (Habermas') contention that becoming moral is signaled by "the transition from normatively regulated action to practical discourse" (p. 170). In other words, the development of morality is indicated by people's ability to detach themselves from everyday thinking and decide (after participating in discussions with others about the ethical justifications of various approaches to situations) how to act in ways that are not ideologically predetermined. Moral consciousness emerges as a person "passes into the post-conventional stage of interaction" in which "the adult rises above the naïveté of everyday life practice" (p. 160). Passage into this postconventional stage is marked by the adult becoming aware of life's contingencies, by her recognizing the contextuality of beliefs, and by the ability to understand that thought is ideologically shaped. To Habermas, "only at the post-conventional stage is the social world uncoupled from the stream of cultural givens" (p. 162).

What does it mean for an adult to be "uncoupled from the stream of cultural givens"? Here Habermas harks back to Marcuse's emphasis on the need for distance, privacy, and isolation as necessary to the development of critical consciousness. If people are to act morally, they need to learn how to view their immediate concerns without the pressures put upon them by the imperatives of the situation or the force of "common sense." One way to do this is to talk with others who have different experiences of these concerns, or who interpret the same concern in markedly different ways. As the adult "becomes a participant in discourse, the relevance of his experiential context pales" (1990, p. 161), and it becomes easier to separate out the generic elements of a situation from its context-specific features. The "relevance of the experiential context" is often judged as an unalloyed good in adult education circles (experience being thought of as something positive that should always be tied to learning), so it is interesting to read this critique of its potential for domination. Here Habermas is pointing out the dark side of experience, the way its familiarity and immediacy can foreclose new and surprising understandings. Discussing different perspectives on experience helps people think "independently of contingent commonalities of social background, political affiliation, cultural heritage, traditional forms of life, and so on" so that they "can now take a moral point of view, a point of view distanced from the controversy" (p. 162).

In an interview in *Autonomy and Solidarity* (1992a), Habermas clarifies the meaning of a moral point of view, seeing it as an awareness of the contextuality of one's own beliefs and values. Hence "to see something from a moral point of view means that we do not elevate our own understanding of the world or our self-understanding to the status of criteria for universalization of a mode of action" (Habermas, 1992a, p. 269). We recognize the provisionality of our convictions even as we act as if they were certitudes. Those holding moral viewpoints are open to "test their universalizability from the perspective of all the others" (p. 269) that pertain to that particular situation. Acting morally, in other words, involves a degree of circumspection regarding the correctness of one's own actions, no matter how carefully these have already been scrutinized.

Habermas is careful to acknowledge that he is describing only the possible development of adult moral consciousness and that its existence is relatively rare. He admits that "empirical investigations come out strongly against the idea that all adult members of a society, even of modern Western societies, have acquired the capacity for formal-operational thought (in Piaget's sense) or for post-conventional judgments (in the sense of Kohlberg's theory of moral development)" (1992a, p. 165). But he does hold out the possibility that widespread independent moral thought could at some point form a hedge against the lifeworld's occupation. In this he is once again practicing that affirmative brand of Marcusean critical theory he finds so appealing. In his words, "I maintain only . . . that individuals can develop structures of consciousness which belong to a higher stage than those which are already embodied in the institutions of their society" (p. 165).

In speaking of the widespread possibility of adults across a society being able to move to a postconventional stage of reasoning, Habermas is exhibiting a universalistic emphasis that has aroused strong criticism. He is aware of the intellectual unfashionability of his position, acknowledging that "I am defending an outrageously strong claim in the present context of philosophical discussion; namely, that there is a universal core of moral intuition in all times and in all societies" (1992a, p. 201). However, he is not arguing that this core assumes the same shape in all contexts. What he does contend is that these moral intuitions spring from the same origin— "from the conditions of symmetry and reciprocal recognition which are unavoidable presuppositions of communicative action" (p. 201). In other words, communicating in good faith is an inherently moral act based on certain presuppositions. The giving of reasons for action is one such presupposition, the readiness to grant to others the same communicative rights as oneself, another.

We must always remember, though, that Habermas' position of moral universalism is, paradoxically, a rejection of cultural universalism. He defines a universalistic value orientation as one entailing the rejection of the universal validity of one's own beliefs. A morally universalistic outlook means that "one does not insist on universalizing one's own identity" and that "one does not simply exclude that which deviates from it" (1992a, p. 240). Instead of a xenophobic certitude, "one relativizes one's own way of life with regard to the legitimate claims of other forms of life" (p. 240). One also "grants to the strangers and the others, with all their idiosyncrasies and incomprehensibilities, the same rights as oneself" (p. 240). Habermas' believes that with the adoption of such a perspective "the areas of tolerance must become infinitely broader than they are today" (p. 240).

The Theory of Communicative Action

As we saw in the previous section, communicative action is action undertaken by adults to reach understanding and agreement. Indeed, my phrase "action taken by adults" probably implies more intentionality than Habermas intends. In social living, such action is unavoidable. As Habermas declares in a 1994 interview, "I never say that people *want* to act communicatively but that they *have to*" (Habermas, 1994, p. 111). In his opinion, "in everyday communicative practice, sociated individuals cannot avoid (also) employing everyday speech in a way that is oriented toward reaching understanding" (p. 101). As long as we live in association with others, and as long as we accept that our lives are better without constant conflicts and disputes, then communicative action is required. This is because "there are elementary social functions that can only be satisfied by means of communicative action. Our intersubjectively shared, overlapping lifeworlds lay down a broad consensus, without which our everyday praxis simply couldn't take place" (p. 111). Rearing children, cooperative action of any kind, solving problems "without the costly recourse to violence" (p. 111) are all examples of these social functions in his view.

At the heart of human speech lies the desire for mutual understanding. In Habermas' view, "reaching understanding is the inherent telos of human speech . . .the concepts of speech and understanding reciprocally interpret one another" (1984, p. 287). The point of speech, indeed in many ways the point of life, is to come to understandings with others. Such understandings allow us to build relationships and alliances, thereby giving our lives meaning. When people agree on something, they enjoy "the intersubjective mutuality of reciprocal understanding, shared knowledge, mutual trust, and accord with one another" (1979, p. 3). This kind of agreement represents the sort of solidarity that Habermas earlier described as the most endangered resource on the planet. The solidarity arising from agreement also underlies social action.

Without agreement, the intersubjective energy that propels collective action in the pursuit of common goals cannot develop. As such it is integral to the kind of political will formation so necessary to democracy.

In Habermas' view, reaching agreement is inherently democratic since true agreement springs from the freely given assent of the parties concerned. Hence, "a communicatively achieved agreement . . . cannot be imposed by either party (whether instrumentally via intervention or strategically via undue influence)" (1984, p. 287). Embedded in authentic human communication—especially that concerned with how to live as a community—are certain democratic norms. First, as we have seen, "coming to an understanding requires the rider uncoerced" (1984, p. 392). Those involved must feel that the understanding has been reached of their unforced volition. Second, coming to an understanding is based on the truthful giving of reasons for various actions. It is "a process of mutually convincing one another in which the actions of participants are coordinated on the basis of motivation by reason" (1984, p. 287). Third, "coming to an understanding means that participants in communication reach an agreement concerning the validity of an utterance; agreement is the intersubjective recognition of the validity claim the speaker raises for it" (1987a, p. 121). When we agree to something, we implicitly acknowledge that the views of others involved in the agreement have some validity.

The concept of validity claims features strongly in the early Habermas, particularly in *Communication and the Evolution of Society* (1979) and in *Theory and Practice* (1973). Learning to assess the validity of speech is for him a crucial adult learning project. As already discussed, Habermas believes adult learning happens primarily through speech. In social systems, "subjective learning processes take place and are organized within the framework of ordinary language communication" (1973, p. 12). When we engage in "ordinary" conversation, we are continually learning to assess the validity claims embedded within another person's words. Validity claims are the unspoken assumptions we make regarding the truth and sincerity of another person's comments. Is the person talking to us interested in stating her views as clearly as she can so we have a good chance of understanding what she's trying to say? Or is she appearing to be open and honest so as to get us on her side in order to make it easier for her to influence us for her own ends? Habermas believes that each time we enter into a conversation we are continually judging how far we can trust what our partner is saying. In effect, we are assessing a number of validity claims implied in the other's attempt to speak to us. Habermas argues that "in action oriented to reaching understanding, validity claims are 'always already' implicitly raised" (1979, p. 97). Furthermore, "these universal claims . . . are set in the general structure of possible communication" (p. 97). Whenever people, irrespective of time or place, try to reach understanding, they act according to these claims. Hence "in communicative action, the validity basis of speech is presupposed" (p. 118).

What are these validity claims Habermas identifies? The first is "the comprehensibility of the utterance" (1973, p. 18). We ask how clear and understandable are the words the other person is using. This is the claim of comprehensibility, and it requires speakers to strive to use language that stands the best chance of being understood by hearers. When we hear a sentence, we also try to gauge "the truth of its propositional component" (p. 18); that is, whether or not the words used accurately represent some state of affairs in the wider world. This is the second claim of truth. Is the speaker doing her best to give us the fullest possible information about the matter under consideration? The extent to which the speaker sticks to the rules of talk that prevail in our community is a third feature we pay attention to. A sentence is judged partly according to "the correctness and appropriateness of its performatory component" (1973, p. 18); that is, whether or not it is stated in a form that is familiar and likely to be understood the way it is intended. Communication is impossible without people observing the intuitively understood norms and rules governing speech, the broadly accepted road map of talk. In Habermas' view, "all communicative actions satisfy or violate normative expectations or conventions" (1979, p. 35), and when we speak to someone we continually judge their adherence to these. This is the claim of rightness. Finally, we need to know that the person speaking to us is sincerely interested in reaching understanding. This is the claim of authenticity, particularly "the authenticity of the speaking subject" (1973, p. 18). We must be able to trust that others in conversation sincerely wish to make themselves understandable and to understand us in turn.

If meaningful conversation is to occur, these four validity claims have to be satisfied. For Habermas, "communicative action can continue undisturbed only as long as participants suppose that the validity claims they reciprocally raise are justified" (1979, p. 3). When speakers involve themselves in communicative action—when they talk to each other with the intention of reaching common understandings—they rely on the fact that the four claims could be demonstrated if any of the speakers requested this of any of the others. Each person assumes that, if necessary, the others in the conversation could show how they are trying to satisfy these claims. So in any genuine speech "there is a common conviction that any validity claims raised . . . could be vindicated because the sentences, propositions, expressed intentions and utterances satisfy corresponding adequacy conditions" (1979, p. 4).

Learning to recognize when, or how far, these validity claims are being met is an unending adult learning project, one crucial to democratic life. If we haven't learned to distinguish between propagandizing and a genuine statement of deeply held views, or to discern those times when apparent truthfulness masks coercive intent, then our ability to defeat subtle demagoguery within the public sphere is severely curtailed. It is in everyday communicative action that adults learn to recognize the kinds of sophistry and manipulation of speech that, on a larger scale, diminish the public sphere. The chair of a community gathering who, in giving the "sense of the meeting," carefully slants his summary to highlight his preferred view; the adult education facilitator who sums up the main points of a discussion and gives an account that some in the room barely recognize; the spouse or lover in a supposedly open conversation who skillfully manipulates the outcome so that the blame for any marital stress or interpersonal tension always rests on the other's shoulders— all these communicative actions are violating one or other of the validity claims Habermas identifies as endemic to communicative action. In learning how to detect when these violations are happening, and how to bring these to people's attention, adults prepare themselves for conversations in the public sphere. They show that they are learning communicative competence.

One of Habermas' ideas that has drawn criticism is his emphasis on the giving of reasons as a universal feature of speech. To him "even the most fleeting speech act offers, the most conventional yes/no responses, *rely on* potential reasons" (1996, p. 19). If asked, we could supply the reasons why we propose something or respond to another's proposal in the ways we do. Reasons, therefore, "are the primary currency used in a discursive exchange that redeems criticizable validity claims" (p. 35). The reasons given for various proposals or assertions can, of course, be false, wrong, exploitative, or immoral. But the giving of reasons is universal. We may appeal to authority (do this because I tell you to) or supernatural powers (do this because the rain god will be displeased if you don't), but we always cite reasons to justify our beliefs or actions to ourselves and others. Speakers engaged in communicative action assume the responsibility to give grounds for the validity claims implicit in whatever they say. Habermas summarizes the responsibilities entailed by communicative action as follows: "The speaker, in a cognitively testable way, assumes with a truth claim, obligations to provide certain grounds, with a rightness claim, obligations to provide justification, and with a truthfulness claim, obligations to provide trustworthy" (1979, p. 65).

Nowhere is this giving of reasons more important than in deliberations within a democratic public sphere. As we have seen, Habermas believes a speech community is also a democratic community, and the rules that govern communicative action are therefore the same as those informing the democratic process. If learning to participate in communicative action is a universal adult learning project, then learning democratic process is its political counterpart. When we learn to talk to each other in ways that are comprehensible, truthful, appropriate, and authentic, we are learning an analog of democratic process. This is because the standards and rules with which we learn to judge the rightness of our participation in a conversational community are very similar to those we adopt when assessing whether or not a democratic decision has true legitimacy. In both instances, "participating actors must conduct themselves cooperatively and attempt to reach an agreement about their plans (in the horizon of the shared lifeworld) on the basis of common (or sufficiently overlapping) situation interpretations" (1992b, p. 79). In pursuing agreement as citizens or as "ordinary" speakers, adults apply communicative rationality, "the rationally motivating force of achieving understanding" (p. 80). Communicative rationality is centered on the fulfillment of validity claims, on being able to explain how one's assertions and proposals are comprehensible, sincere, truthful, and appropriately expressed. Communicative rationality thus "provides a standard for evaluating systematically distorted forms of communication and of life" (p. 50). The same criteria of validity that we apply to judge the effectiveness of our communicative efforts can be applied to assess the legitimacy of our social, political, and economic institutions. After all, these institutions are determined by our communicative efforts, and if participants within them do not act understandably, sincerely, truthfully, and appropriately, then they can easily become instruments of ideological manipulation. For Habermas, then, "those aspects of validity that undergird speech are also imported to the forms of life reproduced through communicative action" (1996, p. 4). The most important of these forms is the democratic way of life.

A Discourse Theory of Democracy

In a rare (and welcome) burst of lyricism concerning the limits of communicative rationality, Habermas acknowledges that "communicative reason is of course a rocking hull—but it does not go under in the sea of contingencies, even if shuddering in high seas is the only mode in which it 'copes' with these contingencies" (1992b, p. 144). Perhaps the most turbulent waves—the tsunami of communicative action—are produced when people try to work with the inherently contradictory and uncontrollable political arrangement we call democracy. Nonetheless, from *Theory and Practice* (1973) to *The Postnational Constellation* (2001a), Habermas is consistent in his argument that the rules of discourse represented by communicative reason are also the basis of democratic process. Adult educators will recognize these discourse rules as informing the conduct of many adult discussion groups. The rules Habermas specifies are "that (a) all relevant voices are heard, (b) the best of all available arguments, given the present state of our knowledge are accepted, and (c) only the non-coercive coercion of the better argument determines the affirmations and negations of the participants" (Habermas, 1992a, p. 260). In other words, good discussion, and therefore good democratic process, depends on everyone contributing, on everyone having the fullest possible knowledge of different perspectives, and on everyone being ready to give up their position if a better argument is presented to them. Taken together, these rules constitute an ideal which citizens can use to judge the effectiveness of political deliberations, and adult educators can use to judge the validity of adult education programs and adult learning activities.

Of course the problem with this ideal is that judgments as to which voices are relevant, how relevance itself is to be determined, how we decide which are the best arguments, and who estimates exactly what is the present state of our knowledge are all highly contentious. If we're not careful, we end up asking those in authority to decide these things, privileging the very experts Habermas is trying to restrain. Not surprisingly, Habermas is quick to recognize this danger. In an interview in *Justifications and Applications* (1993), he voices his regret at coining the term "ideal speech situation," calling it "a term whose concretistic connotations are misleading" (p. 164). He acknowledges that "language is also a medium of domination and social power" that "serves to legitimate relationships of organized force" (Habermas, 1988, p. 172) as well as being the medium through which democracy can be learned. He continually points to the ways in which ideology works "to conceal the asymmetrical distribution of chances for the legitimate satisfaction of needs" (Habermas, 1975, p. 27), particularly the chances different people have to join a deliberative speech community. If a society maintains itself by subtly discrediting or marginalizing certain voices, then "communication between participants is then systematically distorted or blocked" (p. 27). However, Habermas does not believe that these drawbacks inevitably render rules of discourse as useless. To reject these rules because they can be co-opted and manipulated by dominant groups is to throw the baby of communicative reason out with the bathwater of potentially distorted communication.

For Habermas the ideal rules of discourse, embedded as they are in the universal processes of speech, offer the best hope of keeping democratic forces alive. We can use these rules to determine whether a speech community (of, say, elected representatives) is reaching its decisions in a fair and morally defensible way. Since the members of such a community are all those affected by the matters being discussed, we can check whether or not they are all present. We can assess how far "all motives except that of the cooperative search for truth are excluded" (1975, p. 108) in the community's deliberations. Deliberations conducted around "a common interest ascertained without deception" in which "the constraint-free consensus permits only what *all* can want" (p. 108) are admittedly rare. But their rarity does not render these rules irrelevant. A genuine attempt to adhere to these rules, while recognizing that people will always fall short of them, is what grants legitimacy to adult educational processes and to the broader workings of democracy. A democratic decision—what should comprise the curriculum of a graduate adult education course, the way in which wealth should be distributed among the population, or whether or not the citizenry should authorize its government's invasion of another country—only has legitimacy if it is reached after an attempt to follow the rules of discourse.

From a discourse theory standpoint, the fact that a decision represents the will of the majority is no guarantee of its legitimacy. Habermas echoes Fromm's and Marcuse's warnings about the dangers of automaton conformity and repressive tolerance. What is crucial in determining the legitimacy of a majority decision is the way this is reached, particularly whether or not it has "an internal relation to the competitive quest for truth" (Habermas, 1992a, p. 256). If the standards already discussed are observed when people come to a decision, then Habermas believes we can call it reasonable. Such a decision is reasonable because it represents "the rationally motivated, although fallible, result of a discussion which was prematurely ended under the pressure of the need for a decision" (p. 256).

Between Facts and Norms (1996) is the book in which Habermas' discourse theory of deliberative democracy is most fully laid out, though its elements are addressed much earlier in books such as *Toward a Rational Society* (1970). Habermas argues that "according to discourse theory the success of deliberative politics depends . . . on the institutionalization of the corresponding procedures and conditions of communication, as well as on the interplay of institutionalized deliberative processes with informally developed public opinions" (Habermas, 1996, p. 298). The rules of discourse implied in the simplest speech acts provide a model for the formal workings of democratic process and for debate about these within the public sphere.

At its most basic level, democratic decision making represents "a consensus arrived at in discussion free from domination" (Habermas, 1970, p. 7). However, as societies grow ever larger and more complex, a domination-free consensus arrived at through town meetings or other inclusive community conversations becomes increasingly impossible to achieve. In the twenty-first century, Western societies are "pluralistic societies in which comprehensive worldviews and collectively binding ethics have disintegrated" (Habermas, 1996, p. 448). Legislative procedures become increasingly concentrated in elite circles and distanced from the everyday lives of citizens. Existing laws, and the ways these are made, can also be changed at any moment by lawmakers.

In this situation, where the populace is often deeply alienated from the legislative process, how can the laws that are produced by that process have any validity? It is Habermas' contention that "the democratic procedure for the production of law evidently forms the only postmetaphysical source of legitimacy" (Habermas, 1996, p. 448). In other words, the only hope we have that people will accept as legitimate a decision they don't agree with is if they see that decision as clearly the result of genuinely democratic deliberations. As we have already seen, these democratic procedures themselves arise out of communicative action. Hence, from the viewpoint of discourse theory, "the discourse principle acquires the legal shape of a democratic principle" (p. 458) because it works "to legally institutionalize those communicative propositions and procedures of a political opinion and will formation" (p. 458). The only chance that laws have of being perceived by the populace as legitimate is if they are democratically arrived at. If political actors acknowledge the validity claims that Habermas sees as endemic to human speech, then citizens will regard the decisions they make as rational; that is, as being in the best interests of those they affect. Thus, "discourse theory explains the legitimacy of law by means of procedures and communicative presuppositions that, once they are legally institutionalized, ground the supposition that the processes of making and applying law lead to rational outcomes" (p. 414).

These are weighty roles for discourse and democracy. In Habermas' words, "the *democratic process* bears the entire burden of legitimation" (1996, p. 450) where the law is concerned. Citizens act under "the promise that democratic processes of law making justify the presumption that enacted norms are rationally acceptable" (Habermas, 1996, p. 33), and people carry the expectation that democratically decided laws are fair, contingent, and revisable. This foregrounding of democratic process as the guarantor of legislative legitimacy raises significant questions for adult education. If people are to judge whether or not "democratic processes of law making justify the presumption that enacted norms are rationally acceptable" (p. 33), then they need to learn ways of recognizing when democratic processes are being conscientiously followed. This is not just a matter of learning democratic theory. People need to experience the contradictions and tensions of democracy, and to learn how to navigate through these while also learning the uncomfortable ontological truth that they are often unnavigable. Learning democracy is a matter of learning to live with ambiguity and contingency as much as it is learning how to apply deliberative decision-making procedures. As such, it connects directly to the development of postconventional judgment that Habermas identifies in *Moral Consciousness and Communicative Action* (1990) as an adult learning project.

Habermas' work on adult political learning explores three avenues through which adults can learn democratic procedures and dispositions. First, societies can institutionalize evolutionary learning processes so that knowledge of democratic practices can be handed down from generation to generation. In *Communication and the Evolution of Society* (1979), Habermas argues that organized learning processes are successful if they result in "the production and utilization of technically and practically useful knowledge" (p. 173). Democratically speaking, this means that adult education must give plenty of opportunities for people to learn about the technical aspects of democratic procedures and the typical, predictable diversions and blockages that arise when working within these. Welton (2000) argues that initiatives such as the Canadian Citizens' and Farm Forums of the 1940s and 1950s represented "institutionalized opportunities to exist and act as citizens, as participants in public life" (p. 214).

As far as formal adult education is concerned, learning democracy suggests that the negotiation of curriculum and of classroom process among members of the learning community should constitute the norm rather than the exotic exception. The kinds of negotiations over purposes and activities that are the common conversational currency in community action groups would become prominent in adult education programs. If this happened, then adult education as part of civil society could constitute a mini-laboratory in which people could learn and practice democratic dispositions that could then be transferred into the public sphere. Such protocols and dispositions comprise what Welton (2003) describes as the "pedagogics of civil society . . . the optimal learning conditions that enable open, uncoerced and respectful communication amongst citizens who engage each other towards the creation of a common world able to attend to the needs of its citizens" (p. 198).

Everyday conversations represent a second avenue for learning democratic process. Seeing things from another point of view, taking different perspectives, suspending judgment about something contentious until we hear what the other person has to say about it—these are all communicative acts we engage in during conversations about apparently nonpolitical matters. In discussion groups within both liberal and radical adult education, many of these everyday communicative behaviors are explicitly identified as the ones around which discussion should be organized. For example, Bridges (1988) urges discussion participants to learn how to build a moral culture for discussion; Burbules (1993) sketches out the necessary communicative virtues adults need to learn if they are to talk across differences; and Brookfield and Preskill (1999) outline dispositions of mutuality and reciprocity that must be learned if democratic discussion is to occur.

Eduard Lindeman is the American adult educator who has argued most prominently for democratic discussion as the quintessential adult educational method. In papers such as "The Place of Discussion in the Learning Process," "Group Work and Democracy," and "Democratic Discussion and the People's Voice" (all in Brookfield, 1987b) and in books such as *The Meaning of Adult Education* (Lindeman, [1926] 1961) and *The Democratic Way of Life* (Smith and Lindeman, 1951), Lindeman's vision of democracy and his emphasis on the need for adult citizens to learn a number of democratic disciplines through discussion participation have distinctly Habermasian overtones. Although Lindeman cannot be located within critical theory's central discourse, his concern to help adults learn conversational processes that are central to democratic functioning does anticipate Habermas' work in this area. As Welton (2003) points out, "commitment to educating the communicatively competent citizen has deep roots in adult education traditions" (p. 207), and one of the deepest of these is Lindeman's work on dialog and discussion. The rules and dispositions of discourse proposed by Welton himself—inclusiveness, openness, lack of coercion, tolerance, tact, civility, and solidarity—parallel in many ways the democratic disciplines outlined by Lindeman.

Habermas' work on the development of moral consciousness offers clues towards a third, somewhat contradictory, approach to the project of learning democracy. As discussed earlier in this chapter, Habermas sees the development of postconventional judgment, and the consequent tolerance of multiplicity and contextuality this entails, as something that is paradoxically learned when people are removed from their experiential context (see Habermas 1990, pp. 161–162). A separation from immediate experience allows adults to reflect back on this—usually in conversation with others—in a way, and with a critical edge, that is difficult in daily life. This is the essence of adult critical reflection.

Critical reflection, in Habermas' view, is chiefly an adult phenomenon. He believes we cannot talk about critically reflective learning until uncritical, unreflective learning has occurred, usually at earlier stages of life. In his opinion, "we are not able to reflect back on internalized norms until we have first learned to follow them blindly through coercion imposed from without" (Habermas, 1988, p. 170). So critical reflection in adulthood depends on an uncritical assimilation of norms in childhood and adolescence. One cannot reflect in a vacuum, there must always be something to reflect about. Learning about oppression or ideological domination, for example, is not just a theoretical exercise. It only has true meaning when we have lived through the consequences of domination, felt the cracks in the smooth façade of the administered life. Until adult life grants us enough diverse experiences to provide the comparative data for critical reflection, we are unable to judge the accuracy or benevolence of rules and perspectives learned in childhood. Reflection, therefore, "is condemned to operate after the fact" (Habermas, 1988, p. 170). However, this does not render it irrelevant since "operating in retrospect, it unleashes retroactive power" (p. 170). This is the retroactive power of criticality, the capacity to "become critically aware of the meaning of . . . the sequence of identifications and alienation" (p. 183) that comprises our life histories.

This vision of adults separating themselves out of everyday life and joining with others to discuss what it means to live democratically is at the core of residential adult education. Residential experiences offer participants the distance and ready-made speech community necessary for them to reflect on their experiences with democratic process. The residential workshops of the Highlander Center in Tennessee, in which activists learn from each other's experiences of building democracy in an oppressive world, represent an attempt to reflect critically on democratic participation (using appropriately dialogic approaches) that is very much in tune with Habermas' thinking on this matter.

For many North American adult educators, Habermas remains the only show in town where critical theory is concerned. In this chapter and in Chapter Eight, I have tried to illuminate the reasons for his prominence in our field. Although his body of work is intimidatingly wide, certain themes close to adult educators' concerns repeatedly emerge. There is the belief that adult learning is the engine of social change and that understanding its dynamics is as important as understanding mechanisms of production and exploitation. There is also the contention that critical reflection is a learning process observable mostly in adulthood, and a consequent emphasis on the possibility of adults reflecting back on ideological norms and behaviors internalized uncritically in childhood. Along with this is the stress on the way standards of conversation derived from communicative action can provide a methodological ideal against which dialogically inclined adult educators can gauge their effectiveness. Finally, there is the connection constantly returned to between the behaviors and dispositions of communicative action and the democratic process. Drawing on both Marxist and pragmatic traditions, Habermas reaches the same conclusion as Lindeman regarding the workings of democracy—that it must be understood as a lifelong learning process in which learning to live with contingency and contradiction is of equal importance to learning a set of procedural arrangements. In the next chapter this radical democratic fusion of ideology critique and pragmatic experimentation, and the place this fusion might occupy in the field of adult education, is explored further through an analysis of the work of several contemporary African American intellectuals, particularly Cornel West.

Chapter Ten

Racializing Criticality

In the introduction to his influential anthology on African American thought, *Philosophy Born of Struggle*, Leonard Harris observes that "the works of Afro-Americans are trapped, as it were, in a labyrinth where even the walls are white" (1983, p. ix). As readers will by now be well aware, this applies just as much to the philosophical tradition of critical theory as to analytic philosophy, empiricism or, idealism. Criticality's theory is undeniably Eurocentric, in Yancy's (1998) words "the history of white men engaged in conversation with themselves" (p. 3). Although conducted as an intellectual project for the liberation of all humankind, critical theory's location in White male discourses means that it may well function as yet one more "site of white cultural hegemony, sustained and perpetuated in terms of the particularity of race and gender related institutional power" (pp. 8–9). This is why Yancy argues that "there is a need to de-center Euro-American philosophy" (p. 11). Yancy believes that "African-American philosophers, within the context of American racism, share a certain *Othered* experiential reality in which the motif of race, its historical reality, its cultural dimensions, its heinous weight, its political importance, and its philosophical problematicity, is both explicitly and implicitly operative" (p. 11). Given that White European critical theorists are unlikely to reframe critical theory in the service of a different racial group, some African American intellectuals have tried to interpret this tradition in terms that serve African American interests. Others feel these interests are best served by instigating a separate Africentric discourse.

In the present chapter I respond to Yancy's call to de-center critical theory by examining how some African American intellectuals (in particular, Lucius T. Outlaw, Jr. and Cornel West) draw explicitly on critical theory but reinterpret its contributions from a racialized (to use Outlaw's term) African American perspective. These theorists believe that concepts prominent in the critical tradition have a utility in furthering African American interests but that these ideas must be viewed through, and fundamentally changed by, the prism of African Americans' experience of racism. For adult educators of all racial identities, critical theory can inform our understanding of how adults learn to assimilate, and sometimes to resist, racist ideology. As Outlaw (1983b) observes, it is contradictory for a theory that purports to help adults liberate themselves from injustice not to address how ideology buttresses racial oppression. In his view, if it is to have any meaning in a multicultural society, critical theory "must be reviewed critically to determine why, as both theory and praxis, it has dealt so inadequately with the matter of race/ethnicity and racism in the American social order" (p. 119). Outlaw's project is to sculpt an analysis of emancipation "in terms that are drawn from both the critical theoretical tradition of Marxism and from the tradition of Black Nationalism" (Outlaw, 1983b, p. 118).

Using Outlaw's work, along with that of Karenga and West, I wish to examine how the factor of race intersects with those learning tasks of adulthood—challenging ideology, overcoming alienation, contesting hegemony, unmasking power, and so on—that are the focus of this book. However, I should acknowledge that the intersection of critical theory and Black Nationalism explored in different ways by the writers discussed in the present chapter is but a small corner of the multilayered quilt of African American thought. Many African American intellectuals (including prominent adult educators) explicitly reject Eurocentric critical theory as a perspective that can be used to understand the African American experience. In their view, this experience (including the experience of African Americans learning and teaching within adult education) must be understood in terms drawing on African cultural traditions; in other words, from an Africentric perspective. In works such as *Afrocentricity* (Asante, 1998a) and *The Afrocentric Idea* (Asante, 1998b), the Africentric perspective articulates a position derived from an analysis of the indigenous elements of African culture. To adult educators Scipio Colin III and Talmadge Guy, "Africentrism is a sociocultural and philosophical perspective that reflects the intellectual traditions of both a culture and a continent. It is grounded in the seven basic values embodied in the Swahili *Nguzo Saba*" (Colin and Guy, 1998, p. 52). The Africentric position toward the field of adult education "asserts that adult educational policies, practices, experiences, philosophies, ethical issues, theories, and concepts must be considered and evaluated on the basis of the perspective and experience of African Ameripeans/African Americans" (p. 52). In particular, an Africentric perspective explicitly excludes the understanding of adult education from a Eurocentric theoretical perspective such as critical theory.

In the white-walled labyrinth described earlier by Harris (at least where critical theory is concerned), all paths lead to a preoccupation with class, rather than race or gender. Critical theory as explored by the White males whose works have been reviewed in the previous chapters foregrounds class analysis. Adult identity is understood primarily as a function of the adult's class location and relationship to the means of production. Adult alienation is viewed as the adult's separation from the process and products of her or his labor. Ethnicity emerges as a factor from time to time (as in Marx's analysis on the hostility of English workers to Irish immigrants) but is not generally treated as a separate analytical category. The role of racially oppressed groups as catalysts of revolutionary change also receives occasional attention, as in Marcuse's view of the Black Power movement as a powerful force for disturbing the smooth façade of the administered life. In general, though, race is not featured consistently as a central, separate category of analysis in the work reviewed so far. Instead, the class reductionist perspective "tacitly assumes that racism is rooted in the rise of modern capitalism" (West, 1993c, p. 262).

There is no doubt that important interconnections do exist between class and race. In *Dusk of Dawn,* his autobiographical analysis of the concept of race, Du Bois ([1940] 1968) describes how his journey to Africa helped him "more clearly to see the close connection between race and wealth," in particular "the income-bearing value of race prejudice" (p. 129). But the racist conceptualization and treatment of people as subhuman based on physical characteristics such as facial features, hair type, and skin pigmentation constitutes a dimension of oppression that cannot be explained away purely by the economic benefits such practices accrue for the dominant class.

In recent times African American philosophers such as Boxhill (1983, 2001) and Karenga (1983) have argued that omitting race from critically inclined theory ignores the empirical reality of contemporary multiculturalism and the persistence of racist oppression. In Boxhill's view, "class analysis must either be scrapped altogether, or amended with a qualitatively new and theoretically independent conception of race, if it is to be of any use in understanding multiracial societies" (1983, p. 108). To Karenga, racial and ethnic particularities "are constitutive of human and social identity and in a racist social context, determine life-chances and social treatment" (p. 219). Consequently, in his view, "it is incorrect and analytically unproductive" (p. 219) to view racial oppression as a subcategory of class oppression. Because African Americans are reduced "to a permanent underclass set off from the rest of the American working class by systematic racist discrimination (they) are not simply alienated from their labor as workers, but also as Blacks" (p. 217). Consequently, "racial alienation joins class alienation as a fundamental problem of Black self-consciousness" (p. 217).

The pertinence of race has not been lost on adult educators of a critical cast who have argued that scholarship and practice in the field mirrors and perpetuates the racism of the wider society. During a symposium at the 1992 Adult Education Research Conference in Saskatoon, Canada, several participants protested vigorously over the way literature in the field—particularly the then newly published text *Adult Education: Evolution and Achievements in a Developing Field of Study* (Peters, Jarvis, and Associates, 1991)—excluded non-White non-male voices. This galvanized some theorists' energies and led to a series of important edited collections that focused on illuminating racism and sexism within the field and on widening its frame of inquiry (Hayes and Colin, 1994; Guy, 1999; Peterson, 2002; Sheared and Sissel, 2001). The emergence of the African American preconference preceding each annual meeting of the Adult Education Research Conference (AERC) is another indicator of the way in which race has been foregrounded as a crucial factor in adult education research and scholarship. Other AERC preconferences have been arranged on the perspectives and experiences of Indigenous People, the Asian Diaspora, and Chicanas(os)/Latinas(os). The racial membership of adult classrooms, the racial composition of the adult education profession generally and its professoriate in particular, the racist character of certain adult education policies, practices, and instructional materials, the racial positionality of authors and conference presenters, the racially skewed valorization of certain figures as "experts" in the field, the dominance of theories and concepts that appear race-blind, and the racial make-up of gatekeeper boards, committees, and editorial collectives are now emerging motifs in critically inclined adult educational discourse.

Considerations on Racializing Critical Theory

Before engaging with the racializing of critical theory, however, I wish to make some important caveats. The first concerns the selection of an African American perspective as the racial perspective to explore most deeply. Why de-center critical theory through this lens rather than a Latino, Native American, Hmong, Pakistani, Chinese, or Aboriginal perspective? Where does the work of a Caribbean Marxist like C.L.R. James fit in, or that of the Afro-Caribbean British cultural studies theorist, Stuart Hall? Are the philosophical worldviews of indigenous, First Nation peoples not equally deserving of attention? Are we in danger of erecting a racial hierarchy that privileges certain previously excluded bodies of thought over others?

My choice of the African American perspective as the one to explore in depth in this chapter springs from my own practice as an adult educator. As a White Englishman, the group of non-White adult learners with whom I have had the most contact over the years is that of African Americans. So I should be honest about having a selfish, vested interest in understanding how my own practice— sculpted in a society 3,000 miles on the other side of the Atlantic ocean—is constantly widened, challenged, and problematized by working with this group of learners. Part of my effort to become aware of the condescension and unacknowledged racism implicit in my own practice has involved me reading in the literature reviewed in this chapter. In this regard I have been fortunate enough to have cotaught several times with the foremost Africentric adult education theorist in the United States, Scipio A. J. Colin III. Dr "C." has been a valued mentor to me in guiding me through the multiple literatures of African American thought, though the misunderstandings I am guilty of are no responsibility of hers.

My own positionality as an English male, and more specifically my own racial membership as White, is an important element to acknowledge in this chapter. In their analysis of Black intellectual life, Cornel West and bell hooks discuss the ways in which, according to hooks, "White theorists draw upon our work and our ideas, and get forms of recognition that are denied Black thinkers" (hooks and West, 1991, p. 36). She speaks of how "there is a feeling now that a White academic might take your idea, write about it, and you'll never be cited" (p. 36). In the same conversation, West observes, "White scholars are bringing certain baggage with them when they look at Black culture, no matter how subtle and sophisticated the formulations" (p. 36). I have learned from Dr C. that the baggage of my racial membership and identity means I cannot be an Africentric theorist whose being, identity, and practice spring from African values, sensibilities, and traditions. I can appreciate the accuracy and explanatory power of something like Du Bois' concept of double consciousness. In so doing I can reflect on how being both African and American means that one is "always looking at oneself through the eyes of others, of measuring one's soul by the tape of the world that looks on in amused contempt and pity" (Du Bois, 1995, p. 45). But though this may illuminate what some of my learners and colleagues are experiencing, I can have no real understanding of what this means. As a White Englishman, I have no experiential, visceral access to the philosophy born of struggle that comprises the central dimension of African American thought. My skin pigmentation, White privilege, and collusion in racism places me irrevocably and irretrievably outside the Africentric paradigm. I can learn from and honor this scholarship. I can be grateful for the way it questions and reformulates aspects of critical theory, or the way it shatters (in a helpful way) my own understandings and practices. But I can never claim to work as an Africentric adult educator. No matter how much I wish to honor this tradition, my racial membership precludes me making such a claim. In the words of a provocative volume, it is problematic to be *Teaching What You're Not* (Mayberry, 1996).

My third caveat has to do with the positioning of this chapter within this book. After all, this chapter on racializing critical theory comes after nine chapters focused exclusively on its Eurocentric variants. Conducting this discussion in Chapter Ten may appear an instance of subtle (or maybe not so subtle) marginalization, relegating African American scholarship to the status of the exotic "other" in contrast to the Eurocentric center. The chapter could be seen as an example of the kind of repressive tolerance discussed by Marcuse in Chapter Seven, whereby an apparent embrace of a different perspective serves only to neuter that same perspective. There could easily appear a suggestion of tokenism, or of intellectual colonialism, with critical theory raiding African American scholarship as a means of reinforcing critical theory's prominence. Under the guise of appearing to honor African American intellectual traditions, such an effort would only marginalize African American thought even further. So let me emphasize that one important reason for writing this chapter is to urge interested readers to engage with the multiple bodies of African American scholarship and with the expression of an Africentric paradigm on its own terms. This chapter is not just an exploration of important and interesting theoretical perspective on critical theory, but a starting point for a whole new analysis.

Fourth, I want to say something about my adoption of Outlaw's (1996) concepts of "raciation" and "raciality" (his words). To Outlaw raciation and raciality are important and unavoidable social facts. They describe the way people's racial histories and identities inform how they "organize meaningfully, give order to, and thus define and construct the worlds in which we live, our life-worlds" (Outlaw, 1996, p. 5). Raciality, ethnicity, and gender "are constitutive of the personal and social being of persons . . . they make up the historically mediated structural features of human life-worlds and inform lived experience" (p. 174). Taking a racialized view of a phenomenon, in Outlaw's terms, means that we view it through the distinctive lens of a racial group's experience of the world. This chapter acknowledges the struggle against racism as a crucial element of African American raciality.

Outlaw emphasizes that raciality is a positive phenomenon, and he stresses that "racialism neither is nor need become racism" (1996, p. 8), though keeping the two from conflating is sometimes a struggle. Racism comprises "sets of beliefs, images and practices that are 'imbued with negative valuation' and employed as modes of exclusion, inferiorization, subordination, and exploitation in order to deny targeted racial or ethnic groups full participation in the social, political, economic, and cultural life of a political community" (p. 8). Racialism is the positive recognition of how the constitutive features of one's lifeworld, one's positionality and sense of historical and cultural identity, comprise a set of preconscious filters and assumptions that frame how life is felt and lived. Racialism's valuation is positive, not negative. It recognizes the contributions and particularities of one's racial identity. We can celebrate the constitutive elements of our and others' raciality in a way imbued with generosity and recognition quite different from the brutal, negative celebration of one's racism.

It is important to note that most philosophical discourse as a product of European, Enlightenment rationality is already racialized. To Outlaw (1996) philosophy has already engaged in "the racialization and coloring of reason" (p. xxx) by valorizing European cultural modes of analysis within Harris' "white walled labyrinth." As a branch of European philosophy, critical theory too is already racialized. This Eurocentric body of work represents a White, Enlightenment rationality and celebrates how this intellectual project is dedicated to the realization of a more humane world. In Outlaw's terms, the current chapter is about re-racializing critical theory, viewing it through an African American rather than Eurocentric lens. We should always remember, too, that adult educational theory and practice is also already racialized. Andragogy, self-direction, critical reflection, transformative learning—all the most frequently cited concepts that purport to define what is distinctive about the field and that comprise its dominant discursive boundaries—are valued positively and identified mostly with scholarship conducted by White American, European, and Commonwealth males. Acknowledging that concepts and practices are racialized is not to say they should be abandoned. After all, Davis, Outlaw, Karenga, West, hooks, and others discussed in this and the next chapter do not abandon critical theory but rather reinterpret it to serve particular racial interests. But a racialized perspective means that adult education scholars should be much more intentional in their efforts to trace the racial dimensions of the field's dominant discourse.

The Importance of Terminology

Before exploring a racialized view of critical theory, a word should be said about its terminology. Scholarship conducted by American philosophers of African descent is referred to by those same scholars in a number of different ways, each of which signifies an important element in that scholar's analysis. The descriptors of African-American philosophy (Yancy, 1998), Black philosophy (Hord and Lee, 1995), Afrocentric philosophy (Asante, 1998a, 1998b), Kawaida (Karenga, 1983), African American philosophy (with no hyphen, see for example Peterson, 2002), Africology (Outlaw, 1996), and Africentric paradigms (Colin, 1988, 2002) are not interchangeable. Viewing adult education through an Afro-centric paradigm is, in Colin's view, not the same as viewing it through an Africentric paradigm. Colin points out that "for many scholars of the African Diaspora the conceptual connections between race (how they identify themselves) and knowledge production is extremely important relative to meaning, interpretation and analysis" (S.A.J. Colin, personal communication, 2002). Thus, the use of the hyphen in African-American is objectionable to many. As Colin puts it, "Some scholars of the Diaspora don't use the hyphen because they don't view themselves as 'hyphenated Americans' but rather as Africans in/of America" (S.A.J. Colin, personal communication, 2002).

The use of the hyphen in terms such as African-American, Afro-centric, or African-Ameripean also contradicts a tenet of the philosophy such terms are sometimes intended to illuminate. In the Africentric paradigm, "a traditional value of African society . . . is an irrevocable bond between the members of the race and the collective whole" (Colin, 2002, p. 62). This bond rejects what is seen as the false dichotomy between individual and group identity. From Colin's point of view, a hyphen is a punctuation device that emphasizes the separation, rather than the interconnection, of two words. When those two words refer to racial and cultural characteristics, such as African and American, it implies for her a separation of identities that is empirically false. Applied to her own theory of the need for selfethnic reflectors among African Ameripeans, she writes, "This writer's use of the term selfethnic without the hyphen reflects the underlying principles of influence and reciprocity that form the foundational basis of the relationship between African Ameripeans and their race" (p. 62).

As you may have noticed above, Colin proposes the term African Ameripean to describe adult educators and adult learners of African descent living in the United States. For her, the use of the word *African* "denotes the primary genetic roots and land of origin" of this group of people. The term *Ameri* "reflects the voluntary assimilation with various Native American tribal societies (particularly Cherokee and Seminole)," and *Pean* "reflects the forced assimilation with various European ethnic groups, particularly the British, French, and Irish during the period of slavery in the United States" (Colin, 2002, p. 62). Consequently, Colin's body of work on Africentric interpretations of adult educational theory, philosophy, and practice consistently employs the term *African Ameripean*. This usage, which challenges dominant notions of what constitutes a distinctly American identity, illustrates how the scholarly language we use to describe our work (in this case the work of adult educators of African descent) is often contested. For example, in an edited collection in which she used this term (Colin, 2002), the publisher inserted a note at the head of her chapter, in boldface, stating that the term *African Ameripean* and other terms in this chapter were reflective of the Africentric perspective of its author. The statement went on to say that the publisher did not condone the use of the term, that it was used at the insistence of the author, and that the publisher thought it best to let readers decide on the term's applicability.

It is hard to imagine such a caveat being issued at the head of a chapter in which the term *andragogy*—itself a new word generated within adult educational discourse to describe particularities of adult educational practice—was used. There are no publisher disclaimers, as far as I'm aware, of the use of new terminology in adult educational discourses around transformative learning or critical reflection. Yet Colin is always very careful to follow scholarly conventions of giving a precise rationale for her choice of terms. In another publication (where no publisher disclaimer was deemed necessary), Colin and her co-editor explain their use of terms as follows: "The term African Ameripean is used . . . because of the authors' belief that terms such as colored, black, Negro, Afro-American, and African American are culturally inappropriate and historically incorrect" (Hayes and Colin, 1994, p. 3). It denotes "any person of African descent born in America" (p. 3) and thus describes an important group of participants in many adult education programs. Colin and Hayes then go on to explain their use of Africentric and Africentrism, rather than Afrocentric or Afrocentrism. For them, "Africentrism is a sociocultural and philosophical perspective that reflects the intellectual traditions of both a culture and a continent" (p. 3). It is grounded in the seven basic values of *Nguzo Saba* (to use the Swahili term), one of which—*Ujamaa*—underpins Julius Nyrere's exposition of an African socialism (Nyrere, 1968). In contrast to Africentrism's grounding in African cultural values, "Afrocentrism is considered by these authors to represent an integrationist perspective that incorporates elements of European traditions" (p. 3). So in adult educational discourse the presence, or lack of, a hyphen and the use of an "o" or "i" in Afro or Afri have important implications (to hark back to Colin's terms quoted earlier) for knowledge production on race and adult education.

Connecting Critical Theory to African American Philosophy

Although this chapter explores an African American perspective on critical theory, it should be unequivocally stated that most of the writers I review deny that there is any such thing as a unitary, African American philosophy. This is well illustrated in the interviews in Yancy's (1998) *African-American Philosophers*. In his introduction to the volume, Yancy eschews any "ontological essentialist foundationalism that forms the sine qua non of African-American philosophical identity and thought" (p. 10). About as far as he will go is to observe that what emerges in his book is "a complex set of philosophical positionalities and thoughts exhibiting areas of commonality and diversity broadly informed by, though not simply reduced to, African-American culture" (p. 10). West (1998) declares there is no such thing as a general African American philosophy that somehow transcends history, though there is "a certain cultural response to the world" (p. 38) informed by a particular African American "deep blues sensitivity that highlights concrete existence, history, struggle, lived experience and joy" (p. 39). To Harris (1998), "African-American philosophy is simply the history of

African-Americans engaged in doing philosophy . . . with conscious recognition of the African-American heritage and the kinds of issues and problems which that heritage emphasizes" (p. 214)—in particular the heritage of struggle. Outlaw (1998) too points out that "African-American philosophy does not refer to a single anything, but rather to a collectivity . . .. to the philosophizing of persons who are Americans of African descent" (p. 313).

So to talk of African American philosophy as if it were a distinctive, unified body of work is inaccurate and condescending. One would not talk of British philosophy as if everyone born in Great Britain philosophized in the same way. African American philosophy exhibits the same kind of subtlety, difference, and disagreements as does the philosophizing of any other group of people. To take just one recent example, the emergence of critical race theory (Delgado, 1995; Crenshaw, Gotanda, Peller, and Thomas, 1995) in legal studies has generated a vigorous intellectual debate amongst African American intellectuals (as well as in the wider world) that in its energy, sophistication, and rigor parallels anything in the white-walled philosophical labyrinth. The relevance of this debate for Africentric adult education has been well summarized by Peterson (1999). There is also a wide-ranging debate within African American philosophical circles surrounding the validity of the Africentric philosophical paradigm that illustrates a range of principled positions on the issue (see for example Hountondi, 1983; Serequeberhan, 1991; Appiah, 1997, 2001). So as Outlaw (1998) maintains, "There is nothing automatically conveyed about their philosophizing when we say that there are African-Americans who philosophize" (p. 314). The African American theorists discussed in this chapter represent but one of many philosophical orientations evident amongst African American intellectuals. They have been chosen because they have drawn explicitly on ideas in critical theory to interpret and illuminate aspects of African American experience. More particularly, they have applied these ideas to understanding and combating racism. But it is important to remember that, to other African American intellectuals, critical theory is just one more hegemonic Eurocentric discourse representing a White, Anglicized view of the world.

The African American theorists considered in the following paragraphs are explicit in acknowledging their study of the critical tradition. In Outlaw's and West's work in particular, references to Marx, Horkheimer, Habermas, Gramsci, Foucault, and Marcuse are interwoven into their discussions of Garvey, Du Bois, Locke, Cruse, and Fanon. One of the most well-known connections between African American intellectuals and critical theory is that between Angela Davis and Marcuse. In a 1998 interview, Davis declared that "I think of both Baldwin and Marcuse as mentors who helped me to conceptualize a relationship between theory and practice, a challenge that I continue to struggle with today" (Davis, 1998b, p. 20). Davis was Marcuse's student at Brandeis University, and after being introduced to German idealism, she decided to study in Frankfurt, there attending lectures by Adorno and Habermas. She returned to the United States to work closely with Marcuse "because he maintained a sense of the connectedness between emerging social movements and his larger philosophical project" (Davis, 1998b, p. 23). Lucius T. Outlaw also describes how as a student he was "impressed and inspired" by the "provocative, interesting and insightful" (Outlaw, 1998, p. 321) work of Marcuse which led him to a deeper engagement with critical theory, especially Habermas (Outlaw, 1996, pp. 159–182).

Both Davis and Outlaw are drawn to Marcuse's engagement with contemporary social and political movements, to his idea that philosophizing is endemic to social activism. As expressed by Davis, "Critical theory . . . has as its goal the transformation of society, not just the transformation of ideas, but social transformation and thus the reduction and elimination of human misery. It was on the basis of this insistence on the social implementation of critical ideas that I was able to envisage a relationship between philosophy and Black liberation" (Davis, 1988b, p. 22). In their use of critical theory to illuminate racism, Davis, West, and Outlaw emphasize how racist ideology is buttressed by other forms of oppression based on economics, gender, sexual preference, physical capability, and so on. Consequently, they frame the fight against racism as necessarily entailing a fight against these interlocking systems of oppression. Although these critically inclined African American scholars highlight race as a central category of analysis, and though they all identify racist beliefs and practices as lying at the heart of dominant ideology, they also all acknowledge that in fighting racism they are fighting for a broader social transformation. To them dismantling racism does everyone a favor, it benefits all racial and ethnic groups. As Outlaw (1983a) puts it, "Our struggle for liberation as a people is but a part, a moment, of a wider struggle that embraces other peoples, groups, and classes within the social order" (pp. 83–84).

Combating Racist Alienation

One of the most explicit attempts to explore how concepts drawn from critical theory can be combined with Black nationalism to inform an understanding of American racism is Maulana Karenga's articulation of *Kawaida,* a "synthesis of the best of nationalist, Pan-Africanist, and socialist thought" (Karenga, 1983, p. 212). In West's view, the sophistication of Karenga's analyses means they "stand shoulders above much of the theoretical reflections on African-American's oppression proposed by the Black Marxist left" (West, 1993c, p. 263). Outlaw (1996) places Karenga's work alongside that of Asante (1998a, 1998b) in the school of Africology since it proposes as "the core of a 'Black value system,' the *Nguzo Saba,* provided to guide cultural and social change, and the organization of black life" (Outlaw, 1996, p. 119). In his articulation of *Kawaida* in *Philosophy Born of Struggle* (Harris, 1983), however, Karenga emphasizes that his position also draws on a Marxist-influenced concept of alienation. It is important to note that not all African American scholars agree that alienation is a central construct for understanding African American experience. McGary (1997), for example, argues that the ability of African Americans "to form their own supportive communities in the midst of a hostile environment" allowed them "to maintain healthy self-concepts through acts of resistance and communal nourishment" (p. 292). For him a continuing (and in his view mistaken) emphasis by liberals and Marxists on African Americans' alienation only serves to deepen the perception that African Americans are rootless victims without deeply forged cultural traditions and community supports.

Alienation as a central unit of analysis for Karenga is grounded in his investigation of the ways in which European dominance of Africa represented a systematic dispossession of African culture from the continent's indigenous people. Colonial rule ensured its own perpetuation by destroying African family forms, oral traditions, customs, and belief systems, thereby inducing a form of cultural amnesia. With "no historical memory to draw from and no future to look for out-side a servile association with white history and future" (Karenga, 1983, p. 215), African people were alienated from the cultural tradi-tions and practices that defined them. Now, with little awareness of their African cultural heritage, and under the harsh realities of con-temporary American capitalism, members of the African Diaspora are reduced to "a permanent underclass set off from the rest of the American working class by systematic racist discrimination" (p. 217). This is because "the ruling class and the ruling race overlap to form a ruling *race-class* that imposes both racist and capitalist views on soci-ety" (p. 220). As a result African Americans "are not simply alienated from their labor as workers, but also as Blacks . . . racial alienation joins class alienation as a fundamental problem of Black self-con-sciousness" (p. 217).

Karenga defines alienation in familiar Marxist-inclined terms as the "estrangement and separation of humans from all or any-thing through which they can realize themselves" (1983, p. 216). For African Americans the dominant ideology of White supremacy is a crucial source of alienation in that it blocks efforts at self-recognition. In common with West and Outlaw, Karenga analyses race as an ideological construct that prevents the development of oppositional consciousness. Racial stereotypes and racist under-standings are viewed as part of the regime of truth, an example of the way knowledge construction is intertwined with power. In this regime, power and knowledge combine to allow a small group of White Europeans to assign worth and status to other human beings on the basis of phenotype (people's facial features, hair, and skin pigmentation). The more that non-Whites try to emulate Euro-pean behaviors, appearance, and practices, the closer they move to become the targets of patronizing tolerance. Overt exploitation, violence, and brutality are replaced by condescension and cultural genocide. As part of dominant ideology, therefore, racism com-prises "an elaborate system of pseudo-intellectual categories, assumptions, and contentions negative to Third World peoples" that is designed "to create a non-historical dehumanized being who could not merit freedom and equality even by his own justification and dared not attempt rebellion" (p. 218).

Ideological dominance sooner or later begets ideological resis-tance in Karenga's view, and he has a clear program of intervention to combat racist ideology. Breaking epistemological oppression means breaking "the monopoly the ruling ideology has on Afro-American minds" and beginning "to lay the basis for a critical Afro-centric alternative" (1983, p. 220). Such an alternative would be generated from and act on behalf of a Black nationalist culture that represented African traditions and African epistemology. Karenga contends, "it is the ruling ideology that prevents Afro-Americans from perceiving their objective situation and real interests" (p. 223) meaning that socioeconomic liberation is premised on epistemological liberation. Karenga urges the building of a Black nationalist culture as a form of "self-conscious, collective thought and practice through which a people creates itself, celebrates itself, and introduces itself to history and humanity" (p. 224). Citing Gramsci in his support, Karenga sees the need for a Black intellectual vanguard to lead this cultural, and ultimately political, struggle. This vanguard would work as African American organic intellectuals to build and proclaim "an Afro-centric theory, i.e. one that rises from, is focused on and behalf of them" (p. 223). As well as drawing on analytical constructs from Marxism, Karenga thus also embraces an Afrocentric perspective drawing on indigenous African cultural traditions in the manner of Asante (1998a, 1998b).

Turning to the African American Lifeworld

A call that echoes Karenga's emphasis on the development of theory focused on behalf of African Americans is Outlaw's insistence on the need for a hermeneutics of the African American lifeworld. Outlaw is consistently explicit about the influence of critical theory (especially Marcuse, Horkheimer, and Habermas) on his work. He also acknowledges how Foucault's elaboration of disciplinary power "supports some of the criticisms of 'Eurocentric' intellectual endeavors advanced in African-American studies" (Outlaw, 1996, p. 101). Mostly, though, Outlaw is concerned with Habermas' project to defend the lifeworld from attacks by capital and state power by refocusing this through the lens of African American interests. He positions himself as a philosopher of African descent who shares critical theory's conception of philosophy as a tool for social change. In Outlaw's view, "the vocation of philosophizing . . . is to share in the refinement and perpetuation of critical intelligence as a practice of life" (1996, p. 29), with this practice leading to "life expressed as qualitatively-progressively-different" (p. 29). To live philosophically is to "live life conditioned primarily by the activity of critical, dialectical thinking" (p. 30). More particularly, to live as a Black philosopher is to be "guided by the interest (i.e. the value commitment) to serve the emancipatory efforts of people of African descent" (1983a, p. 66). This project necessarily entails the widespread "revolutionary transformation of the American order" (p. 66).

Doing philosophy within the particularities of the African American experience helps reveal the true needs, interests, values, and contributions of African Americans. Outlaw argues that philosophizing in the interests of people of African descent develops a distinctive Black philosophical identity based an awareness of Black intellectual traditions. A primary purpose of African American philosophers is to "become transparent to ourselves as a class in terms of our history, our responsibilities, our possibilities" (1996, p. 27). Black intellectuals "need to be clear as to our grounding as black thinkers (in) the long history of struggle on the part of our people for an increasingly liberated existence" (p. 27). One chance to develop a philosophy that will serve African Americans' interests is to combine Black Nationalism and critical theory. Outlaw believes that both traditions are necessary to clarifying African Americans' real needs and the means by which these might be met.

Why is critical theory an important partner to Black Nationalism? Outlaw argues that critical theory "seeks to cut through the veil of socially unnecessary domination by socially unnecessary systems of authority and control via the praxis of critical reflection" (1983a, p. 72). As such, it provides a framework "within which we people of African descent (and others) can assess our situation and achieve clarity regarding which concrete historical possibilities are in our best interest" (p. 83). Reframed in the interests of African Americans, critical theory "has as its primary interest the liberation of black folk, and others, from domination, to the greatest extent possible" (p. 72). If critical theory is to be a useful partner in a fusion with Black Nationalism, however, it must incorporate an analysis of racism, and how this might be challenged, into its workings.

How might a racialized interpretation of critical theory serve the interests of people of African descent? Here Outlaw draws explicitly on Habermas' concept of the lifeworld to argue that critical theory's most useful contribution is to elaborate the contours and constitutive elements of the African American lifeworld. He commits himself as a philosopher to understanding and communicating "the life-world of African-American people, in all of its ambiguities, complexities, contradictions, and clarities; to our concrete life-praxis, in search of our distinct orientation" (1983a, p. 66). Where Habermas is concerned chiefly with the colonization of the lifeworld by the exchange dynamic of capitalism and the logistics of bureaucratic rationality and state power, Outlaw focuses is on its invasion by the dynamics of racist ideology. When the African American lifeworld is distorted by White supremacist ideology, then its members are hampered in their understanding of their current situation and future possibilities. An emancipatory philosophical project, therefore, is to illuminate the African American lifeworld in a way that reveals racial identity as a positive constitutive element of the lifeworld, rather than as a source of shame or internalized self-loathing. A racialized turn to the lifeworld would explore "the lived experiences of persons within racial/ethnic groups for whom raciality and ethnicity is a fundamental and positive element of their identify" (Outlaw, 1983b, p. 177). Difference based on racial heritage would be celebrated as a crucial part of the African American lifeworld, not viewed as something to be erased in the name of racial integration.

What elements comprise this lifeworld? Outlaw looks to the different forms of expression produced in efforts to communicate the history of African American struggle. These include African folk tales, religious rituals, political practices, music, poetry, art, and the language of common currency. As concrete expressions of the African American lifeworld these elements, in Outlaw's view, contain fundamental meanings and orientations that can guide a program of political reconstruction serving African American interests. Reclaiming these meanings and orientations from a lifeworld distorted by White supremacy "will provide understandings of the historically conditioned concerns of black people (and) provide the clarified historical grounds for the orientation of present and future philosophical and practical activities in the interest of African-American people" (Outlaw, 1983a, p. 66). As the contours of African Americans' response to racism are drawn, this will lead to "increased self-transparency—a broadening and intensification of our personal and collective self-understanding" (p. 69). For Outlaw this is "a condition necessary for restructuring present and future projects." A hermeneutics of the African American lifeworld will also help in "the restoration and repair of broken communication among the various groupings of our people" (Outlaw, 1996, p. 30).

This mapping of the contours of the African American lifeworld represents a project for critical reflection very different from most adult educational work in this area. Instead of reflection being used to uncover the individual adult's assumptions informing her experience, reflection here has as its focus the reclamation of a lifeworld from the distortions of racist ideology. Learning to be critically reflective in this instance contributes to the building of identity and political purpose amongst members of African American communities and becomes an important element in learning antiracist perspectives and practices. Learning to understand and appreciate the cultural and epistemological topography of the African American lifeworld is an adult education project that is explicitly geared to the furtherance of African American interests. Although any curriculum produced by this project might seem to be sectional, it will, in Outlaw's opinion, ultimately serve the broader social good of all groups and communities since "many of the more fundamental needs of black people are shared by many others" (Outlaw, 1996, p. 29).

Restoring Critically Tempered Hope

Learning to understand and dismantle racist power structures as part of a broader movement of social transformation is a project that is also endorsed by Cornel West, perhaps the most prominent of contemporary critical African American intellectuals. Like Outlaw, West draws strongly on critical theory to understand and advance African Americans' interests, though unlike Outlaw he turns away from Habermas. In West's opinion Habermas has only a "tenuous relation to Marxism" with his work serving to provide "an innocuous badge of radicalism . . . a kind of opium for some of the American left-academic intelligentsia" (West, 1993, p. 88). The figures in the critical tradition most consistently acknowledged by West are Marx, Foucault, and Gramsci, all of whom in his view have

RACIALIZING CRITICALITY 293

much to contribute to keeping revolutionary hope alive in the African American community. As bell hooks comments in the "talking book" she produced with West, "Cornel West is unique among Black intellectuals in that he has always courageously identified himself with Marxist social analysis, and socialist political movement in the United States" (hooks and West, 1991, p. 22).

West defines himself as "an American Democratic Socialist of African descent" (1991, p. xi) in his introduction to *The Ethical Dimensions of Marxist Thought,* thereby signaling his intent to use critical theory in the interests of African Americans. In *Prophesy Deliverance* (1982), he proclaims his "abiding allegiance to progressive Marxist social analysis and political praxis" (p. 12), an allegiance that informs his understanding of the struggle for Black freedom as "a struggle that is a species of a radical democratic project that empowers and enhances the wretched of the earth" (West, 1993a, p. x). West's own role in this struggle is "first and foremost an intellectual freedom fighter" (p. 87) who works as a critical organic catalyst; "a person who stays attuned to the best of what the mainstream has to offer—its paradigms, viewpoints and methods—yet maintains a grounding in affirming and enabling sub-cultures of criticism" (West, 1993c, p. 27). This Gramscian-influenced model of intellectual activism links oppositional work within the academy "with political activity in grass-roots organizations, pre-party formations, or progressive associations intent on bringing together potential agents of social change" (p. 103). At the core of West's intellectual vocation is his "profound commitment to what I call a prophetic vision and practice primarily based on a distinctly black tragic sense of life" (p. x). This vision and practice is premised on "the love ethic of Christian faith—the most absurd and alluring mode of being in the world—that enables me to live a life of hope against hope" (p. xi).

In these self-designated identities—democratic socialist, intellectual freedom fighter, critical organic catalyst, radical Christian—we can see West's celebrated refusal to remain bounded by traditional categorizations. As commentaries on West have noted (Yancy, 2001; Wood, 2000), his eclecticism has led to criticisms of superficiality and dilettantism, of touching on a concept here, alluding to an intellectual position there, with no deep articulation of these traditions. My belief is that West's eclecticism is a principled eclecticism and a strength of his work as a connected, engaged organic intellectual. It is principled because it stands in support of his overarching project to keep activist hope alive. West ranges far and wide in his studies because he wishes to indicate the support for social transformation implicit in so many different intellectual traditions. He draws enthusiastically on any insights, from any source, that suggest ways of making democracy a reality in the United States. This breadth is a strength in that it allows him to speak to a wide array of constituencies and enclaves and to show their points of connection and interest.

West's traversing of multiple intellectual terrains means he engages with bodies of thought that are often regarded by their proponents as diametrically opposed. For example, he steadfastly retains "an affinity to a philosophical version of American pragmatism" (1982, p. 12) that is distinctly at odds with critical theory's mistrust (discussed in Chapter One) of pragmatism as self-interested, vulgar opportunism. But West's affinity to pragmatism and his belief in individuality are part and parcel of his enduring faith in the possibility of democracy. The encroachment of the state on individual freedom is, for him, a major threat to democratic processes. Individuals may be formed by culture and society, but they are not purely the sum total of traditions and forces. West also counters the radical pessimism of books such as *Dialectic of Enlightenment* with his optimistic belief in possibility and love. Despite his preoccupation with the tragic dimension of existence, his Christianity fuels his enduring sense of hope, a theme common to other fusions of Marxism and Christianity (MacIntyre, 1968; Marsden, 1991). He refuses to fall foul of a numbing despair, though in no sense does he underestimate the power of racist, antidemocratic forces, or dismiss the constant presence of disease and death. West's commitment to the absurd yet alluring love ethic of Christianity allows him to "keep alive a tempered hope for the future" (West, 1993c, p. xi).

A Racialized Engagement with the Critical Tradition

As already mentioned, West consistently exhibits a racialized engagement with three major figures in the critical tradition—Marx, Foucault, and Gramsci. The importance of considering seriously but critically the first of these figures is a theme that threads throughout his work. For West, Marx's ideas are "indispensable—although ultimately inadequate—in grasping distinctive features of African-American oppression" (West, 1993c, p. 259). In his view, however, the "richness of the Marxist methodological orientation and analytical perspective in relation to race remains untapped" (p. 261). This is partly because Marx himself did not conduct an analysis of race as a separate dimension of oppression nor did he anticipate how "a common denominator of white supremacist abuse cuts across class, gender, sexual orientation" (West, 1993b, p. 131). In the words of the title of West's best seller, Marx failed to anticipate that *Race Matters* (1993d). There are other silences and blind spots in Marx; "a relative inability to understand the complexity of culture—issues of identity and so forth" (1993b, p. 139) and a lack of understanding of how power is "tied to the microphysics of a society" (p. 139). Furthermore, Marxism is irrevocably linked in the American imagination to totalitarianism and Stalinist oppression, which ensures its continuing exclusion from mainstream consideration as a means of understanding American life. In his talking book with bell hooks, West speaks of how "any critic of capitalism in the United States is marginalized, and therefore it's very difficulty for them to speak a language that is intelligible to large numbers of people" (hooks and West, 1991, p. 44).

Yet, time and time again, West urges the importance of engaging with Marx as "an inescapable part of the intellectual weaponry for present-day freedom fighters" (1991, p. xiv). While he acknowledges that contemporary matrices of oppression—nationalism, racism, homophobia, patriarchy, ecological abuse—are not accounted for by Marx, he remains convinced that "these complex phenomena cannot be grasped, or changed, without the insights of Marxist theory" (hooks and West, 1991, p. 44). Why should this be so? For West it is the rise of global capitalism and the ever-increasing power of multinationals that make Marx indispensable. In an interview with George Yancy (1998), West states his case as follows: "I don't see how, in fact, we can understand the market forces around the world and the fundamental role of transnational corporations, the subordination of working people, the tremendous class conflicts going on around the world at the market place between management and labor without understanding some of the insights of the Marxist tradition" (p. 41).

In *Prophesy Deliverance* (1982), West proposes a blending of Marxism with Black theology, to him the single most important source of philosophical energy for African American activism. Black theology and Marxism both employ a methodology of unmasking falsehood, but in his opinion "Black theologians barely mention the wealth, power and influence of multinational corporations" (West, 1982, p. 113). Neither do they make the link between "the way in which the racist interpretations of the gospel they reject encourage and support the capitalist system of production, its grossly unequal distribution of wealth, and its closely connected political arrangements" (p. 113). Inserting a Marxist element into Black theology would ensure that Black oppression in capitalist America was understood as linked to Black and Brown oppression in the third world.

As a way of illuminating the interconnected nature of racial and class oppression, West also calls for a "Marxist influenced genealogical materialist analysis of racism" (1993c, p. 268). This would probe the logic of White supremacy through a "micro-institutional (or localized) analysis of the mechanisms that promote and contest these logics in the everyday lives of people" (p. 268). Such an analysis would explore "the ways in which self-images and self-identities are shaped, and the impact of alien, degrading cultural styles, aesthetic ideals, psychosexual sensibilities and linguistic gestures upon peoples of color" (p. 268). Concurrent with this microinstitutional analysis would go a macrostructural exploration of "class exploitation, state repression and bureaucratic domination, including resistance against these modes, in the lives of people of color" (p. 268).

This emphasis on a genealogical analysis of racist practices in everyday life demonstrates West's acknowledgment of another major figure in the critical tradition, Michel Foucault. West declares that "Foucault's perspective can be valuable for Afro-American philosophers whose allegiance is to a revolutionary future" (West, 1983, p. 58) because it helps illuminate how the power of racist ideology is made manifest in daily conversations, gestures, rituals, and interactions. By fusing Foucault's ideas with a neo-Marxist analysis, "Foucault's viewpoint can be creatively transformed and rendered fruitful for a genealogy of modern racism, in both its ideational and material forms" (p. 58). This genealogy of racism would not just analyze the way dominant discourse inaugurated the category of race and excluded positive notions of Black beauty, culture, and character from its discursive field. It would also "put forward an Afro-American counter discourse, in all its complexity and diversity, to the modern European racist discourse" (p. 58). Such a discourse would "exercise and evaluate how the Afro-American response promotes or precludes a revolutionary future" (p. 58). In *The American Evasion of Philosophy* (1989), West does criticize Foucault for his surreptitious ascription of agency to discourses, disciplines, and techniques (1989, p. 225), but overall he acknowledges that the particular philosophical stance of prophetic pragmatism "promotes genealogical materialist modes of analysis similar in many respects to those of Foucault" (p. 223).

Finally, West peppers his works with approving references to Gramsci, describing himself as a Gramscian Marxist and calling Gramsci "the most penetrating Marxist theorist of culture in this century" (West, 1982, p. 118). Explaining his affinity to Gramsci he writes "my particular stand within the Marxist tradition is linked primarily to that of Gramsci, which always places stress on historical specificity, on concrete circumstances and situations" (1998, p. 41). Just as he claims Foucault's work reflects the spirit of prophetic pragmatism, so he believes that "prophetic pragmatism is inspired by the example of Antonio Gramsci [who] exemplifies the critical spirit and oppositional sentiments of prophetic pragmatism" (West, 1989, p. 230). West is drawn to Gramsci's (and also Raymond Williams') idea that hegemony is always contested and open to being undermined by specific actions taken in specific situations. He is drawn also to Gramsci's emphasis on cultural products—films, books, rap music CD's—as sites of resistance and has himself produced a rap CD, *Sketches of My Culture* (West, 2001). In particular, West refers repeatedly and explicitly to Gramsci's idea of the organic intellectual as a useful descriptor both for his own work and for the work of critical Black intellectuals in general. He believes, as did Gramsci, that "the aim of philosophy is . . . to become part of a social movement by nourishing and being nourished by the philosophical views of oppressed people themselves for the aims of social change and personal meaning" (1989, p. 131).

This situating of philosophy in everyday practices and struggles is a defining feature of the organic intellectual. In *Keeping Faith* (1993c), West reframes the concept slightly as that of the critical organic catalyst, "a person who stays attuned to the best of what the mainstream has to offer—its paradigms, viewpoints and methods— yet maintains a grounding in affirming and enabling sub-cultures of criticism" (p. 27). In his view, Black intellectuals should function as organic intellectuals. They should be scholar-activists who are grounded in the experiences and struggles of the African American community while being informed by the wisdom of allies outside that racial group. This model of intellectual engagement "pushes academic intellectuals beyond contestation within the academy . . . and links this contestation with political activity in grassroots groups, pre-party formations, or progressive associations intent on bringing together potential agents of social change" (p. 103). Such groups include activists of color, feminists, lesbians and gays, black churches, ecological movements, rank and file labor caucuses, and Black nationalists.

As organic intellectuals, African American philosophers have specific responsibilities in West's view. In a Foucaultian vein, they must "articulate a new 'regime of truth' linked to, yet not confined by, indigenous institutional practices permeated by the kinetic orality and emotional physicality, the rhythmic syncopation, the protean improvisation and the religious, rhetorical and antiphonal repetition of African-American life" (1993c, p. 82). They must also conduct "a critical self-inventory" (p. 85) and work to create and reactivate "institutional networks that promote high-quality critical habits primarily for the purpose of black insurgency" (p. 83). West is clear on the need for organizing and is critical of overly charismatic activists who leave no organizational or community structures in the communities they visit. In approving contrast to this, he cites Martin Luther King as "an organic intellectual of the first order—a highly educated and informed thinker with organic links to ordinary folk" (p. 273). King's roots in the black church "gave him direct access to the life-worlds of the majority of black southerners" (p. 273). His education provided him with an analysis of anticolonialism as well as bringing him respect within the Black community, and he "facilitated relations with progressive non black people, thereby insuring openness to potential allies" (p. 273).

As the foregoing discussion clearly shows, West's work draws strongly on critical theory—in particular the work of Marx, Foucault, and Gramsci—as one of the central intellectual traditions contributing to African American philosophy. His project is summarized by the titles of two of his books *Restoring Hope* (West and Sealey, 1997) and *Keeping Faith* (West, 1993c). To him "the principal task of the Afro-American philosopher is to keep alive the hope of a revolutionary future . . . in which the multifaceted oppression of Afro-Americans is, if not eliminated, alleviated" (West, 1983, p. 57). In pursuing this task, West believes that African American philosophers must preserve critical theory's notions of negation and transformation and initiate "a serious confrontation with the Marxist tradition and, among others, the recent work of Michel Foucault" (p. 57). But African American philosophy must also be "indigenously grounded in the prophetic religious and progressive secular practices of Afro-Americans" (p. 57) and have as its particular project the generation of guidelines for social action that springs from the true needs of African Americans. He summarizes "the major function of Afro-American critical thought" as being "to reshape the contours of Afro-American history and provide a new self-understanding of the Afro-American experience which suggest guidelines for action in the present" (West, 1982, p. 22).

There are several elements to this project. One is, as we have seen, to conduct a genealogy of racist ideas and practices. Another is "to provide a theoretical reconstruction and evaluation of Afro-American responses to white supremacy" (1982, p. 23). A third is to explore the cultural roots and sensibilities of African Americans. A fourth is "to present a dialogical encounter between Afro-American critical thought and progressive Marxist social analysis" (p. 23). This encounter is much more than an interesting philosophical confluence for West. Indeed, he sees such an intellectual fusion as crucial to democratic social reconstruction declaring confidently that "in an alliance between prophetic Christianity and progressive Marxism . . . lies the hope of Western civilization" (p. 23). Finally, West sees the task of African American critical thought being to disentangle and interpret the African, European, and American elements in Black experience. As West writes, "The life-worlds of Africans in the United States are conceptually and existentially neither solely African, European, nor American, but more the latter than any of the former" (p. 24). As mentioned earlier in this chapter, the intertwined intersections of African, Native American, and European cultures is one important reason why the Africentric adult education scholar, Scipio Colin III, has generated the term "African Ameri-pean" as an alternative to "African American."

Infusing Pragmatism into Criticality

To critical theorists and Africentrists alike, the most challenging (and, to many, perplexing) aspect of West's thought is his constant attempt to integrate the philosophical spirit of pragmatism into his project for African American reconstruction. After all, pragmatists do not usually describe themselves as organic intellectuals or free-dom fighters. But West is very consistent in declaring his "affinity to a philosophical version of American pragmatism" (1982, p. 12) alongside his recognition of Marxism. Despite pragmatism's avoid-ance of racial analysis, and the conduct of its discourse in the white-walled labyrinth mentioned earlier, its contributions to African American thought are "enormous" in West's view (1982, p. 21). He writes of pragmatism that "through its historicist orien-tation, for example, Afro-American thought can avoid both abso-lutist dogmatism and paralysis in action" (p. 21). For West "pragmatism provides an American context for Afro-American thought, a context that imparts to it both a shape and a heritage of philosophical legitimacy" (p. 21). In a conversation with bell hooks, he says that "to talk about America is to talk about improvi-sation and experimentation" (hooks and West, 1991, p.34), themes at the core of pragmatism.

Why should African American intellectuals take seriously a philo-sophical tradition viewed as a compromised element of White supremacy by some in the African American intellectual commu-nity—as "bourgeois through and through" in McClendon's (1983, p. 38) words? West makes his case by citing two distinctive contribu-tions pragmatism can make to building an African American praxis. First, he reads Emerson, Peirce, James, and Dewey as spokespersons for a morally grounded philosophical tradition tied to the creation of a true democracy. In his major book on the subject, he speaks of pragmatism's "unashamedly moral emphasis" (1989, p. 4) and its "yearning for principled resistance and struggle that can change our desperate plight" (p. 4). He locates its impulse in "a plebian radi-calism that fuels an anti-patrician rebelliousness for the moral aim of enriching individuals and expanding democracy" (p. 5). Prag-

RACIALIZING CRITICALITY   301

matism "tries to deploy thought as a weapon to enable more effective action" (p. 5), particularly action taken to promote "the flower-
ing and flourishing of individuality under conditions of democracy"
(1993a, p. 32). Pragmatism does not support action for action's sake.
Although it puts "a premium on human will, human power and
human action" (p. 37), it is neither vulgar practicality nor unprin-
cipled opportunism. In an unconscious echo of another pragmati-
cally inclined intellectual activist (the adult educator Eduard
Lindeman) West sees pragmatism as "preoccupied with . . . the
democratic way of life" (West, 1993a, p. 31)—coincidentally the title
of one of Lindeman's last books (Smith and Lindeman, 1951). A
democratic society is one comprised of "unique selves acting in and
through participatory communities (in) an open, risk-ridden future"
(West, 1993a p. 43).

Its self-critical strain is a second argument West adduces in support of his advocacy of pragmatism. He particularly admires Dewey's
belief that philosophizing requires the constant critical analysis of
assumptions. Although West works outside the adult education discourse community, his emphasis on the importance of critical analysis is framed in terms very familiar to adult education scholars
preoccupied with critical reflection and transformative learning.
Thus, a pragmatic orientation "constantly questions the tacit
assumptions of earlier interpretations of the past. It scrutinizes the
norms these interpretations endorse, the solutions they offer, and
the self-images they foster" (West, 1982, p. 20). To pragmatists (as
to critically reflective adult educators), "norms, premises and procedures . . . are never immune to revision" (p. 20). Pragmatism is
defined by its "calling into question any form of dogmatism" and
its belief in a form of fallibilism in which "every claim is open to revision" (West, 1993a, p. 43). It is not to be confused with an antithe-
oretical stance, or with the idea that anything goes depending on
the context. Instead, "it subtly incorporates an experimental temper within theory-laden descriptions of problematic situations (for
instance, social and cultural crises)" (West, 1993c, p. 137).

This antifoundational strain of pragmatism, in which experimentation and problem solving run strong, is fused with West's religious beliefs and his commitment to critical theory to produce a
new variant of pragmatism—prophetic pragmatism. Prophetic
pragmatism is West's unique blend of Judeo-Christian traditions,

European critical theory, American pragmatism, and Black theology, a blend that to him best fits the fight against the nihilism and cynicism he sees as destroying both the African American community and the broader society. In its religious affiliations, prophetic pragmatism draws on "traditions of Judaism and Christianity that promote courageous resistance against, and relentless critiques of, injustice and social misery" (1993c, p. 139). In Biblical fashion these traditions "help keep alive collective memories of moral (that is anti-idolatrous) struggle and non-market values" (p. 139). From critical theory, prophetic pragmatism incorporates that tradition's microstructural and macrostructural analyses of the dynamics of oppression embedded in the works of Marx, Gramsci, and Foucault. Prophetic thought and Marxism "both focus on the plight of the exploited, oppressed, and degraded peoples of the world, their relative powerlessness and possible empowerment" (West, 1982, p. 107).

From American pragmatism, its prophetic variant draws the spirit of self-criticism and the pursuit of the democratic way of life. Hence, "critical temper as a way of struggle and democratic faith as a way of life are the twin pillars of prophetic pragmatism" (West, 1993c, p. 140). Here the antifoundational willingness of Dewey to experiment with multiple approaches to realizing democracy is harnessed to the project of combating racist ideology and practices. Finally, from Black theology, prophetic pragmatism draws the desire "to bestow dignity, grandeur and tragedy upon the denigrated lives of ordinary black people and to promote improvisational life-strategies of love and joy in black life-worlds of radical and brutish contingency" (p. xii). Like critical theory, Black theology begins with negation, in this case "negating white interpretations of the gospel" (West, 1982, p. 108). Deconstructing these interpretations is the necessary precursor to "transforming past understandings of the gospel into new ones" (p. 109). Black theology also shares with critical theory a desire "to link some notion of liberation to the future conditions of the downtrodden" (p. 108). However, because of the lack of class analysis in Black theology West views it as insufficient to be a stand-alone tool for the furtherance of African American interests.

The element of fallibilistic self-criticality endemic to prophetic pragmatism has a particular resonance for the practice of adult education. In its skepticism regarding theoretical dogma and reified, standardized models of practice, prophetic pragmatism provides a justification for a critically reflective practice of adult education emphasizing openness, flexibility, and contingency. In West's words the "critical temper" of prophetic pragmatism "promotes a full-fledged experimental disposition that highlights the provisional, tentative and revisable character of our visions, analyses and actions" (West, 1993c, p. 140). In adult educational terms, possessing a critical temper means avoiding a slavish adherence to a particular methodology, whether this be andragogical, self-directed, transformative, or didactic. It means that continuously researching the different contexts in which adults are learning, whether these be adult basic education programs, community action groups, organizational teams, or higher education classrooms, becomes an imperative of good practice. A critically reflective stance toward adult education practice, like a prophetically pragmatic one, abandons any premature commitment to one approach, no matter how liberatory this might appear. Instead there is a principled methodological eclecticism, a readiness to experiment with any and all approaches in the pursuit of emancipatory learning. This is particularly the case with adult education initiatives that see themselves as anti-racist (Hayes and Colin, 1994).

When applied to adult education, the methodological eclecticism of prophetic pragmatism can be called principled for two reasons. First, it eschews any pretence that adult education lacks a sociopolitical dimension and acknowledges instead that practice is driven by moral and political impulses. In West's case his practice is geared toward the furtherance of African American interests, the fight against racist ideology, and the democratic transformation of society. A prophetically pragmatic approach (and, by implication, a critically reflective form of adult education) "begins with social structural analyses" and "makes explicit its moral and political aims" (West, 1993c, p. 23). Such an approach is unashamedly "partisan, partial, engaged and crisis-centered" (p. 23). Yet, combined with its openly acknowledged intent of changing minds, practices, and structures, prophetic pragmatism "always keeps open a skeptical eye to avoid dogmatic traps, premature closures, formulaic formulations or rigid conclusions" (p. 23). Its solicitation of critiques of its aims and procedures is a defining feature of its internal logic.

Second, a prophetically pragmatic approach is principled because it shares with a critically reflective orientation a commitment
to the collective creation of knowledge. Prophetic pragmatism con-
ceives of knowledge as developed "within the conceptual framework of intersubjective communal inquiry" (West, 1982, p. 21) in
which "knowledge claims are secured by the social practices of a
community of inquirers" (p. 21). As such, prophetic pragmatism
exhibits a direct connection to one of the strongest traditions in
the adult educational field. This is the tradition of community-
based, dialogically inclined, groups of activists and citizens working collaboratively to examine their experiences and practices with
a view to transforming society in democratic directions. This is the
tradition of Lindeman, Horton, and Freire and, in Gyant's (2002)
view, also that of Alain Locke, the first African American president
of the American Association for Adult and Continuing Education.
It ascribes an explicit social purpose to adult education and frames
adult educational practice as an analog of the very participatory
democracy it is intending to bring about. It privileges collaborative
dialog over individual analysis and fights any tendency to the pri-
vatization of knowledge.

It is interesting that the White and Latin American adult educators emblematic of this tradition—Lindeman, Horton, and Freire—
toward the end of their lives exemplified the spirit of critical temper
that West associates with his own formulation of prophetic pragmatism. Although a theme in much of these three adult educators' earlier work is the importance of nondidactic modes of practice, after
a lifetime's practice all three advocated a principled methodological eclecticism. Lindeman declared that he was open to using any
methodology in adult education for social change depending on the
circumstances and learners' past experiences (Brookfield, 1987b).
Horton admitted that at times he would give presentations as a way
of building trust and meeting activists half way before moving to
work dialogically, and that the timing and modalities of how he contributed to dialog depended very much on his understanding of a
context (Horton 1990; Horton and Freire, 1990). Freire reversed his
condemnation of lectures as the epitome of banking education, emphasized the importance of rigorous, line-by-line critical reading
(with a dictionary if necessary) of texts, and allowed that lectures
could be critically stimulating while apparently dialogic groups could

be exercises in insidious manipulation (Shor and Freire,1987; Freire and Macedo, 1995). All three also committed themselves to anti-racist practices, with Lindeman being one of the few White adult educators to publish in the *Journal of Negro Education,* and the High-lander Folk School becoming an adult educational center for Civil Rights' activists.

The Africentric Paradigm as an Alternative Discourse

The work of Karenga, Outlaw, and West is paralleled in recent years by the emergence within adult education scholarship of a racialized analysis of African American learners' alienation from mainstream adult education practices and African American schol-ars' alienation from the field's dominant discourses and scholar-ship (Smith and Colin, 2001). Concepts central to the field such as andragogy, self-directed learning, critical reflection, and trans-formative learning have been generated by White male scholars based on studies of mostly White, middle-class adult learners. Explicit or implicit claims that such ideas comprise the corner-stones of a distinctive universal theory of adult learning and edu-cation are not just empirically suspect but also highly exclusionary, in themselves a form of racism. If philosophical inquiry represents a white-walled labyrinth (in the terms quoted by Harris at the beginning of this chapter), so does adult education scholarship. The ways that American members of the African Diaspora experi-ence participation in adult education, and in particular how this represents an alienation from African traditions, sensibilities, and practices, have traditionally been ignored.

In the last two decades or so, however, several theoretical lines of inquiry have emerged that explore an African American, racial-ized interpretation of adult educational practices and adult learn-ing concepts. We have Colin's (1988, 2002) theory of the importance of selfethnic reflectors in adult education (drawing on the work of Marcus Garvey), the documentation of African American learners' and academics' entries into, and negotiations of, higher education (Johnson-Bailey, 2001; James and Farmer, 1993), and the celebra-tion of African American women leaders and activists (Easter, 2002; Peterson, 2002; Brown, 2001). There have been efforts to develop Africentric models of curriculum for graduate adult education

(Colin and Guy, 1998; Colin, 1994) and the exploration of African influenced adult learning and educational practices (Smith, 2001). The intellectual history of the field has been reframed as influenced significantly by the debates regarding the fight against racism conducted by Du Bois and Washington (Potts, 2002), Marcus Garvey (Colin, 2002), Alain Locke (Guy, 1994; Gyant, 2002), and Malcolm X (Smallwood, 2002) amongst others. Peterson (1999) has also outlined the contribution of critical race theory to the continuing dialog amongst African American adult educators regarding anti-racist practice.

This body of scholarship represents a contestation of the dominant White conceptualization of adult education history and practice. Furthermore, the creation of the AERC African American preconference (which some believe overshadows the official mainstream conference in terms of its intellectual vigor) represents a potent oppositional discourse community within which the development of Afrocentric and Africentric theories of adult education are emerging. In Karenga's terms, the initiatives described above certainly meet his criterion that an Afrocentric theory must rise from the experiences of African Americans (in this case their practices as adult learners and adult educators) and be focused on and behalf of them. It also serves the larger social good of the field to have such an emphasis at the forefront of adult educators' concerns, irrespective of these educators' racial background.

However, as Smith and Colin (2001) document, the struggle by African American adult education scholars to bring African American perspectives into the field's discourse and thereby "make the invisible visible" (Smith and Colin, 2001, p. 65) is one of continued marginalization. Africentric adult education scholars tell of White faculty's and graduate students' perceptions of them as ignorant of Eurocentric perspectives, only interested in pushing one racialized paradigm, and intellectually limited. Respondents in their study of African American professors of adult education talk of the "hell" that is their life as an academic, of having strangers automatically turn to them in a university office expecting them to be a secretary, and of being heard but not listened to. In their terms, "the disacknowledgment or debasement of an Africentric Paradigm serves as a form of 'public invalidation' which is rooted in an ideology of racial superiority and inferiority by both students and colleagues" (Smith and Colin, 2001, p. 64).

What comprises an Africentric approach to adult education theorizing and practice? Guy and Colin (1998) write that Africentrist adult education texts "approach their subject from the cultural reference point of the African-American experience . . . are written by persons who have direct cultural knowledge as African Americans, and . . . represent classic or seminal statements or analyses of adult education from an African American perspective" (p. 86). As a philosophical orientation, Africentrism is "reflective of the sociohistorical context in which African Ameripean/African American individuals lived. The salient feature of this context, regardless of time period, was racism" (Colin and Guy, 1998, p. 44). Hence, an Africentric approach to adult education "addresses sociocultural and educational goals in light of the African Ameripeans'/African Americans' striving against racism" (p. 44). The Africentric focus of practice is consistent with adult education's traditional learner centeredness in that Africentric adult education builds on the core experience of its adult learners (that of experiencing racism) and explores how learners can be empowered though action (by dismantling racism).

To Colin and Guy, the Swahili concept of *Nguzo Saba* is at the core of the Africentric paradigm. Its values—*Umoja* (unity), *Kujichagulia* (self-determination), *Ujima* (collective work and responsibility), *Ujamaa* (cooperative economics), *Nia* (purpose), *Kuumba* (creativity), and *Imani* (faith)—stress community, interdependence, and collective action. In Colin and Guy's view, "this differs significantly from traditional Eurocentric perspectives of individualism, competition, and hierarchical forms of authority and decision-making" (1998, p. 50). The seven principles of *Nguzo Saba* match a particular curricular orientation to adult education, one that focuses on selfethnic liberation and empowerment. Drawing on Marcus Garvey's philosophy of selfethnic reliance, Colin and Guy argue that African American adult education programs must be "designed to counteract the sociocultural and the socio-psychological effects of racism" (Colin and Guy, 1998, p. 47). They should be developed by members of the ethnic or racial group that have lived the experience of racism in the "firm belief that members of the race are quite

capable of assuming leadership roles in their own liberation: psychologically, educationally, and socially" (p. 47). Crucially, Africentric
adult education practices and understandings must be generated
outside the dominant Eurocentric ideology. Instead of andragogy or
criticality as intellectual lynchpins of practice, the principles of *Nguzo
Saba* move center stage. In Colin and Guy's opinion, "from an adult
educational standpoint, this means that the selection, discussion and
critique of African Ameripean/African American content must not
occur based on using standards or criteria arising from traditional
Eurocentric perspectives. Rather, selection of content about African
Ameripean/African American adult education is based on an Africentric perspective" (Colin and Guy, 1998, p. 51).

This perspective raises problems for those who seek to racialize
critical theory in the interests of African Americans. As a Eurocentric discourse, the racial membership of its authors appears to prevent critical theory from having any connection to Africentric adult
education. However, many within critical theory would dispute that
it represents a traditional Eurocentric perspective, arguing instead
that it represents a perspective that has been subjugated and marginalized within dominant Eurocentric discourses for being too contentious, too ideological, too subversive. Those in the tradition who
were forced to flee Nazi Germany and the Holocaust knew viscer-
ally the experience of genocide. The themes of individualism, competition, hierarchical authority, and decision making attributed to
traditional Eurocentric perspectives are, as the previous nine chapters demonstrate, the themes also challenged by the counterdis-
course of critical theory.

Others would argue that the values of community, interdependence, and collective action that lie at the heart of *Nguzo Saba* are
also the basis of European working-class political movements and
cultures, and the normative basis of critical theory itself. In this
regard adult educational practices derived from critical theory
share some of the emphases of Africentric adult education—for
example, breaking the individualization and competition implied
in interpretations of self-directed learning and privileging the collective cocreation of knowledge within collaborative work groups.
For critical theory, authority and identity are viewed as residing in
the collective, not the individual, and decision making becomes a
community process. For an adult educational interpretation of

these values, and the difficulties of realizing them within hierarchical structures, see the discussion by Avila and others (2000) of an attempt to recast graduate adult education as a process of participatory learning.

Of course what is missing from critical theory, and what is crucial to Africentrism, is a consistent and clear focus on race as the central construct. Critical theory's focus on alienation, and its attribution of alienation to capitalism and bureaucratic rationality, do not lead it to an historical focus on understanding and combating racism through selfethnic or other forms of liberation. Critical theory does not dismiss the racism embedded in dominant ideology, but neither does it highlight such racism as its overarching concern. An Africentric orientation on the other hand sees race, not class, as the central problem of our time (to borrow Du Bois' formulation). As such, Africentric adult education incorporates, in Colin's (2002) view, Marcus Garvey's emphasis on race first, race pride and race unity.

However, an Africentric adult education does not seek to imitate European ethnocentrism (in which Whiteness is placed as the unacknowledged conceptual center) by regarding all things African as inherently superior. Colin points out that Africentrism is not ethnocentrism and that "the Africentric approach does not view other racial and cultural groups as being comparatively inferior" (Colin, 2002, p. 57). What is important in Africentric adult education is to "present and preserve the intellectual and philosophical traditions in African Ameripean/African American history and culture" (Colin and Guy, 1998, p. 49), not to denigrate other cultures and traditions. In Colin's view, the adult education practice of Marcus Garvey represented this Africentric emphasis in that it "reconceptualized the purpose and aims of adult education for those people who bear the burden of institutional racism" (Colin, 2002, p. 61).

In this chapter I have attempted (within the limits of my racial membership) to explore racialized interpretations of critical theory that incorporate some of its analytical approaches and conceptual tools in the broader project of understanding and combating racist ideology. In the next chapter I take this process one stage further by examining how scholarship on gender that draws on the critical tradition influences the conduct of critical adult education.

Chapter Eleven

Gendering Criticality

As will be all too clear from earlier chapters, the Frankfurt School of first-generation critical theory was largely generated by men for men. Concepts central to its discourse such as the commodification of labor, the alienating character of work, the oppositional role of the organic intellectual, and the re-creation of a public sphere were all articulated against the backdrop of a mostly male-conceived world of work and politics located in factories and bureaucracies. Since capitalism is viewed as an all-enveloping oppressive system, most critically inclined theorists are ready to admit to the importance of liberating all people—men, women, and children—from its constraints. But, as with race, gender is undertheorized in the male-authored Frankfurt canon. First-generation critical theory is strong on the analysis of alienated labor or the way repressive tolerance effectively neuters alternate ideologies but weak on the analysis of patriarchy as a source of female alienation or the way patriarchy allows a degree of carefully managed feminist critique as a way of heading off a more sustained challenge to the system.

Feminist responses to critical theory's exclusionary tendencies have taken many forms. One major movement has been the articulation of distinctively feminist epistemologies. This perspective emphasizes gender-based modes of cognition such as connected knowing (Belenky, Clinchy, Goldberger, and Tarule, 1986) and maternal thinking (Ruddick, 1995). There has been a vigorous debate in feminist literature regarding the validity of feminist epistemology and the extent to which this analysis promotes or impedes women's interests (see, for example, Chodorow, 1989; Alcoff and Potter, 1993; Grant, 1993; Fluss, 1989). Writers such as Fraser (1989, 1997), and Gore (1993) have pointed out the dangers of a kind of essentialism that confines women to an ethic of care (Gilligan, 1982). In their view, this emphasis on traditional feminine qualities of nurturance, by implication, reserves the exercise of rationality for men.

By way of response, those identified as arguing for the recognition of gender-based modes of cognition sometimes argue that their position has been oversimplified as representing a wholly biological determination of cognition. For example, in the follow-up text to the influential *Women's Ways of Knowing* (Belenky, Clinchy, Goldberger, and Tarule, 1986), Nancy Goldberger observes that "we did not claim that the five perspectives or ways of knowing that we described were essentially female" (Goldberger, 1996, p. 7). Goldberger insists that the volume's authors wished only to demonstrate that "there are hidden agendas of power in the way societies define and validate and ultimately genderize knowledge" (p. 7). In a new preface to her 1989 book, *Maternal Thinking*, Sara Ruddick pointed out that "there is nothing foreordained about maternal response" (p. xi), that "mothering is construed as work rather than as an identity or fixed biological or legal relationship" (p. xi), and that "there have always been men who mother" (p. xii). Mechtild Hart (1992) argues that mothering by either sex can be viewed as an inherently critical project, particularly when viewed from the social margins rather than from the center of established White masculinist norms. To Hart a crucial element of motherwork is "raising the child against these norms, teaching her about their power, but also about their built-in injustice" (p. 185). Hart draws on critical theory to propose "an alternative concept of work, where the involvement in body and mind, in nature and culture, is seen as creating and nourishing life" (1995, p. 101). Like Ruddick, Hart argues that motherwork—living and working with children—is something that everyone, regardless of gender, is connected to. Her vision is of a society in which such work "would become an issue for all workers . . . where the very term 'worker' would include this reality" (p. 119).

In this chapter I begin by focusing attention on the particular feminist response to critical theory represented by women educators and theorists who have taken some of the tradition's concepts and reinterpreted these in women's interest. Some of these feminists engage with particular male critical theorists such as Marx (Hartmann,

1995; MacKinnon, 1989), Habermas (Meehan, 1995: Fleming, 1997, Gouthro, 2003), Foucault (Diamond and Quinby, 1988; Sawicki, 1991), and Gramsci (Kenway, 2001). Others (Hirschmann and Di Stefano, 1996; Hernandez, 1997) focus more on gendering broad concepts of democracy, civil society, autonomy, community, obligation, and care. Whatever their focus, these writers are trying to take from critical theory those elements that best explain and further the position of women. Just as the theorists reviewed in the last chapter were attempting to racialize critical theory to serve African Americans' interests, so the theorists reviewed in the current chapter are engaged in the project of gendering critical theory to serve women's interests. This project involves both challenging the centrality of male worldviews within critical theory, and attempting to build on the elements of these that are most productive for advancing women's interests.

However, as Luke (1992), Fraser (1995), and others have pointed out, talking in a generic way about women's interests, as if the universality of gender membership trumped all other differences of race, culture, education, ethnicity, and ideology, is to privilege gender in a way that is contested by women of color. Collins (1990), hooks (1984), Davis (1998a, 1998b), James and Buisa (1993), and others have argued that focusing solely on gender oppression and neglecting racial or class identity is yet another illustration of White privilege. To them the White, heterosexual feminists who assume an unproblematized unity of gender oppression amongst all women have underplayed the potency of interlocking systems of oppression, neglecting particularly the effects of race and class. Recently White feminists have begun to acknowledge their own complicity in this situation and to question the accuracy of their own analyses. I end this chapter by reviewing analyses of these interlocking systems that draw on the critical theory tradition, focusing particularly on the work of bell hooks and Angela Davis.

Critical Theorizing as the Exercise of Male Privilege

It is no surprise, to many feminists, that the classical canon of critical theory is produced by men. Given the unequally gendered access to the resources that make all kinds of theorizing possible— a room of one's own, for example—it is very predictable that so many theoretical traditions (at least as far as the publishing of texts is taken to represent a tradition) would be male-dominated. As Luke (1992) observes, "Critique and action are not generally available to unwaged housewives or, for that matter, to half the labor force of women working double jobs in predominantly part-time clerical and service employment, and in full-time child care, sexual and domestic service work" (p. 30). Theorizing of all kinds is, in this analysis, skewed in favor of men. From this perspective, the revolutionary intent of Gramsci's aphorism that "all men are intellectuals" becomes tinged with a cruel and unintended irony. Weiler's (2001b) edited collection of feminist engagements with male critical theorists constantly points out this irony. She argues, "Historically, the exclusion of women from the public sphere has meant that men alone had access to the resources that allowed them to become socially respected and acknowledged intellectuals. As a result, men have claimed the authority to speak for all, to define human concerns" (p. 1). Luke (1992) too observes that "critical inquiry . . . is fixed most profoundly to gendered privilege" since social structures "have historically situated the male individual at the center of theoretical, public discourse" (p. 29).

When we turn to the particular discourse surrounding the educational practice of critical theory, we can see that, in Lather's (2001) words, it is "still very much a boy thing" (p. 184). To Lather critical theory focuses too much on male concerns and experiences that are explored against the backdrop of male locations. It also exhibits a "masculinist voice of abstraction, universalization, and the rhetorical position of 'the one who knows' (p. 184). Drawing on the work of psychologists such as Chodorow (1989) and Gilligan (1982), Luke (1992) hypothesizes that the male sense of self is a separatist sense, and that the male "expresses relationality through the production, competition, control and exchange of objects and objectifies others (e.g. knowledge, commodities, nature, women)" (p. 43). For Luke, however, this is not an essentialist analysis. These characteristics, which are often assumed to be genetically wired, are political constructs. They are the result of a process of cultural socialization that assigns competitive rationality to men and collaborative nurturance to women.

To feminist critics the male domination of critical theory and its educational implementation in critical pedagogy has consequences that work against women's interests. Perhaps the most important is that the analysis of patriarchy as a central prop of dominant ideology is undertheorized. Heterosexual marriage, homophobia, childrearing as female-only work, women's economic dependence on men—the whole "set of interrelations among men that allow men to dominate women" in Hartmann's (1995, p. 189) words—receives occasional genuflections but little else. In discourse influenced by critical theory, there is not enough sustained analysis, using female-authored texts that reflect the wide range of positions in feminist scholarship, of how "in capitalist societies a healthy and strong partnership exists between patriarchy and capital" (p. 189). As the body of work seeking to implement the educational tasks and promises of critical theory, the literature of critical pedagogy is also criticized for its neglect of gender issues. It creates, in Ellsworth's (1992) view, "the category of generic critical teacher . . . young, White, Christian, middle-class, heterosexual, able-bodied, thin, rational man" (p. 102). In a narrow sense this ignores the fact that the feminization of the teaching profession means a large number of women are engaged in critical work. In a broader sense it mistakenly perpetuates the illusion that there is one standardized form of critical practice available to teachers and one ideal type of educator (male) able to execute it effectively.

This chapter explores the way in which some feminists who have been influenced by (but refuse to be constrained within) the critical theory tradition have fought the illusions and misunderstandings outlined above. I begin by exploring how feminist critics and educators have engaged with the men of critical theory—particularly Marx, Habermas, and Foucault—to fight the gender blindness in the tradition and to develop a gendered criticality. I then review the serious criticisms many feminists have made concerning the "masculinist prescriptive understanding" (Lather, 2001, p. 186) that informs much writing on the educational application of critical theory (that is, critical pedagogy). These criticisms focus on the unacknowledged role of the teacher as potential oppressor, the alienating language of critical discourse, and the ways that emancipatory intentions (such as bringing students into voice) can be experienced as arrogant and condescending by those who are supposed to be the target of liberatory practices. I conclude the chapter by exploring the works of two contemporary African American feminists, bell hooks and Angela Davis. The work of both these theorists is located at the intersections of critical theory, feminism, and racial analysis.

Both draw explicitly on Marx and subsequent critical theorists (Marcuse and Freire in particular), but both believe the critical tradition needs to be reconfigured to focus on gender and race as well as class.

Gendering Marx

In the 1960s and 1970s a vigorous debate began between Marxism and feminism as women intellectuals and activists attempted to address the gender blindness in Marx's work, while integrating its revolutionary insights into the women's movement. Whole collections of articles were published on the unhappy marriage of Marxism and feminism (Sargent, 1981) with some arguing for a more progressive union (Hartmann, 1995), some questioning whether the marriage could be saved (Ehrlich, 1981), and some pondering whether a trial separation was called for (Vogel, 1981). In a prominent essay (first published in the 1970s), Hartmann (1995) argued that both Marxist and feminist understandings were necessary to disentangle the ideology and practice of patriarchy. For Hartmann "the struggle against capital and patriarchy cannot be successful if the study and practice of the issues of feminism is abandoned" (p. 195). This was because "a struggle aimed at only capitalist relations of oppression will fail, since their underlying supports in patriarchal relations of oppression will be overlooked" (p. 195). This position significantly extended Horkheimer's insistence (documented in Chapter One) that critical theory was dominated by "a single existential judgment" (Horkheimer, 1995, p. 227) concerning the need to abolish the exchange economy of capitalism.

Subsequent analyses have underscored the force of the feminist critique of Marxism. Benhabib and Cornell (1988), for example, feel that the gender blindness of Marx requires a paradigm shift for Marxism toward the articulation of "a minimal utopia of social life characterized by nurturant, caring, expressive and nonrepressive relations between self and other, self and nature" (p. 4). Perhaps the most consistently expressed criticism concerns Marx's emphasis on the ways in which the conditions of industrial labor were emphasized as the overarching source of contemporary alienation. Since working-class, male laborers were most subject to these conditions, the suggestion was that these were the people most injured by alienation. Marx's analysis of alienation focused itself

almost entirely on how the forces of commodification and objectification played themselves out on the shop floor. In Luke's view it
is clear that in Marxism "alienation is posited as a male condition"
(Luke, 1992, p. 31). The domestic work of childbearing and childrearing is not seen as inherently alienating in this analysis. Luke
points out that in Marx's references to domestic labor "the products of that labor (meals, clean clothes, socialized children) do not
confront and alienate the domestic worker" (p. 31). To her Marx
implies that "the natural, unwaged (private) labor of species production, family and child care, by virtue of being outside visible
exploitation and appropriation by the capitalist wage system, constitutes a non-alienating condition" (p. 31). Others, such as Mac-
Kinnon (1981) and Gimenez (1997), contest this vision of Marx,
arguing that implicit in his work is an analysis of patriarchy that
highlights its indispensability to capitalism. To Gimenez, for example "the control exerted by the capitalist class over its own conditions of reproduction and over the conditions necessary for the
reproduction of the laboring classes determines, in the last instance,
the nature of the relations between the sexes and the relative significance of the family within social classes" (Gimenez, 1997, p. 81).

In the 1970s a vigorous debate was initiated regarding the alienating nature of housework and the degree to which domestic labor
represented a form of unwaged capitalist exploitation. Summarizing the materialist feminist perspective Hennessy and Ingraham
(1997) argued, "women's cheap labor (guaranteed through racist
and patriarchal gender systems) is fundamental to the accumulation of surplus value—the basis for capitalist profit-making and
expansion" (p. 3). Amongst a growing number of feminists who
declared themselves socialists, the organization of work and family
life in industrial America was analyzed as representing a sexual division of labor that was necessary to the efficient functioning of capitalism (Kuhn and Wolpe, 1978). Prominent among such theorists
was Zillah Eisenstein (1979) who argued that capitalism and patriarchy were inextricably intertwined and that "the sexual division of
labor is at the structural and ideological base of patriarchy and capitalism" (Eisenstein, 1990, p. 134). Capitalism required ordered production, a line of authority stretching from stockholders to
managers to supervisors to shop floor workers. In Eisenstein's view,
"male supremacy as a system of sexual hierarchy supplies capitalism

. . . with the necessary order and control" (p. 135). Learning to accept such control as legitimate and natural was "necessary to the smooth functioning of society and the economic system" (p. 135). One of the primary sites in which children and adults of both sexes learned to accept the legitimacy of patriarchy, and in which they learned to enact this system of control, was the nuclear family. As we shall see later in this chapter, much of bell hooks' work focuses on how the family is the crucible in which people learn a "politic of domination" (hooks, 1989, p. 175).

The 1980s brought a critical analysis of this position with writers such as Barbara Ehrenreich arguing that "the family, so long reified in theory, looks more like an improvisation than an institution" (1990, p. 275). As many males simply exited the nuclear family, it became harder to argue that the family was the prime site within which patriarchy was learned. Writers such as Vogel (1983) also pointed out that women's oppression predated the onset of capitalism and was not exclusive to capitalist societies. Additionally, concerns were raised about the alienating nature of socialist feminist language that could itself become oppressive. For example, in an impassioned denunciation Christian (1990) declared herself "appalled by the sheer ugliness of the language, its lack of clarity, its unnecessarily complicated sentence construction, its lack of pleasurableness, its alienating quality" (p. 573). To her, such language "mystifies rather than clarifies our condition, making it possible for a few people who know that particular language to control the critical scene" (p. 572). The control of feminist discourse by a small cadre of White academic feminists is a theme echoed later in this chapter by both bell hooks and Angela Davis.

Critiquing Habermas and Foucault

In recent years some critically inclined feminists have conducted a sustained engagement with Habermas and Foucault, both of whom are seen as having particular relevance for feminist analysis. Habermas' communicative theory of learning, and his analysis of the lifeworld as a potentially emancipatory hedge against the swamping of life by the systems of money and power, have received particular attention from feminists interested in the ways in which critical theory can be reconfigured to serve women's interests. In her opening essay of a volume of feminist scholarship reappraising Habermas, Meehan (1995) opines that his work "offers a framework for analyzing the structure of modern life, its potential for both emancipatory forms of life and forms of life issuing in political repression, market manipulation and domination" (p. 1). She feels, however, that this analysis is in need of gendering, of being reappraised in terms of how it can inform specifically the emancipation of women. One example of a feminist development of Habermas' thought is Braaten's (1995) reframing of the idea of communicative rationality as communicative thinking. Just as Habermas sees communicative rationality as rooted in discourse communities, so Braaten sees communicative thinking as rooted in discourse communities arising out of expressions of feminist solidarity. In such groups solidarity is realized through the exchange of women's stories of struggle against patriarchy. The thinking demanded in such exchanges is "defiantly holistic" (p. 157) according to Braaten, since "it seeks intricacy, complexity and multidimensionality" (p. 157) in understanding the multi-layered nature of women's experiences.

But while Habermas has been a departure for some contemporary feminists, they have also criticized his work. Fraser (1995) and Fleming (1997), for example, argue that he overemphasizes the split between the system and the lifeworld. In their view when Habermas stresses how the repressive steering mechanisms of money and power dominate the system, he conveys the implicit assumption that the lifeworld tends to resist these pressures. Fraser (1995) argues strongly that this system-lifeworld split is oversimplified and that feminist empirical analyses of familial decision-making, handling of finances, wife battering, and so on have proved "that families are thoroughly permeated with, in Habermas' terms, the media of money and power" (p. 28). By overstating the contrast between the capitalist economy and family life, Fraser feels that Habermas "blocks the possibility of analyzing families as economic systems that is, as sites of labor, exchange, calculation, distribution, and exploitation" (p. 28). She also criticizes him for restricting the analysis of power to bureaucratic contexts and urges that he place more attention on domestic patriarchal power, on recognizing that "actions coordinated by normatively secured consensus in the male-headed nuclear family are actions regulated by power" (p. 29).

Foucault has also received critical approbation from some contemporary feminists who have built on his analysis of the way knowledge generated within dominant discourses (such as the assumption that male thought is inherently more rational and therefore superior) inevitably supports existing power structures and relations (such as patriarchy). They appreciate particularly his understanding of the complexities of the exercise of power and surveillance and his placing the analysis of sexuality at the center of his concerns. In Sawicki's (1991) view, "feminist appropriations of Foucault have resulted in pathbreaking and provocative social and cultural criticism" (p. 95) such as studies of anorexia nervosa, female desire, and the social construction of femininity. Lather (1991) and Gore (1993) have made particular use of Foucault in their critique of the essentialist certainties of critical pedagogy. They draw on his emphasis on the uncontrollability and oppressive dimensions of supposedly rational, emancipatory practices and his acknowledgment of the unpredictability and contextuality of educational practice. Foucault's work, in their view, helps move critical theorists toward a pedagogical stance that is "tentative and contextual in confronting complicity, incompleteness, and dispersion" (Lather, 2001, p. 188), and that leads to "the construction of complicated, disturbed answers" (p. 191).

Sawicki (1991) does acknowledge the criticism made by some feminists that "Foucault's discourses on subjectivity, power and resistance threaten to undermine the emancipatory project of feminism" (p. 96). After all, stressing how opposition movements can themselves manifest unintended oppressive tendencies "might undermine the self-assertion of oppositional groups and suppress the emergence of oppositional consciousness" (p. 107). But Sawicki values above all the element of productive uncertainty that Foucault brings to the analysis of political action. Drawing on Foucault, she argues that "one must always feel uncomfortable with one's political principles and strategies lest they become dogma" (p. 103). Consistent with Marcuse's assertion that critical theory must always be critical of itself, and West's belief in the continuing relevance of prophetic pragmatism, Sawicki values the openness to experimentation and rejection of fixed strategies that she feels Foucault's analysis brings to contemporary feminism. This emphasis is confirmed by Lather (2001) who feels that it is important to be "reflexive without being paralyzed" (p. 191) and that postmodern and poststructuralist perspectives are helpful in informing reflexively considered action.

Feminist teachers who draw on critical theory in their efforts to work critically have returned again and again to the importance of questioning the uncritical application of Marx, Habermas, or Foucault to their attempts to fight patriarchy through education. Grounding their work in specific classroom contexts, these educators stress the naiveté of assuming that teachers can work unproblematically for the emancipation of learners, particularly adult learners whom those teachers view as peers. In stressing the arrogance and condescension of assuming that one can bring students into voice, or empower them to exercise agency, feminist critiques of critically inclined pedagogy undermine the confidently masculine tone they hear in its texts. Practiced in a feminist key, critical pedagogy is never innocent, never uncomplicated, never without contradictions. Specific practices (such as putting students into circles, running leaderless discussion, or adopting learning journals) are analyzed not as inherently emancipatory but as sometimes emphasizing teacher power and increasing students' sense of being under covert surveillance. It is to a deeper exploration of this analysis that we now turn.

Deconstructing Critical Pedagogy

In recent years an enormous amount of interest has been generated by the attempt to derive educational practices from the study of critical theory. Most of this work has focused on analyzing how teachers can help adult learners realize and confront the controlling power of dominant ideology. As a shorthand descriptor, the term *critical pedagogy* has been given to this body of practice, and in recent years a vigorous discourse has been generated around this work. There are numerous texts exploring critical pedagogy, an annual conference devoted to studying the pedagogy and theater of the oppressed, and even a newly created doctoral degree in critical pedagogy. In adult education the critical pedagogy discourse is one of the dominant discourses informing work around critical reflection and transformative learning.

Critical pedagogy as articulated most prominently by McLaren (1995, 1997) and Giroux (1983, 1988) focuses on galvanizing students' oppositional consciousness and helping them translate this into action. Feminist analyses of critical pedagogy frequently place it as the realization through educational practice of critical theory. Lather (1992), for example, describes critical pedagogy as "constructed out of a combination of Frankfurt School critical theory, Gramscian counter-hegemonic practice and Freirean conscientization" (p. 122). Gore (1993) underscores how the language of critical pedagogy is "borrowed from Neo-Marxism, the Critical Theory of the Frankfurt School, and oppositional politics generally" (p. 109). Drawing explicitly on Marx, Gramsci, and Habermas, critical pedagogy emphasizes the struggle of teachers and students to fight classism, racism, and sexism inside and outside their classrooms. Part of this struggle involves the creation of democratic dialog within educational communities, part of it entails teachers working as organic, critical, or transformative intellectuals to connect classroom learning to broader social movements. Central to this struggle is an emphasis on the agency of teachers and students in classrooms and communities who learn how to advocate for social justice, how to work tactically and strategically to advance the interests of the disenfranchised, and how to confront and undermine dominant ideology.

The variant of critical pedagogy represented by Freire's work (Freire, 1994) has had particular resonance within adult education. Its focus is on helping adults analyze their experiences collaboratively and critically so they can uncover the knowledge, insights, and skills they possess that will help them fight their own oppression. Although Freire developed his own ideas on educational methodology while working with illiterate adults in northeast Brazil, his work has found a receptive audience in North America and Europe. For example, in a series of provocative books that focus on the specifics and contradictions of dialogic, democratic practice, Ira Shor, and his sometime coeditor Caroline Pari, interpret Freire's ideas in the context of American higher education (Shor, 1987a, 1987b, 1992, 1996; Shor and Pari, 1999, 2000). Freire has himself assisted the extension of his work to North American contexts by holding a series of conversations with American-based educators such as Shor (Shor and Freire, 1987), Donaldo Macedo (Freire and Macedo, 1987), and Myles Horton (Horton and Freire, 1990). In these conversations he explores concepts and practices that are of

concern to feminists such as bringing students into voice, the importance of inclusionary practices, the co-construction of curriculum
through problem-posing education, and the extension of democratic communication. As a result, Freire has had a significant influence on feminist pedagogy, being quoted extensively (and often
approvingly) by such ideologically diverse writers as the *Women's Ways
of Knowing* (Belenky and others, 1986) group, Antonia Darder
(2002), and bell hooks (1994). Along with Foucault, he is one of the
most highly quoted male theorists in this discourse. Gore's (1993)
book analyzing critical and feminist discourses of truth acknowledges
the contributions of both these men to emerging efforts at feminist
pedagogy.

Freire's work has not been uncritically received, however. Some
feminists, including hooks (1994) herself, take Freire to task for the
unequivocal certainty they hear in his voice and his lack of serious
engagement with feminist perspectives. Weiler (2001a) notes that in
an interview with Macedo (Freire and Macedo, 1995), Freire talks
in general terms of " 'the feminists,' as though there were a single
movement or voice" (p. 81) and that he fails "to analyze the underlying patriarchal assumptions of the European intellectual tradition
from which his own thought has emerged" (p. 81). Others, such as
Kenway and Modra (1992) comment on the worrying aura of hero-
worship that obscures a critical appraisal of his work. In their words,
"it looks very much as if Freirean idolatry is taking the place of the
development of critical consciousness *in the very project of liberatory
education itself*" (p. 157). Weiler (2001a) echoes this criticism and
notes that Freire "never put forward a self-critique of his tendency
to glorify the revolutionary leader" (p. 76). She laments that his "fundamental framing of oppression remains in class (and occasionally
racial) terms" (p. 79) and how this framing leads him to imagine the
revolutionary hero "as male and as existing solely within the public
world, a vision which discounts the world of personal relationships
or of everyday life—the world of women" (p. 76).

But perhaps the most serious and sustained feminist criticism
of how critical theory has been translated into pedagogical practice
has focused on the work of Giroux and McLaren, the strand of critical pedagogy that draws clearly and explicitly on critical theory via
Marx, Habermas, and Gramsci. The reverberations that were produced by Ellsworth's (1992) critique of the (to her) unwarranted

masculinist certainties of critical pedagogy and the responses of Giroux and McLaren to this, are, as Lather (2001) notes, still in the air. Some of the general criticisms of the Giroux-McLaren strand of critical pedagogy made by feminists are that there is a remarkable lack of self-criticality evident in critical discourse, that the discourse is itself oppressive and functions as a form of repressive tolerance (though Marcuse's use of this term is not invoked), and that the teacher as benevolent, freedom-fighting agent of emancipation is unproblematized. To them there is a paternalistic arrogance—a sense of "teacher knows best"—pervading critical pedagogy. More particular criticisms focus on the unacknowledged impossibility of realizing Habermas' ideal speech situation, the contradictions of encouraging voice amongst learners, and the lack of specificity around vague notions of empowerment. In the next few paragraphs I review both these general and more specific criticisms.

As already mentioned, a general lack of self-criticality in the discourse of critical pedagogy is commented on by several feminist critics. For example, Gore (1992) writes "the 'self-critical' nature claimed for critical discourses seems more rhetorical than actual" (p. 60), and "the possibility that their own academic construction of critical pedagogy might not be the emancipatory discourse it is intended to be is rarely articulated by these theorists" (p. 60). Kenway and Modra (1992) criticize in particular the lack of engagement with feminist theorizing such theorists exhibit. Writing of male critical pedagogues they assert, "it is uncommon for them to either examine the gendered assumptions embedded deeply and subtly in their theoretical premises or to grasp the full significance of the presence and power of gender in educational settings" (p. 138). Given that critical pedagogues claim that they are "quintessentially engaged in democratizing the educational process" (p. 138), Kenway and Modra conclude that "this failure to engage with feminism casts considerable doubt on their authenticity" (p. 138). As Luke (1992) observes, for critical pedagogues simply to cite a few prominent feminists in passing does not constitute a sustained engagement with the complexities of this perspective.

A second criticism of critical pedagogy articulated in feminist analyses concerns the ways in which its discourse, supposedly emancipatory in intent, becomes oppressive in its functioning. The substance of this criticism concerns the authoritative tone permeating

324   THE POWER OF CRITICAL THEORY

discussions of the teacher's presumed emancipatory authority. By foregrounding the teacher's role as central, critical pedagogy's discourse implies that without a teacher's presence adults will be too ideologically duped to discern their manipulation. Gore (1993) finds the concept of the teacher's emancipatory authority as actively dangerous "in the extent to which it primarily functions to emancipate both the theorist and the teacher from actively worrying about inconsistent effects of their pedagogy" (p. 102). She explores typical emancipatory practices such as having students rather than teachers facilitate classes and builds on a Foucaultian perspective to argue that "in this specific pedagogical technique, the circulation of power is, potentially, both repressive and emancipatory" (p. 120). Ellsworth's (1992) study of her class on anti-racist practice at the University of Madison is one of the most quoted empirical studies in critiques of the potentially oppressive nature of critical pedagogy. Although she does not cite Marcuse's (1965) analysis of repressive tolerance (discussed in Chapter Seven), it seems to me that she provides a telling example of how that process works. Ellsworth observes how her classroom discussions around race and gender worked to exclude those they were designed to include, and how they exacerbated the very racist, sexist, classist, and authoritarian conditions they were designed to ameliorate. She argues that notions of empowerment, learner voice, dialogue, even the idea of being critical, "are repressive myths that perpetuate relations of domination" (p. 91). For her the discourses and practices of critical pedagogy "were working through us in repressive ways, and had themselves become vehicles of repression" (p. 91).

One of the chief sources of oppression that the feminist critique of critical pedagogy reveals is the way the pedagogical role itself is conceived. When the teacher as freedom fighter is at the center of the discourse, there is a grave danger that those who are the "target" of emancipatory efforts will see chiefly the paternalistic arrogance of critical teachers. In Orner's (1992) view, critical educators mistakenly believe they are the only ones who truly understand patriarchy and ideological subjugation. In this scenario Orner believes that "the only people who get 'worked over' are the students" (p. 87) who are the unwitting target of educators who are presumed to be free of ideological distortion and oppressive tendencies. However, as Ellsworth (1992) writes concerning her own attempts at emancipatory pedagogy, "I cannot unproblematically bring subjugated knowledges to light when I am not free of my own learned racism, fat oppression, classism, ableism, or sexism" (p. 99). Teachers' have their own positionalities which must be taken into account just as much as those of their students.

Much of the feminist critique of critical practice concerns the division between the "us" of critically aware teachers and the "them" of ideologically duped students. This distinction is inherent in critical theory's formulation of ideological control. Ideology is learned, hegemony is embraced, and control is internalized by the masses with only a few enlightened individuals able to penetrate the ideological smokescreens that obscure the reality of unjust structures. Feminists of a poststructural persuasion such as Gore (1992, 1993) and Lather (1991, 1992, 2001) have been particularly adept at highlighting the contradictions of such a position. It is not that this position is inherently arrogant. Ideological control certainly exists and some are clearly better than others at detecting its presence. The problem is rather that a sense of total certainty creeps into the minds of those critical educators who are convinced of the correctness of their ideological reading of the world. The reading may indeed be correct; but as soon as it is taken for granted it becomes as potentially oppressive as dominant ideology. Gramsci, Marcuse, Foucault, and West are amongst those who urge strongly the need for critical theory to retain a degree of self-criticality and to be ever on the alert for its own reification. The feminist critique underscores this necessity. In Gore's (1992) view the us/them relationship becomes problematic when the focus is only on the "them" of learners. As she points out, "When the agent of empowerment assumes to be already empowered, and so apart from those who are to be empowered, arrogance can underlie claims of 'what we can do for you'" (p. 61).

A particular concern of feminist critics of critically inclined pedagogy is the emphasis in its discourse on bringing students into voice. Giving voice, discovering voice, encouraging voice, and finding voice are phrases frequently used to describe practices designed to develop in learners a confidence to name the world in ways that feel accurate to them and that match their experiences. There is an assumption that people who have found their voices speak in ways that represent

the core of their being. Instead of speaking the language of the oppressor, with its self-blaming vocabulary, adults who have found their
voices are thought now to speak in ways that truly represent who they
are. The agent who facilitates this finding of authentic voice, the
leader on the trek of aural discovery is, of course, the teacher.

Three problems are raised by feminist critics regarding the discourse and practice of helping learners discover their voices. First,
there is the questionable modernist assumption that a core authentic self exists which can find true expression in a certain voice. This
is a form of highly dubious essentialism. As Orner (1992) points
out, "Calls for student voice in education presume students, voices,
and identities to be singular, unchanging and unaffected by the
context in which the speaking occurs" (p. 80). Second, there is the
presumption that when this voice is spoken the truly attentive critical teacher will recognize its presence. This grants to the teacher
a potentially oppressive degree of control to define what is true
and authentic. Thirdly, there are many times when speaking in
one's voice is clearly not safe. Critical pedagogy cannot assume that
teachers have the power to create speech safety zones in their classrooms that are free of prejudice and hate. Those who feel they
have managed to do this are, in the eyes of feminist critics, fooling
themselves in a very dangerous way. As Ellsworth (1992) points out,
it is mistaken for critical teachers always to assume that silence represents voicelessness or loss of voice. This view "betrays deep and
unacceptable gender, race, and class biases" (p. 105) and neglects
the possibility that silence is often a politically sophisticated, deliberate choice. Orner (1992) and Ellsworth (1992) observe that
students will not speak when they perceive threatening body language amongst peers, when the teacher is not viewed as an ally,
when they have bad memories of speaking out in the past, and when
they resent having to teach privileged students about the nature of
oppression.

Feminism as a Transgressive Pedagogy: bell hooks

A critical appraisal of voice is offered by the African American theorist, bell hooks, in her analysis of feminism, *Talking Back* (hooks,
1989). hooks acknowledges that for women of color in working-
class communities "coming to voice is an act of resistance . . . a way

to engage in active self-transformation and a rite of passage where one moves from being object to being subject" (p. 12). However, she shares the skepticism of Orner, Ellsworth, and others regarding the idea that each of us has a unique voice representing our individual identity and declares herself more interested in the struggle of groups to recover their collective voice, a voice "embodying collective reality past and present, family and community" (p. 31). hooks is also skeptical of the way oppositional voices can easily be co-opted by the dominant culture. Although she does not cite Marcuse directly, her analysis of the way dominant culture neuters criticism, while appearing to encourage it, is very close to Marcuse's description of repressive tolerance. She writes "in a white-supremacist, capitalist, patriarchal state where the mechanisms of co-optation are so advanced, much that is potentially radical is undermined, turned into a commodity" (hooks, 1989, p. 14). This commodification is achieved by radicals themselves who, in their eagerness to communicate with as many people as possible, find themselves using metaphors and analogies that reinforce dominant ways of knowing. In hooks view, "it is easy for the marginal voice striving for a hearing to allow what is said to be overdetermined by the needs of that majority group who appears to be listening, to be tuned in" (p. 14). In an effort to connect with the majority group, radicals are tempted "to describe and define experience in a language compatible with existing images and ways of knowing, constructed within a social framework that reinforces domination" (p. 14).

The quotes above illustrate how hooks works within the critical theory tradition, though she draws less frequently and explicitly on particular authors and ideas from that tradition than Davis. Nonetheless, her work is replete with references to concepts familiar within critical theory. In *Talking Back* (1989), for example, she writes of the commodification of knowledge, the reification and commodification of Blackness and the way this leads to alienation and estrangement, and the ways "women can and do participate in politics of domination, as perpetrators as well as victims" (p. 20). Her comments on the politicization of love (hooks, 1989, p. 6) draw on Freire and can therefore be connected to Freire's own reading of Fromm. She also returns again and again to the importance of class analysis, so strongly argued by Marx, and to the importance

328 THE POWER OF CRITICAL THEORY

of attaching a critique of capitalism to any attempt to understand Black experience. In her talking book with Cornel West, she laments "the reluctance of Black people to engage in any critiques of capitalism today" (hooks and West, 1991, p. 100). She notes how "we deal with White supremacist assault by buying something to compensate for feelings of wounded pride and self-esteem" (p. 98) and how "murder can be justified in pursuit of the right status symbol, e.g. a pair of sneakers" (p. 99).

For hooks class analysis must always stand alongside the analysis of racism and sexism. In *Where We Stand: Class Matters* (hooks, 2000b), she laments the fact that in critically inclined conversation "the uncool subject is class" (p. vii) and that "there is no organized class struggle, no daily in-your-face critique of capitalist greed that stimulates thought and action-critique, reform and revolution" (p. 1). The fact that much feminist analysis concentrates on gender oppression is seen by her as a reflection of the way the concerns of White middle-class women have come to be universalized as the concerns of all. In her view "had poor women set the agenda for feminist movement they might have decided that class struggle would be a central feminist issue" (hooks, 1984, p. 61). Additionally, the analysis of class and gender oppression cannot be conducted without attention to racism. In *Feminist Theory* (1984), she argues that "class structure in American society has been shaped by the racial politic of white supremacy" (p. 3) and that "it is only by analyzing racism and its function in capitalist society that a thorough understanding of class relationships can emerge" (p. 3). Hence, "class struggle is inextricably bound to the struggle to end racism" (p. 3), and race and class issues should be "recognized as feminist issues with as much relevance as sexism" (p. 25).

So in hooks' view feminism is not an attempt to gain equality with men but a fight against the whole ideology and practice of domination constituted by the interlocking systems of sexism, racism, and classism. Since women's identities are fundamentally affected by all three systems, she argues that "feminist thought must continually emphasize the importance of sex, race and class as factors which *together* determine the social construction of femaleness" (hooks, 1989, p. 23). That this has not generally happened is a central critique of *Feminist Theory* (1984) where hooks critiques feminism consciousness-raising because it "has not significantly pushed women in the direction of revolutionary politics" (p. 159). Her experience of feminist consciousness-raising groups is that they have not done enough to help women understand how capitalism works to exploit female labor, reinforce sexism, or create an addiction to consumption. Neither has consciousness-raising pushed women to learn about alternate political systems such as socialism.

In *Talking Back* (1989), hooks defines feminism specifically as "a struggle to eradicate the ideology of domination" (p. 24) and points out how sexism is "the practice of domination most people are socialized to accept before they even know that other forms of group oppression exist" (p. 35). The family is an important location for people to learn patterns of domination whether this is learning how to discriminate against others or learning to accept the right to be dominated. Even in single-parent families with no male figure "children may learn to value dominating, authoritative rule via their relationship to mothers and other adults" (p. 36). Given that domination involves a mix of class, racial, and gender oppression, any attempt to challenge the "politic of domination" (hooks, 1989, p. 175) must involve fighting all three systems. One cannot just confront gender oppression "since all forms of oppression are linked in our society because they are supported by similar institutional and social structures" (1984, p. 35). Any attempt to challenge sexism also involves fighting racism and classism, just as any attempt to challenge racism involves confronting sexism and classism, and so on.

hooks identifies some of the specific elements of contemporary ideological domination in *Teaching to Transgress* (1994). Chief amongst these are the belief that deep racism doesn't exist anymore, that any Black person who works hard enough can become economically self-sufficient, that women have gained equality with men to the extent that White males are now the victim of minorities and domineering women, and that those who are poor and unemployed are in that state by choice. Ideological domination maintains itself by the fact that people have "a lack of meaningful access to truth" (p. 29) so that they view the ideology described above as self-evidently true. In hooks' view, "this collective cultural consumption of and attachment to misinformation is coupled with the layers of lying individuals do in their personal lives" (p. 29).

Such self-delusional mendacity only serves to rob people of the necessary energy for change. This ideological double whammy of cultural socialization and personal self-delusion means that "our capacity to face reality is severely diminished as is our will to intervene and change unjust circumstances" (p. 29).

An important element in combating the "collective cultural consumption of and attachment to information" described above is adult education. Unlike many of the theorists addressed in this book, hooks lays out an educational agenda for combating ideological domination in quite specific terms. Central to this agenda is the reliance on small groups as crucibles for feminist consciousness-raising and, hence, resistance. In terms that call to mind Horton's work at Highlander, hooks argues that small groups are particularly suited to the integration of critical analysis into discussions of personal experiences. Small groups more easily allow for the democratization of conversation, and they stress the importance of an oral sharing of information, which reduces the relative dominance of White academic feminists. As such they are good settings for "the politicization of the self that focuses on creating understanding of the ways sex, race, and class together determine our individual lot and collective experience" (hooks, 1989, p. 24).

hooks has less to say about the pedagogy of small groups, however, than she does about her own practice within formal classrooms. She views the feminist classroom as an arena of struggle distinguished by a striving for a union of theory and practice. One of the most striking elements in her analysis is her emphasis on the inevitability of teacher power and the ways in which its exercise is often unavoidably, even necessarily, confrontational. In her judgment the role of teacher "is a position of power over others" with the resultant power open to being used "in ways that diminish or in ways that enrich" (hooks, 1989, p. 52). She freely admits that sometimes the exercise of power to force people to confront their own uncritical acceptance and practice of dominant ideology is fraught with risk. To emphasize the commitment students should have to the learning of others, hooks takes attendance, a practice reminiscent of elementary school for many skeptical adult students. To underscore the importance of attendance she lets students know that poor attendance negatively affects their grade. She requires all to participate in class discussion, often by reading out paragraphs they have already written. Such practices inevitably lead to negatively critical comments by students, a fact that she admits has been difficult for her to accept. Because "many students find this pedagogy difficult, frightening, and very demanding" (hooks, 1994, p. 53), teachers who use it are bound to be resisted, even disliked. This is why hooks insists that students' perception of the classroom as a safe, positive, or congenial environment for learning is not a good criterion to use in assessing teacher competence.

In emphasizing the kinds of confrontational practices outlined above, hooks demonstrates her liking for pedagogic flexibility. In methodological terms, she comes close to Cornel West's position of critical pragmatism, whereby the pursuit of revolutionary ends is distinguished by a continuous readiness to experiment with different approaches. hooks believes that "to make feminist classrooms the site of transformative learning experiences, we must constantly try new methods, new approaches" (1989, p. 54). In reflecting on her pedagogy in *Teaching to Transgress,* she observes that "there could never be an absolute set agenda governing teaching practices. Agendas had to be flexible, had to allow for spontaneous shifts in direction" (1994, p. 7). One interesting authorial manifestation of her experimental disposition is her use of the pseudonym bell hooks (her real name is Gloria Watkins). By using a pseudonym, she frees herself to leave behind ways of thinking that now seem inaccurate, without feeling she has somehow compromised her basic identity. As she puts it in *Talking Back* (1989), "In using the pseudonym I consciously sought to make a separation between ideas and identity so that I could be open to challenge and change" (p. 163). The public perception of her as bell hooks frees her "to change perspectives, to let them go if necessary, to admit errors in my thinking" (p. 163).

Finally, hooks' privileging of openness and inclusivity is seen in her willingness to work with Whites and with males in the struggle against White supremacy. Once again, the similarities between her stance and that of Cornel West's on this issue are apparent. Both emphasize that confronting systemic forces requires allies drawn from all segments of society, and that the building of such alliances can be done without compromising one's racial identity. In hooks' view refusing to work with Whites in the struggle against White supremacy "is a gesture that undermines my commitment to that struggle" (hooks, 1989, p. 118). Similarly, in critiquing exclusively anti-male conceptions of feminism, she argues that such an orientation alienated many non-White, poor, and working-class women from the feminist movement. Such women believe "that they have more in common with men of their race and/or class group than bourgeois white women" (hooks, 1994, p. 68). In particular, Black men and women are united by the ties of collective struggle for liberation.

Since men as well as women suffer from being bound by rigidly conceived stereotypical sex roles, hooks believes that fighting to end sexism is something that benefits men as well as women. In her intentionally populist primer and manifesto *Feminism Is For Everybody* (2000a), she writes that, although most men are disturbed by patriarchal violence against women, the fear of giving up what they see as the benefits of patriarchy means that "they find it easier to passively support male domination even when they know in their minds and hearts that it is wrong" (p. ix). If only men had an accurate understanding of feminism as a fight to end sexism (and by implication to end racism and classism) "they would find in feminist movement the hope of their own release from the bondage of patriarchy" (p. ix). This is why feminism—the fight to end sexism—is for everybody, and why a man who is struggling to recognize and challenge the advantages he gains from patriarchy "is a worthy comrade in struggle, in no way a threat to feminism" (p. 12). More particularly, hooks believes that "men have a tremendous contribution to make to feminist struggle in the area of exposing, confronting, opposing, and transforming the sexism of their male peers" (hooks, 1984, p. 81). Indeed, she argues that without male involvement the feminist movement can never fully realize its transformative intent. Hence, "feminist consciousness-raising for males is as essential to revolutionary movement as female groups . . .. Males of all ages need settings where their resistance to sexism is affirmed and valued" (hooks, 2000a, p. 11). The insistence on the phrase "of all ages" is telling. Men learning how to confront and challenge sexism are truly engaged in a lifelong project that hooks believes we should regard as life-saving. For her "a wise and loving feminist politics can provide the only foundation to save the lives of male children" (p. 71). This foundation can be laid both in all-male groups whose members try to recognize the ways their own sexism harms themselves as well as those they live with, and also through men's struggle to live in anti-sexist ways with women.

One final element of hooks' work that is of particular interest to adult educators who wish to draw on critical theory as they construct and live out their practice, is her insistence on developing theoretical work that is accessible to a broad group of people while losing none of its power to critique. Recalling Gramsci's unwittingly sexist aphorism that "all men are intellectuals" (1971, p. 9) hooks writes that "everything we do in life is rooted in theory" (2000a, p. 19) and that "we all use it in daily life" (1989, p. 38). Since theory is no more than an underlying system of understandings that shape thought and practice, it "is not an alien sphere" (p. 38). Theory, like feminism, is for everybody, and people "practice theorizing without ever knowing/possessing the term" (hooks, 1994, p. 62).

However, although everybody is a theoretician, many people are intimidated by the language of feminist theory. This is ironic since feminist theory, like critical theory, has a deliberately liberatory intent. But in hooks' view, the dominance of feminist discourse by White women academics, overly influenced by French post-structuralism, has meant that for many working women feminist theory "is synonymous with that which is difficult to comprehend, linguistically convoluted" (hooks, 1989, p. 36). Feminist theory has become "a narrow constricting concept" (p. 36) to the extent that "it reinforces the fear, especially on the part of the exploited and oppressed, that the intent of theorizing is not to liberate but to mystify" (p. 37). When this happens the radical, subversive potential of theory is clearly undermined. If the transformative purpose of theory is to be realized, hooks believes it must be written in accessible terms. In her view "theory cannot become the groundwork for feminist movement unless it is more accessible" (p. 39).

Creating theory that is accessible, yet that has critical power, requires some important shifts in direction for feminists, according to hooks. First, academics must rid themselves of the conception that "speaking about one's personal experience or speaking in simple language is . . . a sign of intellectual weakness or even anti-intellectualism" (hooks, 1989, p. 77). This is why the commitment by feminist pedagogy to education for critical consciousness must stress the exploration of personal experiences and "start with examining the self from a new, critical perspective" (p. 109). However, the examination of experiences must not slide into an uncritical celebration of everyone's stories, or a series of untheorized personal disclosures. hooks believes feminist educators "must work to link personal narratives with knowledge of how we must act politically to change and transform the world" (p. 111). There must also be a renewed effort on the part of feminist theorists "to speak simply with language that is accessible to as many folks as possible" (p. 77). This means that colloquialisms, slang, the language of the streets must be used to communicate the insights of feminism to those that habitually use that language. If feminism is to be a mass movement to end sexism, then there is little point, according to hooks, in using theoretical language understood by only a small cadre of intellectuals. As she puts it, "If I do not speak a language that can be understood, then there is little chance for dialogue" (p. 78). For radical intellectuals of color like herself, the issue of language is particularly crucial since a rejection of familiar, colloquial speech patterns that represent distinctive aspects of a person's racial heritage and identity "is one of the ways we become estranged and alienated from our past" (p. 80). This has led hooks to experiment with methods of expression that risk the opprobrium of her peers. Just as Cornel West was seen by some as straying from the intellectual straight and narrow by recording his CD "Sketches of my Culture," so hooks has been criticized for venturing into children's literature with her book *Happy to be Nappy* (hooks, 1999).

Angela Davis: Theorist of Transformative Struggle

Making theory accessible so that it can transform society has also been a major concern of Angela Davis. In a more consistently explicit manner than hooks, however, Davis has always drawn openly on her grounding in Marxism, and her acquaintance—personally as well as theoretically—with figures in the critical theory tradition. In many ways she has remained one of the most prominent socialist-feminists, continually interpreting women's issues (housework, rape, abortion rights) in the light of capitalism's systematic suppression of women of color and poor women in general. It is clear to Davis that "there are forces in society that reap enormous benefits from the persistent, deepening oppression of women" (Davis, 1990, p. 13), but it is also clear that it is not men as an undifferentiated group that are responsible. Rather, it is particular men (and particular women) who constitute the subalterns of the ruling class. Davis writes that "within the existing class relations of capitalism, women in their vast majority are kept in a state of financial servitude and social inferiority not by men in general, but rather by the ruling class. Their oppression serves to maximize the efficacy of domination" (Davis, 1998a, p. 185). Hence, any feminist analysis she conducts starts from an understanding that "the structures of female oppression are inextricably tethered to capitalism" (p. 185).

Her early interest in Marx led Davis to become a student of Marcuse as she saw how "he maintained a sense of the connectedness between emerging social movements and his larger philosophical project" (Davis, 1998b, p. 22). At his suggestion Davis spent some time in Frankfurt, Germany, where she attended lectures by Adorno and Habermas, amongst others. On her return to the United States, she joined the Communist Party and became involved with the Black Panther movement. Whilst teaching philosophy at UCLA (and fighting to keep her job), she became increasingly involved with activism focused on prisoners' rights. As her public profile as a Black communist grew, she began to receive death threats to the extent that campus security guards would check her car for bombs as she left work each day. To provide off-campus security for herself, she legally purchased and registered two handguns, and accepted protection from a variety of bodyguards. One of these was Jonathan Jackson, the younger brother of George Jackson, one of the famous Soledad Brothers (Jackson, 1970) indicted for the murder of a guard in Soledad prison.

In August 1970 Jonathan attempted to gain publicity for the Soledad Brothers by traveling to Marin County, north of San Francisco, entering a courtroom and, along with the prisoners on trial, taking the judge, Harold Haley, the district attorney, and several jury members hostage. One of the guns he used was registered in Angela Davis' name. In the courtroom car park, Jackson, the judge, and two prisoners were shot and killed while the district attorney, several jurors, and a third prisoner were wounded. Davis (who was in Los Angeles at the time) was named as an accomplice and went underground for two months before being arrested in New York as one of the FBI's "Ten Most Wanted" criminals. Whilst in prison Davis worked as co-counsel on her defense and produced her own prison writings (Davis, 1971a). In February 1972 she was released on bail (after the California supreme court abolished the death penalty), and in June 1972 she was acquitted by a jury of all charges against her. In her account of the trial, Aptheker (1999) documents how it triggered a worldwide movement for Davis' release.

Her public notoriety—celebrated by the left, demonized by the right—has meant that, in Joy James' words, "her writings are surpassed in the popular mind by her iconographic status" (1998, p. 19). Yet, after her acquittal she returned to activism, teaching and research, and for the last thirty years has published analyses that consistently link issues such as rape, female incarceration, and women's blues to a larger context of social and political oppression. In James' words, Davis "radicalizes feminism through a class and antiracist analysis and offers new constructions" (p. 15) by exploring "intersectional analyses of Marxism, antiracism, and feminism" (p. 15). Davis herself argues that her use of the term *feminist* is constantly evolving and that she rejects any single definition. For her "the most effective versions of feminism acknowledge the various ways gender, class, race, and sexual orientation inform each other" (Davis, 1998a, p. 304). Feminism is always linked in her mind with "substantive, radical institutional transformation" and specific political action such as "agendas for jobs, student funding, health care, childcare, housing, reproductive rights" (p. 304). She has never abandoned the perspective, grounded in critical theory, that personal relationships (including those that are abusive), feelings (of alienation, racial hatred or misogyny), cultural forms (blues songs, rap, TV sit-coms), and specific social structures (such as education or the prison system) must always be understood as part of a wider system of capitalist exploitation. Like hooks, Davis returns us again and again to Horkheimer's single existential judgment of the importance of abolishing the exchange dynamic of capitalism, but she does so with a contemporary focus on how that dynamic underscores racism and sexism.

Her autobiography, written immediately after her acquittal in the early 1970s, is full of descriptions of moments when critical theory illuminated the connections between capitalism and racism. Perhaps the most dramatic of these intellectual events was her reading of *The Communist Manifesto* which hit her "like a bolt of lightning" (Davis, 1974, p. 109). The vivid intellectual awakening this occasioned is worth quoting in her own words:

> I began to see the problems of Black people within the context of a large working class movement. Like an expert surgeon, this document cut away cataracts from my eyes . . .. It all fell into place. What had seemed a personal hatred of me, an inexplicable refusal of Southern whites to confront their own emotions, and a stubborn willingness of Blacks to acquiesce, became the inevitable consequence of a ruthless system which kept itself alive and well by encouraging spite, competition and the oppression of one group by another. Profit was the word: the cold and constant motive for the behavior, the contempt, and the despair I had seen [p. 110].

Nearly quarter of a century later, she continued to acknowledge how the manifesto gave her some her basic conceptual tools for an analysis of "what we now call intersectionality, or the relationship between race and class" and for a way "to think about social change in a way that moved beyond an exclusive focus on race" (Davis, 1998b, p. 19). As well as using Marxist concepts such as alienation (Davis, 1971b) throughout her work, Davis also exemplifies the Marxist notion of using philosophy to change the world. Like hooks, Gramsci, and others in the critical tradition, Davis regards philosophizing as an activity open to all people, a normal part of daily reality. She speaks of her own philosophical practice as "a quotidian way of living in the world" (1998b, p. 17), and in an interview with George Yancy declares "the theme of my work, of my life, has been the attempt to use whatever knowledge, skills, and wisdom I may have acquired to advance emancipatory theory and practice" (p. 29). Such work is "part of a tradition of struggle . . . connected with a collective effort to bring about radical social change" (p. 29).

For the past three decades Davis has been concerned to mount a critique of capitalism and to combat the ideologically convenient belief that the fall of the Berlin Wall and collapse of Eastern Europe marks the triumph of capitalism. In her view capitalism has been frighteningly successful in spreading its own ideological justification, to the point where it is now seen as the "natural" way of ordering economic affairs to billions of people across the globe. Its crises and contradictions are veiled by people's readiness to view unemployment, homelessness, declining public services, and an assault on welfare as events as much outside their control as are flash floods or hurricanes. Corporations relocate to countries where labor is cheap and nonunionized and where pollution controls are nonexistent. The communities they abandon are left jobless, prey to the drug trade, and lacking the tax base to fund decent education or welfare systems. Their only growth industry is crime and, "in a horrifying and self-reproducing cycle" (Davis, 1998a, p. 67), the only jobs created to replace those that have left are in the prison sector.

Davis laments that "the vast expansion of the power of capitalist corporations over the lives of people of color and poor people in general has been accompanied by a waning anticapitalist consciousness" (1998a, p. 67). In a 1998 interview she stated her belief that "the expansive globalization of capital has led to a predicament in which the everyday lives of people are even more directly and intimately affected by capital than, say, twenty years ago" (1998b, p. 28). This is why, in her view, "the project of developing explicitly anticapitalist theories and practices is of greater importance now than ever before" (p. 28). Davis' own engagement in this project has focused on illuminating the ways racism and women's oppression are accepted as part of dominant ideology, as creations of capitalism necessary to its own successful functioning.

In an anthology of prison writings produced while she was incarcerated, Davis wrote of the "millions of Americans whose senses have been dulled and whose critical powers have been eroded by the continual onslaught of racist ideology" (1971a, p. 25). Sometimes this ideology is overt, but at other times "open, explicit racism has in many ways begun to be replaced by a secluded, camouflaged kind of racism" (1998a, p. 65). In particular, racism has been subtly strengthened by an "ideologically produced fear of crime" (p. 65) which has led to "the naturalization of black people as criminals" (p. 67). If Black people are successfully demonized as innately criminal, then the disproportionate numbers of them who are imprisoned ceases to be remarkable. As these numbers grow more and more, prisons become a source for capital investment, a true growth industry, so that "the ideological construction of crime

is thus completed by the material construction of jails and prisons"
(p. 69).

Davis' writings on women's issues also consistently place these
within a broader critique of capitalism. In a collection of essays on
Women, Culture and Politics (1990), she traces "the parallels between
sexual violence against individual women and neocolonial violence
against people and nations" (pp. 36–37). In the same volume she
argues that the fact that Black women's health was so harmed in
the 1980s by reductions in Medicaid coverage, lack of prenatal
care, and the closure of abortion clinics due to loss of funding is
part and parcel of an ideology that declares that those in power
always know best. She identifies a number of "political forces
responsible for the violation of Black women's health rights" such
as the "increasing militarization of our economy' and the "general
assault on democracy" (p. 62). In her words, "It is no coincidence
that a government that would sabotage the rights of every citizen
of this country by permitting the development of a secret junta
controlled by the Central Intelligence Agency and the National
Security Council also seriously infringed upon the health rights of
Black women and all poor people" (p. 63). Davis' essay "Peace is a
Sisters' Issue Too" also argues that Black women's liberation cannot just be understood as a battle against racist attitudes. Instead, it
must be considered as part of a larger project of economic and
social transformation. Given that "nuclear bombs do not know how
to engage in racial discrimination" (p. 68), Davis argues that peace
is not "a white folks issue" nor "an abstract state of affairs" but
rather "inextricably connected with our ability to achieve racial,
sexual and economic justice" (p. 69).

For adult educators some of the most provocative elements of
Davis' writings are her analyses of the liberatory power of education and in particular the need to build multiracial coalitions and
alliances in the struggle to unmask and confront dominant ideology. She traces her own formation as an educator back to the behavior of her parents. By her own account her disposition toward a
critical, philosophical stance was "a consequence of my parents'
encouragement to think critically about our social environment"
(1998b, p. 17). Her parents taught her "not to assume that the appearances in our lives constituted ultimate realities" and "to look
beyond appearances and to think about ways in which we would,

with our own agency, intervene and transform the world" (p. 17). Central to this effort to penetrate the obfuscations of dominant ideology was a critically inclined education. Davis declares that "I learned very early to value education and its liberatory potential. . . . Education and liberation were always bound together" (1998a, p. 316).

Since Davis believed that "liberation was not possible without education" (1998a, p. 316), it was only natural that she should become a powerful scholar-activist. One of her earliest involvements was in the Liberation School organized by the Los Angeles branch of the Student Non-Violent Coordinating Committee. In her 1974 autobiography she describes this as "a place where political understanding was forged and sharpened, where consciousness became explicit and was urged in a revolutionary direction" (1974, p. 183). The belief that education is inherently political has informed all her later work. She argues that education should give people the tools to critique capitalism, penetrate ideology, and help them realize that their individual situations can only be improved if they build alliances across race and gender identities. Transformative education can never be an individual process in David's view, and neither can it be successful if it is restricted to a particular group. Over and over again she emphasizes the need to ally with others in the struggle for social transformation.

At the heart of Davis' credo of transformative struggle is the phrase "lift as we climb," the motto of the National Association of Colored Women's Clubs (founded in 1896). To "lift as we climb" is to ensure that "we must climb in such a way as to guarantee that all of our sisters, regardless of social class, and indeed all of our brothers, climb with us" (Davis, 1990, p. 5). This effort to build a social movement across lines of race and gender, rather than one based on a single racial or gender identity, must, for Davis "be the essential dynamic of our quest for power—a principle that must not only determine our struggles as Afro-American women, but also govern all authentic struggles of dispossessed people" (p. 5). One of the most important dimensions of this struggle is the building of "a revolutionary, multi-racial women's movement that seriously addresses the main issues affecting poor and working class women" (p. 7). Such a movement would involve Latina, Asian, and also White women. Davis clearly sets out her belief that membership of a movement for struggle on behalf of one group is open to people of all groups, not just those immediately affected by an act of dispossession. Much as do West and hooks, Davis rejects the Africentric emphasis solely on African cultural values as those that should inform the struggle of Black people. She writes, "We do not draw the color line. The only line we draw is one based on our political principles" (p. 7).

An insistence on building coalitions across race and gender springs partly from Davis' suspicion of an uncritical espousal of the politics of race identity. In a provocative passage, she warns of the dangers of "ethnic solipsism," of focusing solely on one's racial and ethnic formation and the struggle to satisfy needs of members of one's cultural group: "Ethnic solipsism is something we have always attributed to whiteness, Eurocentrism. Do we want to accept the notion that discourses about race are essentially about black/white relations? As if to suggest that if you are not either black or white, then you are dispensable?" (Davis, 1998a, p. 227). For Davis political commitments and beliefs are what unite people in collective struggle, not racial identity. She asks "how would you define 'one's own group'? For African-Americans, would that include every person who meets the requirements of physical appearance or every person who identifies as African-American, regardless of their phenotype? Would it include Republican African-Americans who are opposed to affirmative action?" (p. 229). She points out that "an African-American woman might find it easier to work together with a Chicana than with another black woman whose politics of race, class, gender, and sexuality would place her in an entirely different community" (p. 229). Hence, "what counts as black is not so important as our political commitment to engage in anti-racist, anti-sexist, and anti-homophobic work" (p. 229).

As a Marxist, Davis views identity as politically constructed, part of the ideological superstructure of capitalism. What is perhaps more surprising is her criticism of those seeking a unique and distinctive theory of philosophy of African American woman-ness. As a prominent African American woman intellectual Davis is sometimes categorized as a Black feminist, yet this is a label she strenuously resists. In fact her own understanding of feminism is fluid: "My own conception of myself as a feminist constantly evolves as I learn more about the issues that women's movements need to address" (Davis, 1998a, p. 304). Feminism is a discourse with a range of positions, theories, categories, and commitments and in her view the most effective versions of feminism acknowledge the various ways gender, class, race, and sexual orientation inform each other. In her interview with George Yancy, she argues that "there is no such thing as Black feminist theory" (Davis, 1998b, p. 25) if this is seen as a unitary body of work. There are Black feminist theories representing a range of positions, but no one single shared perspective. Davis urges people "not to assume that racialized identities have always been there" and "not to adhere to rigid categories, to the idea that there is something called African-American woman-ness, some essence we can discover" (1998a, p. 300).

Equally, Davis is skeptical concerning claims of a shared women's unity. In common with hooks, she realizes that one's gender position must always be understood in the light of one's race or class positions. Observing that in her view, "there has been a rather naïve approach to women's unity, just as there has been a rather naïve approach to Black unity" (Davis 1998b, p. 25), she concludes that unity cannot be grounded solely in racial membership or gender. Skeptical of a focus on unity for unity's sake, she argues that "unity needs to be produced politically, around issues and political projects" (p. 25).

There may be a generalized unity around the need to overthrow capitalism but this can only be realized in struggles around particular issues—health, rape, abortion rights, prison reform, and so on. In this her position is close to Foucault's analysis of the need for intellectuals to locate themselves in specific sites around specific struggles, and also to the activist emphasis of Gramsci's notion of the organic intellectual. However, activist intellectuals must be wary of reproducing the racial politics of the outside world in their own social movements. Thus, in the struggle for social justice "it will be imperative for whites to accept the leadership of Black people," in fact "for black people to provide the leadership for the total struggle" (Davis, 1974, p. 182).

What lessons can be drawn for the practice of adult education from Davis' analysis of collective struggle? It seems to me that first and foremost is the support she provides for the recognition that all adult educational practice is theoretically informed. Adult education discourse often distinguishes between theory and practice. There is an implication that some people (usually professors in graduate schools of adult education who publish a great deal in journals or write books on critical theory) are theoreticians while others (usually those who do not hold a graduate degree in adult education and publish little or nothing) are practitioners. Within this distinction is embedded an implicit hierarchy. Professor-theoreticians are responsible for the high-level cognitive process of theorizing, in which concepts (andragogy, critical reflection, trans-formative learning) are produced, insights (such as the social nature of transformative learning, the need for critically reflective mirrors, the importance of the adult educator's role modeling) are generated, and hypotheses (such as the prediction that placing learners into circles helps democratize discussion or that using learning journals builds learners' confidence to speak and write in their own voice) are produced. Practitioners such as basic educa-tion teachers, organizational trainers and community activists are then responsible for implementing in their daily work the theoret-ical insights produced by academics within their universities. Im-plicitly such practitioners are held to work at much lower levels of generalization and abstraction.

If we accept Davis' argument that philosophizing and theorizing are quotidian activities—something we cannot help doing on a daily basis—then this distinction breaks down. Practice becomes inherently theoretical, something that either perpetuates or challenges domi-nant ideological beliefs and practices. From this viewpoint one is equally a theoretician whether one teaches philosophy in a university-sponsored, noncredit continuing education course or auto-repair at a community education center. The way we treat adult learners, how we address them, how we explain our teaching processes to them, the extent to which we encourage peer learning amongst them—these are all practice acts with strong theoretical underpinnings. We do these things based on predictive understandings of how we believe people will respond to our actions and on convictions about what it means to act morally. Such understandings and convictions are derived from the empirical data of our experiences rather than from published texts, but they are theoretical nonetheless.

A second element of Davis' work has particular resonance for those within adult education who see their practice as a force for democratic political change. If you believe, like Davis, that liberation is not pos-sible without education, then adult education becomes, in her words, "a consciousness-raising vehicle . . . imparting political education to the community" (1974, p. 183). Many adult educators would draw back from equating adult education wholly with political consciousness-raising, but for those who do Davis proposes several curricular tasks that bear examination. First and foremost the core curricular task of adult education interpreted through Davis' eyes focuses on understanding and critiquing capitalism. In this she is squarely in the mainstream of critical theory. For her the need to critique capitalism is even stronger in the twentieth century as the influence of transnational and global corporations becomes ever broader, and as the fall of Socialist regimes in Eastern Europe leads people to conclude that history proves capitalism to be the natural way of ordering the economic affairs of life. Much in the way that Fromm advocates teaching a structuralized worldview Davis urges that adults caught at the intersections of race, class, and gender oppression be taught how to place their local problems within a broad socio-political framework. Racism, crime, incarceration, violence, and poor health are all experienced disproportionately by working class people of color. However, ideological mystification ensures that these economically and culturally created experiences are seen as natural and unavoidable accompaniments of being born without a White skin on the wrong side of the tracks. Ideology causes people to believe that the side of the tracks on which they find themselves is a matter of pure chance over which there is no control, and that their innate abilities fit them for the specific social location in which they find themselves.

How can people be taught to recognize and challenge how dominant ideology works to persuade them to accept as unremarkable an inherently unequal state of affairs? I believe Davis' work contains two implicit pedagogic impulses. The first concerns the collectivist nature of teaching. Again and again Davis emphasizes the collective nature of transformative processes, whether these are concerned with learners transforming their consciousness, educators transforming their classrooms, or citizens transforming their communities. She believes that people need each other to make any significant change in the world, that those who see things more clearly have a duty to help others come to consciousness (we must lift as we climb) and that the most effective initiatives are those characterized by collective leadership. She is very consistent on the need for multiracial alliances and for leadership in those alliances to be non-White. This position suggests that the methodologies of team teaching and cohort learning are best suited to the project of helping adults penetrate dominant ideology. In this (though she does not directly address any of the literature in adult education) she is very much in line with a tradition of thought and practice that values collective learning. From Lindeman ([1926] 1961), through Horton and Freire (1990) and up to contemporary examinations of collaborative inquiry (Yorks and Kasl, 2002), adult cohort learning (Saltiel and Russo, 2001), transformative learning (Mezirow, 2000), and critical reflection (Brookfield, 1995) adult educators have consistently emphasized the fact that much crucial adult political education happens in groups and through engagement in collective struggle.

If transformative learning by adult students is a collective process, then we can legitimately infer that adult teachers must model their own engagement in this process. If we accept that adult learners are moved closer to engaging in learning that is potentially transformative by witnessing adult educators model their own public commitment to that process, then team teaching (as against solo teaching) is clearly called for. Team teaching properly conceived and implemented (that is, teaching in which teachers plan processes together, are present for all instruction whether or not they are leading the activity, and debrief their work collectively) models a strong commitment to collective learning for adult students. Just as Davis believes that transformative struggle calls for multiracial coalitions in which people of color assume leadership roles, so we can infer that teaching teams that have potentially the profoundest effect on adult learners are those that are multiracial. In such teams, as in multiracial coalitions, Davis' analysis suggests that senior leadership roles should be taken by non-White faculty. Of course, team teaching itself is not without its own inherent contradictions, particularly when imbalances of power and status (real or perceived) exist amongst team members. If we accept Marcuse's admonitions about the ever-present danger of repressive tolerance, or Foucault's analysis of how superficially democratic or apparently collaborative practices can be experienced by learners as reconfigurations of oppression, then it is clear that the practice of team-teaching risks confirming the very inequities and injustices it purports to challenge. In my experience a good general rule is that in multiracial adult teaching teams, White faculty should speak last and least. On those occasions when White faculty do assume the lead teacher role, the non-White faculty should make it clear to learners that this is a team decision and that the White faculty member has been asked to assume temporary authority at the specific request of the faculty of color in the team.

One particular pedagogic emphasis implicit in Davis' work concerns the potential of art, particularly popular cultural art forms such as Blues songs (Davis, 1999), to trigger learning that can lead to revolutionary change. For her Blues performances are "an alternative site for recovering historical forms of working class women's consciousness" (Davis, 1998a, p. 314) and, as evident in the work of 'Ma' Rainey, Bessie Smith, and Billie Holiday, they inform the development of a distinctive Black feminism (Davis, 1999). In this regard Davis echoes Gramsci's emphasis on the importance of popular culture to revolutionary movements and, perhaps more intentionally, follows in the footsteps of her mentor Marcuse. As Chapter Seven records, Marcuse believed strongly in the productively estranging nature of artistic experiences, attributing to these the power to encourage rebellious subjectivity in adults. Similarly, Davis believes that artistic experience is "a special form of social consciousness that can potentially awaken an urge in those affected by it to creatively transform their oppressive environments" (Davis, 1990, p. 199).

Her analysis contains some discernible differences from that of Marcuse, however, in that she takes more seriously the role of explicitly political art as a force for social change. Marcuse's emphasis on privacy, distance and isolation, on individual engagements with art, is downplayed. For Davis, the most transformative art is created, and experienced, collectively. Also, Davis does not trace the revolutionary significance of art to the learner's being temporarily subjected to the rigors of a different aesthetic form, whether this be Shakespearean sonnets or cubism. Marcuse allows a major role for the transformative potential of "high" cultural forms. Davis is much more concerned with populist expressions of deliberately political impulses. While Marcuse believes there is more revolutionary potential in the poetry of Baudelaire or Rimbaud than in the explicitly political plays of Brecht, I read Davis as much more inclined toward the political theater of Brecht or Boal, or toward the way Blues lyrics challenge racism, rape and patriarchy.

An important function of art for Davis is to be a "sensitizer and a catalyst, propelling people toward involvement in organized movements seeking to effect radical social change" (Davis, 1990, p. 200). Davis departs from Marcuse in allowing a role for explicitly political art. Indeed, she sees a symbiotic relationship between radical social movements and particular artistic impulses. To her "progressive and revolutionary art is inconceivable outside of the context of political movements for social change" (p. 216). Hence, in her analysis of the fight against slavery she sees spirituals as both "cause and evidence of an autonomous political consciousness" (1990, p. 201) and crucial to an emergent momentum of resistance. For Davis spirituals "always served, epistemologically and psychologically, to shape the consciousness of the masses of Black people, guaranteeing that the fires of freedom would burn within them" (p. 202). Work songs with their familiar call and response pattern, gospel, and the Blues are taken by her to comprise "an aesthetic community of resistance, which in turn encouraged and nurtured a political community of active struggle for freedom" (p. 202). A song like Bessie Smith's "Poor Man's Blues" had specific political intent in that it "evoked the exploitation and manipulation of working people by the wealthy and portrayed the rich as parasites accumulating their wealth and fighting their wars with the labor of the poor" (p. 203).

In the development of a curriculum for revolutionary learning, then, we can see a major role for aesthetic creation, according to Davis. This role is not to produce beauty, or induce an estrangement with reality, but to enable the creation of political momentum. An adult education program that has as its purpose the development of political consciousness, particularly consciousness regarding the exploitation of people of color, should involve more than the study of critical theory, or the analysis of activist tactics. It should entail its participants writing songs, producing plays, filming dramatized vignettes of oppression, painting murals, rapping—using every aesthetic avenue to create the "strong bonds between art and the struggle for Black liberation" (p. 200) that Davis believes characterizes the history of African American culture. Art created explicitly in the service of political struggle, and that addresses that struggle's purpose directly by galvanizing action, plays a crucial role in social movements in her view.

As this chapter shows, Davis' explicit focus on transformative struggle connects her directly to adult education's recent concern with transformative learning and education. Davis places herself squarely in the tradition of transformative learning as ideology critique. For her the purpose of transformation is to uncover and challenge dominant ideology. She sees the necessity to critique the influence of capitalism in all spheres of life (intimate relationships, personal health, crime, housework, and so on) rather than limiting such a critique to the world of politics formally defined. She also shares the inclusive orientation of Cornel West and bell hooks, in which people of different colors and genders unite around specific transformative initiatives. In her view the key to successful transformation is membership in a multiracial alliance, an emphasis not especially prominent in adult educational treatments of this topic. Davis also exemplifies the sort of willingness to engage in self-criticism that is often claimed as being as crucial to critical thinking (Brookfield, 1987a). Much in the spirit of her mentor, Herbert Marcuse's, tenet that "critical theory is, last but not least, critical of itself and of the social forces that make up its own basis" (1989, p. 72), she is open to constant critical reappraisal of her own work. She admits that "many of us can be very critical when we are doing our research—but not necessarily in relation to the ideologies that inform our lives and ideas" (1998a, p. 227) and follows her own admonition to "try to take critical thinking seriously" (p. 227). For example, she problematizes notions of women's unity and describes her own self-identity as a feminist as constantly evolving. She criticizes Africentrically inclined notions of woman-ness and ethnic solipsism, stressing instead the importance of political commitment over ethnic identity, and the need for multiethnic alliances. And, finally, she rejects the conventional wisdom that the fall of Eastern European regimes means there is no longer any need for a critique of capitalism. Instead, she argues consistently and resolutely that feminist advocacy and women's liberation in an era of global capitalism must always be tied to a critique of capitalism. Those involved in the growth industry that is research and scholarship on transformative processes in adult learning and education ignore her work at their peril.

Chapter Twelve

Teaching Critically

One of the most frequent assertions of the critical tradition is that separating our practice from our theorizing, as if these existed in two wholly separate domains, is untenable. The tradition sees these two processes as conjoined; on the one hand, all practice is theoretically informed, on the other hand, theory always contains practical implications. So although this book is "officially" about critical theory, it is also, implicitly, about critical practice. In this final chapter, then, it seems fitting to review and integrate the pedagogical suggestions made by the theorists reviewed in the previous eleven chapters. I do this in three ways. First, I explore what it means to teach critically, arguing that doing this is a matter of focus as much as method. Teaching critically is not just a question of how we teach. It is also about what we teach. Second, I examine some of the methodological approaches that emerge in critical theory's analyses. These in no way comprise a unified stance. The previous chapters will have made it clear that there is a considerable eclecticism in the methodological injunctions of critical theory. Indeed, sometimes these injunctions seem directly in contradiction. As an example, consider how Marcuse's emphasis on the need for privacy, isolation, and cultural detachment stands against Fromm's or Habermas' insistence on dialogic teaching, collaborative learning, or the collective creation of knowledge. Finally, I reflect on the pedagogic lessons I have learned in my own experience teaching critical theory within graduate education.

The Practice of Teaching Critically

The practice of teaching critically is inherent in critical theory's formulations. From Marx's eleventh thesis on Feuerbach onwards, it is clear that the theory is full of activist intent. Indeed, as Horkheimer (1995) argued in his essay defining critical theory (first published in 1936), the theory can only be considered successful if it produces revolutionary change. Theorizing exists so that people can understand the dynamics of political, economic, racial, and cultural oppression. With that understanding they can then begin to challenge these dynamics and learn to create new social forms, particularly new conditions of labor, that allow them to express their creativity. So to teach informed by critical theory is, by implication, to teach with a specific social and political intent. Critical theorists intend that their analyses and concepts will help people create social and economic forms distinguished by a greater degree of democratic socialism.

Although teaching critically has a transformative impetus, there are noticeable differences in the ways different theorists pursue this. However, one theme—the inevitably directive nature of education—remains constant across all the theorists reviewed in these pages. Critical teaching begins with developing students' powers of critical thinking so that they can critique the interlocking systems of oppression embedded in contemporary society. Informed by a critical theory perspective, students learn to see that capitalism, bureaucratic rationality, disciplinary power, automaton conformity, one-dimensional thought, and repressive tolerance all combine to exert a powerful ideological sway aimed to ensure the current system stays intact. Critical thinking in this vein is the educational implementation of ideology critique, the deliberate attempt to penetrate the ideological obfuscation that ensures that massive social inequality is accepted by the majority as the natural state of affairs. Adults who learn to conduct this kind of critique are exercising true reason, that is, reason applied to asking universal questions about how we should live. Two of these questions might be: What kind of societal organization will help people treat each other fairly and compassionately? How can we redesign work so that it encourages the expression of human creativity?

This form of critical thinking is, however, only the beginning of critical theory's educational project. The point of getting people to think critically is to enable them to create true democracy—what Fromm, Marcuse, West, and others regard as the cornerstone of socialism—at both the micro- and macrolevel. If adults think critically in this view, they will be demanding worker cooperatives, the abolition of private education, the imposition of income caps, universal access to health care based on need not wealth, and public ownership of corporations and utilities. Critical thinking framed by critical theory is not just a cognitive process. It is inevitably bound up with realizing and emphasizing common interests, rejecting the privatized, competitive ethic of capitalism, and preventing the emergence of inherited privilege.

Teaching in a manner informed by critical theory is, therefore, teaching that is inherently political. It is political because it is intended to help people learn how to replace the exchange economy of capitalism with truly democratic socialism. It is political because it makes no pretense of neutrality, though it embraces self-criticism. It is political because it is highly directive, practicing, in Baptiste's (2000) terms, a pedagogy of ethical coercion. This politicized emphasis is scattered throughout the history of critical theory. It is there in Marx's belief that the point of philosophy is to change the world. It is there in Gramsci's view of the adult educator as a revolutionary party organizer working to direct and persuade the masses to replace ruling class hegemony with proletarian hegemony. It is there in Marcuse's urging the practice of liberating tolerance involving exposure only to dissenting viewpoints and in his acknowledgment that clear differences exist between teachers and learners.

Teaching politically is evident too in West's conception of the adult educator as a critical organic catalyst galvanizing activists in grassroots oppositional movements. hooks' recognition of the need for teachers to confront students with the reality and injuries of dominant ideology embodies this directive spirit; so too does Davis' insistence that teaching about women's issues such as rape, abortion, access to health care, domestic violence, and sexual harassment cannot be separated from a broader analysis of the destructive effects of capitalism. Foucault's analysis of how specific intellectuals fight repressive power at specific sites, Fromm's belief that learners must be taught to realize how individual problems are really produced by structural forces, and Habermas' urging that educators illuminate how the lifeworld has been invaded by capitalism and bureaucratic rationality—all these indicate the inescapably political nature of critical teaching.

Methodological Approaches

Although critical theorists share a common recognition of the politically directive nature of education, they do not advance any kind of methodological orthodoxy to describe how such education should take place. However, four contrasting methodological clusters or emphases are discernible in the work of the writers I have surveyed. One of these is the importance of teaching a structuralized worldview, something well conveyed in the title of C. Wright Mills' book *The Sociological Imagination* (1959). In the preface to *One Dimensional Man* (1964), Marcuse wrote of "the vital importance of the work of C. Wright Mills" (p. xvii) that had successfully interpreted individual experience in terms of broader social and economic forces. A structuralized worldview always analyzes private problems and personal dilemmas as structurally produced. At root, this idea is grounded in Marx's theory of consciousness with its argument that what seem like instinctive ways of understanding the world—our structures of feeling to use Williams' (1977) phrase— actually reflect the material base of society. This idea recurs throughout critical theory in concepts such as the colonization of the lifeworld, one-dimensional thought, and disciplinary power.

Two theorists who strongly advocate teaching a structuralized worldview are Erich Fromm and Angela Davis, though to a degree all in critical theory advocate this. Fromm's perspective as a therapist and social psychologist is that adults' intellectual development means they are much better equipped than children to realize that forces external to their own whims and inclinations shape their lives. He feels that adults' accumulated experience of life provides the curricular material that can be analyzed for evidence of the impact of wider social forces. Davis consistently urges that any teaching about women's issues must always illustrate how individual lives are shaped, and injured, by the workings of capitalism. For her this is crucial to the development of political consciousness and to women's psychological well-being. They learn that what they thought were problems

visited on them by an arbitrary fate, or the result of personal inadequacy, are in fact the predictable outcome of the workings of capitalism and patriarchy. This is a life-saving realization.

A second pedagogical emphasis in critical theory explores the
need for abstract, conceptual reasoning—reasoning that can be
applied to considering broad questions such as how to organize
society fairly or what it means to treat each other ethically. Critical
theorists, particularly Marcuse and Habermas, argue that critical
thought is impossible if adults have learned only to focus on particulars, on the immediate features of their lives. For example, people need some basis for comparing the claims of various groups
that they should be treated differently because of their history,
race, culture, religion, and so on. As long as we live in association
with others, there has to be restrictions placed on the liberty of
those who behave in ways likely to injure others. How we decide
what these limits should be is based on some broad concepts of
fairness or social well-being. Your right to smoke a cancer-inducing
cigarette cannot be exercised regardless in a small room containing asthma, lung cancer, or emphysema sufferers. So if living socially requires the development of rules of conduct that have a
level of generality beyond that of individual whims, then we need
to be comfortable thinking in broad abstract terms. Deciding
which rules should be followed, and how these might be established in ways that ensure their general acceptance, are matters
that require a level of thought beyond that of saying, "This is what
I want because it works for me in my life." Freedom, fairness,
equity, liberation, the ethical use of power—all these "big" ideas
are central to the critical tradition and all contain a level of universality entailing the exercise of abstract, conceptual thought.

A third element stressed in some variants of critical theory is
the need for adults to become "uncoupled from the stream of cultural givens" to use Habermas' (1990, p. 162) phrase. This momen-
tary separation from the demands and patterns of everyday life
allows them to view society in a newly critical way. Both Gramsci
and Marcuse argue that a temporary detachment from social life
is a necessary spur to critical thought, with Marcuse conducting a
sustained analysis of how separation, privacy, and isolation help
people to escape one-dimensional thought. I have argued that this

strand of critical theory connects directly to adult educators' concern with self-directed learning and the practices that foster this. This element in critical theory receives less contemporary attention probably because privacy is now, as Marcuse admits, a resource available chiefly to the rich. Also, Marcuse's emphasis on how a powerfully estranging, private engagement with a work of art leads to the development of rebellious subjectivity smacks to some of elitism. It also raises the specter of unrestrained individualism, an element of dominant ideology that prompts deep skepticism amongst many of a critical cast. Collins (1991), for example, has authored a well-framed critique of the individualist and technicist nature of much of what passes for the facilitation of self-directed learning.

In my own practice I believe there is still a place for separation, privacy, and isolation, despite its compromised nature. One of the approaches I use in my own teaching—the emphasis on students doing private, separated, and isolated reading of original critical theory material before engaging in small group discussion of this— is a small variant of this idea. I believe that self-directed learning still offers a valuable language and practice of critique and that it can be interpreted to fit squarely into the radical tradition of adult education (Brookfield, 2000). I have also argued that a source of necessary detachment can exist in such an unlikely setting as accelerated learning programs, often regarded as the apogee of fast buck, cash cow, capitalist adult education (Brookfield, 2003). An argument can also be made for a greater degree of individual disengagement from cohort programs that are often lionized as the best of alternative adult educational practices. Cohorts can readily exhibit automaton conformity, generate a tyranny of the majority, and uncritically reproduce dominant ideology.

Cohort groups are themselves one setting for a fourth pedagogic emphasis in critical theory, that of dialogic discussion. Fromm and Habermas are the two theorists discussed who emphasize this approach most strongly with both of them viewing a widespread facility with dialogic methods as the guarantee of democracy. Fromm's emphasis on the dance of dialogue in which speakers lose their ego in a selfless attempt to understand the positions advanced by others is very much a forerunner to Habermas' ideal speech situation. Both theorists believe that decisions arrived at through fully participatory, inclusive conversation are the cornerstone of democracy, and both believe education can play a role in teaching adults the dispositions necessary to conduct such conversations.

As a teacher I share this dialogic emphasis, though my use of it has changed greatly over the years. When I began teaching I viewed discussion leadership as a wholly artistic process, one distinguished by creativity and constant improvisation. I still believe these factors are important in discussion, but they are very far from being the whole story. Too often what is justified as a laissez-faire approach meant to demonstrate the teacher's refusal to dominate conversation actually serves to bolster wider social inequities that have been imported into the group. The people who talk the loudest and longest inside the classroom are often those whose social locations mean their voices get the most attention in the world outside. A misplaced belief that teacher interventions automatically represent an unwarranted domination also led me to think that the best discussion leaders were those who were invisible. If a discussion leader said or did nothing during the conversation to indicate his or her role as the teacher, then I used to argue that this person was an emblematic adult educator. Now I am not so sure. While remaining silent is a legitimate stance in some situations, there are others in which the teacher is required to be strongly interventionist. This does not necessarily mean talking a lot. One can be silent, for example, but have played a strong role in determining the inclusive ground rules governing conversation.

I have argued in an earlier book coauthored with Stephen Preskill (Brookfield and Preskill, 1999) that most discussions are not distinguished by automatic goodwill on the part of all participants. After all, most people do not have the chance to practice the kinds of democratic dispositions good discussions require. Ideal speech situations are virtually extinct for many of us. We must not assume that adult education classrooms are safe havens or power-free zones. Neither learners nor teachers leave their racial, class, or gender identities at the classroom door, nor do they forget their previous participation in discussions with all the humiliations and manipulations these often entailed. For an adult education group to look anything remotely like the egoless dance celebrated by Fromm, or the ideal speech situation described by Habermas, its participants will need to evolve and adhere to rules of discourse that exemplify these features. Since the exercise of these rules cannot be left to chance, the group will have to find some way to monitor observance of these.

Because groups are often unwilling to acknowledge and confront the hierarchies and power dynamics they import into the classroom, teachers can help illuminate these. Discussion leaders can consistently draw attention to the need for inclusive models of conversation such as the circle of voices, circular response, snowballing, or newsprint dialog (Brookfield and Preskill, 1999). They can intervene in conversations to stop the most privileged and vociferous from dominating by declaring a ground rule that the next couple of minutes of conversation are reserved for those who up to now have not had a chance to contribute. They can also democratize the conversation by advocating the three-person rule. This rule holds that once someone has made a comment they are not allowed to contribute again until at least three other people have spoken. The only exception to this is if someone else in the group directly asks a speaker to say more about their original comment. Teachers can also distribute to the group the results of anonymous student classroom evaluations if these reveal that some people feel shut down and unheard. And they can acknowledge constantly the fact of their own power and how this is being exercised to create conversational structures that equalize participation and prevent the emergence of an unofficial pecking order of contributions.

The methodological eclecticism evident in critical theory suggests that a range of approaches be adopted with adult student groups. Given the range of cultural backgrounds, learning preferences, intellectual abilities, and mix of racial, class, and gender identities evident in many adult education classrooms, a variety of approaches and methodologies seems both necessary and inevitable. Situating pedagogy in the realties of classroom dynamics, cultural traditions, and learning rhythms, while simultaneously attempting to introduce people to a critical theory perspective, could be described as a kind of critical pragmatism. As an approach to practice, critical pragmatism emphasizes the continuing relevance and applicability of critical theory's understandings at the same time as it takes a self-critical perspective on that theory. In Cornel West's words, "the degree to which one is willing to be self-critical and self-questioning" is taken as "a sign of commitment" (West, 1999b, p. 295) to critical practice.

Critical pragmatism also supports an experimental orientation to adult education practice and rejects any one approach as representing the core of critical pedagogy. It views all four emphases discussed in this section as valid depending on the context involved. If anything can be argued as endemic or core to adult education, I believe it is the creation of a moral and political tone in which adults are treated as adults. And if anything can be argued as core to critical teaching, it is a focus on the learning tasks—challenging ideology, contesting hegemony, unmasking power, and so on—outlined in Chapter Two. How these tasks are pursued depends on the unique and complex configurations of each adult classroom and on the teacher's own positionality, talents, and experience.

Reflections on Teaching Critical Theory

In this section I want to describe some of my own personal experiences teaching critical theory to adults. Because I'm a university teacher, my experience is mostly confined to graduate programs of education and that is the context on which I will focus. Hopefully, the problematic dynamics of teaching and learning that I describe, and my response to them, will illuminate some of the work you do in your own setting.

My work in four specific locations informs this chapter. The first is my full-time home institution, the University of St. Thomas in Minneapolis-St. Paul, Minnesota. Since 1992 I have taught courses at St. Thomas in which critical theory comprises some of the core material. For example, in teaching for the educational leadership program, my course on Leadership as Critical Reflection defines critical reflection as the deliberate attempt to unearth and research assumptions regarding the legitimate exercise of power in education. Additionally, critical reflection is defined as the uncovering of hegemonic assumptions; that is, assumptions about the practice of educational leadership that are embraced as common sense and morally desirable but that actually work against practitioners' best interests and serve to keep an unfair system intact. Consequently, Leadership as Critical Reflection requires students at the outset of the course to engage with Foucault and Gramsci. Also at St. Thomas I have taught a number of different courses in the doctorate in Critical Pedagogy (as far as I know the only such doctorate in existence).

The focus of this program is squarely on the critical tradition and the ideas reviewed in this book are core to the theoretical foundation for the program.

A second setting for teaching critical theory is National Louis University's (Chicago) doctoral program in adult education. Since 1992 I have served as a part-time consultant to the doctoral program and a member of the visiting teaching faculty. The NLU doctoral program explicitly situates the study of adult education within its social and cultural context. Critical theory, along with Africentrism, feminism, and postmodernism are some of the chief theoretical paradigms explored. Teachers College at Columbia University (New York) is a third context in which I have worked with the ideas of critical theory. From 1982 to 1992 I worked as a full-time professor in the adult education doctoral program, and since 1992 I have conducted occasional workshops at the Center for Educational Outreach and Innovation, one of which is titled Critical Theory and Adult Learning. Finally, in 2002, as visiting professor at Harvard University, I taught courses in the Graduate School of Education, one of which was titled Critical Theory and the Practice of Adult Education. Most of the chapters in this book were included in that course's materials and were read and critiqued by the students who attended.

Resistance

On the face of it, the contexts described in the preceding paragraphs seem, at the very least, benign. The students have enrolled to study educational leadership, critical pedagogy, or adult education and have sometimes shown up for courses where critical theory is prominent in the course title. So it may seem surprising to see this section headed "Resistance." But my experience has taught me that the one fact on which I can depend in this work is that students will resist, often quite strongly, learning about this tradition. Five elements in critical theory seem to present particular problems for them in terms of provoking resistance: the emphasis on Marx, the critique of capitalism the theory entails, the questioning of democracy (particularly the identification of the tyranny of the majority), the difficult language used by critical theorists, and the radical pessimism induced by constantly reading analyses that emphasize the power of dominant ideology and the way it effectively forestalls any real challenge to the system. Let me deal with these in turn turning first to the issue of "Marxophobia."

One of the first things I do when teaching critical theory is position it as a response to Marx (much in the way I positioned critical theory in the first chapter of this book). I do this as a matter of scholarly honesty. Since I believe Marx's work to be the foundation and fulcrum of critical theory—its theoretical starting point—it would be disingenuous not to make this clear. Hearing this is difficult for some students who ask, "Does this mean I have to be a Marxist to study critical theory?" The rampant Marxophobia commented on by McLaren and West in Chapter One means that any body of work connecting to Marx's ideas, no matter how critically these ideas are examined, is immediately deemed suspect. Students with a strong commitment to values of individuality, liberation, and creativity—the same values emphasized (as Fromm points out) in Marx's manuscript on alienated labor—see reading Marx almost as an unpatriotic act. It is as if by opening the pages of *The German Ideology* (Marx and Engels, 1970) or *Marx's Concept of Man* (Fromm, 1961), one is rejecting democracy, free speech, even America itself.

It is important to say that it is not only third- or fourth-generation American students who have this difficulty. Students from former communist regimes who have fought in wars, suffered the loss of family members, seen the disappearance of livelihoods, and been forced into exile by those regimes also have an understandable visceral reaction to Marx's association with critical theory. It doesn't seem to matter how many times I point out that critical theorists unequivocally condemn the automaton conformity, surveillance, and one-dimensional thought they see in totalitarian communism, or how many times these theorists assert the primacy of true democracy. Once Marx is mentioned—unless it is to denounce anything associated with him—you've immediately created a problem in several students' minds.

So how do we respond to this situation? One thing I try to do early on in any course is emphasize the self-critical nature of critical theory itself and how this critical perspective is applied to Marx's work as well as to capitalist ideology. I quote Gramsci's warning against the idolatry of Marx, Marcuse's insistence on the need to take a critical approach to critical theory, West's essay on the indispensability yet insufficiency of Marxist theory, and the blindnesses of race and gender in Marx identified by hooks, Davis, Karenga, and others. A useful resource here is Noam Chomsky's essays on "The Leninist/Capitalist Intelligentsia" (Chomsky, 2002) and "Marxist 'Theory' and Intellectual Fakery" (Chomsky, 2002). Chomsky, one of the most prominent leftist scholar-activists in the United States, has a long record of public ideology critique, so his credibility is strong. He is scathing about the way Marxism-Leninism reveals, in his view, strong elements of authoritarianism and condescension. These are seen most prominently "in the very idea that a 'vanguard party' can, or has any right to lead the stupid masses towards some future they're too dumb to understand for themselves" (Chomsky, 2000, p. 226). Chomsky views Marx as a theorist of capitalism who has an interesting abstract model of how capitalism functions, but one that can be improved on, refined, and broadened. He says he hasn't "the foggiest idea" (p. 228) what "dialectics" means and admits that "when I look at a page of Marxist philosophy or literary theory, I have the feeling that I could stare at it for the rest of my life and I'd never understand it" (p. 228). For many students this is enormously reassuring! I also construct an early assignment around a critical appraisal of Marx. This assignment asks students to identify omissions, ethical blind spots, and inconsistencies in Marx's work as well as to consider points of connection or resonance between their experiences or practices and his ideas.

It is important to stress, however, that Marx should not be introduced so circumspectly as to rob his ideas of any force or power. There is a thin line between encouraging a healthy skepticism of Marx, or of any theorist, and predisposing people to dismiss him. The point is not to set him up for easy demolition but to demonstrate that a serious reading of Marx can happen without students feeling they somehow have to "convert" to Marxism. So at the same time as affirming students' right to disagree with and condemn Marx, I also affirm my right as a teacher to insist they engage him before they ritualistically dismiss him. Furthermore, if students' engagement does lead to their dismissing his work, it is not enough for them to dismiss him out of hand. I invite, even require, students to be critical of Marx, but I ask that these criticisms be specific. Students are expected to provide page citations and direct quotes that indicate those aspects of his work they most take exception to. It is not acceptable only to make general criticisms such as Marx is anti-democratic, misunderstands the natural competitiveness of human beings, or has no awareness of the complexities of cyberspace or the postindustrial workplace. If these criticisms are leveled, I ask that each of them be illustrated by at least three specific references to his work. These should be either quoted verbatim in the paper or their location in his work indicated clearly enough for me to be able to find the relevant passages.

The second source of resistance critical theory induces concerns its critique of capitalism. Recall the "single existential judgment" offered by Horkheimer (1995) that critical theory's chief project is studying how to abolish the exchange economy of capitalism. A critique of capitalism—the way it commodifies creativity and labor, makes reason its servant, reduces friendships and intimate relationships to the exchange of personality packages, and fuels spiritual malnourishment—is threaded throughout critical theory. One reason this disturbs students so much is because they recognize features of their own life in this critique. But I think the deeper impact of this critique is that it calls into question the professional location, and by implication, the professional practices and personal identities of the students themselves.

Many of my students work in corporate America, the apogee of capitalism. They live in a country where capitalism is propounded as dominant ideology, as obviously a "good thing" that supports admired values of freedom, liberty, and individuality. Capitalism is lauded for the prosperity it brings, the technological advances it stimulates, and the way it disseminates the innovative spirit of entrepreneurship amongst the population. For those working at the heart of capitalism to hear a sustained critique of its workings, and a documentation of its injuries, is highly threatening.

This is why it's important, early on, to get students to distinguish between capitalism's ideology and functioning and their own role in the system. There are many who work in corporate America who believe strongly in the need for workplaces to be locations for the exercise of human creativity and who think they are working to humanize an inhuman system. When students in my courses read the manuscript on alienated labor, they find it expresses many of their own misgivings about their own workplaces. They would not use Marx's language to describe their reality, but they recognize the spiritual and creative diminution signified by the relentless devotion to the bottom line of corporate profits.

One way to bring students to consider a critique of capitalism is through Fromm's analysis of alienation. As I argued in Chapter Six, Fromm is the critical theorist who had the greatest success introducing a Marxist-inclined analysis of American life to mainstream America itself. His outlines of the social character of capitalism with its stress on punctuality, orderliness, and pulling for the team, his analysis of the marketing orientation with its emphasis on producing attractive personality packages for exchange on the open market of relationships, and his warnings against the pull of automaton conformity are all couched in still recognizable vignettes and accessible language. As a starting point for understanding Marx, Fromm is far more appealing to suspicious students than, say, Gramsci or Althusser. Fromm, like Marcuse and Habermas, is also very good on critiquing statist, totalitarian communism and pointing out the automaton conformity and alienation rampant in totalitarian communist regimes.

A third source of resistance lies in critical theory's condemnation of the way democracy has been distorted to serve capitalism's interests. The radical democratic strain evident in critical theory also regards the realization of genuine democracy as blocked by the simple-minded assumption that a majority vote inevitably ensures the right course of action. Assuming that a majority vote is by definition correct is based on the belief that the choices the majority make represent the free and uncoerced realization of authentically felt needs. Critical theory argues that in reality automaton conformity, one-dimensional thought, self-surveillance, and the steering mechanisms of money and power combine to ensure that these supposedly "authentic" majority needs merely mimic dominant ideology. The radical democratic critique holds that in "comfortable, smooth, reasonable, democratic unfreedom," to use Marcuse's (1964, p. 1) formulation, majority choices are by definition manipulated and compromised-uncritical expressions of needs that capitalism and bureaucratic rationality have created. Contemporary democracy is thus seen as representing the automatic tyranny of the majority, rather than an inclusive, open-ended conversation.

To hear democracy critiqued this way is very tough for a lot of students. They can live with a critique of capitalism, but democracy? How can that be bad? Even some who are relatively comfortable with reading critical theory become very alarmed when democracy is called into question. This makes the idea of democracy a fine example of a premature ultimate; that is, a term that is held in such reverence that its invocation effectively ends any further debate or critical analysis. Adult educators can get away with pedagogic murder if they justify their practice by saying they're striving to act democratically.

One response to the resistance to any critique of the majority vote model of democracy is to remind students that critical theory and democracy are not at odds. There is a radical democratic strand in critical theory that sees genuine participatory democracy as a viable political system but believes that hegemony has co-opted and distorted this idea to reproduce the current unequal system. This strand is evident particularly in the work of Fromm, Marcuse (who says that the fact that democracy has never existed does not mean we give up its dream), Habermas, and West. In fact West positions Marx himself as a radical democrat, arguing that Marx and Engels define communism as a struggle for democracy. This democratic emphasis is evident, in West's view, in the insistence by Marx that "ordinary people, workers, ought to have some control over the conditions of their existence, especially the conditions of their workplace" (West, 1999b, p. 223). To West this is "a profoundly democratic idea" (p. 223) and one, therefore, that can be linked to the mainstream of American ideology. Arguing that Marx is a radical democrat creates some interesting cognitive dissonance for learners used to thinking of him as the antithesis of all that is democratic.

Another useful way to open up a discussion of how democracy allows the tyranny of the majority to reproduce dominant ideology is to ask for a vote in class on a relatively simple procedural matter. Ira Shor has described in great detail the contradictions of the "democracy as majority vote" position in books such as *Empowering Education* (1992) and *When Students Have Power* (1996). But you don't have to experiment with democratic process in as sustained a way as Shor does to get students to realize the tyranny of the majority in their midst. Just ask the class to vote on what time to take a break, or which of the available course texts to focus on, and the minority that has been outvoted will soon be complaining about the unfair nature of majority votes.

As a teacher I have spent several years teaching in doctoral cohort programs at the University of St. Thomas and National Louis University in which the negotiation of curricular and program matters was an accepted part of the program (Baptiste and Brookfield, 1997). Repeatedly, students involved in this negotiation report that the "official" curriculum of the program (even if it includes reading Gramsci, Habermas, and Foucault) is a piece of cake compared to the effort to develop democratic consensus in student governance sessions. Groups that try to work with the majority vote model soon bump up against the fact of the tyranny of the majority. This is particularly the case where a minority of students wishes to explore a topic that seems off center, not part of the official curriculum. If this is proposed, discussion quickly focuses on the costs of doing this. These are almost always expressed as not graduating on time, annoying the faculty, or not achieving the kind of academic record that will help in a job search. Against this background it is easy to teach about the commodification of learning since students realize how in their governance deliberations a concern for good grades and for obtaining the diploma on time quickly outweigh all other considerations. It becomes glaringly obvious how grades and the diploma are seen as tradable commodities on the open market.

Finally on this point one of the things teachers can stress to students new to critical theory is that theory's central concern is with freedom—a libertarian idea very honored in American ideology. For example, Habermas argues that "socialism and liberty are identical" (Habermas, 1992a, p. 75), a sentiment many of my students would regard as contradictory. However, Fromm, Marcuse, and Habermas in their different ways all see socialism as "an attempt . . . to indicate the necessary conditions which would have to be in place for emancipated life-forms to emerge" (p. 145)—to be free in other words.

Critical theory is centrally concerned with releasing people from falsely created needs and helping them make their own free choices regarding how they wish to think and live. Framed this way, it is much closer to democratic ideals than people realize. Although in many students' minds critical theory is essentially a socialistic discourse concerned only with economic arrangements, it can be broadened to privilege freedom as much as common ownership. To North American adult educators suspicious of Marxophobia and wary of all things socialistic, it is the emphasis in critical theory on claiming freedom that stands the best chance of engaging their interest.

A fourth source of resistance to studying critical theory is its often impenetrable language. If you have made it through to this final chapter, and not skipped too much along the way, you cannot have failed to notice this problem. Throughout the text I have tried to use as many direct quotes from the authors reviewed as possible. This has been partly to honor their scholarship and partly to convey as accurately as possible the essence of their thought. You might have spent some considerable time puzzling over the meaning of some of these quotes. You will almost certainly have noticed that after including a quote from an original text I often start the next sentence with the phrase "in other words." This sentence then uses my own words to explain a particularly convoluted sentence or passage drawn directly from a critical theory text.

There are great dangers embedded in the phrase "in other words." The author can use it to introduce his or her preferred reading of the theorist's original meaning, sometimes distorting it beyond recognition in the process. So you should be very suspicious whenever you see me use this form of words. Obviously, whenever I use the expression "in other words" I feel I can justify it by claiming that I am creating access points into a complex and intimidating tradition. But then I would say that, wouldn't I? In my defense I can only point out that it is my sense that for those unused to reading in this area, critical theory can seem like a foreign language in need of translation. Marcuse is one of those who recognizes how the language of critical theory can alienate potential readers and allies. He is particularly perturbed by those who ritualistically invoke terms (proletariat, dialectics, and so on) that are "identification labels for in-groups . . . mere clichés" (Marcuse, 1972, p. 39). Mechanically repeating phrases like *emancipatory praxis* or *proletarian hegemony* can make those outside of the leftist in-group even more convinced that readers of critical theorists live in some kind of fantasy world.

Noam Chomsky is another on the left who is most critical of a specialized language of leftism. He declares that "whenever I hear a four-syllable word I get skeptical, because I want to make sure you can't say it in monosyllables" (Chomsky, 2000, p. 229) and urges people to "be extremely skeptical when intellectual life constructs structures which aren't transparent" (p. 229). In a similar vein, hooks and Davis both argue strongly for an accessible language of critique. Both acknowledge the way everyday language has become distorted by capitalist ideology, and both are quite willing to use many terms drawn from the critical tradition. Both also use auto-biographical reflection as a way to ground critique in contexts that connect to readers outside academe. Davis' own autobiography (Davis, 1974) and hooks' personal reflections in books such as *Talking Back* (1989) and *Where We Stand* (2000b) interweave descriptions of personal episodes with theoretical analyses. Many of these episodes have to do with the excitement of stumbling over a new way of thinking—a theoretical analysis in other words—that explains something in their lives.

Both Davis and hooks believe that much of the revolutionary energy of critical theory has been dampened by its overly convoluted language. How can an adult educator galvanize people's desire to question and then act upon their world if the language used to do this "mystifies rather than clarifies our condition" (Christian, 1990, p. 572). This is where Gramsci's idea of the organic intellectual has a particular resonance. To be able to understand a complicated but powerful vocabulary of critique and to be able to render this in an intelligible and meaningful way to those outside that discourse is a crucial educational role. Erich Fromm worked to do this as do contemporary commentators such as Ira Shor (1992, 1996), Lisa Delpit (1996), Herb Kohl (1994; 2000), and Mike Rose (1990, 1999). Myles Horton's (1990) use of stories, analogies, and metaphors was one of the best adult educational implementations of this, and one that avoided all jargon.

As a classroom teacher I go back and forth on the issue of how much I should function as a translator. When I'm working with students wholly unfamiliar with critical theory, I usually begin a class with some introductory exposition. My assumption is that those who have read little or nothing in the area, and who may be resistant to it for the reasons outlined earlier in this chapter, need me to build a case early on for the relevance of this material. As I summarize the contours of "big" ideas like ideology, hegemony, alienation, or power, I try to talk about their meaning in my own life by

giving examples. I show how dominant ideology shapes my decisions as a teacher, how my practice is commodified, how I engage
in self-surveillance, how repressive tolerance manifests itself in my
attempts to broaden the curriculum, or how automaton conformity
frames my response to new practices or ideas. I also present critical
theory as grounded in three (hopefully) understandable core
assumptions regarding the way the world is organized: (1) that
apparently open, Western democracies are actually highly unequal
societies in which economic inequity, racism, and class discrimination are empirical realities, (2) that this state of affairs is reproduced
as seeming to be normal, natural, and inevitable (thereby heading
off potential challenges to the system) through the dissemination
of dominant ideology (defined as the system of ideas, values, beliefs,
and practices accepted as common sense truth), and (3) that critical theory attempts to understand this state of affairs as a prelude
to changing it.

After this introductory exposition, I often ask students to spend
some time reading extracts from critical theory literature. They do
this individually and privately during classroom time. The extracts
themselves are not long—a few paragraphs here, a page or two
there—since I would prefer students to read carefully a few pivotal
sections than to try and become familiar too early on with the
range of broad debates and interpretations surrounding an idea.
For example, if we are discussing alienation students can choose
to read a couple of pages from Marx's alienated labor manuscript
(Marx, 1961), followed by Fromm's own discussion of that idea
(Fromm, 1961). When this period of private reading is finished,
students work in small groups to discuss their reactions to the reading. Examples of some of the questions I suggest they consider in
these groups are given below:

Ideology

After you have read (privately and individually) the materials on
ideology, please form into groups of four to six and discuss your
reactions to the readings. Some suggested questions:

1. What aspects of the writings on ideology were most resonant
   and most discrepant for you?

2. What are elements of the dominant ideology in the United States today?
3. What hegemonic beliefs and practices have you, or those you know, embraced?
4. To what degree is your learning at this university commodified, and to what degree have you commodified learning for others in your own practice as an educator?
5. Do you see this university or your employing agency as an ISA? If so, how does it work?
6. How did you find the language? Congenial? Intimidating? Puzzling? Illuminating?

Try and bring back one or two questions or issues you'd like addressed in the large group.

Alienation

After you have read (privately and individually) the workshop materials on alienation, please form into groups of four to six and discuss your reactions to the readings. Some suggested questions:

1. What aspects of the writing on alienation were most resonant and most discrepant for you?
2. Do you see your own labor—or other aspects of your life—as characterized by alienation? If so, how?
3. What pressures do you feel toward automaton conformity in your life, your learning, or your practice of education?
4. How does the marketing orientation manifest itself in your life, learning, and practice?
5. How did you find the language? Congenial? Intimidating? Puzzling? Illuminating?

Try and bring back one or two questions or issues you'd like addressed in the large group.

Power

After you have read (privately and individually) the workshop materials on power, please form into groups of four to six and discuss your reactions to the readings. Some suggested questions:

1. What aspects of the writing on power were most resonant and most discrepant for you?
2. What regimes of truth do you see in your learning, life, work, or educational practice?
3. In what ways do you feel under anonymous surveillance?
4. How does your experience of power match or contradict Foucault's idea of power as a chain, flow, or web—both oppressive and emancipatory simultaneously?
5. How have you managed to subvert dominant power?
6. How did you find the language? Congenial? Intimidating? Puzzling? Illuminating?

Try and bring back one or two questions or issues you'd like addressed in the large group.

My work as translator in the classroom is, however, fraught with contradictions. As I have already argued, in translating you inevitably distort and simplify. There is also a strong hint of condescension in adopting this role. To put it bluntly, you're in effect saying that students aren't smart enough to understand an author's ideas in the way he or she originally expresses them. The anger this can produce was brought home to me in a class I taught at Harvard on Critical Theory and the Practice of Adult Education. We had arrived at the point in the course where we were examining the work of Habermas. I suggested that students first read my own summary of Habermas' twenty or so English language texts (essentially an early draft of Chapters Eight and Nine in this book) before they tried to read him in the original. In the anonymous student evaluations submitted for the weeks we looked at Habermas, there was strong criticism of the insult to adult students' intelligence that my supposedly helpful suggestion represented.

One consequence for students struggling to grasp the intimidating vocabulary of critical theory is that of impostorship. Impostorship is the sense that many adult learners have that they are not smart enough to be "real" or "proper" students. They feel they lack the mental agility of eighteen to twenty-two year olds and that sooner or later they will say or do something so awful that their intellectual limitations will be revealed and they will be asked to leave the course under a cloud of shame and humiliation. Impostorship is just as rampant (though often better concealed) in doctoral courses at Harvard or Columbia as it is in a neighborhood adult literacy center. With its complex language, critical theory is particularly suited to inducing impostorship. Students feel like they will never "get" critical theory because its discourse exists in a realm beyond their understanding.

One way to deal with impostorship is to name it early in the term. Teachers can do this themselves or they can invite former students in their courses to visit the new class and talk about how they felt when they first encountered the language of criticality. Invariably the former students will talk about their own sense of impostorship, giving examples of how excruciating this was. When they do this, a collective sigh of relief is often exhaled around the room by all those who felt they were the only ones who felt that way. In my own case I talk frequently about my own struggles engaging with this tradition. I talk about how much time it takes me to read its texts, how I study the same sentence over and over again and still have no idea what it means, and how I frequently feel like an idiot compared to colleagues who seem very comfortable with Althusser, Foucault, or Marcuse. Despite having done this for several years, I am always surprised at what a shocking, though very welcome, revelation this is for students who automatically assume (as I probably would in their place) that as the designated professor I have got critical theory "down." Interestingly, this admission does not seem to weaken my credibility, or if it does, that perception is not recorded on anonymous weekly student evaluations. Instead, students seem relieved that someone who has studied this work for some time still feels like a novice.

The final point of resistance to critical theory is caused by the radical pessimism it induces. For some people new to the tradition, reading analyses of ideological manipulation, the infinite flexibility of hegemony, the pervasiveness of automaton conformity and alienation, the invasion of the lifeworld, and so on is like being hit over the head repeatedly with a padded mallet. There seems to be no end to the unrelieved gloom, no prospect of the clouds of oppression ever being blown away. The two worst phases for many students are when they read Foucault on the nature of surveillance and disciplinary power and Marcuse on repressive tolerance. These writings contain the same message of circumspection regarding actions that seem unequivocally hopeful or liberating. Foucault and Marcuse both warn against the easy and seductive assumption that the sincerity of a teacher's emancipatory intent guarantees that his or her actions will somehow be experienced as liberating. This is sometimes very hard for activist adult educators to hear.

Educators drawn to critical theory are often attracted by its oppositional stance. It seems to hold the promise of helping us overcome alienation, unmask power, or learn liberation. When adult educators encounter an idea like repressive tolerance, it seems to sap their energy. On the one hand, their studies in critical theory have created enthusiasm for the possibility of opening up the curriculum to different ideas, thereby galvanizing their own students' activism and developing their critical thinking. Then they read Marcuse's warning that broadening the curriculum often serves only to emphasize the dominance of the existing center, and they feel robbed of hope. "How can we do anything," they ask, "when Marcuse says that opening things up really only closes them down further, and Foucault tells us our efforts to democratize education will be experienced as oppressive by those we're seeking to help?"

There is not a lot one can say in response to such a question. But just shrugging your shoulders is not an option either. I usually reply by talking about the importance of using whatever energy you have most effectively. More particularly, I focus on the importance of not wasting energy obsessing fretfully over things you can't control. It seems to me that educators trying to get adults to think and act critically need to make students aware of the many traps that lie in wait for those who engage in these activities. One of these is working diligently to promote practices that you feel are unequivocally positive without realizing their potentially negative consequences. To act believing you're changing the world for the better, and then to find out that the converse is the case, is horribly demoralizing. It kills the transformative impulse and induces a profoundly debilitating pessimism.

As a teacher I would rather know of the traps and dangers that lie ahead, no matter how much they might complicate matters. If I am aware of the contradictions and complications of teaching critically, then when these present themselves I am less likely to feel that I have single-handedly caused them to appear. In her book *Practice Makes Practice,* Britzman (1991) identifies the belief that "everything depends on the teacher" as one of the most enduring myths teachers learn early on in their careers. This myth holds that successes are due to your brilliance and failures to your incompetence. We need to dispel this myth with its Copernican emphasis on the teacher as the center of the universe. Given that teaching critically is a pothole-strewn highway, we need to know that the reason the car is banging about in such a perilous and unpredictable manner is because of the holes already in the blacktop, not because we can't drive.

One final thought on teaching critical theory in the face of student resistance. Something I have consistently found to be helpful in this regard is the use of team teaching. I am talking here of team teaching properly conducted, with all members of the team involved in planning and debriefing each class session, and all present throughout each class meeting. The power of team teaching is perhaps not surprising in the light of West's and Davis' stress on the need for multicultural alliances in critical practice. In multiracial teams, particularly those in which women of color outnumber White males, the possibilities of probing how critical theory can be racialized and gendered are often enlarged. It is important to say, however, that an absence of faculty of color, or of women teachers, clearly should not mean an absence of racial or gender analysis.

One reason team teaching works well has to do with the problem of translator distortion discussed earlier. When two or three faculty are in the room together, the chances that distortions or oversimplifications of critical theorists' ideas will go unnoticed are considerably reduced. Even if students notice these distortions, they may be unwilling to bring them to the class' attention because of the power of the teacher. It is much easier for faculty working as a team to point out publicly to each other the potential oversimplifications of a particular teacher's comments. Team teaching also opens up the possibility of structured devil's advocacy with different team members taking turns to argue against the emergence of an easy consensus on difficult classroom issues.

Final Word

There can be no conclusion to a book like this, since the tradition of critique embedded in critical theory emphasizes that this is an open and unending project. So how to end this long and complex journey that *The Power of Critical Theory* represents? Perhaps the simplest way is to reprise the purposes I set myself in writing this book. I wanted to respond to the student who saw no reason to engage with critical theory and who believed there was no way in which her practice as an adult educator was illuminated by its concerns. Hopefully, *The Power of Critical Theory* has built a convincing case that critical theory helps explain many of the dilemmas and contradictions of contemporary adult education practice. If so, readers will be less likely to ascribe these problematic situations to their own incompetence or to the fickle whims of unpredictable fortune.

I wanted too, to put the critical back into critical thinking by carefully elaborating one of the chief intellectual traditions that informs that discourse. I hope that this book will help relocate critical thinking and critical reflection squarely in the tradition of critical theory, with the explicit social and political critique, and activism, this implies. My hope is that in exploring the critical tradition I have argued convincingly that, far from being an outdated perspective, critical theory is relevant as ever in a world dominated by global capital. I hope, too, that the insights of critical theory have been shown to have direct relevance for understanding contemporary adult education practice and for building a critical alternative.

In doing these things I was concerned as much as possible to use the words of the theorists themselves so that distortions and oversimplifications would be kept to a minimum. This is why the previous chapters contain so many quotes drawn directly from texts authored by the theorists themselves. At the same time, I wanted the book to be an accessible entry point into the critical tradition that used language and examples readers could understand. The point was to try and interpret critical theory's tenets in a way that could be understood by those with no previous acquaintance with this work. I wanted to clarify not mystify. Again, this is why that most suspicious of authorial phrases—"in other words"—keeps popping up.

As readers you will judge the degree to which I have had any success in realizing any of these purposes. For me, this book will have been worth it if one, very simple, thing happens. If, after reading these chapters, you feel like you want to get hold of the original texts and make your own (rather than Stephen Brookfield's) judgments about their meaning and utility for your work as an adult educator, then I will feel that *The Power of Critical Theory* will have had some measure of success.

References

Adorno, T. W. *Negative Dialectics.* New York: Seabury Press, 1973.

Alcoff, L., and Potter, E. (eds.). *Feminist Epistemologies.* New York: Routledge, 1993.

Allman, P. *Revolutionary Social Transformation: Democratic Hopes, Political Possibilities and Critical Education.* Westport, CT: Bergin & Garvey, 2000.

Allman, P. *Critical Education Against Global Capitalism: Karl Marx and Revolutionary Critical Education.* Westport, CT: Bergin & Garvey, 2001.

Althusser, L. *Lenin and Philosophy.* New York: Monthly Review Press, 1971.

Appiah, K. A. "African-American Philosophy?" In J. P. Pittman (ed.), *African-American Perspectives and Philosophical Traditions.* New York: Routledge, 1997.

Appiah, K. A. "African Identities." In B. Boxhill (ed.), *Race and Racism.* New York: Oxford University Press, 2001.

Apple, M. W. *Official Knowledge: Democratic Education in a Conservative Age.* (2nd. ed.) New York: Routledge, 2000.

Aptheker, B. *The Morning Breaks: The Trial of Angela Davis.* Ithaca, NY: Cornell University Press, 1999.

Arygris, C. *Reasoning, Learning, and Action: Individual and Organizational.* San Francisco: Jossey-Bass, 1982.

Asante, M. K. *Afrocentricity: A Theory of Social Change.* Trenton, NJ: Africa World Press, 1998a. (Revised edition).

Asante, M. K. *The Afrocentric Idea.* Philadelphia: Temple University Press, 1998b.

Avila, E. B. and others. "Learning Democracy/Democratizing Learning: Participatory Graduate Education." In P. Campbell and B. Burnaby (eds.), *Participatory Practices in Adult Education.* Toronto: Erlbaum, 2000.

Bagnall, R. G. *Discovering Radical Contingency: Building a Postmodern Agenda in Adult Education.* New York: Peter Lang, 1999.

Baptiste, I. "Beyond Reason and Personal Integrity: Toward a Pedagogy of Coercive Restraint" *Canadian Journal for the Study of Adult Education,* 2000, *14*(1), 27–50.

Baptiste, I., and Brookfield, S. D. "Your So-Called Democracy Is Hypocritical Because You Can Always Fail Us: Learning and Living Democratic Contradictions in Graduate Adult Education." In P. Armstrong (ed.), *Crossing Borders, Breaking Boundaries: Research in the Education of Adults*. London: University of London, 1997.

Basseches, M. *Dialectical Thinking and Adult Development*. Norwood, NJ: Ablex, 1984.

Baudrillard, J. *The Mirror of Production*. New York: Telos Press, 1975.

Baudrillard, J. *Simulations*. New York: Semiotext Publications, 1983.

Belenky, M. F., Clinchy, B. M., Goldberger, N. R., and Tarule, J. M. *Women's Ways of Knowing: The Development of Self, Voice, and Mind*. New York: Basic Books, 1986.

Benhabib, S. *Critique, Norm, and Utopia: A Study of the Foundations of Critical Theory*. New York: Columbia University Press, 1986.

Benhabib, S., and Cornell, D. *Feminism as Critique: On the Politics of Gender*. Minneapolis: University of Minnesota Press, 1988.

Billig, M., Condor, S., Edwards, D., Gane, M., Middleton, D., and Radley, A. *Ideological Dilemmas: A Social Psychology of Everyday Thinking*. Thousand Oaks, CA: Sage, 1988.

Boal, A. *Theater of the Oppressed*. New York: Theater Communications Group, 1985.

Borg, C., Buttigieg, J., and Mayo, P. (eds.). *Gramsci and Education*. Lanham, MD: Rowman and Littlefield, 2002.

Borradori, G., Habermas, J. and Derrida, J. *Philosophy in a Time of Terror: Dialogues with Jurgen Habermas and Jacques Derrida*. Chicago: University of Chicago Press, 2003.

Boshier, R., and Wilson, M. "Panoptic Variations: Surveillance and Discipline in Web Courses." *Proceedings of the Adult Education Research Conference, No. 39*. San Antonio: University of the Incarnate Word, 1998, pp. 43–48.

Boxhill, B. "The Race-Class Question." In L. Harris (ed.), *Philosophy Born of Struggle: Anthology of African-American Philosophy from 1917*. Dubuque, IA: Kendall/Hunt, 1983.

Boxhill, B. (ed.) *Race and Racism*. New York: Oxford University Press, 2001.

Braaten, J. "From Communicative Rationality to Communicative Thinking: A Basis for Feminist Theory and Practice." In J. Meehan (ed.), *Feminists Read Habermas: Gendering the Subject of Discourse*. New York: Routledge, 1995.

Bridges, D. *Education, Democracy, and Discussion*. Lanham, MD: University Press of America, 1988.

Britzman, D. P. *Practice Makes Practice: A Critical Study of Learning to Teach*. Albany: State University of New York Press, 1991.

Brockett, R. G., and Hiemstra, R. *Self-Direction in Adult Learning: Perspectives on Theory, Research, and Practice.* New York: Routledge, 1991.

Bronner, S. E., and Kellner, D. M. (eds.). *Critical Theory and Society: A Reader.* New York: Routledge, 1989.

Brookfield, S. D. *Developing Critical Thinkers: Challenging Adults to Explore Alternative Ways of Thinking and Acting.* San Francisco: Jossey-Bass, 1987a.

Brookfield, S. D. (ed.). *Learning Democracy: Eduard Lindeman on Adult Education and Social Change.* London: Croom Helm, 1987b.

Brookfield, S. D. "Self-Directed Learning, Political Clarity, and the Critical Practice of Adult Education." *Adult Education Quarterly,* 1993, *43*(4), 227–242.

Brookfield, S. D. *Becoming a Critically Reflective Teacher.* San Francisco: Jossey-Bass, 1995.

Brookfield, S. D. "Self-Directed Learning as a Political Idea." In G. A. Straka (ed.), *Conceptions of Self-Directed Learning: Theoretical and Conceptual Considerations.* Berlin/New York: Waxmann, 2000.

Brookfield, S. D. "Critical Perspectives on Accelerated Learning." In R. Wlodkowski and C. A. Kasworm (eds.), *Accelerated Learning for Adults: The Promise and Practice of Intensive Educational Formats.* San Francisco: Jossey-Bass, 2003.

Brookfield, S. D., and Preskill, S. *Discussion as a Way of Teaching: Tools and Techniques for Democratic Classrooms.* San Francisco: Jossey-Bass, 1999.

Brown, A. H. "African-American Women of Inspiration." In V. Sheared, and P. Sissel (eds.), *Making Space: Merging Theory and Practice in Adult Education.* Westport, CT: Bergin & Garvey, 2001.

Burbules, N. *Dialogue in Teaching.* New York: Teachers College Press, 1993.

Burman, E. *Deconstructing Developmental Psychology.* New York: Routledge, 1994.

Cale, G. *When Resistance Becomes Reproduction: A Critical Action Research Study.* Proceedings of the 42nd Adult Education Research Conference. East Lansing: Michigan State University, 2001.

Candy, P. C. *Self-Direction for Lifelong Learning.* San Francisco: Jossey-Bass, 1991.

Cherryholmes, C. H. *Reading Pragmatism.* New York: Teachers College Press, 1999.

Chodorow, N. J. *Feminism and Psychoanalytic Theory.* New Haven, CT: Yale University Press, 1989.

Chomsky, N. *Necessary Illusions: Thought Control in Democratic Societies.* Boston: South End Press, 1989.

Chomsky, N. *Understanding Power: The Indispensable Chomsky.* (P. R. Mitchell and J. Schoffel, eds.). New York: The New Press, 2002.

Christian, B. "The Race for Theory." In K. V. Hansen and I. J. Philipson (eds.), *Women, Class, and the Feminist Imagination: A Socialist-Feminist Reader.* Philadelphia: Temple University Press, 1990.

Clark, C., and Wilson, A. L. "Context and Rationality in Mezirow's Theory of Transformational Learning." *Adult Education Quarterly,* 1991, *41*(2), 75–91

Coben, D. *Radical Heroes: Gramsci, Freire and the Politics of Adult Education.* New York: Garland, 1998.

Colin, S.A.J. III. "The Universal Negro Improvement Association and the Education of African Ameripean Adults." Doctoral dissertation, Dept. of Adult Education, Northern Illinois University, 1988.

Colin, S.A.J. III. "Adult and Continuing Education Graduate Programs: Prescription for the Future." In E. Hayes and S.A.J. Colin III (eds.), *Confronting Racism and Sexism.* New Directions for Adult and Continuing Education, No. 61. San Francisco: Jossey-Bass, 1994.

Colin, S.A.J III. "Marcus Garvey: Africentric Adult Education for Selfethnic Reliance." In E. A. Peterson (ed.), *Freedom Road: Adult Education of African Americans.* Malabar, FL: Krieger, 2002 (rev. ed.).

Colin, S.A.J. III, and Guy, T. A. "An Africentric Interpretive Model of Curriculum Orientations for Course Development in Graduate Programs in Adult Education." *PAACE Journal of Lifelong Learning,* 1998, *7,* 43–55.

Collard, S., and Law, M. "The Limits of Perspective Transformation Theory: A Critique of Mezirow's Theory." *Adult Education Quarterly,* 1989, *39*(2), 99–107.

Collini, S. "Is This the End of the World as We Know It?" *Guardian Weekly,* 2000, *162*(2), 2–13.

Collins, M. *Adult Education as Vocation: A Critical Role for the Adult Educator.* New York: Routledge, 1991.

Collins, M. *Critical Crosscurrents in Education.* Malabar, FL: Krieger, 1998.

Collins, P. H. *Black Feminist Thought: Knowledge, Consciousness, and the Politics of Empowerment.* Boston: Unwin Hyman, 1990.

Crenshaw, K., Gotanda, N., Peller, G., and Thomas, K. (eds.). *Critical Race Theory: The Key Writings That Formed a Movement.* New York: The New Press, 1995.

Darder, A. *Reinventing Paulo Freire: A Pedagogy of Love.* Boulder, CO: Westview Press, 2002.

Davis, A. Y. *If They Come in the Morning: Voices of Resistance.* New York: The Third Press, 1971a.

Davis, A. Y. *Lectures on Liberation.* Los Angeles: National United Committee to Free Angela Davis, 1971b.

Davis, A. Y. *Angela Davis: An Autobiography.* New York: International Publishers, 1974.

Davis, A. Y. *Women, Race, and Class.* New York: Vintage Books, 1983.

Davis, A. Y. *Women, Culture, and Politics.* New York: Vintage Books, 1990.

Davis, A. Y. *The Angela Y. Davis Reader.* Blackwell: Malden, MA: 1998a.

Davis, A. Y. "Angela Y. Davis." Interview in G. Yancy (ed.), *African-American Philosophers: 17 Conversations.* New York: Routledge, 1998b.

Davis, A. Y. *Blues Legacies and Black Feminism: Gertrude "Ma" Rainey, Bessie Smith, and Billie Holiday.* New York: Random House, 1999.

Delgado, R. (ed.). *Critical Race Theory: The Cutting Edge.* Philadelphia: Temple University Press, 1995.

Delpit, L. D. *Other People's Children: Cultural Conflict in the Classroom.* New York: New Press, 1996.

Dewey, J. *Experience and Education.* New York: Collier Books, 1938.

Diamond, I., and Quinby, L. (eds.). *Feminism and Foucault: Reflections on Resistance.* Boston: NorthEastern University Press, 1988.

Du Bois, W.E.B. *The Souls of Black Folk.* New York: New American Library, 1995. (Originally published 1903).

Du Bois, W.E.B. *Dusk of Dawn: An Essay Toward an Autobiography of a Race Concept.* New York: Schocken Books, 1968. (Originally published 1940.)

Eagleton, T. *Ideology: An Introduction.* London: Verso Press, 1991.

Easter, O. V. "Septima Poinsette Clark: Unsung Heroine of the Civil Rights Movement." In E. A. Peterson (ed.), *Freedom Road: Adult Education of African Americans* (revised ed.). Malabar, FL: Krieger, 2002.

Ehrenreich, B. "Life Without Father: Reconsidering Socialist-Feminist Theory." In K. V. Hansen and I. J. Philipson (eds.), *Women, Class, and the Feminist Imagination: A Socialist-Feminist Reader.* Philadelphia: Temple University Press, 1990.

Ehrlich, C. "The Unhappy Marriage of Marxism and Feminism: Can it Be Saved?" In L. Sargent (ed.), *Women and Revolution: A Discussion of the Unhappy Marriage of Marxism and Feminism.* Boston: South End Press, 1981.

Eisenstein, Z. (ed.), *Capitalist Patriarchy and the Case for Socialist Feminism.* New York: Monthly Review Press, 1979.

Eisentstein, Z. "Constructing a Theory of Capitalist Patriarchy and Socialist Feminism." In K. V. Hansen and I. J. Philipson (eds.), *Women, Class, and the Feminist Imagination: A Socialist-Feminist Reader.* Philadelphia: Temple University Press, 1990.

Ellsworth, E. "Why Doesn't This Feel Empowering? Working Through the Repressive Myths of Critical Pedagogy." In C. Luke and J. M. Gore (eds.), *Feminisms and Critical Pedagogy.* New York: Routledge, 1992.

Entwistle, H. *Antonio Gramsci: Conservative Schooling for Radical Politics.* New York: Routledge, Kegan and Paul, 1979.

Eribon, D. *Michel Foucault.* Cambridge, MA: Harvard University Press, 1991.

Fay, B. *Critical Social Science: Liberation and Its Limits.* Ithaca, NY: Cornell University Press, 1987.

Fleming, M. *Emancipation and Illusion: Rationality and Gender in Habermas' Theory of Modernity.* University Park, PA: Pennsylvania State University Press, 1997.

Fluss, D. *Essentially Speaking: Feminism, Nature, and Difference.* New York: Routledge, 1989.

Foley, D. E. *Learning Capitalist Culture: Deep in the Heart of Tejas.* Philadelphia: University of Pennsylvania Press, 1990.

Foley, G. "Adult Education and Capitalist Reorganization" *Studies in the Education of Adults,* 1994, *26*(2), 121–143.

Follett, M. P. *Creative Experience.* New York: Longmans, Green, 1924a.

Follett, M. P. *Dynamic Administration.* New York: Longmans, Green, 1924b.

Foucault, M. *The Order of Things: An Archaeology of the Human Sciences.* New York: Vintage Books, 1973.

Foucault, M. *Discipline and Punish: The Birth of the Prison.* New York: Vintage Books, 1977a.

Foucault, M. *Language, Counter-Memory, Practice: Selected Essays and Interviews.* (D. F. Bouchard, ed.). Ithaca, NY: Cornell University Press, 1977b.

Foucault, M. *Power/Knowledge: Selected Interviews and Other Writings, 1972–1977.* New York: Pantheon Books, 1980.

Foucault, M. "The Subject and Power." In H. L. Dreyfus and P. Rabinow (eds.), *Michel Foucault: Beyond Structuralism and Hermeneutics.* Chicago: University of Chicago Press, 1982.

Foucault, M. "Interview." In J. Bernauer and D. Rasmussen (eds.), *The Final Foucault.* Cambridge, MA: MIT Press, 1987.

Foucault, M. *Philosophy, Culture: Interviews and Other Writings, 1977–1984* (L. D. Kritzman, ed.). New York: Routledge, 1988a.

Foucault, M. *A Seminar with Michel Foucault* (L. Martin, H. Gutman, and P. H. Hulton, eds.). Amherst, MA: University of Massachusetts Press, 1988b.

Foucault, M. *Foucault Live: Collected Interviews, 1961–1984.* New York: Semiotext(e), 1996.

Foucault, M. *Society Must Be Defended: Lectures at the College De France, 1975–1976.* New York: St. Martin's Press, 2003.

Fox, D., and Prilleltensky, I. (eds.). *Critical Psychology: An Introduction.* Thousand Oaks, CA: Sage, 1997.

Fraser, N. *Unruly Practices: Power, Discourse and Gender in Contemporary Social Theory.* Minneapolis: University of Minnesota Press, 1989.

Fraser, N. "What's Critical About Critical Theory." In J. Meehan (ed.), *Feminists Read Habermas: Gendering the Subject of Discourse.* New York: Routledge, 1995.

Fraser, N. *Justice Interruptus: Critical Reflections on the "Postsocialist" Condition.* New York: Routledge, 1997.

Freire, P. *Pedagogy of the Oppressed.* New York: Continuum, 1970.

Freire, P. *Pedagogy of Hope.* New York: Continuum, 1994.

Freire, P, and Macedo, D. P. *Literacy: Reading the Word and the World.* South Hadley, MA: Bergin and Garvey, 1987.

Freire, P., and Macedo, D. P. "A Dialogue: Culture, Language, and Race." *Harvard Educational Review,* 1995, *65*(3), 377–402.

Fromm, E. *Escape from Freedom.* New York: Holt, Rinehart and Winston, 1941.

Fromm, E. *Man for Himself.* New York: Holt, Rinehart and Winston, 1947.

Fromm, E. *The Sane Society.* London: Routledge, Kegan and Paul, 1956a.

Fromm, E. *The Art of Loving: An Enquiry into the Nature of Love.* New York: Harper and Row, 1956b.

Fromm, E. *Marx's Concept of Man.* New York: Frederick Ungar, 1961.

Fromm, E. *Beyond the Chains of Illusion: My Encounter with Marx and Freud.* New York: Simon and Schuster, 1962.

Fromm, E. (ed.). "The Application of Humanist Psychoanalysis to Marx's Theory." In E. Fromm (ed.), *Socialist Humanism: An International Symposium.* Garden City, NY: Doubleday, 1965.

Fromm, E. *The Revolution of Hope: Toward a Humanized Technology.* New York: Harper and Row, 1968.

Fromm, E. *To Have or To Be.* London: Sphere Books, 1976.

Geuss, R. *The Idea of a Critical Theory: Habermas and the Frankfurt School.* New York: Cambridge University Press, 1981.

Giddens, A. "Four Theses on Ideology." In A. Kroker and M. Kroker (eds.), *Ideology and Power in the Age of Lenin in Ruins.* New York: St. Martin's Press, 1991.

Gilligan, C. *In a Different Voice: Psychological Theory and Women's Development* Cambridge, MA: Harvard University Press, 1982.

Gimenez, M. "The Oppression of Women: A Structuralist Marxist View." In R. Hennessy and C. Ingraham (eds.), *Materialist Feminism: A Reader in Class, Difference, and Women's Lives.* New York: Routledge, 1997.

Giroux, H. A. *Theory and Resistance in Education: A Pedagogy for the Opposition.* Westport, CT: Bergin & Garvey, 1983.

Giroux, H. A. *Teachers as Intellectuals: Toward a Critical Pedagogy of Learning.* Westport, CT: Bergin and Garvey, 1988.

Goffman, E. *The Presentation of Self in Everyday Life.* New York: Anchor Press, 1959.

Goffman, E. *The Goffman Reader* (C. Lemert and A. Branaman, eds.). Malden, MA: Blackwell, 1997.

Goldberger, N. R. "Introduction: Looking Backward, Looking Forward." In N. R. Goldberger, J. M. Tarule, B. M. Clinchy, and M. F. Belenky (eds.), *Knowledge, Difference, and Power: Essays Inspired by Women's Ways of Knowing.* New York: Basic Books, 1996.

Goldberger, N. R., Tarule, J. M., Clinchy, B. M., and Belenky, M. F. (eds.). *Knowledge, Difference, and Power: Essays Inspired by Women's Ways of Knowing.* New York: Basic Books, 1996.

Gore, J. M. "What We Can Do for You! What *Can* 'We' Do for 'You'?: Struggling over Empowerment in Critical and Feminist Pedagogy." In C. Luke and J. Gore (eds.), *Feminisms and Critical Pedagogy.* New York: Routledge, 1992.

Gore, J. M. *The Struggle for Pedagogies: Critical and Feminist Discourses as Regimes of Truth.* New York: Routledge, 1993.

Gould, R. "The Therapeutic Learning Program." In J. Mezirow and Associates, *Fostering Critical Reflection in Adulthood: A Guide to Transformative and Emancipatory Learning.* San Francisco: Jossey-Bass, 1990.

Gouthro, P. A. "Feminist Perspectives on Habermasian Theory: Implications for the Development of Critical Theoretical Feminist Discourses in Adult Education." *Proceedings of the Adult Education Research Conference,* No. 44. San Francisco: San Francisco State University, 2003.

Gramsci, A. *The Modern Prince and Other Writings.* New York: International Publishers, 1957.

Gramsci, A. *Selections from the Prison Notebooks* (Q. Hoare and G. N. Smith, eds.). London: Lawrence and Wishart, 1971.

Gramsci, A. *Selections from Cultural Writings* (D. Forgacs and G. Nowell-Smith, eds.). Cambridge, MA: Harvard University Press, 1985.

Gramsci, A. *The Antonio Gramsci Reader* (D. Forgacs, ed.). New York: New York University Press, 1988.

Gramsci, A. *Letters from Prison, Volumes 1 and 2.* (F. Rosegarten and R. Rosenthal, eds. and trans). New York: Columbia University Press, 1994.

Gramsci, A. *Further Selections from the Prison Notebooks,/Antonio Gramsci* (D. Boothman, ed. and trans.). Minneapolis: University of Minnesota Press, 1995.

Grant, J. *Fundamental Feminism: Contesting the Core Concepts of Feminist Theory.* New York: Routledge, 1993.

Greene, M. *Dialectic of Freedom.* New York: Teachers College Press, 1988.

Gross, B. *Friendly Fascism: The New Face of Power in America.* Boston: South End Press, 1980.

Guy, T. "Prophecy from the Periphery: Alain Locke's Philosophy of Cultural Pluralism and Adult Education." In M. Hyams, J. Armstrong, and E. Anderson (eds.), *Proceedings of the 35th Annual Adult Education Research Conference.* Knoxville, TN: University of Tennessee, 1994.

Guy, T. (ed.). *Providing Culturally Relevant Adult Education.* New Directions for Adult and Continuing Education No. 82. San Francisco: Jossey-Bass, 1999.

Guy, T. C., and Colin, S.A.J. III. "Selected Bibliographic Resources for African American Adult Education." *PAACE Journal of Lifelong Learning,* 1998, *7,* 85–91.

Gyant, L. "Alain Leroy Locke: More Than an Adult Educator." In E. A. Peterson (ed.), *Freedom Road: Adult Education of African Americans* (rev. ed.). Malabar, FL: Krieger, 2002.

Habermas, J. *Toward a Rational Society.* Boston: Beacon Press, 1970.

Habermas, J. *Knowledge and Human Interests.* Boston: Beacon Press, 1971.

Habermas, J. *Theory and Practice.* Boston: Beacon Press, 1973.

Habermas, J. *Legitimation Crisis.* Boston: Beacon Press, 1975.

Habermas, J. *Communication and the Evolution of Society.* Boston: Beacon Press, 1979.

Habermas, J. *Philosophical-Political Profiles.* Cambridge, MA: MIT Press, 1983.

Habermas, J. *The Theory of Communicative Action.* Vol. 1: *Reason and the Rationalization of Society.* Boston: Beacon Press, 1984.

Habermas, J. "Questions and Counter Questions." In R. J. Bernstein (ed.), *Habermas and Modernity.* Cambridge, MA: MIT Press, 1985a, pp. 192–216.

Habermas, J. "Psychic Thermidor and the Rebirth of Rebellious Subjectivity." In R. J. Bernstein (ed.), *Habermas and Modernity.* Cambridge, MA: MIT Press, 1985b, pp. 68–77.

Habermas, J. *The Theory of Communicative Action:* Vol. 2: *Lifeworld and System—A Critique of Functionalist Reason.* Boston: Beacon Press, 1987a.

Habermas, J. *The Philosophical Discourse of Modernity: Twelve Lectures.* Cambridge, MA: MIT Press, 1987b.

Habermas, J. *On the Logic of the Social Sciences.* Cambridge, MA: MIT Press, 1988.

Habermas, J. *The New Conservatism: Cultural Criticism and the Historians' Debate.* Cambridge, MA: MIT Press, 1989a.

Habermas, J. *The Structural Transformation of the Public Sphere: An Inquiry into a Category of Bourgeois Society.* Cambridge, MA: MIT Press, 1989b. (Originally published in 1962)

Habermas, J. *Moral Consciousness and Communicative Action.* Cambridge, MA: MIT Press, 1990.

Habermas, J. *Autonomy and Solidarity: Interviews with Jurgen Habermas.* (rev. ed.) London: Verso, 1992a.

Habermas, J. *Postmetaphysical Thinking: Philosophical Essays.* Cambridge, MA: MIT Press, 1992b.

Habermas, J. *Justification and Application: Remarks on Discourse Ethics.* Cambridge, MA: MIT Press, 1993.

Habermas, J. *The Past as Future.* Lincoln: University of Nebraska Press, 1994.

Habermas, J. *Between Facts and Norms: Contributions to a Discourse Theory of Democracy.* Cambridge, MA: MIT Press, 1996.

Habermas, J. *On the Pragmatics of Communication.* Cambridge, MA: MIT Press, 1998.

Habermas, J. *The Postnational Constellation: Political Essays.* Cambridge, MA: MIT Press, 2001a.

Habermas, J. *The Liberating Power of Symbols: Philosophical Essays.* Cambridge, MA: MIT Press, 2001b.

Habermas, J. "The Different Rhythms of Philosophy and Politics for Herbert Marcuse on His 100th Birthday." In H. Marcuse, *Towards a Critical Theory of Society.* New York: Routledge, 2002.

Hammond, M., and Collins, R. *Self-Directed Learning: Critical Practice.* New York: Nichols, 1991.

Harris, L. (ed.). *Philosophy Born of Struggle: Anthology of African-American Philosophy from 1917.* Dubuque, IA: Kendall/Hunt, 1983.

Harris, L. "Leonard Harris." Interview in G. Yancy (ed.), *African-American Philosophers: 17 Conversations.* New York: Routledge, 1998.

Hart, M. "Critical Theory and Beyond: Further Perspectives on Emancipatory Education." *Adult Education Quarterly,* 1990, *40*(3), 125–138.

Hart, M. *Working and Educating for Life: Feminist and International Perspectives on Adult Education.* New York: Routledge, 1992.

Hart, M. "Motherwork: A Radical Proposal to Rethink Work and Education." In M. Welton (ed.), *In Defense of the Lifeworld: Critical Perspectives on Adult Learning.* Albany: State University of New York Press, 1995.

Hartmann, H. "The Unhappy Marriage of Marxism and Feminism: Towards a More Progressive Union" In D. Tallack (ed.), *Critical Theory: A Reader.* New York: Simon and Schuster, 1995.

Hayes, E. "Current Perspectives on Teaching Adults." *Adult Education Quarterly,* 1993, *43*(3), 173–186.

Hayes, E., and Colin, S.A.J. III (eds.). *Confronting Racism and Sexism.* New Directions for Adult and Continuing Education, No. 61. San Francisco: Jossey-Bass, 1994.

Held, D. *Introduction to Critical Theory: Horkheimer to Habermas.* Berkeley: University of California Press, 1980.

Hennessy, R., and Ingraham, C. (eds.). *Materialist Feminism: A Reader in Class, Difference, and Women's Lives.* New York: Routledge, 1997.

Herman, E., and Chomsky, N. *Manufacturing Consent.* New York: Pantheon, 1988.

Hernandez, A. *Pedagogy, Democracy and Feminism: Rethinking the Public Sphere.* Albany: State University of New York Press, 1997.

Hesch, R. "Aboriginal Teachers as Organic Intellectuals." In R. Ng, P. Staton, and J. Scane (eds.), *Anti-Racism, Feminism, and Critical Approaches to Education.* Westport, CT: Bergin & Garvey, 1995.

Hirschmann, N. J., and Di Stefano, C. (eds.). *Revisioning the Political: Feminist Reconstructions of Traditional Concepts in Western Political Theory.* Boulder, CO: Westview Press, 1996.

Holst, J. D. *Social Movements, Civil Society, and Radical Adult Education.* Westport, CT: Bergin & Garvey, 2002.

hooks, b. *Feminist Theory: From Margin to Center.* Boston: South End Press, 1984.

hooks, b. *Talking Back: Thinking feminist, thinking black.* Boston: South End Press, 1989.

hooks, b. *Teaching to Transgress: Education as the Practice of Freedom.* New York: Routledge, 1994.

hooks, b. *Happy to be Nappy.* New York: Hyperion Press, 1999. Illustrated by C. Raschka and C. Raschka.

hooks, b. *Feminism Is for Everybody: Passionate Politics.* Boston: South End Press, 2000a.

hooks, b. *Where We Stand: Class Matters.* New York: Routledge, 2000b.

hooks, b., and West, C. *Breaking Bread: Insurgent Black Intellectual Life.* Boston: South End Press, 1991.

Hord, F. L., and Lee, J. S. (eds.). *I Am Because We Are: Readings in Black Philosophy.* Amherst, MA: University of Massachusetts Press, 1995.

Horkheimer, M. *Eclipse of Reason.* New York: Continuum, 1974. (Originally published 1947.)

Horkheimer, M. *Critical Theory: Selected Essays.* New York: Continuum, 1995.

Horkheimer, M., and Adorno, T. *Dialectic of Enlightenment.* New York: Seabury Press, 1972.

Horton, M. *The Long Haul: An Autobiography.* New York: Doubleday, 1990.

Horton, M. *The Myles Horton Reader: Education for Social Change.* Knoxville, TN: University of Tennessee Press, 2003.

Horton, M., and Freire, P. *We Make the Road by Walking: Conversations on Education and Social Change.* Philadelphia: Temple University Press, 1990.

Hountondji, P. J. *African Philosophy: Myth and Reality.* (2nd ed.) Bloomington, IN: Indiana University Press, 1983.

Jackson, G. *Soledad Brother: The Prison Writings of George Jackson.* New York: Coward-McCann, 1970.

James, J. "Introduction." In A. Y. Davis, *The Angela Y. Davis Reader.* Malden, MA: Blackwell, 1998.

James, J., and Farmer, R. (eds.). *Spirit, Space and Survival: African American Women in (White) Academe.* New York: Routledge, 1993.

James, S. M., and Busia, A.P.A. (eds.). *Theorizing Black Feminisms: The Visionary Pragmatism of Black Women.* New York: Routledge, 1993.

Jay, M. *The Dialectical Imagination: A History of the Frankfurt School and the Institute of Social Research 1923–1950.* Berkeley, CA: University of California Press, 1973.

Johnson-Bailey, J. *Sistahs in College: Making a Way Out of No Way.* Malabar, FL: Krieger, 2001.

Karenga, M. R. "Society, Culture, and the Problem of Self-Consciousness: A Kawaida Analysis." In L. Harris (ed.), *Philosophy Born of Struggle: Anthology of African-American Philosophy from 1917.* Dubuque, IA: Kendall/Hunt, 1983.

Kellner, D. *Critical Theory, Marxism, and Modernity.* Baltimore: Johns Hopkins University Press, 1989.

Kellner, D. "A Marcuse Renaissance?" In J. Bokina and T. J. Lukes (eds.), *Marcuse: From the New Left to the Next Left.* Lawrence, KS: University Press of Kansas, 1994.

Kenway, J. "Remembering and Regenerating Gramsci." In K. Weiler (ed.), *Feminist Engagements: Reading, Resisting, and Revisioning Male Theorists in Education and Cultural Studies.* New York: Routledge, 2001.

Kenway, J., and Modra, H. "Feminist Pedagogy and Emancipatory Possibilities". In C. Luke and J. M. Gore (eds.), *Feminisms and Critical Pedagogy.* New York: Routledge, 1992.

Kincheloe, J. L. "Making Critical Thinking Critical." In D. Weil and H. K. Anderson (eds.), *Perspectives in Critical Thinking: Essays by Teachers in Theory and Practice.* New York: Peter Lang, 2000.

King, P. M., and Kitchener, K. S. *Developing Reflective Judgment: Understanding and Promoting Intellectual Growth and Critical Thinking in Adolescents and Adults.* San Francisco: Jossey-Bass, 1994.

Knowles, M. S. *The Adult Learner: A Neglected Species.* (3rd ed.) Houston: Gulf, 1984.

Kohl, H. R. *I Won't Learn From You: And Other Thoughts on Creative Maladjustment.* New York: New Press, 1994.

Kohl, H. R. *The Discipline of Hope: Learning from a Lifetime of Teaching.* New York: New Press, 2000.

Kramer, D. A. "Development of an Awareness of Contradiction Across the Life Span and the Question of Postformal Operations." In M. L. Commons, J. D. Sinnott, F. A. Richards, and C. Armon (eds.), *Adult Development: Comparisons and Applications of Developmental Models.* New York: Praeger, 1989.

Kreisberg, S. *Transforming Power: Domination, Empowerment, and Education.* Albany: State University of New York Press, 1992.

Kuhn, A., and Wolpe, A. M. (eds.). *Feminism and Materialism: Women and Modes of Production.* London: Routledge, 1978.

Labouvie-Vief, G. "Beyond Formal Operations: Uses and Limits of Pure Logic in Life-Span Development." *Human Development, 23,* 1980, 141–161.

Laclau, E., and Mouffe, C. *Hegemony and Socialist Strategy: Towards a Radical Democratic Politics.* New York: Verso, 1990.

Laing, R. *The Divided Self: A Study of Sanity and Madness.* London: Tavistock, 1960.

Lather, P. *Getting Smart: Feminist Research and Pedagogy With/In the Postmodern.* New York: Routledge, 1991.

Lather, P. "Post-Critical Pedagogies: A Feminist Reading." In C. Luke and J. M. Gore (eds.), *Feminisms and Critical Pedagogy.* New York: Routledge, 1992.

Lather, P. "Ten Years Later, Yet Again: Critical Pedagogy and Its Complicities." In K. Weiler, (ed.), *Feminist Engagements: Reading, Resisting, and Revisioning Male Theorists in Education and Cultural Studies.* New York: Routledge, 2001.

Law, M. "Engels, Marx, and Radical Adult Education: A Rereading of a Tradition." *Proceedings of the Adult Education Research Conference, No. 33.* Saskatoon, Canada: University of Saskatchewan, 1992, pp. 150–156.

Lawson, K. H. *Philosophical Concepts and Values in Adult Education.* Nottingham, UK: Department of Adult Education, University of Nottingham, 1975.

Leiss, W., Ober, J. D., and Sherover, E. "Marcuse as Teacher." In K. H. Wolff and B. Moore, Jr. (eds.), *The Critical Spirit: Essays in Honor of Herbert Marcuse.* Boston: Beacon Press, 1967.

Lindeman, E.C.L. *The Meaning of Adult Education.* Montreal: Harvest House, 1961. (First published by New Republic, 1926).

Lindeman, E.C.L. "The Place of Discussion in the Learning Process." (Originally published 1935.) In S. D. Brookfield (ed.), *Learning Democracy: Eduard Lindeman on Adult Education and Social Change.* Beckenham, Kent, UK: Croom Helm, 1987a.

Lindeman, E.C.L. "Adult Education for Social Change." (Originally published 1937.) In S. D. Brookfield (ed.), *Learning Democracy: Eduard Lindeman on Adult Education and Social Change.* Beckenham, Kent, UK: Croom Helm, 1987b.

Lindeman, E.C.L. "New Needs for Adult Education." (Originally published 1944.) In S. D. Brookfield (ed.), *Learning Democracy: Eduard Lindeman on Adult Education and Social Change.* Beckenham, Kent, UK: Croom Helm, 1987c.

Loewen, J. W. *Lies My Teacher Told Me: Everything Your American History Textbook Got Wrong.* New York: Touchstone Books, 1995.

Lorde, A. *Sister Outsider: Essays and Speeches.* Trumansburg, NY: Crossing Press, 1984.

Luke, C. "Feminist Politics in Radical Pedagogy". In C. Luke and J. M. Gore (eds.), *Feminisms and Critical Pedagogy.* New York: Routledge, 1992.

Macey, D. *The Lives of Michel Foucault: A Biography.* New York: Pantheon, 1993.

MacIntyre, A. C. *Marxism and Christianity.* New York: Schocken Books, 1968.

MacKinnon, C. A. "Feminism, Marxism, Method and the State: An Agenda for Theory." In N. Keohane, M. Rosaldo, and B. Gelpi (eds.), *Feminist Theory: A Critique of Ideology.* Chicago: University of Chicago Press, 1981.

MacKinnon, C. A. *Toward a Feminist Theory of the State.* Cambridge, MA: Harvard University Press, 1989.

Marcuse, H. *Reason and Revolution: Hegel and Rise of Social Theory.* New York: Oxford University Press, 1941.

Marcuse, H. *Soviet Marxism: A Critical Analysis.* New York: Vintage Books, 1958.

Marcuse, H. *One Dimensional Man.* Boston: Beacon, 1964.

Marcuse, H. "Repressive Tolerance." In R. P. Wolff, B. Moore, and H.

Marcuse. *A Critique of Pure Tolerance.* Boston: Beacon Press, 1965a.

Marcuse, H. "Socialist Humanism?" In E. Fromm (ed.), *Socialist Humanism: An International Symposium.* Garden City, NY: Doubleday, 1965b.

Marcuse, H. *Negations: Essays in Critical Theory.* Boston: Beacon Press, 1968.

Marcuse, H. *An Essay on Liberation.* Boston: Beacon Press, 1969.

Marcuse, H. *Five Lectures.* Boston: Beacon Press, 1970.

Marcuse, H. *Counterrevolution and Revolt.* Boston: Beacon Press, 1972.

Marcuse, H. *The Aesthetic Dimension: Toward a Critique of Marxist Aesthetics.* Boston: Beacon Press, 1978a.

Marcuse, H. "Marcuse and the Frankfurt School: Dialogue with Marcuse." In B. Magee (ed.), *Men of Ideas.* New York: Viking, 1978b.

Marcuse, H. "Philosophy and Critical Theory." In S. E. Bronner and D. M. Kellner (eds.), *Critical Theory and Society: A Reader.* New York: Routledge, 1989.

Marcuse, H. *Towards a Critical Theory of Society.* New York: Routledge, 2002.

Marks, R. W. *The Meaning of Marcuse.* New York: Ballantine Books, 1970.

Marsden, J. *Marxism and Christian Utopianism.* New York: Monthly Review Press, 1991.

Marx, K. *Economic and Philosophical Manuscripts.* (T. B. Bottomore, trans.). In E. Fromm (ed.), *Marx's Concept of Man.* New York: Frederick Ungar, 1961.

Marx, K. *Capital: A Critical Analysis of Capitalist Production.* Vol. 1. (S. Moore and E. Aveling, trans.). New York: International, 1973.

Marx, K., and Engels, F. *The German Ideology.* (C. J. Arthur, ed.). New York: International, 1970.

Mayberry, K. J. (ed.). *Teaching What You're Not: Identity Politics in Higher Education.* New York: New York University Press, 1996.

Mayo, P. *Gramsci, Freire and Adult Education: Possibilities for Transformative Action.* New York: Zed Books, 1998.

McClendon, J. H. "Eugene C. Holmes: A Commentary on a Black Marxist Philosopher." In L. Harris (ed.), *Philosophy Born of Struggle: Anthology of Afro-American Philosophy from 1917.* Dubuque, IA: Kendall/Hunt, 1983.

McClusky, H. Y. "The Course of the Adult Life Span." In W. C. Hallenbeck (ed.), *Psychology of Adults.* Chicago: Adult Education Association of the USA, 1963.

McClusky, H. Y. "An Approach to a Differential Psychology of the Adult Potential." In S. M. Grabowski (ed.), *Adult Learning and Instruction.* Syracuse, NY: ERIC Clearinghouse on Adult Education, 1970.

McGary, H. "Alienation and the African American Experience." In J. P. Pittman (ed.), *African-American Perspectives and Philosophical Traditions.* New York: Routledge, 1997.

McLaren, P. "Multiculturalism and the Postmodern Critique: Towards a Pedagogy of Resistance and Transformation." *Cultural Studies,* 1993, *7*(1), 118–146.

McLaren, P. *Critical Pedagogy and Predatory Culture: Oppositional Politics in a Postmodern Era.* New York: Routledge, 1995.

McLaren, P. *Life in Schools: An Introduction to Critical Pedagogy in the Foundations of Education* (3rd ed.). White Plains, NY: Longman, 1997.

McLellan, D. *Ideology.* Milton Keynes, UK: Open University Press, 1986.

Meehan, J. (ed.). *Feminists Read Habermas: Gendering the Subject of Discourse.* New York: Routledge, 1995.

Mezirow, J. "A Critical Theory of Adult Learning and Education." *Adult Education,* 1981, *32*(1), 3–27.

Mezirow, J. "Transformation Theory and Social Action: A Response to Collard and Law." *Adult Education Quarterly,* 1989, *39*(3), 169–175.

Mezirow, J. *Transformative Dimensions of Adult Learning.* San Francisco: Jossey-Bass, 1991a.

Mezirow, J. "Transformation Theory and Cultural Context: A Reply to Clark and Wilson." *Adult Education Quarterly,* 1991b, *41*(3), 188–192.

Mezirow, J. "Transformation Theory: Critique and Confusion." *Adult Education Quarterly,* 1992, *44*(4), 250–252.

Mezirow, J. "Understanding Transformation Theory." *Adult Education Quarterly,* 1994a, *44*(4), 222–232.

Mezirow, J. "Response to Mark Tennant and Michael Newman." *Adult Education Quarterly,* 1994b, *44*(4), 243–244.

Mezirow, J. "Transformation Theory Out of Context" *Adult Education Quarterly,* 1997, *48*(1), 60–62.

Mezirow, J. "On Critical Reflection." *Adult Education Quarterly,* 1998, *48*(3), 185–198.

Mezirow, J., and Associates. *Fostering Critical Reflection in Adulthood: A Guide to Transformative and Emancipatory Learning.* San Francisco: Jossey-Bass, 1990.

Mezirow, J., and Associates. *Learning as Transformation: Critical Perspectives on a Theory in Progress.* San Francisco: Jossey-Bass, 2000.

Mill, J. S. *The Philosophy of J. S. Mill.* (M. Cohen, ed.). New York: Random House, 1961.

Miller, J. *The Passion of Michel Foucault.* New York: Simon and Schuster, 1993.

Mills, C. W. *Mass Society and Liberal Education.* Chicago: Center for the Study of Liberal Education for Adults, 1954.

Mills, C. W. *The Sociological Imagination.* New York: Oxford University Press, 1959.

Mills, C. W. *The Marxists.* New York: Dell, 1962.

Mojab, S., and Gorman, R. "Women and Consciousness in the 'Learning Organization': Emancipation or Exploitation?" *Adult Education Quarterly,* 2003, *53*(4), 228–241.

Morrow, R. A., and Torres, C. A. *Reading Freire and Habermas: Critical Pedagogy and Transformative Social Change.* New York: Teachers College Press, 2002.

Morss, J. R. (ed.). *Growing Critical: Alternatives to Developmental Psychology.* New York: Routledge, 1996.

Newman, M. *Defining the Enemy: Adult Education in Social Action.* Sydney, Australia: Stewart Victor, 1994.

Newman, M. *Maeler's Regard: Images of Adult Learning.* Sydney, Australia: Stewart Victor, 1999.

Norris, S. P., and Ennis, R. H. *Evaluating Critical Thinking.* Pacific Grove, PA: Midwest Publications, 1989.

Nyrere, J. K. *Freedom and Unity.* New York: Oxford University Press, 1968.

Oberg, A., and Underwood, S. "Facilitating Teacher Self-Development." In A. Hargreaves and M. G. Fullan (eds.), *Understanding Teacher Development.* New York: Teachers College Press, 1992.

Orner, M. "Interrupting the Calls for Student Voice in 'Liberatory Education.'" In C. Luke and J. M. Gore (eds.), *Feminisms and Critical Pedagogy.* New York: Routledge, 1992.

Orwell, G. "Politics and the English Language." In *A Collection of Essays.* New York: Doubleday, 1946.

Outlaw, L. T., Jr. "Philosophy, Hermeneutics, Social-Political Theory: Critical Thought in the Interests of African-Americans." In L. Harris (ed.), *Philosophy Born of Struggle: Anthology of African-American Philosophy from 1917.* Dubuque, IA: Kendall/Hunt, 1983a.

Outlaw, L. T., Jr. "Race and Class in the Theory and Practice of Emanci-patory Social Transformation." In L. Harris (ed.), *Philosophy Born of Struggle: Anthology of African-American Philosophy from 1917*. Dubuque, IA: Kendall/Hunt, 1983b.

Outlaw, L. T., Jr. *On Race and Philosophy*. New York: Routledge, 1996.

Outlaw, L. T., Jr. "Lucius T. Outlaw." Interview in G. Yancy (ed.), *African-American Philosophers: 17 Conversations*. New York: Routledge, 1998.

Palmer, P. J. *Let Your Life Speak: Listening for the Voice of Vocation*. San Francisco: Jossey-Bass, 2000.

Patterson, R.W.K. *Values, Education and the Adult*. London: Routledge and Kegan Paul, 1979.

Patton, M. Q. *Qualitative Research and Evaluation Methods*. (3rd ed.) Thousand Oaks, CA: Sage, 2002.

Peters, J. M., Jarvis, P., and Associates. *Adult Education: Evolution and Achievements in a Developing Field of Study*. San Francisco: Jossey-Bass, 1991.

Peterson, E. A. "Creating a Culturally Relevant Dialog for African-American Adult Educators." In T. C. Guy (ed.), *Providing Culturally Relevant Adult Education: A Challenge for the Twenty-First Century*. New Directions for Adult and Continuing Education, No. 82. San Francisco: Jossey-Bass, 1999.

Peterson, E. A. "Fanny Coppin, Mary Shadd Cary, and Charlotte Grinkle: Three African American Women Who Made a Difference." In E. A. Peterson (ed.), *Freedom Road: Adult Education of African Americans* (rev. ed.). Malabar, FL: Krieger, 2002.

Peterson, E. A. (ed.). *Freedom Road: Adult Education of African Americans* (rev. ed.). Malabar, FL: Krieger, 2002.

Popper, K. R. *The Logic of Scientific Discovery*. New York: Harper and Row, 1959.

Poster, M. *Critical Theory and Poststructuralism: In Search of a Context*. Ithaca, NY: Cornell University Press, 1989.

Potts, E. "The Du Bois-Washington Debate: Conflicting Strategies." In E. A. Peterson (ed.), *Freedom Road: Adult Education of African Americans* (rev. ed.). Malabar, FL: Krieger, 2002.

Reitz, C. "Liberating the Critical in Critical Theory: Marcuse, Marx, and a Pedagogy of the Oppressed: Alienation, Art and the Humanities." In S. F. Steiner, H. M. Krank, P. McLaren, and R. E. Bahruth (eds.), *Freirean Pedagogy, Praxis, and Possibilities: Projects for the New Millennium*. New York: Falmer Press, 2000, pp. 41–66.

Riegel, K. F. "Dialectical Operations: the Final Stage of Cognitive Development." *Human Development*, 1973, *16*, 346–370.

Rogers, C. R. *On Becoming a Person: A Therapist's View of Psychotherapy*. Boston: Houghton-Mifflin, 1961.

Rogers, C. R. *A Way of Being.* Boston: Houghton-Mifflin, 1980.

Rose, M. *Lives on the Boundary.* New York: Penguin, 1990.

Rose, M. *Possible Lives.* New York: Penguin, 1999.

Ruddick, S. *Maternal Thinking: Toward a Politics of Peace.* Boston: Beacon Press, 1995.

Saltiel, I. M., and Russo, C. S. *Cohort Learning and Programming: Improving Educational Experiences for Adult Learners.* Malabar, FL: Krieger, 2001.

San Juan, E. *Racism and Cultural Studies: Critiques of Multiculturalist Ideology and the Politics of Difference.* Durham, NC: Duke University Press, 2002.

Sargent, L. (ed.). *Women and Revolution: A Discussion of the Unhappy Marriage of Marxism and Feminism.* Boston: South End Press, 1981.

Sawicki, J. *Disciplining Foucault: Feminism, Power and the Body.* New York: Routledge, 1991.

Schutz, A., and Luckmann, T. *The Structure of the Lifeworld.* Evanston, IL: Northwestern University Press, 1973.

Searle, J. R. *Speech Acts.* Cambridge, UK: Cambridge University Press, 1969.

Serequeberhan, T. (ed.). *African Philosophy: The Essential Readings.* New York: Paragon House, 1991.

Sergiovanni, T. J. *The Lifeworld of Leadership: Creating Culture, Community, and Personal Meaning in Our Schools.* San Francisco: Jossey-Bass, 1999.

Shalin, D. N. "Critical Theory and the Pragmatist Challenge." *American Journal of Sociology,* 1992, *98,* 237–279.

Sheared, V., and Sissel, P. (eds.). *Making Space: Merging Theory and Practice in Adult Education.* Westport, CT: Bergin & Garvey, 2001.

Shor, I. *Critical Teaching for Everyday Life.* Chicago: University of Chicago Press, 1987a.

Shor, I. (ed.). *Freire for the Classroom: A Sourcebook for Liberatory Teaching.* Portsmouth, NH: Boynton/Cook, 1987b.

Shor, I. *Empowering Education: Critical Teaching for Social Change.* Chicago: University of Chicago Press, 1992.

Shor, I. *When Students Have Power: Negotiating Authority in a Critical Pedagogy.* Chicago: University of Chicago Press, 1996.

Shor, I., and Freire, P. *A Pedagogy for Liberation: Dialogues on Transforming Education.* Westport, CT: Bergin & Garvey, 1987.

Shor, I., and Pari, C. (eds.). *Critical Literacy in Action: Writing Words, Changing Worlds.* Portsmouth, NH: Boynton/Cook, 1999.

Shor, I., and Pari, C. (eds.). *Education Is Politics: Critical Teaching Across Differences, Postsecondary.* Portsmouth, NH: Boynton/Cook, 2000.

Shumar, W. *College for Sale: A Critique of the Commodification of Higher Education.* New York: Routledge, 1997.

Simon, R. I, Dippo, D., and Schenke, A. *Learning Work: A Critical Pedagogy of Work Education.* Westport, CT: Bergin & Garvey, 1991.

Smallwood, A. P. "African American Leadership, Religious Expression, and Intellectual Discourse: Uncovering Malcolm X's Legacy to Adult Education." In E. A. Peterson (ed.), *Freedom Road: Adult Education of African Americans* (rev. ed.). Malabar, FL: Krieger, 2002.

Smith, C. A. "The African-American Market Woman." In V. Sheared and P. Sissel (eds.), *Making Space: Merging Theory and Practice in Adult Education.* Westport, CT: Bergin & Garvey, 2001.

Smith, S. E., and Colin, S.A.J. III. "An Invisible Presence, Silenced Voices: African Americans in the Adult Education Professoriate." In V. Sheared and P. Sissel (eds.), *Making Space: Merging Theory and Practice in Adult Education.* Westport, CT: Bergin & Garvey, 2001.

Smith, T. V., and Lindeman, E. C. *The Democratic Way of Life.* New York: New American Library, 1951.

Spring, J. *Images of American Life: A History of Ideological Management in Schools, Movies, Radio, and Television.* Albany: State University of New York Press, 1992.

Sternberg, R. J., and Wagner, R. K. (eds.). *Practical Intelligence: Nature and Origins of Competence in the Everyday World.* Cambridge, UK: Cambridge University Press, 1986.

Stice, J. E. (ed.). *Developing Critical Thinking and Problem-Solving Abilities.* New Directions for Teaching and Learning, No. 30. San Francisco: Jossey-Bass, 1987.

Taylor, E. W. "Building Upon the Theoretical Debate: A Critical Review of the Empirical Studies of Mezirow's Transformative Learning Theory." *Adult Education Quarterly,* 1997, *48*(1), 34–59.

Taylor, E. W. "Analyzing Research on Transformative Learning Theory." In J. Mezirow and Associates, *Learning as Transformation: Critical Perspectives on a Theory in Progress.* San Francisco: Jossey-Bass, 2000a.

Taylor, E. W. "Fostering Mezirow's Transformative Learning Theory in the Adult Education Classroom: A Critical Review." *Canadian Journal for the Study of Adult Education,* 2000b, *14*(2), 1–28.

Tennant, M. C. "Perspective Transformation and Adult Development." *Adult Education Quarterly,* 1993, *44*(1), 34–42.

Tough, A. M. *The Adult's Learning Projects.* Toronto: Ontario Institute for Studies in Education, 1971.

Usher, R., and Edwards, R. *Postmodernism and Education: Different Voices, Different Worlds.* London: Routledge, 1994.

Usher, R., Bryant, I., and Johnston, R. *Adult Education and the Postmodern Challenge: Learning Beyond the Limits.* New York: Routledge, 1997.

Vogel, L. "Marxism and Feminism: Unhappy Marriage, Trial Separation, or Something Else?" In L. Sargent, (ed.), *Women and Revolution: A Discussion of the Unhappy Marriage of Marxism and Feminism.* Boston: South End Press, 1981.

Vogel, L. *Marxism and the Oppression of Women.* New Brunswick, NJ: Rutgers University Press, 1983.

Weiler, K. "Rereading Paulo Freire." In K. Weiler (ed.), *Feminist Engagements: Reading, Resisting, and Revisioning Male Theorists in Education and Cultural Studies.* New York: Routledge, 2001a.

Weiler, K. (ed.). *Feminist Engagements: Reading, Resisting, and Revisioning Male Theorists in Education and Cultural Studies.* New York: Routledge, 2001b.

Welton, M. R. "Shaking the Foundations: The Critical Turn in Adult Education Theory." *Canadian Journal for the Study of Adult Education,* 1991, *5,* 21–41.

Welton, M. R. "The Contribution of Critical Theory to Our Understanding of Adult Education." In S. B. Merriam (ed.), *An Update on Adult Learning Theory.* New Directions for Adult and Continuing Education, No. 57. San Francisco: Jossey-Bass, 1993.

Welton, M. R. "Review of *Teaching Against the Grain* (R. Simon)." *Adult Education Quarterly,* 1994, *45*(1), 302–310.

Welton, M. R. (ed.). *In Defense of the Lifeworld: Critical Perspectives on Adult Learning.* Albany: State University of New York Press, 1995.

Welton, M. R. "Civil Society as Theory and Project: Adult Education and the Renewal of Global Citizenship." In D. Wildemeersch, M. Finger, and T. Jansen (eds.), *Adult Education and Social Responsibility.* Frankfurt, Germany: Peter Lang, 2000.

Welton, M. R. "Civil Society and the Public Sphere." *Studies in the Education of Adults,* 2001, *33*(1), 20–34.

Welton, M. R. "Listening, Conflict and Citizenship: Towards a Pedagogy of Civil Society." *International Journal of Lifelong Education,* 2003, *21*(3), 197–208.

West, C. *Prophesy Deliverance: An Afro-American Revolutionary Christianity.* Philadelphia: The Westminster Press, 1982.

West, C. "Philosophy, Politics, and Power: An Afro-American Perspective." In L. Harris (ed.), *Philosophy Born of Struggle: Anthology of African-American Philosophy from 1917.* Dubuque, IA: Kendall/Hunt, 1983.

West, C. *The American Evasion of Philosophy: A Genealogy of Pragmatism.* Madison, WI: University of Wisconsin Press, 1989.

West, C. *The Ethical Dimensions of Marxist Thought.* New York: Monthly Review Press, 1991.

West, C. *Prophetic Thought in Postmodern Times.* Monroe, ME: Common Courage Press, 1993a.

West, C. *Prophetic Reflections: Notes on Race and Power in America.* Monroe, ME: Common Courage Press, 1993b.

West, C. *Keeping Faith: Philosophy and Race in America.* New York: Routledge, 1993c.

West, C. *Race Matters*. New York: Vintage Books, 1993d.

West, C. "Cornel West" In G. Yancy, (ed.), *African-American Philosophers: 17 Conversations*. New York: Routledge, 1998.

West, C. *The Cornel West Reader*. New York: Basic Books, 1999a.

West, C. "Cornel West on Heterosexism and Transformation: An Interview." In J. A. Segara and R. Dobles (eds.), *Learning as a Political Act: Struggles for Learning and Learning from Struggles*. Cambridge, MA: Harvard University Press, 1999b.

West, C. *Sketches of My Culture*. New York: Artemis Records, 2001 (CD).

West, C., and Sealey, K. S. *Restoring Hope: Conversations on the Future of Black America*. Boston: Beacon Press, 1997.

Wiggerhaus, R. *The Frankfurt School: Its History, Theories and Political Significance*. Cambridge, MA: MIT Press, 1994

Williams, R. *Marxism and Literature*. New York: Oxford University Press, 1977.

Williams, R. *Keywords*. London: Flamingo Press, 1983.

Williamson, B. *Lifeworlds and Learning: Essays in the Theory, Practice and Philosophy of Lifelong Learning*. Leicester, UK: National Institute for Adult Continuing Education, 1998.

Willis, P. E. *Learning to Labor: How Working Class Kids Get Working Class Jobs*. New York: Columbia University Press, 1981.

Willis, P. E. "Labor Power, Culture, and the Cultural Commodity." In M. Castells and Others, *Critical Education in the New Information Age*. Lanham, MD: Rowman and Littlefield, 1999.

Wittgenstein, L. *Philosophical Investigations*. New York: Macmillan, 1953.

Wolff, J. *Why Read Marx Today?* New York: Oxford University Press, 2002.

Wood, M. D. *Cornel West and the Politics of Prophetic Pragmatism*. Urbana: University of Illinois Press, 2000.

Yancy, G. (ed.). *African-American Philosophers: 17 Conversations*. New York: Routledge, 1998.

Yancy, G. (ed.). *Cornel West: A Critical Reader*. Malden, MA: Blackwell, 2001.

Yorks, L., and Kasl, E. (eds.). *Collaborative Inquiry as a Strategy for Adult Learning*. New Directions for Adult and Continuing Education, No. 94. San Francisco: Jossey-Bass, 2002.

Youngman, F. *The Political Economy of Adult Education and Development*. New York: Zed Books, 2000.

Zinn, H. *Declarations of Independence: Cross-Examining American Ideology*. New York: Harper Collins, 1990.

Zinn, H. *A People's History of the United States, 1492-Present*. New York: Harper Collins, 1999.

Name Index

D

Darder, A., 322
Davis, A. Y., 19, 115, 141, 182, 210,
    281, 286, 312, 314, 317, 334–348,
    352, 360, 366, 372
Delgado, R., 285
Delpit, L., 366
Derrida, J., 219
Dewey, J., 15, 63, 224, 302
Di Stefano, C., 312
Diamond, I., 312
Dippo, D., 11
Du Bois, W.E.B., 276, 286, 306, 309
Dutschke, R., 210

E

Eagleton, T., 34, 40, 67, 68, 76, 78, 91
Easter, O. V., 305
Edwards, D., 126, 127, 130
Ehrenreich, B., 317
Ehrlich, C., 315
Eisenstein, Z., 316
Ellsworth, E., 314, 322, 324, 325, 326,
    327
Engels, F., 41, 73, 94, 359
Ennis, R. H., 15
Entwistle, H., 111
Eribon, D., 141

F

Falwell, J., 19
Fanon, F., 286
Farmer, R., 305
Fay, B., 7, 34, 35, 36
Feuerbach, L., 21, 350
Fleming, M., 312, 318
Fluss, D., 310
Fo, D., 186
Foley, D. E., 80, 88, 89, 90
Follett, M. P., 47, 119
Foucault, M., 37, 45, 45–46, 47, 48,
    118, 120, 121–128, 131–133, 134,
    135, 136, 137–138, 141, 142, 143–
    147, 286, 292, 296, 297, 298, 299,
    302, 312, 314, 319–320, 322, 325,
    351, 370, 371

Fox, D., 85
Fraser, N., 310, 312, 318
Freire, P., 7, 9, 26, 37, 86, 89, 109–110,
    111, 209, 304, 305, 315, 321, 322,
    327, 345
Fromm, E., 14, 19, 21, 22, 41, 50,
    51–52, 53, 148–169, 225, 327, 344,
    349, 351, 352, 354, 355, 359, 362,
    363, 364, 366, 367

G

Garvey, M., 286, 305, 306, 307, 309
Gates, B., 91
Gaventa, J., 36
Geuss, R., 26, 40
Giddens, A., 74, 87
Gilligan, C., 311, 313
Gimenez, M., 316
Giroux, H. A., 320, 322, 323
Giscard d'Estraing, V., 143
Goffman, E., 74
Goldberger, N. R., 85, 310, 311
Gore, J. M., 130, 310, 319, 321, 322,
    323, 324, 325
Gorman, R., 11
Gotanda, N., 285
Gould, R., 14
Gouthro, P. A., 312
Gramsci, A., 3, 16, 17–18, 21, 33, 40,
    43, 44, 45, 46, 86, 89, 92, 93, 94, 95,
    96, 97, 98, 103, 104, 105, 106, 107,
    108, 109, 110, 111, 142, 170, 286,
    289, 292, 297, 298, 302, 312, 321,
    322, 325, 333, 346, 353, 359, 366
Grant, J., 310
Greene, M., 60, 63
Gross, B., 90
Guy, T., 275, 277, 306, 307, 308
Gyant, L., 304

H

Habermas, J., 17, 21, 23, 25, 30, 56,
    57, 58, 59, 63, 64, 65, 94, 117, 124,
    125, 157, 162, 181, 195, 221, 222,
    222–246, 247–270, 271–272, 286,
    289, 291, 292, 312, 314, 317–318,

Subject Index

A

AAACE (American Association of Adult and Continuing Education), 137

Abstract conceptual thought, 193–194

ACACE (Advisory Council for Adult and Continuing Education), 220

Active hegemony, 112–114

Adult Education: Evolution and Achievements in a Developing Field of Study (Peters, Jarvis, and Associates), 277

Adult education: Africentric paradigm as alternative discourse in, 305–309; application of panopticon to, 135–136; applying Gramscian protocol for, 111–112; commodification process in, 166; as communitarian socialism, 157; creating opportunities for privacy/isolation in, 198–199; for critical thinking, 205–209; Davis' writings on liberatory power of, 339–340; democratic ideal embraced by, 60–64; development of specialized discourse in, 185–186; feminist attempts to fight patriarchy through, 320; Foucaultian perspective on power in, 125–128; Fromm on structuralized view of world function of, 172–174; Fromm's outline of political literacy project for, 167–168; Fromm's promotion and belief in, 152–153; Gramsci's worker activism analysis and, 107; as ideological state apparatus, 85–87; influence of Habermas on North American, 272–273; learning about democracy as core of residential, 269–272; learning to defend lifeworld as project of, 222; lessons from Davis' analysis of collective struggle for, 342–348; lifeworld discourse of, 56–59; Newman's case for active hegemony in, 112–114; Newman's criticism of liberal-humanist hegemony in, 112; as practice of liberating tolerance, 209–217; race composition in classrooms of, 277–278

Adult Education Research Conference (Canada, 1992), 277

Adult educators: Baptiste's argument for ethical pedagogy of coercion in, 114–115; the circle and, 129–130; "A Critical Theory of Adult Learning and Education" (Mezirow) influence on, 220–221; exercise of power by, 330–331; faith in convictions and practices of, 179–180; Fromm on character of teachers and, 177; Fromm's warning against majority vote used by, 168–169; impostorship myth exposed by, 369–370; as organic intellectuals, 107–111; power and resistance and role of, 138–143; practice of loving adult pedagogy by, 178; repressive tolerance encountered by, 371; teaching critically, 349–373

Adult learning: avenues of democratic, 269–272; as communicative action, 252–256; as democratic participation, 174–176; developing curriculum for revolutionary, 347–348;

408 SUBJECT INDEX

Humanistic (or communitarian) socialism, 156–158, 161

I

Ideology: beliefs supporting, 66–68; capitalism and bureaucratic rationality, 69–73; capitalism's standardization of, 161; as central critical theory concept, 68–69; combating racist alienation and, 288–289; connections between lifeworld and, 57; critical pedagogy work regarding, 314, 320–326; feminism as struggle against dominant, 329–334; hegemony transformed into, 94; learning, 87–92; "mustn't grumble," 69; as permeating all interpersonal communications, 55; of pluralism, 90–91; resisting, 75–80; self-directed learning as deliberate break from dominant, 105; student discussion on, 367–368; systemic critical, 13. *See also* Challenging ideology; ISAs (ideological state apparatuses)

Ideology critique: adulthood as precondition for, 80–82; critical theory tradition of, 13, 42; Habermas on benefits of, 228; ideological formation of self-directed learning and, 83–85

Ideology (Eagleton), 34

"Ideology and Ideological State Apparatuses" (Althusser), 73

Imani (faith), 307

Impostorship, 369–370

In Defense of the Lifeworld (Welton), 59

Individual isolation, 183–184

Individuality, 301

Institute of Proletarian Culture, 95

Institute of Social Research (Germany), 22–23, 69

Instrumental reasoning, 69, 71–72

ISAs (ideological state apparatuses): adult education as, 85–87; described, 73–75; function of, 119. *See also* Ideology

Italian Communist Party, 95
Italian Socialist Party, 95

J

Journal of Negro Education, 305
"Judges of normality," 145, 146
Justifications and Applications (Habermas interview), 266

K

Kawaida (American racism), 287
Kawaida in Philosophy Born of Struggle (Harris), 287
Keeping Faith (West), 297, 299
"Kneejerk marxophobia," 19
Knowledge: critique of Foucault's analysis of discourse and, 319; power, truth and, 136–138. *See also* Learning
Knowledge and Human Interests (Habermas), 257
Kujichagulia (self-determination), 307
Kuumba (creativity), 307
Kyoto Accord, 250

L

Labor: capitalism and sexual division of, 316–317; feminist critique of Marx's emphasis on alienation and, 315–316; feminist debate over alienation and domestic, 316; Fromm on capitalism and, 153–154; product as objectification of, 154–155. *See also* Workers

Language: alienating nature of socialist feminist, 317; art as producing new forms of, 201–202; blinding people to establishment, 185; censorship of, 215–217; conceptual learning and development of new, 207–208; feminism and, 333–334; logocentrism assumption regarding speech and, 255–256; as medium of domination and power, 266; one-dimensional thought and role of, 191–192; oppositional movements use of, 208; Orwell's analysis